IN NAZI UNIFORM

IN NAZI UNIFORM

BY

SIEGFRIED BORN

PENTLAND PRESS, INC.
ENGLAND • USA • SCOTLAND

PUBLISHED BY PENTLAND PRESS, INC.
5124 Bur Oak Circle, Raleigh, North Carolina 27612
United States of America
919-782-0281

ISBN 1-57197-041-X
Library of Congress Catalog Card Number 96-69832

Printed in the United States of America

For Lucie, Anita, Heinz-Gerd, Petra,
Michael, Muff and Sherry

In Memoriam To:

The late Chris J. Delahunty, Hotelier –

The greatest man I ever knew;
My mentor and best friend;
And a philosopher in his own right!

One of his many quotations:

"Never make haste,
unless you withdraw your arm out of the
open mouth of a tiger!"

"Study the past, and you will know the future."
Confucius

TABLE OF CONTENTS

CHAPTERS

FOREWORD

When I first met Siegfried Born in the spring of 1989, I was immediately impressed by his broad-mindedness, sense of humor and warmth. I frankly did not associate such qualities with a man who had a German military background.

Siegfried mentioned that he was writing a book and wondered if I would agree to proofread a chapter. I wondered how he would present his war record given the defeat of Nazi Germany. I also wondered what it had been like to fight for the Third Reich, only to face defeat and unconditional surrender.

Several of my own family members had served and died in the great conflict of 1939-1945 with the Allied Forces. Although peace was attained before I was born, I knew very little about World War II. Most veterans I have known seldom speak about their part in the war effort. I certainly had no knowledge from the perspective of "The Enemy."

Siegfried's chronicle tells the story of a young man caught in the fury of war. The account is honest and compelling, lacking any effort to glorify or degrade his own participation. No attempt is made to justify failed ideologies or discuss dogmas or "-isms." What appears is a clear picture of life in the German military during this troubled period of human history. No embellishment of his story is required as the events are both ordinary and extraordinary at the same time.

The occurrences, characters and settings come alive through the eyes of a Navy private with a knack for observation. Siegfried witnessed the onset and ultimate conclusion of the bloodiest conflict in history and he recounts his participation with a dignity befitting the gentleman he is. The service he gave to MI 6 (British Military Intelligence) at the war's conclusion provides further evidence of the author's belief in responsibility, fairness and decency.

This is not a hero story but a gripping narrative that reveals the spirit and boldness of the soldiers who fought on the *other side* in the "war to end all wars."

David A. Rowe

ACKNOWLEDGMENTS

I am obliged to . . .

Employees of the Sudbury General Hospital's dietary department for the gift of a typewriter, eliminating an excuse on my part for not writing this book.

Numerous classically trained musicians and jazz artists, who kept me company. They provided inspiration and nourishment for my brain cells.

Beverly Sabourin, my former secretary, who faithfully and enthusiastically screened my drafts, corrected my errors, and typed the original version of the manuscript.

Elvy Yost, host of "Saturday Night At the Movies," TV Ontario, for his kind comments and hints.

Walter MacLeod, for plugging part of my manuscript.

My special gratitude is directed to David Rowe, a great friend and gentleman in his own right, for his unerring and unwavering assistance and valuable advice.

Last, I do thank my wife, Lucie, from the bottom of my heart for her patience and understanding. She assured me right from the outset that I could pull off writing this account of events, without any formal literary training in a "foreign language."

Thank you!

MEMO TO READER

It is only fair to remind you that the statements made and opinions expressed by the players in this book do not necessarily correspond with my own way of thinking. That equally applies to most of the coarse language used by some people I met.

—The Author

Summer of 1989

AUTHOR'S NOTE

This book does not pretend to be a literary masterpiece. Rather, it reports in fast-moving and conversational manner significant events that took place in Scandinavia between October 1941 and October 1945.

It is not a book about war per se, but sheds light on the people in war, and how they handled different situations.

The main players appear under their own names, except a very few, whose names have been withheld or changed in order to avoid embarrassment to surviving relatives.

My account of circumstances does not intend to glorify war or violence. Neither do I want to use my eyewitness experience and evidence as a political instrument, though I have made a number of statements favorable to democracy. Nevertheless, facts will speak for themselves.

Various portions of my portrayals do not emerge in history books. Incidents have been described with as much impartiality as is humanly possible for a former member of the German Armed Forces. However, in no way do I attempt to whitewash atrocities committed by the Nazi government in the name of the German people. My opposition to and contempt for the totalitarian systems, under which I grew up, should be evident.

The author at age four.

Occurrences, dates and dialogues are based on my own notes and recollections. I have no apologies to offer for my actions, nor for any unadulterated comments, which will please some, but annoy others.

For good reasons—becoming clear to you, the reader—I have disclosed my services with the British after cessation of hostilities, including my participation in a demobilization task force led by the legendary Captain Cornish from MI-Six.

I am sure you will be enlightened and also entertained by this documentary biography. Lean back and enjoy reading it as I had the pleasure of writing it for you!

Siegfried Born

CHANGING CLOTHES

The Surprise

On 19 September 1941, business had been rather slow at lunch time and in the afternoon, when we served coffee and cake for those who did not have anything better to do than sloughing themselves to the rim with *Torten* (fancy cakes). That afternoon, the slow service led to discussions among waiters, revolving around the chicken and egg issue: "Are these customers eating so much because they are heavy, or are they so heavy because they eat so much?" Needless to say, we never reached an agreement on that topic, no matter how often it came up.

Herr Rudermann, the headwaiter–who had to be called Herr; otherwise he would have been afraid to lose his dignity–sent me home about 7:30 P.M. Only a few customers were having dinner in the eighty-five-seat dining room. There was the overall impression that many were hanging around without really enjoying themselves. It was one of those days we call "*Sauerampfer* (sorrel) days." Some of the men, I was sure, started getting a bit worried, wondering when their "bell would toll" to be drafted to the German Armed Forces. Contrary to popular belief, not all Germans were looking forward to putting their heads in the noose for the glory of the vaterland.

That included some young people who were studying at the university and those like myself, who had finished an apprenticeship training and had just begun to earn a fairly good living. Getting drafted would interrupt all this. For the edification of the North American reader, I should explain that apprenticeship training, at the time, brought in meager earnings, which could not even keep one going for longer than two days a week. But we did not want to complain about this, knowing that parents of prior generations had to pay employers a hefty sum for allowing their children to learn a trade, technology or profession. That surely would have excluded me from learning a trade, not to mention attending a university in preparation for becoming a professional. We simply did not have any money to spare. Period!

As I always did during my walk home, I stopped here and there to look at some of the *Sondermeldungen* (special bulletins) which the government had out in those days. And there were a lot of them, one chasing the next.

As you remember, or have learned in school, on Sunday, 20 July 1941, Hitler ordered his troops to march through the eastern part of Poland, which came under Soviet administration right after the eighteen-day war, when Poland was carved up as a country between Germany and Soviet Russia. Regardless of the fact that the Western World had regarded the ten-year Nonaggression Pact between Germany and Soviet Russia, signed in the wee hours of Thursday, 24 August 1939, a dirty agreement, Hitler's breaking the pact sent shock waves into the farthest corners of the world!

In the USA, Harry Hopkins, Special Advisor to President Roosevelt, together with a number of influential people from the political stage, as well as a great number of industrialists, tried in vain to convince members of the House and the Senate that war should be declared on Germany. The number of countries we annexed before Poland, and those we overran subsequently, should have been sufficient cause to join the struggle against the dictatorship. Another good reason would have been the disregard we showed for the agreements of the Geneva Convention by torpedoing as many merchant ships as we could sink. Many

Americans, having seen Germany reneging on the Nonaggression Pact, began to wonder which of the two evils was worse: Communism or Nazism?

In any case, credit should be given to the Japanese. They eventually convinced Americans of who is who by attacking Pearl Harbor five and a half months later. That automatically changed the "Axis Power" to a "Triangular Power," Germany, Italy and Japan.

Hitler's claim of launching a preemptive strike against Soviet Russia was just as poor an excuse as his claim that provocative activity by Poles along the border served to justify reprisal by the German Army. History has proven, without a shadow of a doubt, in September 1939, Poland was totally unprepared for any serious conflict with Germany; the same with Soviet Russia in July 1941.

After the war, I had the opportunity to discuss both occurrences with a number of Germans who were on location when it happened. That includes my own father-in-law, who was promptly drafted on Wednesday, 30 August 1939, two days before the outbreak of war. He, with many others about his age, had served in World War I. Because of their previous war experience, most of them were drafted as corporals and, together with professional soldiers of all ages, sent to what was commonly referred to as the Eastern Front. On both occasions, in September 1939 and July 1941, the German Army marched for days before encountering any resistance! I mentioned the reasons before. These were absolute facts, though some members of my generation would like to call it another version. It is not!

Germans were delirious, with the exception of a few who had continued the practice of thinking for themselves. None of them would dare to admit their different thoughts for fear of ending up in a concentration camp. It could easily happen. An acquaintance of mine, four years my senior, had made the grave mistake in 1938 of collecting selected statements from the German Nazi press which contradicted themselves and of showing those clips during a friendly gathering in a *Gasthaus* on the Hofstrasse in Wuppertal. A loyal party member denounced him. He spent two years in a concentration camp. Before his release, he had to sign a declaration, under penalty of death, that he would never reveal to anybody what he had seen and experienced during the time of his confinement. He did not, not even to us. But it convinced me that something horrible must take place behind those barbed wires.

Germans, by and large, were jubilantly intoxicated by all these victories. Who could possibly stay calm? Did these successes not prove what each German soldier had engraved in his belt buckle? *Gott mit uns* (God with us). Never mind the other factors–total censorship of the press and other news media; the forced unions' integration, serving the Reich; the public burning of books; indiscriminate arrests and confinement of people without orderly legal procedures; or even the clipping the wings of the churches after the NSDAP, the *National Sozialistische Deutsche Arbeiterpartei* (National Socialistic German Workers Party) took power.

Every week you would see in newsreels how the German Luftwaffe "gave it to the Tommies" by pounding British cities, none of which were safe from the bombing onslaught. The populace in Brighton, Southampton, Bristol, Plymouth, Birmingham, Coventry and London had a tough time finding sleep. For them, the Battle of Britain had begun.

Then there were all those countries that had been conquered almost in sandwich fashion. Poland was first. Then the German offensive began in the West. Belgium and Holland fell like tenpins. France and Luxembourg fell soon after.

German forces swept through Denmark with the goal of Norway as the next victim in mind for occupation. It turned out to be kind of a cliffhanger. We now know that the Allies, particularly Great Britain, made overtures to convince the Norwegian government of the imminent invasion by German forces. With the goal in mind to make Norway safe, their appeal was directed to the Norwegian Parliament, allowing them to occupy the country before we did. But the Norwegians did not want their country to be occupied by anybody. Nevertheless, we struck twenty-four hours before Britain was ready to invade. The rest is history.

Like so often before, whenever I saw and heard the average German in jubilation, I started wondering whether this would last. I came to the conclusion that the few friends I had all seemed to have one thing in common: an intense dislike of coercion of any kind and more so for the marching brownshirts. We were a small bunch of dissidents, who said and did darn well what we wanted. Being between the ages of eighteen and twenty-two, we could not claim to have a real understanding of what politics was all about. We knew only about the system we grew up under and did not like what we saw. But we sure as heck could distinguish between a system which would allow choice and one that would not tolerate any deviation from the party line. There had to be something else out there.

My closest friend, Fritz Rethmeier, and I had been picked up twice by regular police for not attending Hitler Youth meetings, with the understanding that, if there was a third time, the Gestapo (Secret State Police) would invite us without ceremony. We searched for a loophole and found one. A physician who sympathized with people like us promptly attested to our frailties, which exempted us from all military-like exercises. The Hitler Youth group leader came close to a fit when he saw our diagnoses. We gracefully agreed to become paying members of the group, which pacified him a bit. That took care of it. We had no more problems with him.

In September 1940, Fritz and I had made another move that came under suspicion by irate Nazi thinkers. We enrolled at the Berlitz School of Languages in an English course. How could we ever be so stupid as to throw our money away by learning English? The English and their Allies certainly would lose the war and the language, therefore, would be stamped out. We had to listen to so much crap like this that one day I gave the daring reply, "First of all, who wins the war has not yet been decided. And if so, do you think we could stamp out the English language, which is spoken and understood by two-thirds of the world population." I knew I had hit a bloody sensitive spot!

I did not tell my parents about that incident, if only for the simple reason to not disappoint my dad. We had deep love and affection for each other, but politically we were at odds, to say the least. The following couple of days I frequently woke up in the middle of the night expecting knocks at the door. They did not come. But I still remember vividly when four years earlier some of our neighbors had been picked up exactly in that fashion for similar "demoralizing" remarks. They simply vanished in thin air and were never heard from again. Relatives were not given any information after the arrests when they inquired about the whereabouts of husbands and fathers. In some cases, when relatives kept insisting on knowing the fate of their loved ones, they received one more chance to smarten up—read: stay quiet or else.

As I reached Oberstrasse, the street where we lived, I climbed the precipitous lower part for the umpteenth time. Children were playing, their happy laughter echoing from stone walls of apartment houses, unaware of any danger. For a moment I thought how nice it would be to turn back the clock and be a child again without any worries. I did then fully realize how difficult it must have been for my parents to have me grow up with an extremely limited income, yet be protected from danger and want.

I opened the front door of the apartment house and habitually counted the eighty-one steps that led to the fourth floor. That reminds me of a baffling opposing concept between

Europeans and North Americans. The higher an apartment is located in Europe, the cheaper it is. Here we have exactly the opposite.

Upon entering the apartment, I immediately sensed that something unusual had happened. My mother's eyes were moist, while my father was standing in the door frame between the kitchen and living room, smiling broadly. It just did not make any sense! What kind of news would make Dad happy but Mom sad?

"What is going on?" I asked.

"We will tell you later, after dinner," was my father's reply.

We sat down for dinner, but the atmosphere was loaded with tension. No matter how I tried, I could not figure out the reason. There was nothing wrong with the meal. Yet I noticed Mother chewing as never before. She had a big lump in her throat for sure. We finished with our plates fast. Nobody felt like having dessert.

Father went to the living room, motioning me to follow. "Sit down, my son," he said. He walked over to a small desk and picked up a letter, as Mother walked in. Her eyes were still wet and red. Dad handed me an already opened letter. I took it out. I should have known: A "welcome letter" from the Fuehrer, advising I had been drafted into the navy to serve Fuehrer, Volk und Vaterland. Bang! There went my stomach. But wait, why the navy? That branch of the armed forces hardly ever took anybody but "suitable" volunteers. What happened? Then I recalled the day in June I spent the previous year before the Muster Examination Board.

Getting Ready

The German government at the time had a rather ingenious way of getting hold of young people early in life, realizing, like all dictatorships, that the mind of the young is easiest to form and bend. Hitler's doctrinairism started out with youngsters between the ages of six and fourteen, who were indoctrinated by the Jungvolk, one of the two Nazi Youth organizations. Then followed the Hitler Jugend (Hitler Youth) from fourteen to eighteen. After that, and before the draft, you had better join the Party (there was only one, of course, the NSDAP) to become *ein Parteigenosse* (a party member). The term *Genosse,* by the way, is synonymous with "*Kamerad,*" or "comrade." Sound familiar to you? It should. The word is borrowed from the communistic ideology and was widely used by the Nazis, both as political and military address.

Officially joining any of these organizations was not compulsory until 1940, but parents were well-advised to make sure their kids joined the *Jungvolk* and subsequently the Hitler Youth. Otherwise they would be open to harassment and worse consequences. Also, breadwinners had better be members of the Party or their jobs were in jeopardy, followed by arrests. One sarcastic definition of this catch twenty-two, squeezed-in situation jokingly described it as *freiwillig gezwungen* (voluntarily forced).

The Physical

I had not quite turned eighteen at the time, when the Muster Examination Board called me in to have my frame examined. But the idea of looking at able-bodied men that early was simple. It suited a dual purpose: One, let's find out how soon we can assign this body to a six-month service in the *Freiwilligen Arbeitsdienst* (Voluntary Work Service). There you were given the opportunity to sacrifice a free work service voluntarily to the country, before carrying your bones to war for the fatherland.

Here I was, with a bunch of other youngsters, lined up, crawling from one room to the next, stripped naked except shorts, with all other clothing carried over one arm. By and large, most examiners behaved just like any other doctor. Some others, with their assistants, were determined to give us "softies" an idea of how rough a future we faced. One bastard made the muster particularly degrading. When my turn came, he shouted at me, "Bend down lower, lower, you idiot, so I can see your damn hemorrhoids!" And that was kind of a mild approach. The number and types of flattering statements defy description. Many of us were scared stiff, not at all looking forward to *Kommissleben* (military life).

When this "dance" was over, I was informed that I was exempted from work service. "We have no use for feeble individuals like you, performing work with pick and shovel" I was told, which gratefully hit my ear. "But you have been classified as an army gunner and will be drafted some time next year. Any questions?"

I asked whether I could be considered for another branch of the armed forces. I was referred to the third floor, where the screening of volunteers would take place. Now I must say I did not feel like volunteering for anything, but sooner or later I would have to wear a uniform. I set myself in motion by seeing somebody from the Naval Administration Draft Board.

The Volunteer

There were no elevators. So I used this opportunity to test the fitness of my heart and lungs by quickly jumping up the huge marble steps, until I landed on the floor where at least part of my future would be decided.

Arrows with signs pointed you in the desired direction and offices without any other help–much better than in many North American buildings, including hotels, hospitals and official buildings. German thoroughness is unsurpassed, which is a positive trait, as far as I am concerned. Nothing is left to chance. If you ever want to see a typical example of that thoroughness, get hold of a German railway schedule. The main schedule is as big as the Chicago telephone book! But that is not all. The time table is strictly adhered to anywhere in the country. For instance, if a train is expected to arrive one or several minutes behind schedule, it is announced over the public address system with an apology. (I thought I should throw in a good word for my former fellow countrymen.)

When I reached the landing, I turned to the left, where an arrow with the words "*Deutsche Kriegsmarine Nur fuer Freiwillige*" (German Navy–for Volunteers Only) indicated which direction I had to take.

Soon I was standing in front of a thick oak door with the letters "Navy Volunteers." I knocked and a pleasant voice said, "Come in, please." That already astonished me, since the use of the word "please" was undesirable and discouraged from use within the German military.

I walked in and, to my surprise, a *Bootsmann* (navy sergeant) with a friendly smile, about twenty years my senior, came around his desk. His outstretched hand shook mine and he motioned me to take a seat. I could not believe it; if this was the accepted conduct in the navy, it was certainly for me!

He returned to his leather-upholstered swivel chair, leaned back and said, half asking and half making a statement, "So you want to join the navy?" I told him I did and handed over my muster papers. He glanced at them, then asked, "Why do you want to join the navy?"

I told him the truth–that I simply did not like the idea of becoming an army gunner. Since none of us would have a choice of whether or not we would wear a uniform, I felt I would fit in better with the navy than any of the other military branches. Besides, I loved the sea.

Bootsmann Wallreich (I found out his name much later) opened his desk drawer, took out a form and handed it to me across the desk with the remark, "If you are serious with your intention of joining the navy, here is a form which you should fill out and sign after reading it. Take it home and have your dad or guardian sign it as well. You will need his approval. Then return the application to me, either by mail or in person. Do you have any questions?" he added. I did not have any.

He asked me about my trade and I gave him my background, stating I would be finished with training in September 1940. Then I asked him a question; when could I expect to be drafted?

"Probably not before the end of summer next year," he replied. "The army might induct you earlier than that. But you still will have a chance to earn some money by then." He got up to indicate the interview was over, and shook my hand again. I thanked him politely for his time and left the room.

When I came home that evening, I had a closer look at the application form. The questions to be answered were simple enough. There seemed to be no small print anywhere. I had turned to page three. Hold it! There it was. In order to be accepted by the navy, the applicant had to commit himself to serve for a minimum of four years. I consulted my dad at this point, asking his opinion. He should know about the military since he had served during the entire World War I.

He expressed some doubt about the four years. Peacetime military service, unless one wanted to become a professional soldier, was two years. Maybe it would be better if I did not volunteer after all, mused Dad. Germany had beaten all her enemies so far. Poland had fallen in eighteen days. And only a few days prior, on Saturday, 22 June 1940, an armistice agreement had been signed with France. What else could possibly prevent Germany from being victorious to the end?

"Would you sign, Dad, if I volunteered?" I asked.

"Of course, my son," was his answer. "Even though you are not quite eighteen, you have your muster papers, which entitles you to officially smoke and drink Schnapps or beer. That also makes you old enough to make your own decisions. I guess these benefits are awarded to anybody who, willingly or not, puts his life on the line for the fatherland."

I completed the form and Dad gave his signature. Then, on second thought, instead of mailing it, I put it in a drawer. The four-year service duty commitment had created a knot in my stomach. I never mailed in the application.

1 OCTOBER 1941

It's Getting Serious.

As you might remember, Fritz and I had been exempted from active duty in the Hitler Youth, thanks to the understanding physician who had declared us unfit for participating in semi-military exercises. The group leader disliked, if not hated, our attitude right from the beginning. It might be frustrating for a drill sergeant who is expected to reshape the minds of individuals who stubbornly stick to their views, refuse to be indoctrinated and, therefore, cannot be changed. He must have had a feeling of having failed.

This particular individual suffered from delusions of grandeur–a typical paranoiac. Can you imagine how much he hated us when he could not enforce his will on us and we slipped through his fingers?

Immediately at the outbreak of hostilities in 1939, this Hitler Youth leader, who was then twenty years old, had enthusiastically volunteered to serve in the navy. We knew this from other active members of the group. I guess it was with some glee that Fritz and I went to his office with my draft papers. For a moment he was speechless. Then he grew furious. He shouted, "Damn shit. Here I am, loyal as anybody could be to the fatherland. For two years I am tried to be accepted by the navy, and what happens? They draft a good-for-nothing like you." He continued working himself into a frenzy, like his idol Adolf did during his numerous speeches. We knew we had hit the bull's-eye with our message. When he finally ran out of profanities, we left his domain, laughing about his powerlessness. Revenge may not be noble, but it sure can be sweet.

All draftees had been instructed to report at the railway station with not more than one suitcase. "Once you have received your military uniforms, other clothing and accessories, you cannot wear civilian clothes anymore and, therefore, do not need them," we were told.

I was to report at 1800 hours at the central railway station in Wuppertal. On 1 October, which was a Wednesday, most of my friends were off in the evening or had a day off. They all came to see me off.

I had said good-bye to my relatives, most of whom lived close by. I sent a note to those living in other communities. Private telephones were practically nonexistent at the time. Only rich people could afford them. How times have changed!

It was a rather overcast day, though it did not rain. We gathered in front of the station with a number of other draft victims and their families and friends, making some meaningless conversation in the attempt to adapt to situation that cannot be changed. Not that the crowd was void of devoted National Socialists, but I am sure none of these parents cherished the idea that they may never see their sons again. We are all vulnerable and have feelings.

My mother tried to put on a show of bravery, but the quivering and twitching corners of her mouth belied her front.

I remember well the last conversation I had with my father on that evening. He knew I was kind of a tenderfoot and lacked the courage to face military life. Trying to console me he said, "Siegfried, you will see, the war will be over in one year or so and you will return home."

I replied, "Father, I thank you for your thoughts, but that I do not believe. Three to four years would be more realistic." Little did I know then that I was fairly close.

When Bootsmann Wallreich arrived on the scene, he briefed us on the forthcoming transport to Kiel, German Naval Headquarters, and on expectations of conduct during the trip and later expectations when in uniform. My curiosity got the better of me. While my chums gathered around, I asked him how I got drafted into the navy without having volunteered—remembering quite well the application form that still lay in the drawer of our living room.

He answered, "Well, I'll tell you. On one or two rare occasions during the year, members of the draft board are allowed to induct a few birds like you. I figured you would really like to join the navy but got cold feet when you saw the four-year commitment you would have to make. So we mixed you and a few others here together with volunteers. Right now you belong to a minority of four out of a total of 148."

I thanked him for the information, expressed my gratitude and joy, and promised to become a worthwhile member of the "elite in blue."

A shrill whistle got our attention. It was time to board the train. We said our last goodbye and were herded through the boarding barrier to the train, which had been put together on platform two. A loud-mouthed sergeant from the army told us in no uncertain terms to "move your arses." Three minutes later we were on our way.

The distance from Wuppertal to Kiel is about 500 km. A *D-zug* (fast train) covered that in six hours actual travel time. A *Fern D-zug* (far distance train) managed it in less than five hours. Nowadays, the average speed of a far distance train is 160 kilometers, or one hundred miles, per hour.

Accidents are rare—and that's on European railway nets which have forty times more density than those in North America, plus the fact that they are earning a profit. Maybe we should look over the fence once in a while and learn from management, maintenance procedures and efficiencies in European countries.

The lack of belligerency between labor and management has a lot to do with Europeans' success in the field of transportation. Add to this the owners and shareholders to reinvest capital in the operation—rather than stripping everything bare—and you have a pretty good explanation for their superior service to the public. I hasten to add that postal services are equally good and efficient, much better than in the US and absolutely superior to the atrocious mail deliveries Canadians have to endure.

The troop transport train was neither an FD nor a D train. At best, it could be called an SS train. To remove any possible misconception, the SS does not refer to the political terror organization of the time, but in this case stands for slow-slow. This was understandable, because the train had to pick up new conscripts in each town it passed. Most of us did not mind. We were in no hurry to wear a uniform, not to mention the probability of meeting with danger.

Most inductees engaged in conversation, speculating on where we would receive our basic military training and the future beyond. Others simply played chess or cards to kill time.

From the end of the car we heard loud voices and singing, which seemed to indicate that bottles of Schnapps had been passed around. I had only three possible explanations for this: First, some fools were really celebrating their induction. But then, I thought, why not? After all, they had volunteered. Second, some were trying to hide their fear of things to come and drown their sorrows, like the convict on death row who is to be executed and is allowed one last meal. In this case, it was a last hurrah! Third, some believed this to be the beginning of one big adventure. Well, they would have a thing coming!

Right next to my compartment I heard a guy complaining. He seemed to be in a hurry to get killed. "What is the damn dawdling all about? Is it really necessary to stop at each mailbox?" Another chap had a comment for him, "What the hell are you in such a hurry for? Want to bring a larger distance between yourself and the girl you knocked up?" Following that flattering statement, everybody else got into the act with smart aleck remarks.

Nothing significant happened during the trip. When midnight came around, several men tried to get some sleep. But that was sort of difficult, with the sudden braking, stopping and banging of doors. It was no problem for me, though. When I had finished my detective story, I fell asleep. Once asleep, artillery fire could not wake me up. That came in handy later on. Sometimes, during transport troop travels, there was no space to lie down or sit. I promptly learned how to sleep standing up. Need creates flexibility and inventiveness.

A friend of mine developed an ingenious method of regenerating quickly. He calls it *Schlusselprobe* (key test). It works like this: He sits down in an armchair, leans back, stretches out one arm over the armrest, slips a bundle of keys on a key ring over the middle finger, then closes his fist and eyes. Usually, after three to five minutes, his fist begins to open, the keys clink to the floor; voilà, the key test is finished. He claims to be thoroughly refreshed any time he goes through this exercise. To this day I am not sure whether he was serious about this or was trying to pull people's legs.

Because of the stop-and-go situation, we arrived in Kiel the next morning at 0930 hours. The five hundred kilometer trip had lasted fifteen hours, instead of the regular six, an average of 33.3 kilometers per hour. That was slow, but not the slowest railway travel by any means, as I would find out in 1943 when I returned from Germany to Scandinavia.

KIEL

The Formal Induction

German Navy Headquarters, with the naval branch which processed inductees, was situated in the city of Kiel, at the northeastern tip of the state of Schleswig-Holstein. It was a tremendous complex, capable of accommodating, feeding and screening up to four thousand greenhorns. Because of its hugeness, a maximum number of future members of forces other than naval personnel and some destined for semi-military service were also processed here; but in each case by members of the respective branch.

At Kiel station a number of troop transport trucks awaited to take us to learn about stage one of military life. We were swished to our destination with maximum speed.

All were very tired from the exhaustive trip, particularly the all-night card players and the celebrators. We needed a break. But that was out of the question. When somebody close by me suggested it, the sergeant snapped at him, "Are you nuts? This quiet civilian life is finished at last. You had better get used to stepping in big shit without wincing." Clearly, we had better prepare ourselves for an altogether different kind of education. This was only the beginning of a continuous and obstinate attempt to change people by hook or by crook.

I do realize from my own experience how necessary it is for the military to keep control of the troops. A breakdown of discipline, especially during battle, can be catastrophic and jeopardizes human life. There is no room for different opinions. Only strict adherence to the chain of command produces good results in times of war.

On the other hand, we all know how devastating the legitimizing of murder can be for the individual. How many war veterans have problems readjusting to civilian life once they have been dehumanized by military indoctrination?

When the importance of order, hierarchy of ranks and the deviation of functions or tasks are addressed, it becomes easier for the individual to point fingers. As you know, even war criminals have used the excuse of following orders as a carte blanche for murder!

After the war, my British and Canadian counterparts had several discussions with me on the subject of war in general. Nobody claimed not to have been scared like hell when a tricky order had to be carried out. I concurred and admitted to always having been scared of the unknown, even if there was no apparent danger.

The late German general and military tactician Karl Von Clausewitz once stated, "War is nothing more than the continuation of policies by other means." This is an astonishingly revealing admission. Maybe it is time to discard war as an option? The question then rises, is peace at any price worth it? Probably not, as long as governments disregard human rights and slaughter their own people by the millions.

Between 1900 and 1988, 37.4 million people have been killed by wars, while 119.4 million have been liquidated by their own governments. Something to think about!

Straighten Up!

All those having been drafted the same day were grouped together for processing. The systematic approach of the administration in dealing with several thousand people is astonishing for the uninitiated. Everything ticked like clockwork: rooming arrangements, staggered meal hours, physical examinations–which were not nearly as coarse as sixteen months before–paper processing, learning to stand at attention, saluting and marching still in civilian clothes.

I admired the organizational talent of those with minute precision, though I grew up in the hotel business, where operating departments necessitates a similar approach. The result of flawless communication and coordination put a stamp on the quality of service and lay the groundwork for a good reputation.

Some of my friends could not understand why I enjoyed working in such a complicated business, a world in itself. It takes training, simplification, professional behavior, organization and, last but not least, teamwork. All these are guarantors for successful ventures.

On the fourth day, we had to march to the supply depot, which took over two hours. There we received our first uniforms, boots, caps, steel helmets, gas masks, belts, underwear, socks and daggers. The procedure of issuing these items was simple. No physical measures were taken. You just lined up until your turn came. The quartermaster or one of his assistants would glance you over, pick some clothing out of a pile and would throw them at you with the remark, *"Passt* (Fits)*!"* nipping any protest in the bud.

One chap dared to remark, "This jacket is too small for me. Can I have a larger one?"

The clerk snapped at him, "That jacket will fit you fine in no time, once we've scaled all that excess fat off your cadaver. That life belt you carry around your belly is not needed in the navy. You will learn to swim without it. Next!" End of argument. These guys who issued the stuff were quick on the draw, and at times even funny, but always at the expense of the inquirer.

While I was still in the room having a quick look at my things, I heard one *Landser* (GI) asking, "When will we get our rifles?"

The answer came from the quartermaster. "Don't make me laugh! You can't even stand straight and your body didn't as yet have a chance to adjust to the uniform. That is bad enough. But brother, we don't want to be responsible when you shoot yourself in the foot. You will get your bloody rifle when your skeleton stops rattling!" Nice, very nice, I thought.

The moment I left the barrack I heard a commotion right in front of the entrance. One man had fallen to the ground, surrounded by others. First I thought the poor chap was exhausted because of the long march. Coming closer, I noticed foam at the corner of his mouth. Obviously it was an epileptic attack, I thought, since I knew a former school friend who, off and on, had light epileptic attacks.

A couple of men, who appeared to know what they were doing, knelt beside the man on the ground and made him as comfortable as possible. The corporal in charge of our group had called a superior, a staff sergeant, who came on the scene only seconds after I did. He confirmed my quiet diagnosis, shook his head and, without hushing his voice, said, "How is it possible to draft such a poor man?" Yes, some in uniform did not lose their compassion for their fellow man.

The next several days we marched and marched and marched. We also got a taste of some military songs. One of the first songs which navy personnel had to learn was, of course, *Wir fahren gegen Engeland* ("We Sail for England"), until it came out of our ears. Indoctrination had definitely begun.

One of the spit and polish exercises which soldiers of all countries go through, to the best of my knowledge, is to have highly shining boots. We became expert bootblacks in no time! I heard all kinds of procedures to get best results.

One man showed me his sparkling boots and told me his secret. "First," he said, "I rinse them thoroughly under running cold water to get rid of all that dirt and shit. Then I dry them with a soft cloth, like discarded woolen long johns. Next I pee over them (he was not kidding!), dry them again, apply a fairly thick sheet of shoe polish, wait three minutes, polish with a brush, then use a bottom of a bottle, scraping over the entire surface, and lastly wipe vigorously with another woolen cloth." I followed his instructions to the letter. Awkward, but they worked well. The only thing was that the third step had to be carefully timed.

When receiving our outfits, I had a close look at everything but the leather belt. It seemed to be like any other belt at the time, dark, with a width of about three centimeters, or a bit more than one inch. As I looked at the iron belt buckle, I could not believe my eyes. Around the inner circle stood the inscription *Gott mit uns* (God with us). What a paradox. How could we possibly claim to have the Lord on our side? The system had done everything possible to suppress free speech, banned and burned books, recordings, surrealistic literature and depraved art. We persecuted the Jews and, for that matter, anybody who fell under suspicion for lack of loyalty to the Party. Last, but not least, we told the clergy to stop interfering with the state under threat of closing thousands of churches. And here now, on this belt buckle, we had the nerve to claim that God is with us. This was a bad joke indeed.

The world certainly knew that we had rapidly developed into an atheistic society like the Soviets. Never mind that our ideology stood far to the right, while that of the Soviets leaned to the extreme left. When one looks closer, it becomes obvious that all these "-isms" have a lot in common: They are built on power, not on principle. No matter what they call themselves, they share similar approaches including inflexibility, lacking realism and denying people the right to choose. They just wrap themselves in different packages. It is most unfortunate, though, that only those who actually have lived under a dictatorship know it when they see one.

When the eighth day came along, most of us had blisters on our feet. Hardly anybody was accustomed to marching for hours, in the first place, not to mention in these *Knobelbecher* (popular German slang for boots), some of which were too tight, others too large. My father had warned me about marches and ill-fitting boots. He gave me on my way a six-month supply of Preservative Kreme, a special German foot cream which prevents chafing and rashes. By greasing my feet with this stuff before each march, I did not suffer nearly as much as most.

After breakfast we had to line up, as usual, for early morning inspection. This time there was a special reason. The camp functionaries had completed the major documentation for nearly thirteen hundred inductees and were now looking for some clerical assistance. Each case had to be summarized and formal marching papers processed for basic military training destinations. Seventy-eight part-time clerks were needed to assist with this task. I was one of them.

Thirteen teams of six each were delegated. The trouble with this was the camp was occupied to the rim. Not to worry! One of the two gymnasiums was converted in a jiffy.

All anticipated transfers had to be handled in confidence. To make it more airtight, it was arranged that each one of us involved in processing did not have to screen documents pertaining to members of the group to which we belonged. If I thought this was a secretive way of dealing with documents, I had a thing coming much later, when I became familiar with the cloak-and-dagger, need-to-know approach.

Anyway, all I could find out was that a limited number of files bore an identifying "S." I could not make heads or tails of it. Nor could anybody else. One joker suggested that those would be sent to Switzerland; another offered Sweden to be a desirable destination.

During dinner the conversation circled around that mysterious "S." Curiosity increased. One guy said, "I think I got it, but it isn't good news if I am right. It might stand for *Sonderkommando* (special detachment). I have heard something like this before. These men will receive accelerated basic military training and will subsequently be sent to the front."

You should have heard the whole mob cursing at the suggestion. I did not like that idea either, but did not want to overreact. After dinner I did become somewhat concerned, if only for the reason that all the speculation did not take us out of the one-way street: destination unknown.

Some of the other group clerks had seen the symbol as well. One of them was particularly curious. He decided to visit other groups in hopes of making a big discovery. Against instructions, he had made himself a list of names whose files showed the "S." He seemed to be the kind of person whose ego does not allow him to not know first. Unfortunately, more often than not, the same type often starts and spreads rumors fast.

He opened his booklet and, as we mentioned our names, flew over the pages. My name appeared. It was the only one from the group. I had difficulty hiding my uneasiness when he supported the theory that "S" means *Sonderkommando*. Appearing to be unconcerned said, "You are only half-right. It does not mean *Sonderkommando*, but *Sonderklasse* (special class)." I heard a few boos. The conversation petered out after a while.

It took until the afternoon of the following day to process the thirteen hundred cases. At 1700 hours we had to line up again to be told that we would be shipped out the next day. The tension increased because we did not know what our destination would be. Some of my comrades could not sleep and played card games till the wee hours of the morning.

Finally, after breakfast, all those whose files bore the "S" were called out to line up for the last time. Funny, the chap who had suggested Sweden as a desirable destination came closest. The "S" stood for Scandinavia which, in our case, meant Norway. I could hardly conceal my relief. Norway had been occupied by us in May 1940. It could only mean that I would become a member of the occupying forces. For the time being, at least, there was no danger of being shot to pieces. Was I ever fortunate! At the time, I did not even have the slightest idea how fortunate I really was!

We had sent our civilian clothes back home, but I retained a couple of stockings, a few handkerchiefs and my best pair of black oxfords. There was just about enough space to squeeze everything into the *Seesack* (naval sack), including my two Berlitz English language study booklets. Whatever might happen, I was determined to hang on to my knowledge of the language, which I liked from the moment that I heard it spoken for the first time. That sound decision did pay off later.

DESTINY: HAON – MILITARY TRAINING

The Voyage

Like in other military formations around the world, every soldier is first exposed to what is generally called basic training, regardless of whether he is a volunteer, a draftee for active service, or a reservist. Officer material or not, he goes through the stages of "boot hill life." So it was with us.

We embarked in Kiel on a troop transport ship, whose name escapes me. The head count was 396. It had a capacity to carry easily six hundred plus. Destination: Larvik, which is situated at the southwestern tip of Sandefjord. There, we would be split up and sent in different directions.

I looked leerily at the steamer. A chap in Wuppertal, who was born in 1921 and had been inducted one year earlier as a volunteer, had told me a horror story about troop transport ships. He had arrived home on his first year leave after I had mustered. Among his unpleasantries were a lack of bunks, overcrowding to such extent that men had to be packed like sardines right on the floor, alternately one way, the next opposite. Each man had the pleasure of getting the smelly feet of his two neighbors in his nose. He complained about the rotten food, *mief* (German slang for badly-used air), headache, stomachache, vomiting, diarrhea and extreme oscillation and vibration, which indicated the ship's lack of equilibrating stabilizers.

The ship we were on did not bear any of these shortcomings. With thirty other men, I had a more than reasonable accommodation on *Zwischendeck* (between decks). The food was quite acceptable. The slightly swaying motion of the boat affected me like a lullaby.

In the beginning, the sea was quite calm. That did not appear to prevent some guys from becoming seasick already after one hour. Only a handful of us had seafaring experience. These were former members of the mercantile marine, who were easy to pick out from the rest of the crowd. Their widespread walks and the ability to swing with the waves gave them away. Often, for them, this was just a matter of readjusting from a smaller ship to a larger one. I guess, in comparison, that is easier than driving a small car and then shifting to a big cruiser.

When we had left the North Sea behind us, we navigated northeast, fairly close along the Danish coast, then entered the waters of the Skagerrak. The waves showed more aggression here. I was glad to have followed the advice of Bootsmann Wallreich from the navy volunteers office. "No matter what you might hear from some who have all kinds of silly ideas about seasickness," he advised, "make sure, you substantially fill your stomach with food. First, you will not get easily seasick that way. Second, if you do, you will have enough in your stomach to vomit." I saw by his face that he was not kidding and he was right.

When I came by boat to Canada in 1956, I noticed everyday one man standing around before the board bar would open. On the fifth day, I could not dampen my curiosity anymore. I had entered the bar only a half-hour after it opened. Here he was again, lifting the elbow and staring with a concentrated-looking face into his glass, which he had set down empty, when I came in. I thought, better ask him that burning question now before he gets so plastered that he can only stammer. Twice before I had seen some other men lifting him under the armpits and halfway carrying him away. I asked the bartender to give him a refill and moved over to take an empty seat at his side. It was quiet at this time of the day.

I started the conversation by mentioning something about the calmness of the sea and the so far pleasant trip. Then, as diplomatically as possible, I added a comment, referring to the salty sea and how easily one could become thirsty with this air. He hooked into that right away and replied, "I know what you people must be thinking, having seen me fairly boozed every day. Ordinarily, I do not drink at all. But on the first day of our trip I did not feel too well. I figured it was the movement of the ship and decided to get loaded. I talked myself into the idea that one can only be loaded or seasick but not both. It works. That is the only reason I have to play barfly."

The author at age twenty.

He was rather serious about the whole affair. I suppressed the desire to burst out laughing and excused myself under the pretext of having to send a telegram. If I had his problem, I probably would have imitated his behavior.

We had passed the fifty-seventh latitude, when the captain's sonorous voice ordered us on deck to line up on the double. In the military, everything seems to be carried out on the double, even retreating from the enemy. It keeps the joints flexible and the bones moving.

In this case, it was easier said than done. Depending on the area of accommodation, different routes had been established so as to assure quick assembling on deck in case of emergency. Congestion, confusion and unnecessary crossfire—meaning in this case people bumping into each other—had to be avoided. This was fine, but some of the safety ropes that had been spanned along gangways and deck sections when the sea roughened did not correspond with the abandon ship escape route plan.

I disliked even thinking about what would happen if at that moment the British would land a direct hit with a torpedo. We all would have been taken out of circulation before ever getting a taste of what war would be all about. How much worse would it be if the ship was loaded with personnel at full capacity? Men were running into each other, falling, swearing and cursing, entangling their legs, but still moving somehow.

We had been told that in case of an emergency everybody had to be on upper deck within three minutes. If not, we would repeat the exercise until it clicked. Three minutes my foot! The last couple of dozen or so men finally appeared five and a half minutes after the order came over the intercom. Did we hear a lecture! It was not clear whether the captain knew of the obstructions having prevented us from moving faster. I suspect he did. He included in his bawl-out the statement that, regardless of adversities, we had to learn to "Move your arses!"

Suddenly, the ship's engines stopped completely. The troop commander stepped forward and explained we had just reached the precise spot where on 22 May 1940, after the invasion of Scandinavia, the battleship *Bluecher* was sunk by the British. In memory of our fallen comrades, the black flag was raised and for five minutes we stood silently. I did not know at the time that a chap with whom I had attended school for several years had been aboard the *Bluecher* and was among the few crew members who were rescued.

The remainder of the voyage elapsed uneventfully. We arrived in Larvik after midnight. It was now Saturday, 11 October. Disembarkation was planned for the early morning hours. Most of us tried to get a glimpse of the harbor by rushing on deck. Not much could be seen. It was rather dark.

The Fjord

At 0600 hours, the petty officer on duty woke us with his strange-sounding whistle, which I would hear many more times. The beginning sound comes close to a piccolo flute, then trails off. That is followed by the invitation, "Rise, rise, *aufstehen*." The English word "rise" had become a cosmopolitan word among seafaring nations for almost two hundred years. It is one out of a great number of English terms and words that were adopted by the German mercantile marine and spilled over into the navy. For those who had no clue, the German word *aufstehen* was added as the third word, simply meaning "Get up," to avoid excuses and prevent misunderstandings.

Our last three-tier breakfast took place between 0715 hours and 0845 hours. Immediately after each group had finished, the men filtered into a salon which, in peacetime, probably had served as a ballroom, as indicated by the parquet flooring. Each man received a final destination paper. Mine showed Haon, which was meaningless to me. I was not familiar with the Scandinavian territory, except for what one of my former geography teachers, who was a widely traveled man, had told us. All I remembered was that the Norwegians were a major seafaring nation, caught several thousand tons of fish each year, processed wood, had thousands of lakes and many fjords and islands, and were generally friendly people who loved to mind their own business.

After disembarkation, we went ashore and lined up at the quay, designated as congregation area, and identified by name and number. A tough-looking chief petty officer with deep lines in his face, who did not turn out to be nearly as tough as he looked, acted as receptionist. In ten minutes the 162 men whose papers showed Haon were assembled. The last leg of our voyage would be over in a jiffy, he assured us, only a sixty kilometer stretch. "But," he cautioned, "the boats are small; there is standing room only."

The two boats we were about to embark looked slightly larger than nutshells in comparison to the steamer. The decks had been stripped of everything not necessary for the short trip. No lifeboats. If these large-sized fishing boats would sink, you had better use your natural life belt, or you had it! I had to think back about the chap in Kiel, whose uniform did not fit.

German military commanders had confiscated a great number of Norwegian full-sized fishing boats, which were quite modern at the time. Most of them were converted to *Vorpostenboote* (patrol boats) or *Minenraeumboote* (minesweepers). Older or smaller ones were used within fjord waters for short-distance transportation of troops and materials. Manned with Norwegian captains and crews, they could service the civilian population, but had to be kept on call for whenever we needed them.

The *Oberbootsmann* (chief petty officer) stowed a hundred men on the slightly larger boat and boarded with us the smaller one. The cables were hauled in as soon as the last man had embarked, and away we went.

Soon we had passed Sandefjord and entered Oslofjord. We sailed close to the shore. The scenery was most beautiful. Somehow I felt misplaced as a soldier in an environment that could not possibly be more peaceful than this. What was I doing in this country? Thank the Lord it is that peaceful! I had a hunch this venture was going to be a piece of cake. Close, but not that close. I would get my share of danger.

Apparently I was not the only one who was overcome by nature's beauty. There was such a stillness on deck that one could hear one's own breathing. I would have loved to read my comrades' minds. How lucky to be stationed in such surroundings of total tranquillity. The majority of our comrades were facing danger almost daily. Not all of us were enthused about our political system, which made it so much worse to fight for a cause in which one did not believe.

After a while our leader pointed out a small town on the port side and said, "This is Tønsberg. Twenty kilometers beyond is the town of Horten. The Norwegians call it the town of flowers. These are the two towns where you will spend your time when you get a pass. Haon is located on the starboard side, almost in the center of the two communities. I might just as well tell you right now that there is nowhere to go on Haon. You cannot even find the island on a map."

Great news, I thought. When a boy, I was sent twice for six weeks each time to an island off the Holstein Coast on a state-subsidized vacation, for one reason–to put on weight. The two islands are called Borkum and Norderney. Both are small but well-known resorts. I returned there in the early fifties, but still found entertainment somewhat restricted. Maybe because I literally grew up in the hotel business, I was spoiled. How tiny could Haon be if it was not even listed on a map?

I was almost going to direct a few questions to our leader, but, on second thought, refrained from it, not knowing how ridiculing the answer would be. After all, ridicule from above was the order of the day in the military.

In approaching the island, one could see from the landing side a nice-looking private dwelling on a gradual slope. By goalie, if that was the kind of accommodation we were going to get, we had it made! It was better than at home. But, we'd wait and see.

Haon, The Drill Camp

Both boats tied up side by side at the pier, two small landing jetties. We picked up our things and disembarked. After walking three minutes through a winding path, the chief petty officer proudly proclaimed: "Here we are. This is the middle of the island." That sure gave us an idea how small the island really was. He watched our faces and pointed to four barracks in one row, one barrack at each end and a rocky forest behind. "This here," he said, "will be your entertainment center for the next eight weeks. Be assured, we do not need more space to break you in and make soldiers out of you. Tomorrow, Sunday, you will receive your daggers, gas masks, rifles, ammunition and hand grenades. Rifles and hand grenades will be liberally used during your training here. Our drill sergeants are responsible to me for all your military training. I report about your progress, or lack of it, directly to the island commander. That is the way it works.

"Lieutenant Commander Witzfeld dislikes hearing any bad news. So, it's up to you to make sure that everybody correctly and quickly learns target shooting and the use of hand grenades. Shooting yourself in the foot or through your hand (here was the Kieler description again) will not be tolerated! Waldgruber, take over!"

Thirteen leading seamen had formed a half circle behind the petty officer during his presentation. Second in line, Waldgruber, stepped forward and, with heavy Bavarian dialect, read our names aloud from a crumpled list in his hand. The names were called in sequential alphabetical order, corresponding to group one through group twelve. Each group made up a company unit, twelve men, close to a platoon. The island was just about big enough to accommodate twelve units to be trained without actually getting into each other's way. The thirteenth trainer acted as replacement in case one leading seaman would get ill. He belonged to the camp's administrative staff, which had a total of seven men.

When all names had been called, two men were still standing in their original position. "Aha!" said Waldgruber, "here we have the absentees. Where were you when your names were called?" Both men answered simultaneously, "Here, Herr Bootsmannsmaat." One added, "We did not hear our names called."

"Hogwash," replied Waldgruber. "Who is Pratt and who is Brahms?" Both answered in the affirmative. Brahms added, "We beg your pardon, Leading Seaman, sir, we did not understand our names because of your dialect."

"Typical," said Waldgruber, "you Prussians don't even understand German anymore. You two remind me of Patt and Patterchon (two originals like Laurel and Hardy or Pat and Mike), in name and in looks. Are you a relative of Johannes Brahms, the late great composer?" he asked.

"No, sir," was the reply. "I cannot even play the gramophone."

"That figures. I didn't count on it anyway," Waldgruber commented.

Like most Western countries, Germany has one national language which is taught in all schools. Nevertheless, more than one dozen dialects have developed over two centuries. Unless everybody speaks *Hochdeutsch* (pure German) people have to point ears when they communicate with each other. When exposed to the dialects–and the best experience I can think of is as member of the armed forces–one gets used to all of them.

To add a point of interest, for reasons going far back into history, the south-Germans, particularly the Bavarians, disliked the Prussians for decades. Be that as it may, they did make the mistake and lumped all Germans residing in the western and northern part of the country together with the real Prussians.

The generations after World War II, however, have become much more broad-minded with each other. That has a lot to do with the formation of the EEC (European Economic Community), generally referred to in North America as the common market. Indeed, the personal relationship among Germans has improved, and also between all members of that community. Most Europeans today think about themselves as Europeans first. This is an example that nationalism can be overcome under the right conditions. There is no reason why we cannot think about ourselves in terms of being North Americans first, and Americans and Canadians second.

"You have all day tomorrow to make yourself familiar with the terrain," Waldgruber continued. "Your drill instructors will act as guides. It should not take long. As you can see, there isn't much here to begin with. If you are late for scheduled mealtimes, you lose the grub. Tough luck! Any infraction of rules and regulations will result in disciplinary action, mostly in the form of penalty drills. Repeaters will be handled in a special way. We have some fun exercises for them, like crawling through dirt and shit, or cleaning quarters with a toothbrush. You will follow all instructions from your trainer to the letter, or else! Are there any questions?" The tone of his voice indicated finality as if challenging anybody who would dare to ask questions. But some cannot read between the lines.

Ehrhardt, one of my platoon mates, opened his mouth. "Yes, Leading Seaman, sir, what about girls, and when will we get passes?"

Waldgruber's face started to twist at the corners of his mouth. "Confound it, man!" he let go as if in agonizing pain. "You've got a bloody nerve! Is that all your fucking brain can think about? Having a good time and screwing broads? Let me tell you something. This is not the type of entertainment I mentioned before, but serious business. We make sure you have a good chance to survive when in danger. But training to stay alive demands sacrifices." He took a deep breath and continued, "By the end of a day your bones will feel like fiddlesticks; your lungs will be on the verge of exploding; your heart will jump like a high jump pole at the Olympics; your stomach will be hanging below your belt; your bowels will be shitless and no matter how much water you drink, it will have no time to become piss in your bladder. By the time you drag your cadaver to dinner, you will be glad if you can still move your eyebrows. And if you still don't feel dead, we have special assignments lined up for you. But, to make absolutely sure there isn't one inkling of a sex drive left in you, the cooks will put some stuff in your grub which makes it impossible for your prick to do anything but piss." He took a deep breath and we were dismissed.

I had to admit that was one of the most enlightening and picturesque descriptions I had ever heard. It was not very encouraging, but looking at the brighter side, at least we had not been told to commit suicide–yet.

Each squad consisted of twelve members. I was assigned to group four, which was led by an Austrian leading seaman. His first name was Adolf, but there the similarity with our Fuehrer ended. He was in his thirties and had seen the world as a member of the mercantile marine and knew how to handle people to gain their respect rather than demanding it.

He went with us to see our quarters–twelve to a room. The usual double bunks were spread around the walls, four triple lockers were interspersed as were twelve chairs, one table, one cannon oven to the left of the door and one sink two steps away in the corner. That was going to be our home for the next eight weeks.

"Unpack your things, everything orderly in the locker, left jacket sleeve in front for quick identification of your rank during inspection," he said.

Looking at his watch, he added, "It is now 1530 hours." He continued with a friendly grin, "Coffee and cakes, like at home, or teatime like in England, is not a custom here. Dinner will be ready at 1800 hours. If you are hungry now, go to the *Marketenderei* and buy yourselves some cookies, if you haven't spent all your money on booze. The canteen will close in one half-hour. Keep that oven burning. It gets cool overnight at this time of year. I shall return at 1700 hours sharp. We will tour the camp, then have dinner at the mess hall. See you soon."

We threw our stuff on the bunks, unpacked and sorted out everything in our lockers as instructed. One man shook his head from side to side and complained: "Thunderbolt! If I had known all this before, I sure as hell would not have volunteered to go through this nonsense of training like an infantry man." He turned to me. "Would you?" he asked.

"The shoe doesn't fit me," I replied, because I did not volunteer in the first place. Even if I think I know what it is all about, I don't volunteer in principle. When things go sour, I don't have to blame myself and don't feel that bad.

"Hold it," another guy said. "What the heck are you doing here with us if you did not volunteer?"

I replied jokingly, "There are always a very few with special talents, whom the navy needs. The board knows one when it sees one." Then I had to tell them my story.

Adolf returned as promised and gave us the tour through the territory. The four barracks, where we were quartered, were like lemon wedges. No need to visit them. When standing in front of them, the barrack to the left housed food provisions, the mess hall and a canteen. The barrack to the right was equipped with showers and huge wash basins. That took half the length of the barrack. The other half was used as an ammunitions and weapons depot. As soon as I saw this arrangement, I started to wonder what would happen if the Norwegian Resistance–which, from our standpoint, was an underground movement–would manage to blow up the compound while we would shower and wash. I shuddered at my own gruesome imagination, then threw the thought overboard.

Further to the right, but about ten steps recessed into the bush, was the outhouse, where ten men could hold their "sessions" at the same time. The construction could have been worse. Sideways, there were dividing walls, though the front of the individual cubicles were open. At least we had some privacy. Most important, we did not have to squat on wooden beams and aim at the openings!

The quarters barracks run from east to west. Approximately one hundred meters south of them was one more housing facility, looking a bit less primitive than ours. These were occupied by the drill sergeants and corporals. The areas north, northeast and northwest of the barracks were used as actual drilling grounds. All provisions and materials had to be brought in via the fjord by boat. That, however, never posed a problem; not even in the midst of winter. The fjord waters were kept fairly open and free from ice.

Right after dinner, curiosity got the better of me. I was determined to find out how small the island really was. Two from our group joined me in a walk. Since it was easy to remember where we had disembarked, we decided to return to the landing spot, then circle around the island. That turned out to be darn easy. Walking quite slowly, craning our necks around to look at the scenery, we had closed the circle in less than fourteen minutes. Now we knew!

Returning, we reported the news to our comrades, who did not pretend to be enthusiastic. Some simply drew sour faces; others made free use of four-letter words. (Most German swear words have more than four letters.)

The next day, Sunday, 12 October, was occupied by receiving the military goodies we had been promised the previous day. We were told to "clean the whole damn shit" and be ready for inspection before noon. The drill group leaders gave each group a few quick demonstrations of how to dismantle and reassemble the German *Karabiner* (rifle). This time, they refrained from smart aleck remarks and pointed out safety precautions. Naturally, if one of us greenhorns would actually shoot himself in the foot, the trainer would be called on the carpet. Operating manuals were distributed. Then we had luncheon.

Witzfeld, the commanding officer, extended his official welcome to us during the afternoon inspection. His address was sort of a combination of advice and pep talk, but not worse than any other. I had the feeling that behind his mask of military strictness lay a streak of fairness. My assessment of the man was correct, as I found out before the end of my training.

This being a Sunday, we were given the rest of the day off, with the advice to get a good night's sleep before the fundamental change of our personalities would begin. Most of us sat down to write a letter to our loved ones. Based on Waldgruber's colorful description of our immediate future on the island, nobody knew when we would be strong enough again to lift a pen.

On the next day, our basic training began. Some superstitious guys made remarks of this being a "bloody thirteen," but nothing unusual happened.

Having said that, I have to contradict myself in a sense. Everything was unusual for us. It seemed the day would never end. I had the feeling my bones were fractured, as if from an automobile accident or a bad fight, and my joints were inflamed and close to being torn apart. My legs were as heavy as lead. My cervical spine felt as if it was spiked with knitting needles from ducking too often and too fast when the enemy would shoot at me or throw hand grenades. In other words, I felt like the pits! There was one small consolation: Those men who looked like huge cupboards or piano movers were complaining just as loudly. It's nice not to be alone.

After one week, we all believed the training was getting easier. That was an illusion. The human body appeared to have become accustomed to physical strain and abuse. But we also knew that Adolf, in comparison to the other trainers, treated us less roughly. Only when we came close to another platoon during war exercises did he put on a show. He would raise his voice as much as he could and denounce our pitiful condition. On those occasions he would act like a lion tamer, but his well-disposed smile never left his face.

A couple of weeks went by and nobody goofed anymore. The rifle was taken apart in a jiffy, cleaned according to the book, and put together again like a *Blitz* (lightening). Nobody stabbed himself while fixing the rifle with a dagger. After pulling the pin, hand grenades were correctly kept in hand three seconds, as ordered, before throwing them at the enemy. I hated the darn things. They were so difficult to throw with precision. The heavy head and the light handle did not correspond with each other. We heard a number of stories about the much handier and more effective *Eierhandgranaten* (egg hand grenades) which the enemy used. How easy it was to guide and throw these in the desired direction. Only after the war did I find this out to be true.

One habit that stuck with me from my civilian life was reading in the washroom. During the third week of our training, I could not find anything of interest to read. German newspapers reached the island with great irregularity. Besides, I did not feel like swallowing more propaganda than we heard through public loudspeakers. So, I went to the outhouse empty-handed.

The last cubicle to the right was empty. I sat down and, having nothing to read this time, started curiously looking around—not that I expected to see anything in particular. But wait! In a crevice, seven feet high to my left, there was something squeezed, caught by two ill-fitting wooden beams. As I was ready to leave, I threw overboard my reservations not to pick up anything from the washroom. I stepped on the corner edge of the seat I had occupied and tugged at what seemed to be a rolled-together newspaper.

Unfolding it, I saw at one glance that it bore English print. Sure enough, it was the *Daily Herald*, dated Thursday, 9 May 1940. Among other news, it reported that British troops had embarked "this morning" to sail for Scandinavia with the goal of defending Norway and Denmark against a predictable invasion by the Germans. I could not help thinking about the soldier who had left the newspaper there, visualizing that he and his comrades might have had just sufficient time to read the article before surrendering to us. The irony of fate!

Since the newspaper contained past history, I did not think there was anything wrong with showing it to my pals and to Adolf. He was as curious as the others, and wanted to know what else the newspaper had reported. We spent the remainder of the evening sorting that out. I was only too delighted to accommodate them and did my best to give them all the news. It was obvious to me they were hungry for some different kind of news with considerably less propaganda. The German press simply was not allowed to report a balanced view.

When all the print was exhausted, Adolf thanked me on behalf of everybody and said, "Maybe one of these days, when the war is over, your knowledge of English might come in handy." That time would come, but under different circumstances than he expected. We were destined to meet again in the largest demobilization camp in August 1945.

Each one of us, from time to time, had to perform additional duties besides our regular training. These included assembling breakfast for the platoon, helping with unloading of provisions, standing watch at the landing site and generally securing the periphery of the island. The favorite task was assisting in the canteen, which usually paid off with us receiving an extra portion of tobacco, cigarettes or Schnapps.

The least popular assignment was bringing the outhouse cubicles down to zero. In plain English: dismantle the ten seats; lift the huge tubs full of human waste out of the pits; carry them with the help of a lorry about two hundred feet to the designated area; empty them into one large pit; bury the contents; flush out the tubs with hot water and germicide; return them to the outhouse; slide them back into the individual pits; clean the seats and surrounding walls and reassemble the seats. Sounds simple.

The eight-week cleaning schedule had been pinned on the bulletin board in the mess hall. You can imagine how much that attracted our attention.

The job was to be done twice per week. Each time twelve men worked as a team. As I looked closer, I noticed to my delight that our group and group seven were the only two assigned for this so-called special project only once during our eight-week stay.

Our *Stubenaeltester* (the quarter's eldest–responsible for the groups' compliance with rules and regulations) remarked inappropriately: "Hallelujah! How lucky can one get. We get away with looking after this rotten shitting business only once. Should suit us fine. We get enough shit dished out everyday!" Everybody chuckled.

Leading Seaman Herbert Kaufmann was in charge of food provisions, preparation, the mess hall and the canteen operation. He bore the duty rank silver beam, indicating he carried out the functions of a petty officer second class. I was to become quite familiar with functionaries, whose service rank is often different from the duty or assignment rank. It simply means that, because of a temporary assignment, the duty rank of an individual is higher than his normal service rank.

During the week of 27 October, I had breakfast duty. That was when Herbert and I found out that we had been practically neighbors in Germany. He lived in Schwelm, and I resided in Wuppertal, only some twelve kilometers distance.

On the second day, before we attended to our duties, we had a bit of time to chat. When he found out my background, he said, "I tell you something, Siegfried. You could be of help to me when taking inventory control and with a few other things. I know you are here to learn the basics of how to stay alive, which will keep you hopping. So I would not pull any strings with your trainer to load additional duties on you. But I would like to talk to Adolf to see whether he can exempt you once in a while from some regular duties which are not absolutely necessary. I need a guy like you to assist me with keeping the finger on the pulse of the business. I dislike pencil work involving calculations. What about it? I really would appreciate it!"

I agreed without hesitation. He appeared to be reasonable, though I had heard from one chap who previously had been on breakfast duty that he got shit from the quartermaster. For all I knew, he probably deserved it. But, any excuse to avoid any part of military drills was O.K. with me.

For the remainder of the week, I helped out the odd hour here and there during daytime. By Wednesday I had thrown my principle, never to volunteer for anything, overboard. Wednesday and Thursday evening, I spent most of the time figuring out Herbert's entries in the food and supply receiving and requisition book. Some of the pages looked like chickens had run over them, leaving manure behind in a disorderly fashion.

He joined me the next day to see what changes I would suggest. It was almost funny to see his face when I said, "I'll tell you something; let's forget your self-acquired bookkeeping system and start fresh. For reordering supplies, for instance, we should first of all establish a par stock, or low watermark, for each article we carry. That way, we don't run short and don't overstock either. Bin cards would help for faster identification of articles. If you want, I can set up something that is simpler, yet keeps better control. That is not only important for daily requisitions of food supplied by your cooks, but also for your canteen sales."

You can imagine he was delighted, as he stated later, to finally see the light and get somewhere. He was so grateful as a consequence of my efforts, that he arranged for group four to receive a bit extra whenever the situation allowed. By the time the weekend arrived, we knew each other fairly well. He asked if there was anything he could do for me personally. "Yes," I replied. "If you could let me listen to your radio once in a while, I would appreciate it."

"Sure," he said. "Not only when you do some pencil work for me, but also when you are off duty and feel like it. Come over any time. I am mostly here anyway. Are you guys not finished now with your third week of training?" I confirmed that. "Well then," he continued, "when you receive some passes soon to have some fun in Tønsberg or Horten on the mainland, let me know when your turn comes up. I've been stationed here now seven months and know a few girls in town. Maybe I can introduce you to a couple."

"Are you kidding?" I asked in an exaggerated tone of voice. "I couldn't even handle one, not to mention two. This boot hill business sure got to me. And that *Hirschhornsalz* (saltpeter salt) is doing a great job. I wonder how many pounds your cooks use to spike soups and sauces. Bootsmannsmaat Waldgruber was right the first day we arrived. He hit the nail on the head. That stuff uproots any sex drive and just leaves you with wishful thinking."

On Saturday, 1 November, the Watch Duty List was displayed on the bulletin board for the following week. I was required to be on patrol Monday through Thursday, circulating around the isle from 2200 hours to 2400 hours, and from 0400 hours to 0600 hours. It exempted me from military training each day, Tuesday through Friday, from 0800 hours until 1200 hours.

In the morning, we had received a sizable shipment of food provisions and canteen items for sale. Before everything was checked off and stored, I went over in the afternoon to assist Herbert, while starting the new inventory control system. When we had completed the task, Herbert said, "I am really glad that this system is in place now. There is something strange, though. The canteen man is not too enthusiastic about it. Got an idea why not?"

"Well," I replied, "I'll give it to you straight, Herbert. There are two possibilities: One, it is just resistance to change, human nature being what it is. Two, he might have his own iron in the fire. It wouldn't be the first time that somebody exploited the lack of a good control system. Hopefully, I am wrong, but if not, he will not be able to repeat any tricks in the future without you noticing it."

We had a cup of coffee in a small sitting room beside his office. He had heard from Adolf about the English newspaper I had found. I had to fill him in on some of the major points, which, by then, I almost knew by heart.

His radio was playing subdued. The music stopped suddenly and the announcer broadcast yet another special announcement from the Fuehrer's headquarters, claiming some more territorial gain at the Eastern Front. As usual, the report was followed by Richard Wagner's *Overture to Tannhaeuser.* Then came Lale Anderson on and sang *Lilly Merlene.*

I thanked Herbert for *Kaffee und Kuchen* (coffee and cake) and returned to my quarters to write a letter home. It was the first one since we had left Kiel.

On Sundays we could sleep in. In other words, rather than being rudely awakened at 0600 hours, we were left in peace until 0715 hours. Big deal! Talking about "rise, rise, aufstehen," one of the group trainers had a couple of funny verses, with which he provided us as early morning entertainment.

One dealt with a story where a ship is nearing a harbor and prepares for docking. The sergeant-at-arms tells the crew to "wake up your tired bodies; the pier is filled with naked women." It makes a nice rhyme in German. He had about a dozen of these eye-openers up his sleeves. We knew when he was scheduled to cover the graveyard shift and wondered what he would come up with next. He never disappointed us, always having some fresh material. Anything funny is welcome when you are in uniform. It breaks the monotony of military confinement.

On Monday evening, I hit the sack right after dinner, so as to catch a couple hours of sleep before my first watch would begin at 2200 hours. Two of us went down to the landing site at 2150 hours sharp, to relieve the pair who had stood watch from 2000 hours to 2200 hours. They had nothing to report. My companion went clockwise and I went counterclockwise around the island. After about six minutes of walking, we met on the opposite side of the landing place, then continued to finish our circle.

The instructions we had received pointed out the necessity of keeping in motion, like on a picket line, to congregate only when some messages had to be exchanged. There was not really anything on the isle worth defending or protecting, except, of course, the weapons and ammunitions warehouse. Though we were all officially assigned to *Laufbahn Fifteen, Marines Artillerie* (Career Fifteen, Naval Artillery), there were no antiaircraft guns on the island. That training would come later–in my case, much later.

While on duty the next night, I saw for the first time what Scandinavians refer to as the Northern Lights. One way to describe this phenomenon is this: Looking at the northern horizon, you see for a while the radiation of a bluish-tinged white light, which seems to be caused by a huge burning oven below. After twelve to fifteen minutes, it intensifies almost enough to read the newspaper at midnight. White comet-like stripes stream southward from the horizon in the direction of the observer, covering approximately one-fourth of the visible firmament. It hovers a while, then begins to flicker, until the oven is out. One has to see this spectacle, since it pretty much defies any seemingly sufficient description.

There I was, standing still against regulations and staring at the miracle. I had heard in former years about this phenomenon, but harbored some skepticism about its reality. My tendency was to pool it together with unlikely fish stories one hears more often than not. Or I treated it like a fata morgana which happens to the thirsty wanderer in the desert. He sees the oasis in the distance, but never reaches it. Well, the Northern Lights are real and are a fascinating sight!

The following night I did not see it, but I saw something else. On my second watch, around 0430 hours, I was about to complete my third patrol circle when I stopped. I had not noticed before, but coming around the bend, looking at the water gently slapping the reef of the island, I saw a glow of fluorescent light that I could not explain. It was in constant movement. But wait, there were two different movements. It lasted for about one hour, but I had no idea how long this was already going on before I discovered it.

When I met my comrade from the other direction and asked him if he had seen the same, he looked at me as if I had told him that the world was flat. I motioned to follow me around the next bend, where I had seen the spectacle. It was still in action. Looking at it again made it clear to me that there were two different elements competing with each other.

One element consisted of jerky insects, which looked like they were running across the water, imitating a water boatman. The others were tiny fly fish, looking at first glance like glowworms. They seemed to be determined to outdo the insects by zigzagging above the water surface. My pal shook his head. "I see it," he said, "but I don't believe it! I thought you were joking a few minutes ago. I owe you one."

We asked the others whether they had seen it. Nobody had. They had never even heard about it, including those who grew up at the waterfront. The next day we asked Adolf. He had not heard about it, nor had he seen it. He seemed to be only mildly interested. Then he said, "Look, you guys; you may be glad you have something to look at when you make your rounds. But don't get too distracted by it. Remember, you have to keep moving about. And I don't want to see you walking in pairs like an engaged couple, gazing at the stars. You better not become too dreamy and tell me one day you saw an ocean maiden!"

On my last day of patrol at about 0515 hours, I suddenly heard a motor in the distance. "Wouldn't it be funny," I reflected, throwing a joke at myself, "if an invasion would start now?" Then I pointed my ears a bit more, and now more clearly heard the steady tuf-tuf-tuf of an engine. As I continued to walk, I could hear it getting louder until, after three more minutes, a small one-engine fisherman's boat came into view. It advanced in my direction.

Now I could make out that it had been loaded with freshly caught fish, which was piled in a heap aft of the motor in the stern of the boat. The fisherman had pointed himself at the rudder, changing course slightly to pass the island by. Then he obviously had set his speedometer on slowest gear, came out of his little cockpit and gave me a friendly wave with his left arm. In his right hand, he was holding a *Meerschaum*, so traditional among fishermen. Another common sight was the yellow pelerine which he wore. A pointed dark gray fisherman's hat, with upward curled wide brim, which is usually only rolled down over the ears when it drizzles or rains, crowned his head.

He looked quite happy. No wonder, his catch must have been better than good. You could notice that not only by the visible pile of fish, but also by the draft of the boat; the sea water licked to the upper part of her rails.

I continued my round rather slowly, deep in thought. How fortunate to experience such a peaceful scene, while most of Europe is in strife of war! Soon I met my patrol companion for the last time before we returned to report. He had seen the boat from the other direction, but did not pay any attention to what he called "the nutshell."

As I entered the mess hall around noon, after having had a short snooze, I glanced at the bulletin board. A bunch of guys congregated in front of it, reading intensively. Big news! This being the end of the fourth week of training, we were allowed to apply for passes for the weekend. We actually could choose to go ashore either Saturday or Sunday. Surprisingly democratic! Something must be wrong. We were to report our preferences to our trainers Friday evening after dinner.

Since I had nobody waiting for me on the mainland, I did not care one way or the other. But I did remember Herbert's offer to introduce me to a couple of chicks. So, I saw him before dinner. He said, "I am scheduled for a Saturday pass. We noncoms take turns. There is always somebody here to defend the island. Try to get a pass for tomorrow also. If not, let me talk to Adolf."

"Fine," I said, "will do. At what time will the boat cast off tomorrow?"

"At 1130 hours and 0100 hours. We can take our pick. If you prefer 1130 hours, you normally have to skip your luncheon. But I can fix that."

"O.K., then, 1130 hours it is." I rushed back to the mess hall, not to miss the last sitting, and returned to my quarters.

The 1130-hour boat sailed for Tønsberg, while the later one would dock in Horten. The voyage across the fjord took less than one half-hour. We disembarked and split up in different groups. Those of us who did not smoke or drink had a few kroners in our pockets. Besides, there would be little opportunity to spend any money during the last four weeks on the isle. We received thirty-two kroners every ten days–not much, but still better than nothing.

Herbert and I had another four guys in tow, who had nothing else in mind but going to a reasonably-priced cafe and maybe picking up a broad. Herbert did not tell them the irons he had in the fire. There was no use inviting competition.

It was kind of chilly at that time of the year, but not much colder than central Europe, because the Gulf Stream still has an effect on the southern part of Norway. Only when you reach the city of Trondheim and north from there do temperatures differ substantially. The other reason for not sauntering around too long was–I do understand the town has expanded by now–a tiny community. A yardstick I have often used in the past to estimate the size of a settlement is the number of churches it has. There were two in Tønsberg.

The hotel/cafe we had entered looked like nothing from the outside, but was quite homey on the inside. The decor was modest, but everything was kept immaculately clean. "This owner must be a professional," I thought.

The tables were covered with blue-colored checkered tablecloths, and the chairs were more comfortable than they looked at first glance.

This being lunch time, we ordered a seafood plate. The place was fully licensed, but since the Norwegians were only allowed to make and consume *Duennbier* (light beer–two percent by alcoholic volume) since our occupation in May 1940, we ordered, of all things, a bottle of Swedish wine. I had never heard about the Swedes making any wine, but at this stage I was only a half-baked hotelier and restaurateur. I could not possibly have learned everything there is to know about the business.

However, when the wine was served, I knew it was California wine with a Swedish label. Mind you, in November 1941 the Yankees were not yet at war with us. Either the Norwegians did not want to offend the Germans, knowing Hitler's contempt for President Roosevelt, or they were clairvoyant, because exactly four weeks to the day, thanks to the Japanese, we had added the USA as one of our enemies.

The meal was great. If anybody knows how to prepare fish dishes, it is the Norwegians. That I was going to find out soon. The splendid wine assisted in washing it down rather smoothly.

The waitress spoke a bit of German. When we asked her whether we could order the dessert later, she said, "*Das koennen Sie machen* (That is all right)." It surprised me. The place was packed. Later on we discovered that she was impressed to meet some Germans who would appreciate good wine. I thought, "If she only knew that we also like beer and Schnapps."

We continued to chat, mostly about the training and our beloved native country. After a while Herbert asked the waitress to recommend a dessert. She said something nobody understood, but Herbert ordered it anyway. He asked that Schnapps be served with it. "*Haben wir* (We have that)," she answered, "but it comes from Denmark."

"O.K.," agreed Herbert, "as long as it is good and not too expensive."

When she returned, she had two-ounce Martini-type glasses filled with a colorless liquid on her round bar tray. It was indeed Akvavit from Aalborg, the real thing. We nursed that for a while, then ordered a second round.

We were just about ready to pay our bills and leave, when four guys set up music stands on a small stage. It was around 1530 hours. Inquiring about this, the waitress told us that a concert hour would follow. We could stay if we would order one more round. We did. Herbert went to the telephone to make a few calls. Returning, he gave me a signal, which I did not comprehend.

The quartet, consisting of a pianist, a violinist, a string bass player and a drummer played well together. Obviously they could read notes but did not have any experience in improvising. The music was quite rhythmical, though.

After the band had played the second tune, Herbert said to the others, "You probably want to stay for a while longer. Sigy and I have to go." Nobody asked any questions.

I asked the waitress if I could briefly talk to the manager. I had observed a man appearing from the preparation area several times and talking to some customers, who seemed to be regulars. The manager's office was right beside the kitchen. Herbert and I stalked through the kitchen, carefully avoiding the grease on the floor, which is almost unavoidable in food preparation areas. Stepping into his office, which looked like a small anteroom, the man who raised from his chair was unmistakably of Germanic stock–six foot five, blond, pronounced cheekbones, broad shoulders and small hips. Looking at him, one could well imagine him in different dress with a hair band with horns as a descendent of the Vikings, one of the Scandinavian warriors, who harried the coasts of Europe between the eighth and tenth centuries.

This one was rather tame. He quickly moved around his desk and greeted us with outstretched hands, like friends. "Good afternoon, gentlemen," he said in his native tongue. For a moment there was awkward silence. Herbert nor I were fluent enough to converse in the domestic language. So, I asked the giant, "*Sprechen Sie deutsch?*" He shook his head. I switched to English and his face lit up, apparently relieved. "Yes, I do," he replied. "What can I do for you, gentlemen?"

"If you have a few minutes," I stated, "we would like to complement you on your good cuisine, the fine service, and the homey surroundings. My comrade here has patronized your establishment several times before and recommended it to the other comrades."

"Thank you for your kind words," he replied. "We pride ourselves in serving everybody well, uniform or no uniform." A warm smile, bare of sarcasm, flashed across his face. Then, "I need everybody's business to stay in business." The man sure had common sense!

"Before we leave," I continued, "one question. Just as a matter of curiosity, from where did the Swedish wine really come?"

He looked sort of helplessly for a few seconds, glancing about the room, as if looking for hidden microphones. I quickly assured him, "I recently have learned your business and have no intention of squealing on you, if that is what you are afraid of," looking him straight in the eyes.

The tension left his face and he answered, "I trust you. You see, as a matter of precaution, not knowing whether we officially could carry and sell any non-European goods, our Norwegian Hotel and Restaurant Association arranged for its members the purchase of some California wine through an export-import conglomerate in Sweden. The wine arrives in casks, is bottled and labeled in Sweden, and then shipped to us."

"I don't see anything illegal with that," I said, "but then, I do not know any of your regulations, one way or other. For that matter, too many regulations can kill any business. Nothing beats the free enterprise system; in the long run, it serves everybody well." His facial expression showed sincere surprise.

To hear a German in uniform, whose country was totally overregulated, plugging free enterprise was almost equal to seeing a known atheist entering the confession booth. "Besides," I concluded, "I have coined those who believe that, at times, it is better not to ask too many questions. The answers may be unfavorable."

We thanked him again for his hospitality, with the promise to return. While we eggshelled back through the kitchen, I said to Herbert, "See, I should have made a bet with you guys about the wine."

"You can't win them all," he laughed. "Do you have any other cards up your sleeves? First I find out you know the hotel business and then that you speak English. What else is there?"

"Nothing much," I retorted with an air of humility. "I do not have any other talents which I know of. Maybe some are hidden somewhere."

We had reached the exit of the cafe, when Herbert said as an afterthought, "Do you realize we are not supposed to converse in the language of the enemy?" His eyes belied his seriousness.

"I know. But neither of us understand the language of the natives, and I am sure nobody understands Chinese here!"

He was still chuckling when we took the few steps to the sidewalk. He told me he had contacted Astrid, one of the girls he knew. She would pick up her girlfriend around 1900 hours, then meet us at a corner cafe. We had two hours to kill and took another stroll through town. That was the first time I noticed over ninety percent of houses, residential and businesses, having been built of wood. They did look attractive and cozy. The disadvantage, I thought, would be that Norwegians must have to put up with a lot of fires.

How wrong I was going to be! During my four years in Norway I heard of fewer fires—except those deliberately set—than one can count on two hands. Electrical wiring, for instance, rarely ever causes the outbreak of fires, even though regular current is 220 volts, rather than 110 like in North America. The only two reasons I can think of for the Norwegians to have such a good safety record are their safety-consciousness and conscientious maintenance procedures.

Little Las Vegas

It was 1830 hours when we entered the corner cafe. We were the only ones in uniform, but the Norwegians hardly gave us a second glance. They seemed to have become accustomed to the unwelcome visitors from the south.

It was a simple place, but neat. Somehow it reminded me of one restaurant in Wuppertal, my hometown, which had the reputation of serving inexpensive but good food. Without wanting to put a negative connotation to it, people called it *Der Fressladen* (the gorging place), because of the large portions they served. Unless you were starving, you could not possibly finish a meal. The waiters invariably served a large doggy bag with your meal.

This place was patronized by families, most of whom appeared to know each other. Some were hopping from table to table, engaged in lively conversation, a thing which is not only not practiced in Canadian establishments, but even against the liquor law. (The province of Quebec is less stringent in this regard.)

Herbert ordered a couple of beers with the comment we would wait for company, then have dinner. As my eyes glanced around the room, I noticed four slot machines near one corner. Stepping closer, I saw a man fishing a few coins out of a till, which the machine had extruded. I stepped right beside him and tried to read the operating instructions, but I could not make them out. So I watched the chap for a while, then had a go at it myself.

On the upper right hand side of the machine you would insert a five ore coin, then push a lever, like on a pinball machine, forcing the inserted coin to slide horizontally across several vertical tubes. Depending on the force of the sliding coin, it would enter one of the tube openings, then fall vertically in curving fashion, until vanishing in one of several pockets. Some of these pockets showed zeros, others the numbers five to twenty-five. The machine would pay out the ore as the number showed. I tried five coins, got back fourteen. This must be similar to the Las Vegas I have heard so much about, I thought to myself.

What I did not understand then was that one has to stop while being ahead, before one loses everything again, and more. In the long run the house always wins. Nowadays slot machines are rigged by computers. The house can determine the odds against the player in advance. Quite often, machines are reset if the house figures that profits should be higher. On average, slot machines are adjusted not to pay out more than one-seventh of what has been fed in.

This was different. Once you acquired a feeling for the force needed to catapult the coins, so as to enable them to sink into the paying slots, you had it made. During the last four weeks of my basic training, I took every opportunity there was to return to the corner cafe, making a bit of money on the side. While some of the other chums were spending their last kroners on girls, I prepared myself for hard times.

At 1920 hours, Froken Astrid Berger appeared on the scene, alone, without her girlfriend Victoria Sandborg. No need to comment on her being late by twenty minutes. That seems to be universal with women and has not changed throughout the century.

Her chestnut hair nicely surrounded her ascetic-looking face. Her movements were determined but graceful. She was of slender build, about five feet eight inches tall, and twenty-three years of age, as Herbert told me later. Without hesitation, she embraced my outstretched hand with firmness, looked at me with a pleasant smile and said, "*Freut mich Dich kennen zu lernen* (I am pleased to make your acquaintance)." She carried a slight Scandinavian accent, using the more familiar *Du* (in this case *Dich*), rather than the distant *Sie*.

Herbert had good taste. Obviously, she had class. He had told me about this girl and her friend, who both came from well-educated families. The thought flashed through my mind, questioning why they would bother with Germans. I had no idea. But later, during my three and a half year stay in Stavanger, I met a number of girls and women who associated themselves with us. The reasons for doing so, however, were various ones.

The three of us had a marvelous seafood dinner. Astrid explained that the owner went out to sea everyday to catch fresh fish. The sight came to my mind when the Norwegian fisherman had greeted me early in the morning, while I patrolled the island. Maybe the owner was that fisherman?

After dinner, Astrid and Herbert invited me for an evening out. I declined politely, muttering something about the third wheel on the cart. "Next time," I said, "if Victoria would be with us."

The two of them left shortly afterwards. I ordered another light beer and walked over to one of the four slot machines with the intention of milking it.

Operationally, the system is different from ordinary slot machines. At least your arm cannot get tired or strained from pushing the handle down. The movement is replaced by pushing the coin starter, which is done by using one finger. It was 2130 hours when I decided to stop the monotony and went to the pier to catch the 2200 hour ferry. I had done relatively well on that slot machine, ending up with Kr 23.50 winnings. That was about two-thirds of my pay for ten days of service. Not bad.

Returning to my quarters, I found only one comrade from my group sitting at the table writing a letter. He was one of the two married men in our group, had two kids, and in all likelihood suffered more from being separated from his loved ones than the rest of us. He was the eldest, twenty-five, and had been deferred from military service until recently, because of his trade. He was a machine fitter in a factory manufacturing war material.

I joined him writing a letter to my parents, using the opportunity of comparative quiet since I found it difficult to concentrate when surrounded by noise. There was no girlfriend to write to.

The next day we celebrated the half completion of our basic training. Nobody went out of line. Nothing worthwhile to report happened during the next two weeks. At the end of the second week I received another pass for Sunday but made a change with a pal who preferred Sunday to Saturday.

This time Herbert and I chose the 1300 boat. He had called from his office to make sure that both Astrid and Victoria could meet with us. On the one hand, I was curious about the town of Horten, which I had not as yet seen, but my curiosity was greater to get to know Victoria. If she was similar to Astrid, it promised to be an interesting day.

The weather was foggy. Not like that thick London soup, but nevertheless bad enough to miss out on any lighter boat that would be farther away than forty feet. Every few seconds one could hear a fog horn tooting. This is quite understandable when one also considers the narrowness of the Oslofjord at that particular location.

We had participated in the first luncheon session so we could catch the 1300 hour boat. Having arrived in Tønsberg with a full stomach gave me another chance to learn a bit more about the town. The girls had promised to guide us anywhere we wanted to go, but were not scheduled to meet us before 1500 hours at the restaurant on Storgaten.

From where we had landed, the view tower was close by, and it was not a bad idea to have a look at the surroundings from above. In spite of the fog, we had a fairly good look at the islands of Notteroyand and Tjome, though Haon was not visible. One could make out a couple of sailboats not too far out, but most of them were tied up at the sail club. The weather forecast was not conducive to sailing, except for the few who wanted to live dangerously. We stayed one half-hour, chatted with some other soldiers and navy men on shore leave, then left the tower. It was getting chilly.

The Girls

At 1455 hours sharp we entered the restaurant. To my surprise, the girls had already made themselves comfortable, having selected a corner table. When we approached the table, the waitress was serving them coffee and Danish pastries.

As Herbert introduced Victoria to me, Astrid quickly interjected with the remark, "You see, Sigy, girls can be on time if they really want to." It floored me. Had she been able to read my mind last time? If so, I had better start practicing putting on a poker face.

My first impression of Victoria was that of an introverted girl, rather shy, but quite pleasant. Her smile was sincere and just as bright as Astrid's. In contrast to Astrid, her dark hair floated down her neck and ended up in the center of her back. She was quite a sight! Her height was similar to Astrid's. Her features were somewhat more pronounced, with higher cheekbones. She spoke less fluently than her girlfriend, but her voice was soft and well modulated. When speaking German, her accent was easy to make out. The way the two girls talked did not indicate any roughness, but a certain polish that could not possibly have originated by associating with ordinary sailors.

Herbert and I ordered a little something to keep the girls company with their pastries and coffee. Victoria asked me how I liked the military training. "Absolutely crazy about it," was my answer. I tried not to move an eyelid while offering that fast reply. She looked sort of shocked. "Would never have guessed that," she said. "You don't appear to be the type."

"Just kidding," I threw in hastily. She drew in the air slowly, then noticeably exhaled, indicating relief.

"The training shows no similarity with my background whatsoever," I added. "But who has a choice in wartime? If I ever get out of this mess, I will feel like a king."

"I have the feeling you will," she replied. Our conversation turned to the town of Tønsberg, and Victoria said, "We will show you around this afternoon. After that, we have a surprise for you."

I felt like joking. "I hope you are not going to astonish us with the revelation that you are members of the underground and have the assignment to bump us off!?" Smiling, I added, "Keep in mind we are two peaceful visitors from the South, as the Danes refer to us. We have orders to protect you people against the bad Tommies." To cut off that silly talk, Herbert kicked my shinbone under the table.

We left the restaurant around 1630 hours, and our guided tour began. The girls took us on an Oslofjord voyage. The route stretched from Tønsberg to Horten; from there to Moss and Rigge on the other coast of the fjord, and back to Tønsberg. The fog had cleared miraculously the moment we entered the small cruise ship. The waves were smooth as silk.

Not only had the girls paid for the round trip, they also acted as tour guides as promised, pointing out interesting landmarks and historical dates along the way. We were the only two guys in uniform aboard ship. Again, nobody seemed to take any notice. I had counted the number of islands we had passed; there were twenty-seven in all. Even the smallest ones, not much larger than Haon, were inhabited.

When the boat tied up at the landing again, we thanked the girls for the pleasant trip. "Oh," Astrid replied, "you are quite welcome. We have another surprise for you in stock. Let's go." I looked at my watch; it was 1930 hours.

We had walked for about twenty minutes or so through particularly narrow streets which, as the girls explained, represented the old town of Tønsberg, when we veered off in a northerly direction.

"We are almost home," Astrid announced. "The two of you are invited for dinner. That is the real surprise Victoria was talking about." Herbert muttered something like, "Could not really expect something like that," when I nudged my elbow into his side to shut him up. It was kind of a punishable affront to treat a superior that way. He did not seem to mind, but his face wore the expression of anticipation and great surprise. His eyebrows lifted a bit to produce a comically serious look I had not seen on his face before, not even when he tried to figure out a way to juggle his books.

The street we were on now was comparatively wide. Oak and birch trees were lining the sidewalks. Some were harboring mistletoe, a protected parasite, which was widely used in medieval medicine. It is rarely ever found in Norway, except in Horten where it exists in great quantities. It stretches southward to Tønsberg, where it peters out.

Houses were recessed over a hundred feet away from the street, with well-kept front yards. Some properties were isolated from the outside by high black iron fences. These people living here were definitely not on unemployment benefits. The upkeep of these patrician-looking buildings alone would require a small fortune. Walking through an unlocked gate, the house we were approaching appeared more like a mansion rather than a house. The two-story building must have contained at least twenty rooms.

As we came nearer, an English Retriever and a Doberman barked at us in tandem from a fancy-looking doghouse, sizable enough to be equipped with electric heating. It was situated about ten steps away from the gateway and the building. One word from Astrid and they quieted down, still fixing their fiendish looks on us.

At that moment, the front door opened and a butler in formal attire greeted us courteously, led us through a vestibule into a huge foyer, and took our coats.

At one side of the foyer was a cozy fireplace with a rectangular tea table and opposite placed settees close by. Astrid gave some inaudible instructions to the butler, who retreated quietly, only to reappear four minutes later with a wheeled cart, on which a variety of brandies, liqueurs and appetizer wines were displayed. I could not believe it. These people had Cognac and imported liqueurs at their disposal; items which had pretty much vanished shortly after we occupied the country in 1940.

Only about ten minutes went by and two distinguished-looking well-groomed elderly couples descended from the spiral staircase and greeted us as if we had met before. I was immediately impressed. These people knew how to communicate informally in spite of the reception-like atmosphere!

They introduced themselves in fluent German as Mr. and Mrs. Berger and Sandborg and began the conversation by asking us how we liked Norway, as if we were legitimate tourists or landed immigrants. As always, when one meets new people, the initial awkwardness subsides when the hosts act naturally, a gift few people have.

I immediately answered in the affirmative, speaking well of the people I had met so far and admiring the natural beauty of Norway, cautiously adding that it was not easy to make friends in a country where we had not been invited. Herbert added a few complimentary remarks. Later he told me how astonished he was to hear me making statements "fit to come from a diplomat." Since he said that with sincerity, it was music to my ears.

Mr. Berger turned out to be an emissary of the Quisling government, acting as coordinating diplomat between this Norwegian puppet government of ours and our own German Reich. He was Astrid's father and our host. It occurred to me that, quite naturally, his role was to communicate with us Germans. However, that did not explain why he bothered with little fish like Herbert and me, unless he simply wanted to please his daughter. I could not get the thought out of my mind that there had to be more to it than that.

His friend, Victoria's father, was a nuclear physicist who, among others, was in charge of controlling security at the only Norwegian, but now German-controlled, heavy water plant in northern Norway.

After fifteen minutes of amicable conversation, the butler arrived announcing dinner to be ready. We entered the luxurious dining room, the likes of it I never had seen before. My parents did not walk in those circles.

The table was delicately laid with solid silver cutlery and decorated with late autumn leaves, two centerpieces of flowers and two heavy candelabra. The two gentlemen seated themselves at each end of the table. Herbert and I were placed in the center seat on each side of the table, Herbert with Astrid to his left and her mother to the right. Victoria and her mother flanked my sides. Formal seating arrangements were not new to me, since I had served many times at formal functions of various sizes. Participating in one was another matter altogether! I made a serious attempt to give the impression that this was the order of the day for me.

During the meal we made polite conversation. The two elderly couples wanted to know something about our background. "Aha!" I said to myself. "When you have finished your story, the ax will fall." The reason for this thought was understandable.

Three years ago, I went steady with a lovely girl for about four weeks. Then, one day, her parents insisted on getting to know me. That is quite proper, I suppose. The trouble was, however, that they owned the world-famous Twins Works factory complex (Zwillingswerke A.G.) in Solingen which, to this day, manufactures razor blades and first-rate butcher and kitchen knives. As soon as the girl's father found out my humble background, my relationship with his daughter became taboo overnight. How could a simple hotel employee be possibly good enough for his daughter?

That was not so here. Neither of the two couples gave any indication of disappointment. Before dinner was over, I came to the conclusion that I could not figure out where these people really fit in. Somehow, their democratic approach and behavior contradicted their collaboration with our totalitarian system.

When the main course was removed, we withdrew to a study, where dessert and brandy were served. Mr. Sandborg offered us big cigars, which looked suspiciously Cuban to me. We had not seen any imported cigars for four years, nor should we have expected any, since we isolated ourselves from the rest of the world.

Time flew by. When the great grandfather's clock in the study timed 1000 hours, we thanked our hosts for their hospitality, wished them well, and left. The girls accompanied us to the front gate. We kissed good-bye under a fancy subdued lantern. It momentarily reminded me about Lale Andersen's song *Unter der Laterne, vor dem grossen Tor* (Under the lantern, in front of the big gate).

Outhouse Duty

At breakfast the next morning a group member said to me: "I hope you have not forgotten that this week is brownie week? You know what I mean?"

"No," I replied, boasting that I had such a great time last night, I could not remember anything. There was no use disappointing the guy by telling him the truth, which he likely would not believe anyway.

"Then I will enlighten you," he said. "This week is our turn to clean the latrine, something we have looked forward to for the last six weeks. Tuesday is the big day."

"Scabby dog," I said, somewhat upset, because it was not my style to use strong language. "Could you not wait until after breakfast to give me such rotten news?"

I tried to enjoy my breakfast as usual, but it was not easy. Before returning to my quarters, I dropped in at Herbert's office just to say hello and to ask if he could have my Tuesday luncheon refrigerated until later. "Sure thing, Sig," he replied. "One hand washes the other," he continued. "Need your help again in a couple of days this week with the books. You had better train me before you leave here in December. Otherwise, I will get stuck." We had a deal.

Tuesday rolled around, and the sewer team lined up at 1000 hours. One smart aleck played sick, but did not get away with it. One guy from the next team replaced him, but only to be replaced in turn later by the "sick" guy. The group leader made it clear that nobody was going to leave this island without benefiting from the experience of what perfect sanitation was all about.

The twelve of us got cracking, following the procedure I described before. When we had cranked the second round tub out of the pit and proceeded to load it on the lorry, the chap to my left said spontaneously, "Man, I have never seen so much shit on one pile!" He probably did not even intend to be funny, but his remark instantly hit the funny bone. Convulsive laughter made us put the tub unevenly on the edge of the lorry. All four large-holed handles were vibrating and some of the human excrement spilled over onto the lorry, the ground, and our drill clothes. In the real sense of the word, we now could call ourselves the dirty dozen. Only at that time, it did not have any meaning. The team leader remarked, "Now you do not need a calling card. You smell ten miles against the wind."

One guy added smartly, "We should have had more foresight to use our gas masks. Now it's too late."

When the task was finished, we surrendered our work clothes to the laundry, which was located beside the noncom barrack. Relieved to have completed this popular task, we hit the showers singing, "Happy times are here again." I cannot remember ever having used that much soap and water on my body. The smell seemed to have engraved itself into the skin.

It was now 1330 hours, just enough time to join the last luncheon session. Nobody felt like it. Instead, we went to the canteen and had a stiff drink, chased down with pretty good beer which was brewed for the forces in the town of Drammen. The taste came close to Schwelmer lager beer. When I asked Herbert about it, he said, "You know your beer! Yes, it is the closest taste to my hometown beer. That's why I draw it from Drammen. Besides, it's easier to bring in, since that brewery has its own boat for transporting it right to this island."

Friday, 5 December, was the official last day of basic training. We were told we had to write two examinations on the following Monday, then wait for our detached service papers. By Sunday, 7 December, we felt relieved. Anticipating our first commando, we could relax for a while. Suddenly before dinner the alarm system started to blast. My first thought was, "Another exercise?" But we slipped into our combat-ready outfits and, within four minutes, lined up outside. Nobody had an idea of what was going on, but that was nothing new.

Bootsmannsmaat Waldgruber appeared on the scene, visibly disturbed. Something must have happened! All other drill corporals and sergeants joined in minutes. Everybody seemed to be flustered.

Waldgruber stepped forward and announced, "Men, in a few minutes, Commandant Witzfeld will make a special announcement."

Two group leaders, carrying a long colored cord, went from group to group to make sure the front would be straight. I remembered the first day of exercises, when we had to learn lining up straight and practice saluting. The group leaders could not get their men lined up straight, no matter what. One almost gave up and complained, "Damn it! The whole front is crooked! Some of your potbellies don't even fit between lines. Absolutely disgusting!"

The Attack

At that moment I saw Witzfeld step out of his house, stepping down the couple of steps to the ground, and walk in our direction with the usual military determination. He held something in his hand which, at first glance, looked like a scroll that town criers used in old English times.

He briefly acknowledged Waldgruber's report, then came out with the bombshell. "Comrades," he began, "we just have received a cablegram from the Fuehrer's headquarters in Berlin. A few hours ago, the Royal Japanese Air Force levied a tremendous blow to the US naval contingent, which anchored at Pearl Harbor, Hawaii. According to estimates, over two-thirds of the US naval ships in that harbor have been destroyed. We thank our Japanese friends for keeping the US busy in the Pacific theater. That way, they won't have any time to meddle in our affairs here in Europe." Then he added on his own, "That very likely means that the US has to enter the conflict in that theater. We now have extended the Axis (Berlin-Rome) to a troika, adding Tokyo."

He added a few remarks referring to the conclusion of our basic training and indicated that special permission would be granted to hold a well-deserved celebration before the end of the week. We were dismissed.

Upon returning to our quarters, my comrades immediately engaged in speculation regarding this new development. Some, without actually expressing concern, raised some doubts whether this event would assist us in bringing this war to a victorious end. I abstained from the discussions, since my views were not in line with that of the Party. It was too dangerous to open my mouth, I decided.

As promised, I went to Herbert's office in the evening. We made a few entries and calculations, following an easily applicable step-by-step procedure. Afterwards, to no surprise of mine, he wanted to know what I thought about the Japanese getting into the act. I did not know more about these people than anybody else. We all had heard about the fanatical fighting spirit of the people of the rising sun, how their traditional upbringing demanded sacrifices from them hardly imaginable for us. I had heard about the kamikaze flyers, who were trained for emergency cases, not knowing at the time what it meant. I guess we all know by now.

These flyers would, if there was no alternative, steer their planes to the target, dive and go down with the plane full of explosives. The story that was making its round after the Second World War goes like this: Three former air force pilots meet after the war and exchange notes. The German says, "I was a fighter pilot, and I shot down twenty-six Tommies with my Stuka (diving fighter plane)." The American says, "That's nothing. I knocked the hell out of people in Cologne; flattened two streets in one shot." The Japanese blinks, then says, "I was a kamikaze flyer." The German says, "How is that possible? If you were a kamikaze flyer, you wouldn't be here now!" "Well," the Japanese explains, "I was chicken kamikaze."

When I finished at Herbert's office, I asked if I could listen to his radio the next day around noon. "O.K.," he replied, without asking for the reason. I knew that President Roosevelt held his fireside broadcast every Saturday evening. Based on the new development, he probably would make an important public statement soon. I was right.

Monday I went over to Herbert's office around 1100 hours to tie up a few loose ends. At 1150 hours, he excused himself to hold an eye-to-eye meeting with the canteen operator. I switched the radio dial to the BBC long wave, which, because of its powerful transmitter, could be received quite well in Norway. In crisp clear Oxford-English the announcer gave through some gobble-di-gobble words with numbers, which did not make any sense. Obviously, I was listening to coded messages for spies.

Roosevelt's Speech

A few seconds before noon, Big Ben came on, followed by the Greenwich time signal. The BBC news at noon started. I heard the Japanese attack being described as one of the most vicious ever having taken place without provocation. A major portion of the US Navy in Pearl Harbor was declared destroyed. "Please stand by," the announcer said, "as we will bring you, at the end of the newscast, the unabridged address of President Roosevelt to the American nation."

When his settled voice came on, I could not help admiring the man. He had just received the worst news any national leader could possibly get. Yet, his voice was calm, though determined. While he talked, I remembered my father telling me when I was about fifteen or so how the final participation of the Americans during World War I had been instrumental for the breakdown of the Kaiser Reich. A repeat of that situation loomed in my mind.

The President appealed to his fellow Americans to pull together, and face this grave event and its consequences bravely. He lined out the gradual shifting over of the American industries and the general economy from peacetime production to wartime production. The war act was officially proclaimed to be in force, and a list of industrial changes with some specific logistics was read. Then he offered an estimate of how long it would take to complete the shift over to war production: two to three years. That statement got stuck in Hitler's throat, as I was soon about to find out.

Following his speech, a spokesman of the British War Ministry read a statement from the Prime Minister, who rejoiced that "with our American cousins at our side, we will be victorious and bury this Nazi dictatorship once and for all."

The Last Few Days

Not to be thrown out of the cot on Monday and Tuesday was like a small miracle. We had become so adjusted to the rough life, that it seemed to be difficult for most of us to shift back to normal. We had become creatures of habit.

On Wednesday afternoon, around 1600 hours, we received a special shipment of Schnapps, beer and cigarettes. When we unloaded the boat, I could not believe that all this was meant for us. Accompanying the shipment were several crates of ducks that had been noodled for immediate consumption. Did we ever look forward to that feast. Not that our food was not good, but duckling dinner was really something special for us Germans, and still is. It is just as festive a meal as turkey in North America.

Once more I had to be on patrol, from midnight to 0200 hours; only one stretch. Now that the days of my stay on Haon were counted, I looked with some reflection on the past weeks. Overall, it had been interesting and, in certain ways, educating as well. Proof had been rendered of how much the human body can endure without ill effect. *Kameradschaft* (camaraderie), from which I had heard so much in the distant past, was evident, even in a noncombat situation. I guess it had something to do with herd instinct. Part of it was the ability of people to endure hardship together and overcome it by cracking jokes, even at the worst of circumstances. It is the kind of feeling and attitude that women cannot comprehend.

As I patrolled I looked out for the flying fish, but could not see any this time. The ants had left the scene too. The two hours seemed to pass faster than before. That is nothing unusual, as it compares with taking a trip by car for the first time. It appears to stretch much longer than on subsequent trips.

The following day was the day we expected to be told where we would end up when transferred to our first official commando. Then we would begin our big celebration.

Herbert asked for some volunteers to slaughter the ducks. Groups two and nine had each one butcher aboard. They willingly carried out the task. Having done so a thousand times, it did not affect them. I cannot even see a duck's head chopped off, the blood flowing and the nerves of the animal twitch for a few seconds. A chap who watched the procedure, described to me on purpose how one duck had run around the yard with his head chopped off, zigzagging frantically. He could not refrain from giving the tenderfoot a lesson.

In order to line our stomachs in preparation for the celebration, we were served Pork Hocks and Sauerkraut for luncheon. The ducks were prepared for dinner.

At 1430 hours everybody had to line up on the drilling ground to receive our marching papers. About fifteen had to serve on different boats as navy artillerists, our actual career branch. Some were sent to Trondheim, Narvik, Bergen, one to Kristiansund, two to Lillehammer in the eastern part of Norway, and forty, including myself, as relief detachment to the Stabs and Wachkompanie (the area commander's Staff and Guard Company) in Stavanger. I had once heard my history teacher mention Stavanger as one of many coastal cities in Norway, but that was all I knew about the place. I would come to know it very well. "You will all be sent off next Sunday," pronounced Waldgruber. "So glad to get rid of you," he added, but with a broad grin on his face. "My next victims will already arrive two days later," he said with finality. The forty men we were about to replace had been transferred to other bases.

As a matter of common procedure and policy in the military, not peculiar to the war years, most military personnel is systematically replaced after about two to three years of service in one unit or company. Those who are actually engaged in combat, however, must be relieved after a few months, in order to avoid combat fatigue. There are exceptions to this rule under noncombat conditions whereby an enlisted man has special assignments. For the sake of continuity, he is kept in that slot longer than usual.

The other reason for changing scenes is the simple fact that some guys either become too complacent, or start rubbing elbows with civilians. That is looked upon by base, company or unit commanders as undesirable, particularly in occupied countries or territories during wartime.

In the evening we enjoyed our duckling dinner. Then, unit by unit, we drew supplementary Schnapps and beer to celebrate the successful completion of our basic training. Suffice it to say, it was the biggest blowout in which I had ever participated. It went right through the night and through Friday, until nobody could walk anymore by Saturday. Every room got fogged in by the penetrating smell of cold tobacco smoke, stale beer and spilled whiskey. We totally incapacitated ourselves to the point of silliness. It would have been a splendid time for the Western Allies to invade.

Some of the men visited other guys and never found their way back home. In retrospect, it was an absolutely disgusting sight. Most of us needed until Sunday afternoon to sober up, myself included. My head seemed to be split wide open, and my legs were collapsing. Our two medical orderlies had seen this sight before, and in foresight, had stocked up with aspirin. Sure enough, the consumption of ASA jumped during these two days over five hundred percent. I swore to myself never to get that stinking drunk again. I almost kept my pledge, with one exception in 1943, of which I shall report later.

I had learned enough in the hospitality field to be disgusted with some drunken guests or patrons, men and women. That in itself served as a warning to me not to let drinking get out of hand. If one can control the consumption of alcoholic beverages, there is absolutely nothing wrong with drinking. We should have learned from the time of prohibition that only criminal elements win when the use of it is outlawed. Besides, it is an established statistical fact that from all those who do drink only five percent are unable to control it. Should we therefore penalize the other ninety-five percent by prohibiting alcohol? It would be unfair to them and, besides, it did not work in the twenties.

Having said that, those who fall prey to "devil alcohol," as the great late writer Jack London used to call it, must be helped to overcome their addiction before it becomes a human tragedy. Excessive drinking usually begins at home. If children see their parents drink in an uncontrolled fashion, it sets a bad example. On the other hand, if wine, for instance, is served in moderation with meals to improve the taste and aid digestion of food, why not serve it? In European countries, where the restriction of the use of alcoholic beverages is not nearly as great as here, you do not find more intoxication than is found here. Consumption of alcoholic beverages is part of the process of growing up. Often, children of grade-school age are allowed a little glass of wine with a meal at home. Since it is not a big deal, and is part of everyday life rather than being hidden behind a veil of secrecy, these children do not create a craving for it. We need to learn from other civilized countries who have solved this problem of alcohol consumption.

Wine, by the way, is not considered an alcoholic beverage in the real sense of the word, but rather a temperate drink. Monks have cultivated the growth of grape vines for centuries, and not exclusively for sacramental use! Even the Bible proclaims: "Drink no longer water; drink a little wine for the stomach's sake." And the word "wine" appears sixty-four times in the greatest Book ever written. There must be something good about it. It has been clinically established without any doubt that wine is the most hygienic drink there is, followed by pasteurized milk. (No, I do not own any stocks in wineries.)

The Trip West

On Sunday, 14 December, we had our last breakfast on the island and immediately prepared ourselves to be shipped out. We were divided into two large groups. Those whose destiny lay west of the Oslofjord, including Bergen, were brought to Larvik by boat, then transported the remainder of the stretch by rail. Comrades traveling to the eastern, central and northeastern part of the country sailed to Oslo, where our naval headquarters for the entire Norwegian territory would take over to organize the rest of the trip.

We left Haon at 1300 hours, tied up at Larvik two hours later, and continued our journey at 1630 hours by rail. Though the train does not pass close to the coast from Larvik to Kristiansund, it was a very scenic picture. As strange as it might seem, considering the condition under which I was sent to Norway, I began to look forward with optimism to whatever assignments would come my way. The chap who was detailed to Kristiansund said good-bye to report to his new unit. It was like parting from a friend.

We were transferred into trucks. At the time, railway tracks had not been laid between Kristiansund and (I believe) Flekkefjord. It took us until 1944 to drill through rocks and mountains to finally complete the rail-net through to Stavanger. A large column of engineers and pioneers had to be put into action fulfilling a monumental task. It was one of few positive steps we took on behalf of the country we occupied.

The trip was breathtaking! We passed through small communities and valleys, over winding mountain roads, unable to avoid dangerous precipices to one side of the unpaved road and looking in awe at sky-reaching hills on the other side.

Three combination trucks/busses for the men and two trucks for the gear and equipment laboriously crawled along the snaking road. In each vehicle was a Norwegian driver and one transport supervisor in charge. The drivers were highly skilled in dealing with the treacherous gravel roads. And yet, it suddenly happened! One truck, with personal baggage and effects, skidded and went down an embankment about sixty feet. Luckily, it came to a halt there on a plateau, which extended out of the mountain before the precipice continued right down to the valley. The convoy came to an instant stop.

By the time we had improvised a rescue team for the two men, two hours had gone by. Miraculously, both men were only slightly hurt. The driver had been thrown out of the vehicle by the impact and had landed fifteen feet away from it, with a few cuts and bruises. The German comrade suffered a concussion, which later was diagnosed as survivable. He seemed to be asleep in the front of the truck, at peace with himself. He had to be cut out of that mess of metal with a welding torch. Nobody could understand why the gas tank of the truck had not exploded.

The senior leader of the convoy reported the accident upon arrival in Flekkefjord. A well-equipped rescue team was sent to the location. We heard later that none of the items transported were usable anymore. Thanks to the German obsession for details, a complete list of the items lost was available, with names and ranks of the owners. Certificates and formal requisition requests were made out in Flekkefjord, signed and countersigned by witnesses, assuring flawless reissue by the new commando.

We boarded a special train and arrived in Stavanger three hours later than expected, at 2330 hours. The Stabs and Wachkompanie was called from the railway station. Transport trucks were promptly sent to pick us up. Since it was late, the arrival report was delayed until the next morning. By 0030 hours the forty of us had bunks under our backs.

HALLO STRAVANGER

The Naval Officers Casino

As the tallest of the group, when lining up for inspection the next day after breakfast, I found myself facing the task of reporting to the *Hauptfeldwebel* (sergeant major), generally referred to as "the mother of the company." To my own surprise, I managed to utter the half dozen sentences or so without stuttering once. Only during my first three years of work training was I able, ever so gradually, to lose my speech impediment, which I had developed after entering grade school. The cause was a madman of a teacher, who daily terrified everybody in class with his sadistic behavior and outbursts.

The sergeant major made a couple of routine statements regarding our future service duties. Then, the company commander, Lieutenant Schmidt arrived. He acknowledged the sergeant major's report and began addressing us.

My first impression of the two men was very good. We were not going to be disappointed. Schmidt was a kind, no-nonsense *Volks-offizier* (grown through the ranks without university education). He surrounded himself with men who understood human nature and the needs and aspirations of the average soldier. Everybody in his company admired the man and would have followed him to hell, if asked. He was a real leader, not a pusher.

The commander gave us a clear picture of what was expected of us, the aims of the area commandant for naval operations in general, and the purpose of the company and tasks to be performed by its members. He stressed the importance of our assignments in a matter-of-fact fashion, without using pep talk. Each assignment, he declared, was of equal importance, from those who would be selected to protect strategic installations to doing ordinary company duty, i.e. providing maintenance back-up to those men who would receive special assignments from time to time, partly based on their civilian backgrounds.

"Before the sergeant major gets down to brass tacks," he continued, "giving you your details, I understand that two of you have a background in hotel and restaurant work. Step two steps forward! We immediately need two stewards to be assigned to our naval officers mess downtown."

As if rehearsed, Otto Januszeit from Essen (a town in Westphalia) and I stepped forward, well-timed. "You are dismissed for now and will report without delay to the quartermaster of the uniform room in the supply building," Schmidt continued. "He already has requisitions for issuing two pairs of brand-new blue navy uniforms for each of you. Your gray-greenish artillery set is to be surrendered. Tomorrow at 0800 hours, you will be picked up from the company entrance by car. The driver will drive you to the casino building, where you will report for duty to Heinz Marzi, the chief steward. Dismissed!"

On the way to the supply building, Otto said, "You know, Siegfried, I had an idea that something like that would come up. What do you think of it?"

"It surpasses my expectations," I replied. "I was already pleased with being detailed to an outfit like the Stabs and Wachkompanie, which carries out peaceful duties only. Now you and I can practically continue where we left off at home. There is hardly any difference between a dining room waiter and an officers mess steward. That much I do know. And make no mistake, I put my reputation on it that we will enjoy the best food available and can live almost like civilians. It suits me just fine!"

Otto and I received specially selected uniforms that fit like they had been made to measure. With this, the quartermaster issued new socks, underwear, overcoats, the pointed service cap, the off-duty round hat with the prominent inscription in front *Kriegsmarine* (war navy) and a navy blue sweater. In leaving the building, I mentioned to Otto, "Now we are fit to be photographed as propaganda models for the navy poster used in peacetime with the slogan, 'Join the navy to see the world!'" I did not know at the time, that the US Navy had used the same slogan for years.

Returning to our quarters, which had turned out to be very temporary for us, our comrades received us with smart aleck remarks, such as "Watch out, the peacocks are coming!"

"Well," Otto retorted, using an old and rather impolite adage, "you guys know how it goes. 'The dumbest farmers harvest the biggest potatoes.'"

Everybody was off for the day. The sergeant-at-arms led us around the company to get acquainted with the environment. Otto and I joined the group knowing that, sooner or later, we would have to return here. The man in charge of food production and enlisted men mess hall service, Leading Seaman (Corporal) Hans Steiner, called the two of us to his office after dinner. He was about ten years our senior and was given the task of feeding the troops well. His background was similar to ours, but when drafted one year earlier, he was employed as assistant chef at the Frankfurter Hof Hotel.

We talked turkey in his office and I had the feeling he treated us differently from the others, not only because we hotel people have a lot in common, but also because of our assignments. We did not mind that at all, of course. Steiner felt that maybe our prospects were better than his. Surely we would not have a chance to rub elbows with officers. But, who knows, we might acquire some kind of influence. Later on, after I returned with Heinz Marzi from the bartering trip across Rogaland, he invited me to one of his private parties at the base. We knew each other better by then and had struck some kind of an agreement, realizing we could be useful to each other.

On Tuesday morning, 16 December, at 0800 hours sharp, the private car of the German Navy area commander stopped in front of the gate. Most of the guys who had arrived with us from Haon bade us good-bye. When they saw the limousine, their jaws opened and their eyes seemed to pop out of their heads. "The two of you really seemed to have fetched the scheme," one said loudly. "For sure," another chap shouted, "they've got it made!"

Before entering the car, I craned my neck around and replied, "No, not yet. But we all will have it made, if we survive this whole bloody war and trade in our uniforms for civilian clothes again!" With that, we cruised off.

The Building

The drive took only fifteen minutes. We encountered no heavy traffic, and the driver made a little side tour. He took us in an east-northeasterly direction down Ovre Stokkevei and its extension of Stokkaveien to the western inlet of Stavanger Harbor, which was still open for naval traffic. It actually never freezes completely, since the Gulf Stream still exerts its affect here, keeping the ocean gulfs open for navigation upward in a northerly direction, passing the town of Bergen, then slightly changing course away from the Norwegian coast and finally veering off in northwesterly lines before reaching the city of Trondheim.

We drove along Strandkaien from northwest to southeast, until we had landed at Kongsgardbakken, the extreme inlet of the harbor. The area naval commander's headquarters came into view. The building was beautifully located at the Breiavatnet Pond, east of where the Atlantic Hotel is now located. I did not have the foggiest idea that, in time, I would serve in that building in several well-staged capacities.

We passed the building to our left, entered Lars Hertervigs Gate and turned right into Ny Olavskleiv. It was then a cobblestone street and had been named after Prince Olav (now Norway's recently deceased king) who, with his father, went to England in self-imposed exile, when we occupied the country.

One of a few stone houses was located on the left side of the street. As we approached, I could plainly read the gold-lettered sign directly to the right of the main entrance which, strangely enough, was positioned four steps inside a lane. We had arrived at our destination.

As soon as we stepped out of the 1938 BMW, a chap with deep lines in his face and not taller than about five feet five inches, sprinted out of the smaller front entrance, which was used by all personnel, and for receiving daily and weekly deliveries of food and beverages. He saluted with a good-natured smile and immediately grabbed part of our baggage, which primarily consisted of the traditional *Seesack* (navy or sailor's sack). Otto also had a light travel bag (not quite in conformity with regulations) in which he carried miscellaneous items. I had two additional pieces with me: my mandolin, without which I did not go anywhere, and a document case from my dad. It contained English Berlitz study books and my waiter's tools–an all-purpose bottle opener, a wine bottle corkscrew, two white service serviettes and the latest German edition of an illustrated book about good table service. I was surely ready for this assignment!

Gottlieb, the commodore's driver, left as soon as we had removed our things. "See you guys one day," he had said in parting.

Inside the building, we had to climb about eight steps before reaching the first landing. We saw a door ajar to the right, which the little guy pried open by kicking it with his right foot. We entered.

"Let us set down your things here for the time being," he said, then introduced himself as *Gefreiter* (Private) Erich Apfel. He had two sheets of paper in his hand. Before we could open our mouths to reciprocate his introduction, he turned to Otto and said, "You must be Siegfried," and swinging around to me, "and you are Otto."

"Dead wrong," I answered. "You must be thinking about Richard Wagner's opera *Siegfried*, where the dragon killer is typically Germanic-blond, like Otto here. I am not, as you can see. My dad picked the wrong name for a dark-haired guy." We all chuckled a bit. The ice was broken.

"Are you in charge here?" Otto asked.

"Oh, no!" Erich replied. "The guy in charge is about twice as big as I am; his voice explodes in your ears when he just chats with you and he surely does not fiddle around with anything or anybody. You will see." I suddenly felt a bit chilly, though the door was closed.

The kitchen was empty. Breakfast had been served to the officer corps between 0715 hours and 0900 hours. The cooks had taken a break before preparing luncheon and were in their quarters. Two Norwegian women were washing the breakfast dishes by hand in a triple sink on one side near the pantry, which was actually only a connecting link between the kitchen and the formal dining room. We said hello to them. They seemed pleasant and glad to work for us. There was no visible resentment.

We took our *Sieben Sachen* (belongings), and Erich led us through the pantry into a large cloakroom, where the officers' coats and sidearms were placed. Turning to the right, we went through an archway that led to a large lobby. The sliding doors to the right led into the dining room. It was set up in U-shaped fashion and could accommodate up to fifty-two diners. The average number of officers reporting to and working directly under the command of Dr. Carlos Mayer-Pantin, the naval area commandant, was forty-six.

Opposite the lobby entrance was a door that led to the salon. It was adjacent to the dining room, but much longer, filling out the end of the ground floor area. This large sitting room was tastefully furnished with arm chairs, settees and the first low-cut tables ever made, like the ones used in the Orient. There was sufficient space for stand-up functions for about a hundred. By rearranging furniture, sixty to sixty-five could be seated at one time. With Spanish walls, as they were then called, the room could easily be divided in two.

Double windows at each end of the room and four large windows at one side of the long wall allowed plenty of light to stream in from the outside when curtains were withdrawn. Blackout curtains prevented any light from filtering to the outside at dusk, making it unnecessary to dim lights.

The opposite wall toward the inside of the building was interrupted by a beautiful archway, leading to the end portion of the formal dining room. Two-thirds of the center was occupied by a double fireplace, adding significantly to the dignity of the lounge. A two-foot ledge ran underneath the windows, decorated with ornaments.

Two large chandeliers hung from the eleven-foot-high ceiling. Dusting in this room could be a nightmare, as I soon found out. Everything had been kept in perfect condition and order. Overall, there was not too much space available for hanging pictures. But when entering the lounge from the lobby, one could look straight ahead at an oil painting depicting Grossadmiral Schroeder (Admiral of the Fleet Schroeder), Supreme Commander of the German Navy.

Underneath recessed window ledges was ample space to allow the storing of foldable card tables. At each side of the two small wall windows hung one sketch showing sailing ships of the seventeenth century.

In the center and at each end of the lounge were pulleys with two-inch thick gold-sprinkled red ropes, which were pulled when requiring service. An electrical impulse would activate a call box beside the pantry inside the kitchen indicating to the steward on duty where service was needed. There were six numbers: three for the lounge, one for the dining room, one for the lobby, and one would fall down when the doorbell rang.

The lobby contained only sparse furniture, just sufficient for a handful of people to sit down. A huge spiral staircase, dominating almost one-third of the lobby, led to the mezzanine floor. The handrail was heavily gold-plated. The structure holding it was an excellent work of art, showing exquisitely carved figurines, daintily filigreed. It was worthwhile looking at this masterpiece of ingenuity and artistry.

The mezzanine floor was framed by a balcony-like balustrade on all sides, allowing a full view of the entire lobby. In intervals of six feet, woodcarvings of notable Norwegian poets, writers, settlers, Viking explorers and, of course, one of my favorite composers, Edward Grieg, plus the great Danish philosopher and theologian Soren Aabye Kierkegaard, were facing the lobby. It was a sight I shall never forget.

Disregarding the interruption by the balustrade, the walls of the lobby seemed to reach to the sky, ending up in swinging arches. Several sky windows in beautiful colors concluded the spectacle of almost unsurpassed sophistication.

Erich had allowed us a quick glimpse of the dining room and lounge. It was hard to digest all this beauty at once. As the three of us went up the spiral staircase my heart jumped for joy. This topped everything anybody could possibly expect. Indeed, this was better than anything I had ever seen. I climbed the steps with great elation, knowing that Otto and I had hit the jackpot. This assignment looked like a piece of cake.

Reaching the balcony, Erich pointed to the first rather small door we passed, explaining this led to the attic, where nothing much was kept. "Part of it we use for excess storage. You know," he continued with a grin, "we sometimes manage to get extra provisions, which do not go through the books. But I guess Heinz Marzi will explain that to you in time."

"Here," he pointed to the next door, "we have the Admiral's room, which is always kept at his disposal when he comes to visit us. His name is Admiral Von Schrader, a little man but a strict disciplinarian." Smiling again, Erich added, "When he is announced to come here to Stavanger, from his headquarters in Bergen, the whole staff officers' corps gets nervous. You wouldn't believe how they fear the old man. By the way, guys, when the admiral comes, one of you will have to act as his orderly."

Otto remarked, "That really must be something to look forward to. Stop giving us any bad news, Erich. We still have a fresh memory, which reminds us of all the shit we got on Haon. We came here to recover from all that bull and take a rest."

"Good luck," Erich replied and continued to explain the layout. "Opposite the Admiral's room are two visitors rooms for high-ranking visitors, commodore or brigadier and up."

"To one side of these two rooms lies Heinz Marzi's domain. The room here, on the other side, is for you two. At the end of this floor are two more rooms; one for our two cooks and the one next to it is used by Heinz as an office. There he makes up his food and beverage orders, inventory reports, monthly charge accounts for all staff officers and his monthly operating statement. He reports directly to the casino chairman, who presently happens to be your company commander, First Lieutenant Schmidt. There are no rooms behind the other long wall, as it runs along the lane. Here we are."

With this he opened the door to the room, which became our home as long as we would hold this assignment. It was roomier than the quarters at the company, which I had to share with nine other guys. Right beside the door was one bed, and the other bed was stationed diagonally in the far left-hand corner of the room.

A table for six sat in the center of the room, covered with a flowered tablecloth. The chairs were solid and comfortable, allowing one's lumbar spine to find rest. It was exactly what one needed for relieving the strenuous half-bending position while performing table service.

On each side of the room, bookshelves had been erected. They were fairly well stocked with a variety of books, from hotel-restaurant procedures through Goethe and, of course, Hitler's *Mein Kampf;* from history books to Karl May western stories and adventure series. You could get stuck in here for a while and not get bored. Books of foreign authors were conspicuously absent. Surprise, surprise! It fit Hitler's isolationistic policy, as I call it.

On a small, mobile tea table right beside the bedside table to the front of the room, rested a Philips radio with medium wave, long wave and short wave bands.

Beside one of the two windows at the end of the room, in the right-hand corner, stood a settee for four. "Nice for two couples," I thought, doing some wishful thinking. A double wardrobe on the left side wall concluded the fixtures, except for one large-sized wash basin with running cold water and a miniature wall water heater above, resting in the front left-hand corner of the room.

"Make yourselves at home," Erich said. "I've got to go." Before leaving the room, he turned around. "By the way, you had better get ready by 1130 hours. The chief steward expects you in the kitchen for a quick orientation. Luncheon service to our members commences at noon sharp. Since your predecessors were marched off yesterday, you will have to serve the meal. We have heard you are a couple of greyhounds," (an occasionally used

German expression for efficient and experienced people). "You should not have any problems shaking this out of your shirtsleeves." He left.

We flipped a coin to see who would get which bed. I got the one behind the door. Unpacking was done with the usual military speed and precision, in ten minutes. The wardrobe had sufficient space to accommodate a total of six uniforms. Even my mandolin, wrapped in the pear-shaped linen sack, fit in there nicely, right beside my oxfords. The latter did not belong to regulation outfits, but when reporting for inspection, before receiving a pass, I had noticed that most noncoms in charge closed both eyes. Here, I even had to use them while on duty. A steward simply did not run around in boots or combat shoes.

I stripped down to my shorts, took a bath towel, a bar of soap and told Otto I was going to wash up. He said, "I'll join you in a few minutes."

I left the room and had a closer look at a sign nearby. It said *Badezimmer und Brause* (Bathroom and Shower). The arrow underneath pointed to the farthest left-hand corner of the mezzanine floor.

The semi-double room I entered had completely white tiled floors, walls and ceilings. Two-thirds of the double room was partially partitioned by an equally tiled two-thirds wall. The larger portion held three showers; the smaller one was equipped with a fancy bathtub, cupboard and towel rack. To fill the tub, a super-modern (at the time) dual water tap was shaped in the center like a lion's head, that would spit out water when opening the taps. The eyes of the lion consisted of small pea-sized, translucent, deep purplish-red rubies. The lion's mane framed his head with glittering bluish splinters of lapis lazuli gemstones, which was quite another sight to see.

The fascinating looking fixtures caused me to choose the tub, while Otto showered. Our conversation circled around this enchanting place and how long we would be part of it. Was this whole thing really true or just a dream?

Back in our quarters, we had not quite finished with dressing, when a sharp knock at the door made us flinch around. We barely had completed our half-turn, when the door was unceremoniously thrust wide open.

The Man In Charge

A dark-haired, brown-eyed, determined-looking man stood in the door frame, almost filling it. He was tall (about six feet one), thirty-six years old and athletically built, with wide shoulders and narrow hips. His well-proportioned frame suggested a weight in the neighborhood of two hundred pounds. I later found out I had estimated both his weight and age on the nose.

He returned our salute smartly. His somewhat hulky appearance did not prevent him from quickly stepping forward with amazing lightness. He offered each of us a firm but friendly handshake, while looking us squarely in the eyes. When he withdrew his hand, I noticed it to be unusually small in contrast to the balance of his features. He introduced himself as *Hauptgefreiter* (one notch higher than PFC) Heinz Marzi. The silvery horizontal beam attached underneath his rank, indicated that he carried out the duties of a petty officer, second class (or sergeant).

"Ready to go down?" he asked, glancing at his wrist watch. "I want you to meet the rest of the staff, before familiarizing yourselves with preparation, service and storage facilities."

As we left the room, he turned around and explained, "We keep all doors here unlocked, except the officers' entrance and the front door for personnel and deliveries. The house is well-protected against burglars and other shady elements. Erich Apfel, the chap who greeted you, has his quarters between the elevated ground floor and the mezzanine, nearby an alarm system." While we descended the spiral staircase, Heinz continued, "He is not only our cellar master, receiving and issuing goods and generally keeping control of inventories, but he is also our watchdog."

Before reaching the exterior pantry door, he said, "The dining room table has been set up today by Erich Apfel and Solway, one of our Norwegian kitchen helpers. We now have seventeen minutes left before luncheon service begins."

We crossed the pantry room and entered the kitchen. He introduced us briefly to the two cooks in between their juggling with pots and pans. Erich Eye, the professional in charge, used to be the top executive chef/steward with the *Hamburg/Amerika Dampfschiffahrtsgesellschaft* (steamship line). He was unquestionably the most top-notch chef with whom I ever had the privilege of working throughout forty-eight years. Incapable of spoiling any dish, his soups and sauces were superb! You would not know it when you saw him, because he was the slimmest of them all, weighing around 130 pounds.

The other chap was a butcher by trade, but the perfect person to complement Erich. His name was Hermann Behrens. Both were perfectionists, but that did not cause them to get into each other's hair. Their pride in work and sense of cooperation was exemplary. They were a great pair.

The entire left wall of the kitchen was stocked with food preparation equipment. Nothing was missing. Opposite, to the right of the kitchen door from the front staircase, was a modern refrigerator. It was well stocked with Scotch whiskey, German Schnapps of all kinds, rum, beer, soda and white wine. Red wine was drawn directly from the cellar, the temperature of which was kept at a pleasant sixteen degrees Celsius (sixty-one Fahrenheit). All food supplies were issued by Erich Apfel upon requisition from Erich Eye.

Another refrigerator in the pantry was stocked with miscellaneous items, such as cheese portions, butter patties, cream, etc. A small cabinet held charge voucher booklets for the officers to sign when ordering items not included in their daily ration supplies, primarily beer, wine and hard liquor.

Along one side of the wall ran a sturdy board at mid-chest height. Stewards used it for writing out orders on charge vouchers, marking attendance lists, and noting messages received by telephone for members of the commandant's officer corps. A small radio in the corner of the shelf beside the entrance to the dining room from that side, provided us with news and music, but could only be switched on outside of regular dining room hours.

The washing of china dishes, silverware, and pots and pans took place inside the kitchen but away from the preparation area and the stewards' traffic paths. All tools for table service were kept in a small walk-in cupboard. Shelves and reach-in spaces were plainly marked. A place for everything and everything in its place seemed to be the order. Good organization wins half the battle in the hospitality field. It cuts down on confusion and prevents things from getting lost. Pilfering is also much more difficult that way.

Heinz quickly went with us to the dining room and showed us the table set-up. Every seat was reserved. Across the butter plate, a clean napkin rested folded in a napkin ring, in which the name and rank of the officer was engraved.

Tables were connected with each other so as to form a U-shape. Six seats were at the outside center of the U, reserved for the area commandant (commodore), captain, commander, lieutenant commander (the adjutant), and the highest-ranking medical officer. The balance of the commandant's staff was seated along the outer and inner legs of the U, with the lowest-ranking officers–second lieutenants or acting sublieutenants–at the ends.

Seating arrangements were in accordance with the command echelon, which is much more pronounced in the military than in civilian life. One of several explanations is, of course, the fact that military organizations are not democratic, nor should they be, or could function in that fashion. The line of command, and consequently, the level of authority and responsibility are effective instruments for clearly defining levels of communications.

In the business world, we too often find either overlapping action levels or loopholes, where nobody seems to be responsible. I would not dare to sell private industries the military way of operating a business; that may be unnecessary or even undesirable. On the other hand, any business, no matter how small, should make clear to its employees on all levels what the function levels are, by at least providing a practical organization chart!

"Get your service napkins ready," Heinz said. "We do not use service carts or trays for table service, but platters and plates, which we carry in our hands and on our forearms." He walked to one side of a huge sliding double door, taking from a fancy hook a gold-plated gong and a drumstick (not from a chicken) with a felt-covered, round head.

"Stand on each side of the door," he ordered. "At noon sharp," he looked at his watch, "in twenty seconds, I will slide open the door and ring the gong, the signal which indicates we are ready for services. You will take turns doing this."

He opened the door and let the gong sound twice. Forty-six officers filed in and took their designated seats. All staff officers were present. They unfolded their napkins. Even that movement seemed to be timed. It reminded me of a symphony orchestra, whose members of the string section would use their violin bows in unison.

We stood at attention at the U ends. The commandant rose and everybody followed. "Gentlemen," Commodore Dr. Carlos Mayer-Pantin said, "luncheon will be served now."

With this announcement, he gave a slight nod to Heinz Marzi, who replied with *"Jawohl, Herr Kapitaen."*

Everybody sat down and we left the dining room to pick up the first course of the meal. The timing of picking up courses in the kitchen, then serving and finally removing them, ran like a clock. Not once was there a need for explanations. The pick-up station in the kitchen had looked rather small when I first looked at it, but the efficiency of the cooks who dished out, and the kitchen helpers who lined up the course, made this a cinch.

As soon as the dessert course was removed and coffee had been served, Heinz instructed, "Don't leave the dining room yet."

He went to the *Seekommandant*, bent down close to his left ear and whispered something. Dr. Mayer-Pantin clinked his wine glass with his coffee spoon (nowhere in the German forces was water ever served, although that might have changed by now) and, remaining seated, announced, "Gentlemen, a brief announcement. As you have noticed, we have two new stewards to serve us: Ordinary Seamen Siegfried Born and Otto Januszeit. Heinz Marzi has told me they just completed their basic military training on Haon. As you observed, they are competent waiters. We welcome you," he looked straight at us, standing side by side at the pantry/dining room entrance, "and congratulate you on your assignment." Polite applause followed. We saluted and left the dining room with Heinz.

When we had reached the kitchen we expressed our delight about that welcome. "It has its reasons," Heinz explained. "The chief steward before me and the two stewards you are replacing received a disciplinary transfer. They milked the naval mess for over two years. It took that long to discover their wrongdoing. A cunning double-entry system camouflaged their embezzlements. Even the previous casino chairman responsible for the operation, got sacked for not discovering the fraud earlier. It was a real mess, I tell you. The resulting deficit surpassed Kr 3,000. I committed myself to iron this out within one year by bartering and buying and selling on the side."

Otto and I alternated keeping an eye on our customers, eating our own luncheon in between. The cooks and helpers joined us. We had set up a foldable double table for eight. The feeling which overcame me was like having been adopted by a nice family. Erich Apfel's remark about Heinz Marzi had to be exaggerated. Sure, he had an authoritative voice, leaving no doubt that he was in charge, but the table conversation was quite amiable. The personnel under his supervision respected the man, but certainly did not fear him. "A relief," I told myself.

Shortly after 1400 hours, when the last officers had left, we stripped the tables, laid fresh tablecloths and exchanged napkins. The service arrangements for dinner were different from those for luncheon. While all officers had to attend luncheon at noon, dinner could be enjoyed individually, between 1730 and 1930 hours.

One steward would set up the tables at 1700 hours. The second would join the service at 1800 hours, then hold himself available for after-dinner service. The first one would take off the rest of the day.

Heinz Marzi took us on a second quick tour around 1400 hours. We breezed through the kitchen and went down to the basement, where the main storage areas and the wine cellar were located. Storerooms were sensibly partitioned, keeping different food groups apart. The wine cellar was something else; nothing was missing. There were white, red, rose and sparkling wines from Germany, Italy and France, even Mum's extra dry. All wines had real corks (that plastic stuff had not been invented yet). Each bottle was stored in a slightly slanted, horizontal position, to avoid the cork from drying out—another sign of professionalism.

In a semi-partitioned area, behind wooden slats, was the liquor, liqueur, and beer storage. A few cases were unpacked, but clearly marked. In one corner of the room three shabby-looking crates held together by rusty metal-strips sat side by side. The crates had been placed for easy identification. The viewer could not mistake the big black lettering for anything else but "Black and White Scotch Whiskey." I scratched my head, then I remembered earlier having seen a few bottles of that Scotch whiskey standing up in the kitchen refrigerator. Pointing to the crates, I said to Heinz, "Don't tell me we do some wheeler-dealer trading with the British in between fighting!"

"Ja," he replied, "isn't that something? It would be similar to the joking statement, 'When it rains, the battle is moved to an assembly hall.'" Then he explained.

"In late September 1941, the commanding officer of the navy, operating along the Norwegian west coast, Admiral Van Schrader (here I heard that name a second time in one day) went out west with his speedboat. It was a foggy day, like London soup. The speedboat was accompanied by one cruiser, one minesweeper and a patrol boat.

"They lost visual sight of each other and suddenly noticed in their midst a British supply ship, which had accidentally strayed from her convoy, as we later found out from rescued British sailors. We sank the supply ship. We fished most of the floating goodies out of the ocean, including this Scotch. It ended up here and at the admiral's headquarters in Bergen. This stuff will last us a while. I was told to hold some of it and use it for bartering with Norwegian farmers. One of you, by the way, will accompany me in May, when I peddle across the county of Rogaland."

We went upstairs to the pantry where Heinz explained how charge vouchers were used and the daily head count (which has nothing to do with headhunters) would be made. One acceptable common procedure was of advantage to the operation. A visiting officer, not belonging to the commandant's staff, would be entered on the extra supply list. His name would continue to appear on that list during the entire month, even if he stayed only one day.

Advancing to Heinz's office on the mezzanine floor, Otto and I commented on the beautiful surroundings in general and the spiral staircase and woodcarvings in particular. Using a softer word for "confiscating," we asked him to whom the building belonged when we "requisitioned" it.

"You had better get prepared for this," Heinz said. "Paradoxically, we confiscated it from the local Norwegian Temperance Society. Mind you," he added, "it is still a decent establishment. There are no women and wild parties here. I guess it strikes one as strange. It does conducively present the atmosphere of a British or American private club."

Heinz was absolutely correct in this, as I later experienced. After a total of seventeen months of service, I did not witness one excess in any way, shape, or form. The stigma of all sailors being drunk most of the time and chasing broads around all the time is, at best, an exaggeration.

Arriving at his office, Heinz told us to sit down. He gave us a good rundown of service procedures and conduct. We asked a lot of questions and received prompt answers. He stressed that polite and efficient service was expected all the time. But he also pointed out that our own dignity as persons would not suffer, based on the philosophy of the casino board.

No officer was allowed to ever enter the kitchen, except the chairman. Both the chairman and the commandant had made it clear to the officer corps that the stewards were here to serve them, but to be treated with human respect. I could not believe my ears! "This means," Heinz continued, "you will be treated well by all. On the other hand, don't get the idea that you can rub elbows with these people. You must keep a certain distance, as you also have to do with hotel guests and restaurant and bar patrons."

Heinz asked us to fill in some blanks about ourselves that did not appear in the files. We did. In turn, we asked him about his background. He reluctantly gave us a few bits and pieces, but not nearly enough to make the picture complete. That came later, when we knew each other better, and when we had inquired with others who knew the man well. You may find his adventurous life interesting. We certainly did.

The Adventurer

Heinz Marzi was born in Italy in 1905. His mother was German, his father Italian, with the name of Antonio Ettore de Marzinelli. They were acrobatic circus people, taking their son wherever the circus went. By the time Heinz was fourteen, he had finished his grade school education, barely squeezing in under the bar. That was not too surprising. In eight years he had attended twenty-three different schools. Under those circumstances, one could possibly call his graduation from grade eight a miracle.

He put up with circus life (his own words) another year, then decided to call it quits. One day in Palermo, the circus leader called all his acrobats, animal trainers, miracle show people and clowns together. It had become more than difficult to keep the circus viable.

Two years after the end of World War I, all European countries faced tough economic times. War production had stopped causing the then Italian government to convert to peacetime production. Money was becoming almost worthless, not as bad as it was to become in Germany in 1922, but bad enough to cause a multitude of problems. Italy was spared that total economic collapse which Germany experienced between 1922 and 1924.

The Italians were looking for a strong leader who would "swing the cart around." That they found with the emergence of the fascist party and its leader, Benito Mussolini, who took over the reins of government and built, in his own words, a "New Roman Empire."

The young Marzinelli drew his own conclusions. That evening, he met by chance some crew members of a Portuguese freighter. They painted a pretty good picture to him about life at sea. What Heinz did not know was that they were looking for another "victim" who would serve on their boat as ship's boy, generally referred to as Moses. (I have no idea where that expression originated, but it also was–and maybe still is–used in the German mercantile marine.) The boy who had come with them from Portugal had vanished into thin air.

Sure, Heinz was interested in seeing the world cheaply. The ship's engineer hired him by a handshake before the evening was over. When the carnival was over for the day, Heinz retreated to the Marzinelli wagon to "prepare myself for the adventure." That was easy. Get a duffel bag; hide some underwear, a pair of running shoes which, for the time being, would have to replace the traditional board shoes, a few pairs of socks and some other oddities.

When his parents were already asleep, he stole himself away from the quarters and wrote outside, by the light of a candle, a good-bye note. The duffel bag he hid under the wagon.

The following morning, before the daily chores began, he made up the wagon for the last time while his parents started their daily acrobatic practice. The note he had written the previous evening, he put on Papa's night table. It was brief, but explained that "I am now old enough to look after myself. It will be easier for you and Mama, now that I am not a burden to you anymore." That was the nucleus of his unselfish note.

Taking another long look at the familiar surroundings, he finally opened the wagon door, suppressed his tears, and quickly went around to the back, retrieving his duffel bag. Since the Marzinelli wagon stood at the outer periphery of the Palermo Plaza, it was easy to leave without being seen.

The engineer had prepared for him a simple drawing which would help him find the ship. He did so, went aboard and was brought to the captain's quarters to receive instructions. The ship put to sea soon afterwards. It seemed the crew had only waited for his arrival. The return trip to Lisbon began.

The New Moses

He signed a ten trip agreement for the Lisbon-Havana-Tampico route. During these excursions he was taught all the ropes a ship's boy has to know. That included assisting with cooking for the crew; serving the crew and officers; keeping officers quarters in tiptop shape and acting as cabin boy. Soon the crew found out they had hired an efficient and willing jack-of-all-trades, who could be trusted with any assignment. In spite of his somewhat limited education, Heinz was a fast learner and maintained an amazing degree of self-discipline for his age.

After one year of cruising the route, he decided to try something different. He had observed the busy trade taking place between Mexico, Cuba, Panama and South America. "Maybe I can get a piece of the action," he told himself. As he described it, "The nomadic and entrepreneurial spirit of my family took over." He got paid off in Tampico. Lingering around, he picked up a few pesos here and there, selling oddities and Cuban cigars.

Captain Blood

After a couple of months went by—it now was December 1920—he came in contact with an all-round smuggler, who dealt in anything illegal under the sun. This was nothing unusual. Tampico had, and still has, the reputation of harboring shady elements of all kinds.

The one-eyed smuggler, who reminded Heinz of Captain Blood, struck a deal with him. "I couldn't refuse. I knew it was shady, but I had run short of cash and needed some transfusion. The idea of giving up my independence, returning home and admitting failure, was too much for me."

The next several months were a real adventure, but only the beginning, not the end. Cuban cigars were bought on the black market for rock-bottom prices, then unloaded in crates in different countries. Most of them bore the inscription "Piezas de Repuesto Electrico" and "Electrical Spare Parts." Underneath appeared two stamps: "Inspeccion Internacional Y Soltar" and "International Inspection & Release," a verification of the goods having passed international inspection. In fact, Capitano Garcia had selected certain cities where harbor officials were either lackadaisical, or could be bribed to pass shipments without inspection. In more tightly controlled harbors arrangements were made with owners of small boats who, for a nominal fee, would pick up shipments off shore and land on isolated coastal areas.

Another most profitable item was rum from Jamaica. Captain Garcia had connections everywhere. He brought tons of non-inventoried rum, which was stored on the northwestern tip of the island. Stories went around, claiming these illegal traders to be a blessing for Jamaica, otherwise the island would tip over because of all that heavy rum stored there. It already was leaning in that northwestern direction.

When Garcia went ashore, he took Heinz with him to learn trading. Heinz did not look like a sixteen-year-old kid, but rather like a tough, young man, at his boss' side like a bodyguard, fending off trouble, when needed. He had learned some English, enough to make himself understood and to translate for Garcia. His Italian and Spanish were fluent. Garcia recognized the usefulness of the young man, paying him the salary of a full-fledged engineer, plus trading benefits. The two of them got along well, sort of a frictionless father-son relationship.

The Great Adventure

In August 1921, Garcia met an Englishman, who was to become instrumental in enabling Garcia and his constant companion to "enter the big time." Their freighter had tied up in Southampton, unloading a big shipment of legally acquired goods, but also several crates marked "machine parts." These had been loaded in New York, where they had made a stopover at the request of a businessman who had identified himself to Garcia in Veracruz as a representative of an American machine parts company. The shipment was under contract to be delivered as soon as possible to England, otherwise a penalty would be levied against the company. He would pay very generously for the "special delivery." Garcia agreed to pick it up in New York. He had sufficient storage space left aboard, and there was no sense in crossing the ocean half empty.

Halfway across the Atlantic, Garcia said to Heinz, "You know, Enrico (he always called him that), I've got a funny feeling about that shipment of machine parts from New York. Let's have a look."

Equipped with a crowbar, the two went down. The first crate they opened already told the story. One five-inch layer of real machine parts; underneath, a variety of handguns, submachine guns, and an assortment of rifles and ammunition. "Mon Dieu," Garcia shouted, getting all excited, "if we get caught with this load, we will hang to roast in hell."

They opened all six crates, and found basically the same contents. In some of them, explosives and hand grenades had been added. In one, Heinz saw a large brown manila envelope stashed between two submachine guns. It bore the name "Jack Jr." The envelope was not sealed. Heinz took out the postcard-size, cardboard-type paper with the message, "When you hold this in your hands, you know we made it. Pay off Lyonel as agreed. Will get in touch soon to discuss alternative delivery routes." There was no date; just an indecipherable scrawl.

Garcia put the note back where it had been and recessed the crates as they had found them. Arriving at Garcia's cabin, they kicked their options around. Either they would have to give the crates a "seaman's funeral" by throwing them overboard, which meant losing (or rather not getting) $15,000 shipment charge, or they had to just play dumb, pretending everything to be in order and see where the chips may fall. They decided for the latter.

The receiver of the hot crates was the first who boarded the freighter, producing his credentials. To Garcia's relief the man declared the entire shipment to have passed harbor inspection. Several seals on the shipment's duplicate receiving papers proved the authenticity of the man's statement. It was no sweat!

They were sitting in the officers' lounge when papers and money changed hands. Transactions such as these were all handled in cold hard cash, of course. Transfer papers were signed. Then, out of curiosity, Garcia asked the agents the definitive question: "What is the final destination of this load, and who receives it?"

The agent hesitated a moment, then said, "Well, I'll tell you. You wouldn't be foolish enough to let this go beyond this door. It is going to be loaded onto another freighter bound for Dublin. From there, the stuff will be picked up by food trucks, leaving for Belfast. That is all I know."

When the man had left, Garcia turned to Enrico and remarked, "I don't feel so well. I shouldn't have asked the guy in the first place. No surprise, though. The IRA has its hands in the game. Since 1919, they have intensified their fight against British rule in Northern Ireland. Let's change the subject!"

As he went up and gathered his papers, a note fluttered to the floor. Picking it up, Heinz read aloud, "If you are interested in more profitable transactions, be at the Harbor Inn at 8:00 P.M. tonight. Check with Leslie, the barkeep."

Garcia said, "It may not be a bad idea to investigate this. We don't have any cargo to ship at this time, but I sure as hell don't want to knowingly get caught with a shipment such as we just unburdened. Whatever it is, it likely won't be quite legal, if it pays well, but smuggling weapons is on our black list from now on."

The Harbor Inn did not turn out to be different from any other seaport dive in Hamburg, Antwerp, Lisbon, Bordeaux, Naples, Barcelona, San Francisco, New York or Tampico. The used-up air went into their fresh sea-air lungs like the smell of a garbage dump. Leslie turned out to be a woman in her late thirties. She was the widowed owner of the inn. It was an unusual sight in those days, but steady customers did not seem to be surprised to see a woman tending bar.

She took a quick look at the manly boy, then turned to Garcia, asking, "Are you the Mexican captain or the German expert who is expected?" Before Garcia could open his mouth in protest against being mistaken for a German, the woman answered her own question. "You can't be the German; you're not tall enough." Pointing to a halfway hidden door behind the bar, she added, "Go right in; the colonel is expecting you."

The two entered a dinky room, poorly lit by an oil lamp hanging high above a large-looking table that seemed to fill the entire room. Five men sat there, sort of hunched, looking up at the newcomers. The eldest, obviously in his late forties, with a handlebar mustache introduced himself as Engineer Ross Sitwell, the expedition leader. Then, with a gracious movement of his hand, he turned to his four companions, who looked a decade younger than he, and identified them as Hans Olson, Swedish geologist; Jan Van Buren, Dutch anthropologist; Chuck O'Brian, navigator; and Jorg Bjornson, Norwegian Antarctic explorer.

In halting English, Garcia mentioned his name, then introduced Enrico Marzinelli as "my trades coordinator and interpreter." Both men took a seat.

"Allow me, gentlemen," continued Sitwell formally, in sharp contrast to the primitive surroundings, "to wait a few more minutes with my presentation. I expect Ernst Loehndorff, the German South American expert, to arrive soon."

Heinz thought to himself, "I hope this is not going to be an international conspiracy. It's too much of a coincidence, such a mix of cosmopolitan participants: one Britisher, one Dutchman, one Swede, one Irish-American, one Norwegian, one Mexican, myself, and now we are waiting for a German to appear." But his mind was soon put at ease. These people were gathering here because of their diversified expertise. This promised to be interesting.

Sitwell, whom everybody around the table addressed as Colonel, had ordered coffee, explaining that "we all need a clear head. Business first, pleasure afterwards." Nobody commented. Clearly, the man, who reminded Heinz of another Englishman, whose acquaintance he had made in Cuba, was in charge here.

Five minutes went by when the door opened. A waiter appeared with a huge tray, containing a coffee pot, cups, saucers, coffee spoons, milk and sugar. He was about fifty and clearly out of breath. He puffed the air in and out, sounding like a locomotive. His face had dark lines, and his skin looked cheesy. "No wonder," Heinz thought, when he looked at the man, "when one works in a place like this, where the air can be cut with a knife!"

Sitwell signed a piece of paper and returned it to the waiter with a "thank you." At that moment, the door opened again and Ernst Loehndorff appeared. He looked suntanned, having just returned from the tropics. Without losing any time, he shook hands all around and took a seat.

Sitwell stood up and switched on a dynamo-operated lamp, which focused on a world map, pinned right behind him on the wall. A complete hush fell over the room. The light fell on the African continent. Sitwell began, "Gentlemen, the plan I am going to expose to you is only partially sanctioned by my government. You will understand, therefore, that we cannot enjoy the official backing of His Majesty's government. Most phases of our operation would fall under a gray area, at best.

"For a number of reasons that will become clear to you, I must ask to refrain from taking any notes during this briefing. If you decide not to participate, after you have heard all the risk factors involved, you can bow out. But then only with the understanding that this conversation has not taken place. Do you agree to adhere to these stipulations?" Everybody nodded approvingly.

"All right then," he continued, "here is the picture. For the sake of simplicity, we shall call each undertaking an expedition consisting of four completely different tasks, or mandates, if you prefer.

"Task number one is to secure large quantities of gold from South Africa without the knowledge of the Kruger Government. Not easy, but not impossible to do. We have some concrete ideas of how this can be accomplished without the South African government getting suspicious. Ernst Loehndorff will answer any questions you may have regarding this when I am finished.

"The receiving government of the gold shipments will pose no problem. This part of the overall plan is not expected to exceed two months." He redirected the light to India.

"Payment for one-half the value of the gold shipments will be carried out in British pounds, US dollars and Swiss francs; the balance in opium.

"Task number two will be to transport that opium from India to China, where we will mainly receive silk for payment." He traced the route from India to China on the map.

"Next, we will return here, not necessarily to Southampton, to unload the silk. It will be paid for in the currency of our choice.

"Project number four is probably the most important one, at least as far as my government is concerned. As you all know, South America, particularly Brazil, pretty well dominates the international rubber market, a monopoly my government is not happy about."

Now he focused the light on Brazil with part of the Atlantic Ocean and Brazil's westerly neighboring states of Peru, Bolivia and Paraguay. "With the help of Ernst here, who has spent some time in South America and knows the territory and its people, we have found a plan that may just work to relieve Brazil of some of her precious rubber. Chuck O'Brian, Hans Olson and Jorg Bjornson have been in on this. The five of us feel it can be done with some Irish luck." He smiled benevolently at O'Brian. "It's Chuck's responsibility, of course, to give us a piece of the Irish luck. Details of this four-stage plan will be revealed during the question period to follow. Please go ahead."

A number of questions were raised, mostly by Van Buren and Garcia, the newest additions to the group. Heinz decided to keep his mouth shut and listen. Sitwell, Olson and Loehndorff provided most of the answers.

By logical sequence of procedures, the question period started with the procurement of South African gold. Sitwell had purchased a freighter that had undergone numerous physical changes to suit the purpose of the expected cargo. Structural changes included the keel of the vessel, her reeling and bulkheads. Provisions were made for all kinds of hidden spaces, to make the discovery of cargo more difficult. Garcia would take full responsibility for transporting the cargo, whatever it may be, from Point A to Point B.

Garcia's own freighter would be used as a decoy. The entire four-part operation would be carried out quite innocently, disclosing details of each operation only on a need-to-know basis.

A large number of South African miners had systematically taken gold out of the mines each day at the end of a shift, by using ingenious ways of hiding it from inspection. Illegal receivers then bought the gold from them.

The same receivers also had a deal going with certain middle management personnel, who had discovered a skimming scheme to enrich themselves. The two crews worked hand in glove. There were only two problems: One, the gold could not be marketed in South Africa or anywhere else on the African continent. Secondly, not only would they have to find foreign buyers, but also somebody with good connections who could arrange for the gold to leave South Africa undetected.

Olson did geological work in South Africa. One day he came somewhat close to one of several abandoned mines where the stolen metal was illegally concealed from authorities. The mine watchdog, whose name was Hendriks, struck up a friendship with Olson. He told

Olson his bosses were looking for a buyer, or several buyers who would take the amassed gold off their hands. Everybody could make a pile of money. Olson promised to keep his eyes peeled.

He contacted Loehndorff who had a contact man in Pretoria. Olson had met Loehndorff several years earlier in South America. Loehndorff was one of few legendary orchid collectors, while Olson was on a legitimate geological expedition on behalf of the Swedish crown.

Olson had great respect for Loehndorff. He held his adventurous life in awe and knew that Loehndorff had all kinds of contacts, practically around the world. When Loehndorff was only twenty, he had fought side by side with the Mexican rebel Pancho Villa to free the country from the clutches of the greedy and suppressing conquistadors. Villa had appointed and promoted the young Loehndorff as the youngest general among his army. The main reason for bestowing this great honor upon Loehndorff was not his heroism, but, believe it or not, because he was the only one among Villa's comrades in arms who actually could drive a car!

The two met in Windhoek, now Namibia. "Tell Hendriks," Loehndorff said, "you may be able to find a buyer, but you doubt he would be willing to pay more than ten percent of the gold world market price. The risk and difficulties are great in sneaking large quantities of gold out of the country. Don't tell him that the buyer will arrange for the transportation. We can use that later as another lever. You will hear from me in a fortnight or so."

Sitwell, Olson and Loehndorff had alternately answered all questions, which now seemed to peter out. Sitwell added, "May it suffice, gentlemen, that the African plan, as well as the Indian and Chinese assignment, are as solid as gold." He had to smile at this term, coincidentally befitting the topic.

"The actual negotiations in Africa have been carried out by Loehndorff here who with the assistance of Jorg Bjornson has also worked out the streamlining of the India/China operations. Risk factors have been minimized as much as possible, though it would be foolish to discount the unexpected. That includes the problem of the freighter's weight load distribution, which has been tackled and solved by O'Brian under full consideration of navigational intricacies."

He took a deep breath, then continued. "The Brazilian plan, assignment four, promises to be the most complex. As I mentioned before, each assignment is planned under the guise of an expedition. The expertise of each one of you fits this camouflage as it will suit the actual projects. Let me give you the skeleton of the Brazilian project, after which you can decide about your participation. You will be briefed about the logistics at a later date.

"We will divide into two teams. Both freighters will be used for this project. Garcia's ship will sail directly into São Paulo. He will be accompanied by O'Brian, Loehndorff and Marzinelli. They will act as coffee merchants, formally purchasing huge amounts of coffee beans for the European markets.

"Meanwhile, Bjornson, Van Buren, Olson and myself will sail for Pôrto Alegre with a shipment of concrete for the modernization of Brazilian roads. Most of them so far have been built with a heavy mix of excess coffee beans, to prevent the world price of coffee from slumping. But we made them an offer the Brazilian government could not refuse. Of course, we assisted some government officials with making up their minds by offering generous commissions. The importance of our mission can excuse almost anything.

"When the concrete has been unloaded, the four of us are going to present our government-approved expedition papers. We have permission to excavate within the quadrant of Pôrto Alegre, Rio Grande, Santa Maria and Passo Fundo. The freighter will remain in Pôrto Alegre for a couple of days, then navigate directly in a southern direction to throw anchor off Rio Grande, outside territorial waters. We intend to use her only as watchdog and back-up vessel in case of emergency.

"The converted freighter will proceed from São Paulo to join in due time. O'Brian, Garcia, Loehndorff and Marzinelli will come ashore in a boat. At that point, secrecy is not needed, since the permit papers bear the number of eight specialists as members of the expedition group. Navigation is O'Brian's responsibility.

"We shall do some real excavation not to arouse any suspicion by the authorities. The real job is to be done at night.

"As I mentioned before, we are after rubber, but not in the sense as it sounds. The milky juice from rubber trees alone would not get us very far.

"Ernst Loehndorff has done a lot of preliminary work to make a tricky job somewhat easier. The quadrant area is densely covered with rubber trees, including young ones. Young enough, we believe, to be replanted after excavation. These are the ones we are after. The mandate, given to me by His Majesty's government, is to provide Great Britain with her own rubber trees, making us less dependent upon buying from foreign sources.

"The trees we intend to take from Brazil will be replanted in Ceylon and India. Although something like this has never been attempted or done–at least to the best of our knowledge–Olson, Van Buren and Bjornson agree with me that this plan is feasible. I should hasten to add that our heads will roll if the Brazilian government gets any wind of this! My government, if approached, will naturally have to disavow any knowledge of our actions. Think about this for a few minutes before you make a final commitment. Remember, you buy the whole package or nothing at all."

Loehndorff was the first one to speak. "I am in, Colonel. (Like the others, he also called Sitwell by his former military rank, which he held while serving in Africa and India on behalf of Great Britain as colonial officer.) For me to pop out now would not make any sense. I want to see the fruit of that preliminary work I did."

Heinz talked for the first time. "If my captain agrees," he looked at Garcia, "I will too. I go where my captain goes. I owe him too much to let him down."

Garcia looked very pleased, as if he had not expected that much loyalty. Apparently slightly embarrassed, he quickly nodded his head and said, "Si, si, we will go." Then, everybody else joined the chorus of consent.

Sitwell smiled broadly. "I thought you all would agree, since each one of you, according to my information, is an individualist and does not shy away from adopting unorthodox methods of meeting a goal. Are there any other questions?"

Heinz raised his hand. "Go ahead, Enrico," Sitwell encouraged, "or should I call you Heinz?"

"Makes no difference, sir," Heinz replied. "I've got two questions. One, can we chop these trees undetected; and, two, how can we get them to the freighter? The Brazilians have a rather tight security patrol system along their coast, as Mr. Loehndorff here is telling me."

"Good question," Sitwell said approvingly. "We will select the trees we want during our daytime excavation activities by marking them, and then we will chop them down at night. The trees are then carried to an assembly area close to the Atlantic Ocean, just south of Rio Grande, at the northeastern end of Mirim Lake, right at the border of Uruguay. Ernst arranged to have about twenty wooden beer kegs brought in from Uruguay around the lake and stored in that assembly camp.

"No," he continued, when he saw a quizzical look on Heinz's face, "we are not going to have a celebration before the project is completed. Hans Olson will carefully store the rubber trees in these kegs, packed in vegetable mold for preservation.

"The rest is easy. At least we think so, thanks to Bjornson and O'Brian. As you know, every twenty-four hours we have two high tides and two low tides. At the time of our operation, one high tide arrives along the Brazilian coast around 2030 hours local time, just about when the sun sets. That is when we will put the barrels with the plants inside into the ocean. As soon as the ebb tide sets in–that will be about 2300 hours–they will be carried out to sea, floating in the direction of our two freighters, which will be positioned barely outside the territorial three-mile limit. When the barrels have come close enough to the freighters, they will be pulled aboard and hidden in our converted freighter.

"Normally, we wouldn't need more than a dozen kegs or so full of plants to reach our goal. Some will definitely survive and strike roots when replanted, but since this is not only a dangerous but also an expensive venture, we are aiming to float at least eighteen barrels. We want to be on the safe side in case the Brazilian coast guard arrives on the scene before we have secured them all aboard. Therefore, two nights of floating barrels should do the trick."

There were no more questions. A target date was set for the commencement of the South African project. Everybody shook hands. Sitwell paid for the coffee and the use of the room. Then everyone left the inn.

When Garcia and Marzinelli reboarded the freighter, the cargo had been unloaded, apparently without any problems, as the agent had assured. Before retiring, Garcia had his usual nightcap, a tequila, while Heinz nursed a glass of Italian vermouth. In most Italian families, kids grow up with Vino Rosso and Vino Bianco from an early age on. They sat together for another half-hour to recapitulate the discussions at the inn, then bid each other "Buenos noches" and turned in.

There is not much to add. All projects worked well. There were no major foul-ups. After the Brazilian adventure–twenty-two kegs with young rubber trees had been successfully siphoned off the bush–everybody had cashed in on a substantial amount of money, which Heinz did not want to divulge.

It was in November 1922 that all eight men met for the last time, this time to reminisce, at the Astor. It was a sentimental kind of gathering. It was time to part, after having proven themselves as an excellent team, complimenting each other well with their skills and actions. Heinz described that day to us as "very sad, my boys."

Two days later, Sitwell received a citation for outstanding achievements on behalf of the crown. Ernst Loehndorff went to Germany for a brief rest, but made it even briefer still when he noticed the hair-raising inflation that rampaged across the country. He quickly retreated to Argentina, where a German-Argentinean ranchero friend had invited him for a summer vacation.

Hans Olson returned to Stockholm in search of another archeological assignment. Jan Van Buren went to the (at the time) Dutch West Indies. Chuck O'Brian replaced the navigator of an American luxury liner who had been temporarily paid off and was on extended sick leave. Jorg Bjornson returned to Trondheim, joining an Arctic explorer team this time. "I've seen the Antarctic six times," he remarked. "Now I want to have a look at the other end of the world axis. Not that I expect the icebergs there to be much different from those in the Antarctic. I am sure, they are not gold-covered either." Heinz returned with Garcia to Mexico, where he got paid up and left for Cuba to relax for a while.

A New Deal

Hardly a week passed when Heinz came in contact with a member of the Dutch Shultz group. His peers called him Angel for two reasons: One, his looks and outward behavior gave one the impression of a caring, nice and totally innocent young man. In reality, he would not mind striking a deal with the devil and could not care less who got hurt as long as he walked on the sunny side of the street. Two, he was also the kind of operator who could have had a great career on Madison Avenue, because he was capable of selling refrigerators to Eskimos.

He talked with Heinz about "that prohibition thing," which gave enterprising guys like him a big chance to make some fast dough without working too hard for it. He explained to Heinz that some useful idiots deserved the credit for what he called "the times of the golden goose." He qualified that statement, "You see, Henry, in 1869, a group of silly blockheads founded the Prohibition Party in the US." He interrupted himself, asking, "How much do you know about the USA?"

"Only what I learned in grade school, which is close to nothing," was Heinz's reply.

"Well, I wouldn't waste any time now to give you a lecture, but it is a great country for people who have brains and organizational talents," continued the man, who had introduced himself earlier as Arturo Toriani. "Anyway, that party was primarily founded by former alcoholics. They were swinging the banner of abstinence with great persistency since they could not control the stuff themselves and, therefore, did not want anybody else to have it. That party became such an influential force that it managed to persuade the US government to enact its eighteenth amendment to the Constitution. It became effective in 1919, barring the manufacture, sale or transportation of intoxicating liquor.

"You can imagine what happened. When scarcity of a product is artificially created, or in this case outright outlawed, the craving for the stuff gets greater. Even those who never touched it became curious about it, and on that factor we have built our business. Right now, I am organizing the shipment of two thousand US gallons of rum for our Chicago-based operation to handle for distribution to reliable customers, and we have loads of them."

"By golly," Heinz exclaimed, getting all excited. Taking a pencil, he did some quick arithmetic and said, "That's 23,800 liters! Sorry to interrupt."

"Not much more to add," said Arturo, "except to say we need a few more guys to help us smuggle Canadian whiskey to the US. The risk is not that great and it pays big bucks. What about it? Are you interested?" Heinz sure was.

"O.K.," Arturo continued, "I am the rum route organizer for the group I represent. But I am also authorized to hire suitable applicants for the job up north. We have a special account at the Cuban branch of the First National Bank. You join me there at 1000 hours tomorrow. It is smack in the middle of Havana. You can't miss it. You will get $500 up front, plus travel expenses to Chicago. But first we have to get you a legal permit to enter the States."

They went to the US Foreign Office with Heinz's release papers signed by Capitano Garcia, verifying his skills as trades coordinator. Heinz signed a declaration, stating he would not become a burden to the US. A health checkup was arranged on the spot, certified and sealed by an official representative of the States. He was told, "Your official status is that of a visitor. It will guarantee you free movement within the States. Immigrants have it much tougher. They are carefully screened one by one on Ellis Island, and sometimes have to wait for months until they are allowed to enter the mainland."

Arturo and Heinz met the next day at the bank as planned. Heinz received his money after producing his permit to enter the States. Then he received some last-minute advice from Arturo, "Here is a letter of introduction from me, directed to Cramp Dempster, who is one of Dutch Schultz's aides. You ask for Joe Campani. The address is on the outer envelope. Book yourself a passage to Miami, then take a train. Don't fiddle around here any longer. And listen, buy yourself a decent suit here in Havana at Logiani's. It will cost you only one-fourth of what you would have to pay in Beeftown (referring to Chicago). You got to make a good impression when you report to Campani. My neck is on the line. Besides, you are not a better class sailor anymore, but a businessman. Good luck!"

Heinz thanked him for the advice, promised to live up to expectations, and the two parted. He arrived at Joe Campani's modest ten-room apartment on the eve of Christmas Eve. Long before entering the house he heard blaring noise. The place was full of Italians, and Campani had his record player on full volume. Enrico Caruso was singing an aria with gusto, which the partying guests tried to drown out. Whole families were celebrating, and Vino Rosso flowed like blood at the Chicago cattle slaughterhouse.

Campani asked Heinz to join the fun after he had glanced at Arturo's letter. "Rest a couple of days," he said to Heinz. When he heard that Heinz did not have any relatives or friends in town, he offered him one of his guest rooms. "We'll talk business after Boxing Day."

Heinz worked for the mob for over four years. He had a few close calls, but nothing he could not handle. The first two years he drove trucks. The Organization–that is what they called themselves–had a whole fleet under different names. Confederate Trucking Company was one. They would leave Chicago and Buffalo twice per week.

The Chicago convoy would leave empty, picking up fresh fruits and vegetables from Wisconsin–in winter months, they picked up processed canned goods–for delivery to Sault Sainte Marie in Canada. They would unload the cargo, then reload with Canadian whiskey brought in from Alberta where the distilling took place.

Buffalo delivered machine spare parts and some surplus steel to Hamilton, Ontario, Toronto and Montreal. A lot of milk trucks were also moving back and forth. They were loaded with milk in the US and loaded with whiskey in Hamilton, Ontario, where the gang had its Canadian headquarters.

In January 1925, Campani got shot by federal agents in a skirmish along the Canadian-US border. By then they had worked out nine different routes for bringing in the illegal booze from Canada. Heinz had particularly earned his spurs by his sense of anticipation, which was kind of rare. Not only had he predicted the routes that would become too hot to be used, but he also seemed to be able to pin down the unexpected in advance. At one point in time, a leak from a federal source indicated sharpened surveillance at certain border lines and surrounding territories. Heinz correctly analyzed this information as an attempt for entrapment by the feds. Plans were changed accordingly, after Heinz picked out two other routes as more endangered. The feds were the ones who lost this game of hide and seek.

After Campani's funeral, Dempster called Heinz to his pompous office on Lakeshore Drive and offered him the position as shipping coordinator. Heinz accepted without hesitation. "I got fed up with riding these trucks," he told Otto and me, "and besides, I was going to get a job which I had already filled with one shoe for some time. Who would refuse a better job and better pay?"

Nineteen twenty-six was a particularly successful year for the FBI and the Drug Enforcement Agency. They closed the net more and more. As soon as Heinz had worked out a new route, an old one became inoperative. "I guess I got cold feet," he confessed. "I became aware of the fact–rather late–that I was walking a very thin line, to say the least. My conscience really started to bother me. I had made a pile of money, but illegally. No matter how often I told myself, 'You never participated, never killed anybody.' It didn't make me feel better. So I decided to call it quits. Needless to say, I didn't bother to give notice. That would have been like committing suicide.

"I knew a guy on the south side of Chicago, who had been a makeup artist at the defunct theater. I left all my belongings at the small flat I had rented and went to Nick in the evening, never to return. He did a marvelous job on me. He made me look twenty years older, but also relieved me of $800, a lot of money at the time. The disguise worked well.

"I wanted to bring as much distance as possible between myself and the boys. I had heard a lot about sunny California. A ticket to San Francisco took me there. In those days it took almost three days to get there.

"I had decided to look for some legitimate work, no matter what kind, but soon got discouraged by seeing all those 'no help wanted' signs. Now that I was ready to earn a decent living, there was no work. Not that I needed it. I had enough cash on me to last at least three years without bending a finger. I played beachcomber for a while, but I gave that up after a couple of months. It was too damn hot in June and July. It was time to go home."

Going Home

It was Wednesday, 10 August 1927, when Heinz arrived in his land of birth. He had been away for seven straight years. The problem began when he disembarked in Palermo. With an Italian name, no passport, no other identification but his American visitor's status and Captain Garcia's papers, harbor control did not know how to categorize him. He was referred to an immigration official for individual screening. Fortunately, his mother tongue made it possible to clarify his situation, even though it took an hour to do so. He did not tell the whole story, but just labeled himself as one of many runaways from home who ruefully returned now to be united with his family.

He found a sympathetic ear. The official gave him a few lira to check into a nearby adobe hotel, with the instructions to come back in a couple of days. In the meantime, efforts would be made to find the whereabouts of his parents. Heinz did not dare tell the man that he carried enough money around to buy the Ritz.

Checking back two days later as instructed, he was given a contact address in Naples. He took a train to Messina, crossed with the ferry to Reggio di Calabria, then took another train, along the Tyrrhenian Sea, via Paola and Salermo to Naples.

Heinz described his family reunion as "out of this world!" I fully appreciated that statement, since I had worked with some Italian colleagues and knew well how close Italian families are.

The circus had shut down two years after Heinz had left home, but his dad had found steady work in Naples at a garment factory which processed fine yarns. Since the quality of the materials was second to none, the business had no problems marketing the bales. Wholesalers would buy them on a regular basis and deliver them to Italian tailors, who had well-heeled customers.

For the next ten years Heinz worked as waiter, captain, bartender and maitre d'hotel in restaurants, hotels and nightclubs. His Italian citizenship was reestablished and everything seemed to go well. Then, his mother took quite ill. She needed surgery which, as Italian doctors admitted, they were not prepared to carry out without great risk. Heinz got in touch with one of his uncles, who resided in Germany. Yes, he would contact a bone specialist, with whom he had studied at the University of Goettingen. His mother was flown to Goettingen for a checkup. The diagnosis sounded encouraging.

Heinz quit his job in Naples and moved in with his uncle in nearby Goettingen. Without the knowledge of his parents, he and his uncle arranged with the surgeons to pay the substantial surgery costs not covered by the German state health care plan.

He had never touched a cent from the money he brought with him to the old country. Interest he had received during those ten years alone would cover most of his mother's surgery expenses. He felt good about finally being able to pay back a little bit in return for his parents' care for him during hard times.

When Heinz's mother had recuperated, she accepted the invitation from her sister to take a vacation and spend some time in Dortmund. Heinz contacted his father who, like his son, "would do anything for Mama." Within a day, Heinz found a job at the Hotel Handelshof.

Germany had experienced a complete turnabout, at least economically. From a bankrupt country in 1932, when one of five able-bodied men was unemployed, it had risen to become an industrial giant once more. The government had already zeroed in on heavy steel production, in preparation for the great conflict that had to happen to give Germany more living space.

Heinz's mother became a permanent visitor. She wanted to spend the rest of her life in the country of her birth. Again, his father agreed and applied for a resident visa. That was easily granted at the time. Germany and Italy were hand-in-glove. It was 1938, two years after Germany and Italy had formally signed to coordinate the economic and foreign policies between the two countries.

It was clear to Heinz that his parents would stay in Germany. Consequently, it did not take too much persuasion by one of his co-workers for Heinz to become a German citizen. It did not matter to him where he lived. When he told us this, I stated that maybe without realizing it, he had adopted the approach of a cosmopolitan. In the process of becoming a German citizen, he dropped the last two syllables of his name and shortened it to Marzi.

During September 1939, when Germany attacked Poland, Heinz was called before the military examination board to register. He passed muster as K.V.I. (*Kriegsverwendungsfahig einz*, or top category for war service). He would be drafted soon.

In January 1940, Heinz received his letter of welcome from the government. Because of his background, the *Kriegsmarine* inducted him. His basic training took place in Wilhelmshafen. "I first thought," he told us, "we were singled out for extra tough treatment, but realized soon that was just the way in the German forces." What he described was exactly the same over-disciplined sweatshop type treatment Otto and I went through. A small consolation for us.

Heinz's case was somewhat different from ours, though. Right after eight weeks of basic training, he received special training together with another 80,000 men of all the armed forces. This was done in preparation for a speedy invasion of Denmark and Norway. It included, among other assignments, parachute jumping.

On Monday, 8 April 1940, he was assigned to a troop transport ship with the invasion force, sailing for Norway's main ports. His convoy arrived at the Oslo Fjord the following day. "It was almost like a picnic," he described. "Sure, we had some resistance, but really nothing we couldn't handle. It would have been much worse, of course, if we hadn't arrived about twenty hours or so ahead of the British."

Heinz was to open the first naval officers club in Oslo. "They kept me there only until everything ran smooth enough. Then," he said, looking at his watch, because it was close to the time for us to set the tables for dinner, "I was sent to Trondheim to set a few things straight there. Then I received a transfer to Bergen, where I looked after Admiral Von

Schrader and his officer corps. A couple of weeks ago, when these stewards here were caught stealing from the mess, I was given this assignment. We didn't manage too badly. We borrowed two waiters from the Victoria Hotel downtown, who helped out with the service."

He looked at his watch again. "Time to get moving," he said and got up. We left the room.

I could not remember ever having been so fascinated by any lifetime story. I guess that is the reason for remembering it so well after forty-seven years.

When we went downstairs, I had to force myself to wake up to the present for the job at hand.

CASINO SERVICE

Holiday Surprise

It took Otto and me only a few days to adjust to the new environment and routine service procedures.

On Thursday, 18 December 1941, Hitler was scheduled to speak to the German nation at 1800 hours. The newscaster at noon had announced that part of the content of the address would be kind of a reply to President Roosevelt's speech after the attack on Pearl Harbor by the Japanese Air Force. I asked Otto to cover the dining room for me. This was not a problem since our members arrived in trickles during dinner service, making it easy to handle.

I detached the radio from the wall in the small pantry and plugged it into a kitchen outlet. As usual, Hitler started his address forcefully, but in slightly moderate fashion. Then he worked himself more and more into a rich lather of intense excitement and agitation, ripping into Roosevelt with the claws of the German eagle. He rambled on for an hour and a half, calling Roosevelt a "senile fool, incapable of doing anything but playing with the knickknacks on his desk."

Replying to Roosevelt's appeal to the American nation to pull together, stating that it could take the American economy two to three years to fully convert to war production, Hitler delivered the final blow by shouting, "I have news for that cripple in a wheelchair. By then, he will have missed the bus by a long shot!" He threw a few final insults at the Allies in general and concluded with inflammatory words of victory. The *Reichstags* crowd (former legislative rubber-stamp assembly) jubilantly rose and replied approvingly with the Nazi salute, shouting "Sieg Heil, Sieg Heil, Sieg Heil!"

I returned the radio to the pantry, still hearing Hitler's screaming insults blaring in my ears. As often as I had heard him talk, I simply could not understand the fascination with which the German masses regarded that man. Something inside my stomach twisted. I just could not get the hang of the masses' enthusiasm. As I reconnected the radio, the Berlin Symphony Orchestra had started playing *Die Meistersinger von Nurnberg*, one of Hitler's favorite Wagnerian overtures.

In the late afternoon on Monday, 22 December, a mercantile ship, fully loaded with Christmas goodies for the troops, anchored in the harbor at Strandkaien. The German dock master, an officer responsible to the harbor captain, requested the cargo to be unloaded by a small detachment the following morning.

However, in the wee hours of the twenty-third, we all awoke from a shattering explosion. A single Mosquito bomber had managed to avoid the attention of German naval personnel manning our antiaircraft coastal defense systems. The pilot came in low, flying from the northeast over Steinkarkaien, Kirkegata and Skagenkaien, promptly landing a bomb laterally into the belly of the freighter tied up at Strandkaien and disappeared as fast as he had arrived. He surely did not suffer from blurred vision, and must have known exactly where the target was, since the supply ship was positioned between six other vessels at Strandkaien. Three years and seven months later, my question was answered. By coincident, I met the navigator and copilot of that plane in a demobilization camp in Mandal, Norway. He had left Stavanger in a hurry when we invaded Norway and signed up to serve in the Royal Air Force.

The ship sank right at the pier and spread a heck of a mess around. We had to drag the harbor for two days to rid it from all that floating chocolate coating. It was easy, of course, to find a scapegoat for the event. The investigation that followed established that the ship could have been unloaded the previous evening. The officer in question received a disciplinary transfer. In the meantime, the navy ration warehouse had to be raided to make up for part of the losses.

We had decorated the dining room, the lobby and the salon with Christmas ornaments. On Christmas Day, after luncheon service, Heinz, Otto and I received a Christmas parcel from Dr. Carlos Mayer-Pantin, who added a few words of praise for the good service.

Our company commander, Lieutenant Schmidt, chairman of the officers casino, went with us to the kitchen, unpacked a bottle of Asbach Uralt (German brandy) and killed it with the eight of us: Heinz Marzi, Otto Januszeit, Erich Eye, Hermann Behrens, Erich Apfel, and Solvay and Karen, our two Norwegian kitchen helpers, plus myself. We drank to each other's health and had no problem finishing the bottle in no time.

The remainder of the holidays passed by peacefully. Being kind of a sentimental man, like most Germans and Irish are, I missed the old country, but then again, I was grateful for my fate.

On Monday, 5 January 1942, Heinz rushed into my room and came right to the point: "Forget about taking off this afternoon. Lieutenant Schmidt just called. He wants us to set up the salon after luncheon service for a special briefing. He said to make sure all of his staff officers can be accommodated for a special meeting following luncheon. The commandant is in a terrible mood."

Heinz reported to Mayer-Pantin at the end of the luncheon that the salon was ready to be used as instructed. When everybody had moved to the salon, the commandant joined with his aide and began, "Gentlemen, I am outraged that the British have pulled another trick on us and have gotten away with it. Early this morning, our intelligence sources reported and have confirmed that a larger number of Norwegians that last year who are serving with the British Armed Forces have secretly landed at several points along the Norwegian coast to spend their holidays at home with their families. Indications are that they have been brought close to the coast by submarines and have been picked up by dinghies under cover of darkness and returned back to England the same way. In spite of our intensified vigilance, based on last year's experience, we did not catch one.

"It is particularly embarrassing for us, since the navy is responsible for not allowing any penetration from sea by the enemy, no matter what the purpose. Further investigations into this matter have been ordered by me. I can assure you if this should happen again some heads will roll, though the admiral agrees with me that it is almost an impossibility to seal off the entire coastline."

There was utter silence. Nobody had any comments to make. For several days after that, the whole officer corps seemed to be rather subdued. The holiday spirit had been dampened. What nobody knew at the time was that several Norwegians, trained by the MI Six had also been filtered into the country to strengthen the Norwegian Resistance Movement.

The Bartering Trip

We followed our daily routine without anything unusual happening. Heinz had a number of ingenious ways to bring down the deficit which he had inherited from his predecessor. For instance, he struck an agreement with a Norwegian fisherman, who would actually catch lobsters according to order. On Saturdays, he would deliver X number of lobsters of various sizes and pick up a new order.

We stewards would ask the officers what size lobster they wanted. A lobster, for which the fisherman received Kr 3, would be sold for Kr 6. Since we did not have to recover preparation and service expenses, nor any other operating costs like in commercial establishments, the extra Kr 3 went to bring down the deficit.

In May 1942, Heinz requested from the casino chairman a temporary replacement for me. He made the request by telephone in my presence without using the word temporary. I was flabbergasted. I had not created any problems and always followed instructions to the letter.

What I did not know was that Heinz had discussed the situation with Schmidt before, who had agreed in principle that I should assist Heinz with his bartering trip across the county of Rogaland. Only the time had not been established. My apprehension disappeared when he explained what this was all about. The trip had a dual purpose: to build up extra food supplies and to reduce the deficit which, thanks to our concerted efforts, had already been brought down in six months to less than Kr 2,000.

An ingenious mechanic with the navy truck division at the corner of Ny Olavskleiv and Lokkeveien, had converted a transport truck, so that several different animals could be transported together. He also equipped the vehicle with a four-wheel-drive mechanism, which was revolutionary at the time. (I sometimes wonder, if the same man sold his invention to the Jeep division of the American automobile industry in the early seventies.)

Heinz already had civilian clothes for missions such as this one. I was given permission to select inconspicuous civilian clothing and decided on a hunting shirt and cap, dark trousers and boots worn by mountain climbers, and a windbreaker. We did not look different from any Norwegian civilian. The fact that Heinz and I were both dark-haired would not arouse any suspicion either, since one of four Norwegians is dark, contrary to popular belief. The vehicle also looked like any other run-of-the-mill truck.

Early Thursday morning, 14 May, the truck backed up at our front entrance. Inside the hall along the wall, Erich had already lined up the items we were about to take with us. The bartering ware primarily consisted of Wachholder Schnapps (gin-type whiskey), some Weinbrand (brandy), six crates of German Rhine wine, bales of tobacco, several chests of cigars and cardboard boxes of cigarettes. Loading took only fifteen minutes and we were ready to roll.

Then it dawned on me. Did we not forget to prepare for an important aspect of the operation? Who was going to be the interpreter? The driver? When I asked Heinz, he remarked casually, "I will look after that, don't worry."

I could not believe my ears. I knew he had a Norwegian girlfriend, whom I had met several times when she visited Heinz. But, when others were present, they had always conversed in German. Was Heinz able to pick up yet another language in two years? Then nothing would astonish me anymore about that man.

Heinz handed us our special ID cards, signed by our area commandant, Dr. Carlos Mayer-Pantin. We were only to use these in case we would run into army MPs. Then he said, "In case of emergency," and gave the driver a rifle, me a Mauser and pocketed his own 0815. I looked at the automatic weapon and asked, "Why do I get the heavy stuff?"

"Simple," he replied. "I've read your file. You have been graded as a mediocre soldier, but quite a marksman with a rifle and a pistol. If that's so, you should be able to mow down half a company with that Mauser. As long as we are on this assignment, you will act as the walking Siegfried line, and you had better live up to it!"

We took off south to Sandness, then via Klepp, Byrne, Naerbo, Varhaug, Vigrestad and Sirevag to Egersund. Along the route, we branched off the main road whenever we saw a farm nearby. My admiration for Heinz rose, while hearing him chatter and negotiate with Norwegian farmers. There was not one moment that his conversation became halting.

It was about 1600 hours when we bartered with a farmer south of Vigrestad. He pretty much reminded me of a Viking, like the restaurateur in Tønsberg. The exchange of goods took place in a most amicable atmosphere. He did not seem to be a bit afraid or suspicious and treated us like equals, if not like friends. Even his wife and a boy and a girl in their early teens felt free to join the conversation without any shyness. It was too bad I did not understand one word! All I knew so far was *vennligst* (please), *mange takk* (many thanks), *god* (good), *god morgen* (good morning), *god day* (good afternoon), and *adjo* (good-bye), plus one phrase Erich Eye, our chef, had taught me: *Skjonn pike, jeg elske deg* (Beautiful girl, I love you). Not much with which to start a conversation.

The Friendly Farmer

When the trading was completed, the farmer invited us for dinner and offered us overnight accommodations. Dinner would be served at 1800 hours. Until then we would have time to see the farm if we were interested. We were. He would be delighted to show us around, he said, with pride in his voice. The tame rabbits and the geese we had bartered could be loaded tomorrow morning. He would feed the two pigs we had acquired at another farm when he fed his own. Heinz accepted the offer without asking our approval. Fair enough, since he was in charge.

The farmhouse was in tip-top shape. The barn, the cow shed and the henhouse were in good repair. Even the perch seemed to have been cleaned recently. Who said chickens and ducks enjoy wading around in their own droppings? He had about forty chickens, most of them leghorns, several geese, a dozen or so ducks and two hogs in the barn. Though it was early in the year, his cows were in the meadow, nibbling at the first sparse grass blades.

The farmer took four horses out of the corral, saddled them, and away we went on a casual round trip. I noticed that the horse he had taken for himself was particularly high-stilted and heavy, quite appropriate for a giant.

His property was about six hundred acres in size. I looked in vain for a fence. I asked Heinz about that, who conveyed my query to the farmer. "You will hardly see any fences in Norway," the man replied. "Most of us make due by placing some rocks around our properties for general markings. Some don't use anything. We try to be good neighbors, who don't get into each other's hair."

During our ride I counted forty-seven cows, nine steers and eight calves. I had seen three more horses in the corral, besides the four we were riding. Not bad livestock for a small farmer.

When we returned to the farmhouse, dinner was ready. The ride made me hungry, and I was really looking forward to the farmer's home cooked meal, though I certainly would not have had any reason to complain about navy food. And I am not only talking about the food in the officers casino, but also on the base. Hans Steiner, the man in charge there, had strict instructions from the base commander to prepare the best food possible. Schmidt cared about his people, as they cared about him.

We cleaned up and filed into the dining room, which was adjacent to and semi-detached from the living room by a light teak sliding door. The heavy wood-carved furniture included a huge chest of drawers, a triangular cupboard in one corner of the dining room displaying fine china and glassware, and a nineteenth century grandfather clock, standing in the opposite corner from the triangular cupboard. These items provided for a magnificent and dignified atmosphere I had never seen on any farm. Momentarily, I forgot where we were. The tablecloth bore a beautiful Norwegian design, showing a forest at each end of the cloth with deer running about, with a fjord flowing through the center and mountains in the distance. It was just marvelous!

One glance showed me, the old waiter, that the two children had laid the silver in correctly neat rows, glasses at the tip of knives and a napkin neatly folded on the bread-and-butter plate. As we approached, the youngsters laughingly skipped behind their mom into the kitchen to help with the dishing up and serving of the meal. Through Heinz, I politely offered my assistance with the service, but the patrician-looking woman did not want to hear any of this. "*Mange takk*," (many thanks–also meaning a polite thank you) she said twice, "you are our guests tonight and guests are not allowed to do any work here," she asserted with a twinkle in her eyes.

Heinz took me aside and said, "Get a bottle of Saar-Ruwer (one of the few German red wines of good quality) from the truck and a couple of chocolate bars for the kids. This much hospitality from people whose country we occupy!" He shook his head in disbelief, looking almost ashamed. "Ha," I thought, "this tough-looking and tough-acting guy does have a heart and a conscience." Then he added, "I hope this whole thing is not a trick."

"No, it isn't," I retorted. "I can tell when people mean what they say, even though I do not understand their language. Don't be so suspicious. You have dealt with too many shady elements in the past."

I had hardly finished the sentence when my heart started pumping for fear of getting kicked in the pants. For a moment he looked thoughtfully at me then, to my relief, he smiled. "I guess you are right," he agreed. "If we should get bumped off by the Undergrounds we wouldn't have to worry about being court-martialed." A typical Heinz Marzi statement.

When I returned, armed with the bottle of wine and two large chocolate bars, everybody was seated. The lady of the house cast a friendly, motherly smile when she saw me handing the bars to her kids. Both youngsters looked unmistakably Nordic with their blond hair. The girl was about fifteen and the boy maybe twelve. "*Mange takk,*" both said with a delightfully bright smile. Then I noticed the only empty chair around the table was between the two of them. Somebody must have figured that milk-face me should make up the trio of teenagers. I did not mind.

Before I sat down, Heinz instructed me to open the bottle and serve the wine. I let him taste the wine first and placed the cork beside his wine glass. He sniffed at it and nodded his approval. I poured the wine for the grownups, each glass two-thirds full. Then I placed the still half-full bottle in front of the farmer.

I had skipped my own glass on purpose. Not to make the two youngsters feel bad, I had grabbed three bottles of lemonade from the truck as well, which I served to the three teenagers. Then I took my assigned seat.

Soup was served from a tureen, passed around the table. The farmer said a brief grace and we started what turned out to be a hearty meal. As soon as the soup course was finished, the tureen was removed and a platter with roast pork and thin-sliced beef was served; square dishes with cream-mashed potatoes; two gravy boats with pork and beef gravy; another dish with macédoine vegetables; and a huge wooden salad bowl. It was too early in the season to have fresh vegetables, but you could not tell by the taste that they had been preserved from the previous harvest.

To my astonishment, I saw a bottle of H.P. Sauce on the table, but did not ask any questions. I did some speculation, though, how that bottle might have landed there. Maybe the farmer had had a visit last Christmas by some chaps who were serving with the free Norwegian forces in England? Never mind that!

Not being able to follow the conversation, Thomas, the driver and I felt kind of left out. The two youngsters tried hard to get me involved in a conversation, but all the gesticulation did not get me anywhere.

After dinner, the two kids were told to round up the beef. The farmer explained to Heinz that he did not like the idea of keeping them on the meadow overnight at this time of the year. Besides, he wanted them to be corn-fed as well as allowing them to graze.

The grownups—this time I was included in the term—retired for a nightcap to the living room. The farmer brought out a bottle of Danish Aalborg Akvavit. Knowing we would have to leave early in the morning, we turned in at 2100 hours.

After a hearty breakfast on Friday morning, we loaded our truck and were ready to say good-bye to our gracious hosts. Then I suddenly remembered a piece of history which our geography and history teacher in grade school had given us. In 1814, Sweden had forced Denmark to cede Norway. Norway refused to acknowledge that treaty and, instead, convened the Storting (National Assembly), and adopted its own constitution on 17 May. The Danish prince was promptly elected King of Norway.

That attempt to be independent was snubbed and it angered the Swedish kingdom (not necessarily the people). The ensuing war between the two countries in July and August of that year resulted in Norway's defeat. The king resigned and the Norwegian Storting had no choice but to agree to join a union with Sweden. The first attempt for independence had failed.

It took ninety-one years to dissolve that forced union with Sweden. Norway had finally achieved her independence and elected Prince Carl of Denmark to be her king. Carl took the name of Haakon VII. The day the Norwegian constitution was adopted in 1814, the seventeenth of May had not been forgotten. It was declared as Independence Day by the Storting with the consent of the king.

This was Friday morning, the fifteenth. I reminded Heinz of the fact that Norway's Independence Day was only two days off. He looked at me as if I were a ghost. "What on earth do you know about Norwegian history?" he asked.

"My memory is somewhat better than yours," I replied. "After all, I am seventeen years younger." He laughed good-naturedly. "Have you checked the crates?" he asked the driver. Thomas nodded his head. "Come with me," Heinz said. We took a few more goodies out of the truck, then went to the four of them, who were standing beside the road.

Heinz pointed to me and said, "This young history professor just reminded me of your upcoming holiday. We hope you have a nice weekend and thank you again for your hospitality. We shall remember you."

You could see their radiant smiles. The farmer's wife, it seemed to me, had to suppress her tears. Somehow, I felt I had known these people for years and would have to leave them now. Since I had been accused many times of being a sentimental fool, I could better read my own feelings, though without shame. In any case, from that day on I felt close to these Norwegians. My fondness for them kept growing in years to come.

We left and waved back to this wonderful family until the bending road hid them from our view. Sirevag, the last community before we would reach Egersund, was not far away. My mood was great. As we rumbled along the country road, I took my mouth organ, without which I never left home, out of my pocket and started to play *Always*, while Thomas and Heinz joined in with the German lyrics, which are quite different from the original. They both sang with full force, *Weisst Du was das heisst, Heimweh?,* a sad, blues-type song, which asks the question: "Do you know what homesickness is?"

The Phony Norwegian

Between Sirevag and Egersund we made one more deal with a farmer that included a hog. As we left the farm, the sun came out. We slowed down and enjoyed the beautiful countryside. Approaching the northern outskirts of Egersund, we noticed the road was blocked by a number of uniformed people and civilians. To one side of the road, an army truck sat in the ditch, while a farmer's milk truck had overturned and spread a couple of dozen milk cans all over the place. When we came closer, we heard some loud voices arguing back and forth in German and Norwegian.

Having come close enough to the scene, we stopped the truck and joined the commotion. A German major gesticulated around with a civilian, who turned out to be the driver of the milk truck. I heard the major shouting, "You fool. You have to move immediately when you see an army car!"

The farmer obviously did not understand one word. He just kept grinning, trying to look apologetically. That poured acid on the major's wound. Heinz had told us to get out, but not to say anything. Before the major could really work himself into a lather and collect foam at his mouth, Heinz slipped out of the truck.

He politely approached the major and, pretending to be a Norwegian, said, without addressing the man by rank, "I speak a little German. Can I help?" The major, visibly relieved that somebody could speak his language, simmered down.

Heinz explained to the farmer that the major was a bit upset because any time an accident like this happens, the army personnel involved is unpleasantly interrogated. Turning to the major, he relayed the farmer's apologies for not having been fast enough to get out of the way. Then he added, drawing a wide circle with his right arm, "We are willing to remove this obstacle quickly, so that you can continue your trip, sir." I almost wet my pants! This was top-notch acting, for sure.

The major did not once question Heinz's legitimacy as a civilian. In answer to his questions, Heinz told him a story about having attended a German school for several years. He also assured the major that he really liked the Germans, without so much as dropping an eyelid. I could not stand it anymore and turned around, blowing my nose.

Heinz gathered everybody together and in no time the mess was cleaned up, the road clear and free again for traffic. We proceeded on our journey as if nothing had happened.

In Egersund, we had a good luncheon in a cafe at the eastern outskirts. The owner had started to set up tables and chairs outside on the terrace to serve some of his guests there, anticipating extra business over the holiday weekend. By now we felt quite at home everywhere we went. Of course, wearing civilian clothes did help.

Returning Home

We had made an inventory before we sat down for the meal. There was very little left with which to barter. On the one hand, we should have returned without making any side trips because the animals, though confined reasonably separate, started to smell in the truck. The sun had been shining brightly for several hours on the roof, which did not make things better either.

On the other hand, we felt like seeing a bit more of the countryside. The opportunity to linger a little longer in a civilian environment was particularly attractive to me, since the only uniform I had ever liked was a tuxedo.

It was decided to visit another two farms or so, then select another route to drive back to Stavanger. We chose to go north via the Bjerkreim district to Vikesa, Aalgard and Sandness to Stavanger, using what is now the E-18 Route which, in southern direction, leads to Kristiansund and Oslo.

When we left Egersund the next day, the preparatory work in anticipation of the big holiday was in full swing. We visited only two more farms, one south of Vikesa and the other one between Vikesa and Aalgard, when our supplies ran out. We had done all the bartering for the time being.

Outside Aalgard we put up a tent in the early afternoon and decided to camp overnight. With a couple of blankets each, we would not freeze to death. During the day, the weather was not warm enough to take a swim, or even lie in the sun. We parked the truck away from the camp, with the wind, to spare the intense smell of the animals.

I had a refreshing sleep. The sound of nature did not wake me once. We arose around 0800 hours on Sunday morning and drove on an empty stomach to Sandness, where we arrived one half-hour later. The distance between Aalgard and Sandness is about the same as between Sandness and Stavanger, twenty kilometers.

We had left the truck carefully locked at the southern outskirts of town. Heinz put a sign on with the message in Norwegian, "Temporarily out of order." It took us fifteen minutes to walk to town. The shops were closed. But we found a small restaurant near the harbor inlet open for breakfast. We rushed in there like a flock of geese to the feeding trough. The walk through the rugged but fascinating countryside had made us hungry.

Heinz persuaded us to order a typical Norwegian breakfast, unknown to Thomas and me. When the steaming plates were served, Heinz explained that all the fish was fresh, having been caught early in the morning. First, I did not understand why he emphasized the word "all." There was only one fish on the plate, one of my favorites–poached salmon in butter-mustard sauce. When I asked him about it, he just said, "Eat; I'll explain later."

The oval china platter was divided like a silver platter used for Russian service, with which I was quite familiar. The two slices of Atlantic salmon were already deboned and rested in the sauce. The cavity beside it contained two ball-shaped potatoes, similar to deep-fried croquette potatoes. The next sunken partition contained three thick stalks of white asparagus, decorated with half-moon tomatoes and what looked like English cucumbers.

With this, crisp rolls were served. After that everything was topped off with a dessert, which had a similar look to caramel pudding. Luckily, we were hungry like bears. Otherwise, it would have been difficult to eat that much for dinner, leave alone for breakfast. A pot of fresh-roasted coffee crowned that great meal. What a feast!

When Heinz and Thomas had lit their cigarettes, I asked Heinz, burning of curiosity, what he had meant by "all the fish."

"Well," he explained, "you know, of course, that you had poached salmon in butter/mustard sauce. But that wasn't the only fish you had. The half-moon vegetables were *fiske vegetabilsk* (fish vegetables); the deep fried brown round potatoes that looked so similar to croquette potatoes were actually *fiske boller* (fish potatoes). The dessert was also made of fish called *fiske pudding*."

"That can't be possible!" I exclaimed. "You are pulling our legs."

"No, I am not," replied Heinz. "It shows you how inventive Norwegian cooking is. But, for that matter, the Swedes have been doing the same for two hundred years. The original smorgasbord, for instance, solely consisted of fish items." I had never heard of something like this. But I did not kid myself; there sure was more to come and more to learn.

We decided to stay and join the festivities, at least for part of the day. Thomas, who was an ardent angler in Germany–only commercial fishermen call themselves fishermen–had noticed a shop right beside the restaurant which sold and rented fishing tackle. On the way to town he had noticed a few spots that looked promising for fishing. Heinz talked him out of renting tackle. "You still can fish another time," he said. "We have to buy fodder, and feed the animal farm in our truck first. That will keep us busy part of the day. In the late afternoon, we had better get ready to return to Stavanger and check in before we are declared AWOL."

We mixed with the crowd in town without sticking out. Thomas and I pretty much kept quiet. In the early afternoon, there were several celebrations going on all over town. It was delightful to see the folks dressed in their national costumes and dance in the streets. The children were especially colorfully dressed and enjoyed the festivities with innocent pleasure. It was a scene difficult to forget. We became quite engrossed and had a great time.

At 1730 hours we said good-bye to Sandness and went on our way back home. The animals in the back of the truck made quite a racket. Maybe we had left them alone too long, or the penetrating sun got into their system and drove them nuts. In an attempt to quiet them down, Heinz drew his 0815 and released one shot out of the open door window. That made it worse. Whatever noise we made, the animals beat.

In any case, we arrived safe and sound at 1830 hours. My co-steward Otto, Erich Eye, the chef, Hermann Behrens, the cook, Erich Apfel, the cellar master, and our two Norwegian kitchen helpers, Solvay and Karen, all greeted us with a great hello, as if we had been away for a year. In my mind, I really had adopted this marvelous place as my home. Later on in life, I found it increasingly easier to adapt to new surroundings. I do thank Providence for having become a cosmopolite!

They all helped unpack the truck. When Erich Apfel craned his neck into the back of the truck, he quickly withdrew. "My God, one can easily throw up. What a cussing stink!" he complained, holding his nostrils.

He rushed into the house, shouting back, "I've got to get my gas mask!" Little did he know that gas masks offer some protection, but are practically useless against animal odor. He soon found out.

Returning with his mask on, he confidently stepped into the rear of the truck, only to turn around and jump off like he was bitten by a tarantula. Ripping off his gas mask, he looked at the thing with astonishment and complained, "Shit! This stink is worse than before. I have to turn in this useless piece of rubber," adding jokingly, "before the Tommies invade here."

We laughed heartily and continued unloading the vehicle. Erich Apfel had done some preparatory work while we were gone. There were several wooden cages in the fairly sizable backyard, in which we placed the tame rabbits, sixteen in all. The geese, the ducks and two chickens we released in the yard, which had a high enough fence to prevent them from escaping. Before we were finished, we threw some fodder for the remaining pigs into the back of the truck. Thomas had to drive them to the army slaughterhouse. After processing the meat, including the making of sausages, the stuff would be held for us to pick up when needed.

The local army commandant gladly arranged this for us, reciprocating for a favor we had done for the army the previous year. By order of the military veterinarian, they had to slaughter a number of chickens, which had been taken with a mysterious illness. The meat was declared unfit for human consumption. That is when we had helped them out with some of our extra stock.

THE COMMANDANT & HIS STAFF

Dr. Carlos Mayer-Pantin

Kapitaen zur See (Commodore) Dr. Pantin was our naval area commander. Born in 1882, the son of a German aristocrat-philosopher, he grew up in Argentina, north of Bahia Blanca, on the east coast. He learned to love the ocean at an early stage in life, though he also became familiar and content with Pampa living. When he turned seventeen, his parents consented to his attending two naval academies, first in Buenos Aires, and then in São Paulo, Brazil.

While studying in São Paulo, he had spent most of his free time with his uncle, his mother's brother, who had a hacienda near Ponta Grossa. His frequent visits led to a friendship with an auburn-haired Brazilian beauty, Juanita Delgado. The two had to part, though, when he returned to Argentina, where his first commission was that of a navigational junior engineer with the Argentine coast guard in 1907.

The two corresponded with each other and, as the saying goes, absence made the heart grow fonder. During his second biannual leave in 1909, Carlos decided to ask for Juanita's hand in marriage. Juanita's parents, generations long well-established in Brazilian society, were not enthused. They nevertheless agreed, realizing that their independent-minded daughter would have her way, even if she would have to leave home.

Carlos completed his three-year stint. Then the pair married in 1910, during the carnival season in Rio de Janeiro. It was more or less a spontaneous event. The two had not even decided where they would settle down. When the commodore granted me a formal interview in 1944, he admitted this act to have been totally atypical of his otherwise well-planned and disciplined life later on. Relatives from his father's side extended an open ticket to live with them in Germany any time they wished. That remained in Carlos' mind.

Never short of money, Carlos and Juanita picked up that rain check and temporarily moved to Germany in 1912. Curious about German strategic naval thinking, he enrolled in a refresher course at the Naval Academy in Kiel. He had had a private tutor while growing up in Argentina, who had taught Carlos how to communicate well in German.

Germany impressed the couple with her Kaiser tradition. Carlos quickly moved to the top of his naval technology class. His classmates identified him as a natural leader. Not only was he a brilliant student, he also impressed everybody, including the faculty, with his good manners and looks. Ascetic-looking, six feet five inches tall, slim, with deliberate movements and a pleasant tone of voice, his assets put him in the "outstanding" category as an individual.

When leaving the academy in May 1914, he was immediately offered and accepted a commission as Naval Advisor in matters of foreign affairs. Having dual citizenship—Argentinean and German—allowed him to wear the uniform of the German Kaiser's Navy. His rank: Commanding Officer.

Serving during World War I as technical advisor to the Kaiser's Navy Warfare Department, his prime effort was to shield it from becoming decimated. Though his assignment was fundamentally administrative, he liked to be "out there where the action is." He personally assembled and guided many convoys. Whatever he tackled he successfully concluded, so well that in 1916 the Royal British Admiralty had a file on him as one of the most effective foreign naval tacticians of its kind. Carlos' convoys hardly ever got caught in a squeeze, and if so, they always managed to not only get out of it, but before doing so, caused damage to the enemy.

Promotion came fast. Within four years, he had been promoted three times, previously unheard of in naval annals. When Germany surrendered in 1918, he had reached the rank of commander. Disillusioned and disgusted by the Kaiser's abdication from the throne and his subsequent move into self-imposed exile, he shed his uniform, sold his estate at the outskirts of Kiel and returned with his wife to Brazil.

They bought a small three thousand-acre hacienda in a choice agricultural area west of São Paulo, which included a coffee plantation. His herd of cattle was watched by six gauchos, with whom he frequently roamed the Pampas, a term they all used, though it was originally coined for the wide-open treeless plains south of the Amazon River.

His men loved to work for Carlos because he treated them better than most other rancheros had done. They would talk with their counterparts when in town, affectionately referring to their employer as *El Patron magnifico* (the great boss).

He frequently visited former friends and new ones he had made since his return from Germany. Most of them resided in or around São Paulo, which was beginning to become the hobnob commerce and banking city in Brazil, if not in South America.

Many of them did not have any military background. But they were well-heeled and well-educated, several of them having attended universities in South America, Mexico and the US. All were doing well financially, having established themselves as medical doctors, scientists, lawyers, bankers, engineers and high-ranking military officials.

In 1920, Carlos decided to round off his education by enrolling at the University of São Paulo to work on his Ph.D. Because of his outstanding record as a military man and former student of three academies, his credits were such that he was able to reach his goal within two years. Another first!

He called Carlos on that same evening, suggesting that they join to tackle the challenge together. They both signed two days later for the first stage of the contract. Carlos and Juanita appointed an executor for the estate and promoted their most trusted employee as hacienda foreman during their absence. Then they moved to San Bernardo, south of Santiago de Chile.

Hans and Carlos worked well together. They introduced a number of measures, most of them new, some unorthodox, but all resulted in improvements. It was exactly what Chile needed to beef up her navy.

Their success made international waves. The Argentine government, among others, started wondering why it had not caught on that one of the country's sons had that much talent. It realized that, in spite of all that outward glitter, the fleet needed an overhaul, maybe more so than Chile. Through his dad, the Argentine government contacted Carlos in 1930, during the sixth year of his contract with Chile, suggesting he come home and serve his country rather than signing up for the second term. It was easy for Carlos to accept. He did not even have to switch uniforms again, since the Chilean government had made a rather unusual concession, allowing Carlos to wear his Argentinean uniform during his service with them.

While Hans finished his second term in Chile, Carlos kept straightening out the blue boys of Argentina. He used his Chilean experience as a pattern for success, realizing that there are great similarities in naval functions in any country. He was right. The authority given to him was almost unlimited. Argentina was able to borrow sufficient funds from a variety of international sources so that penny-pinching was not necessary.

I have been informed by reliable sources that at the time Chile improved her navy, Argentinean government officials were afraid they would be surpassed by the "little neighbor out west." The two governments had been suspicious of each other for some time, which went far over and above the normal competitive spirit people often carry around for purely nationalistic reasons.

Hans' contract with the Chilean government ended in October 1934. Carlos finished his special assignment in April 1935. He and Juanita went on an extended trip to Germany, curious how that country had developed after having hit the bottom in 1932-33. They found the economy to be on the upswing, only two years and three months after President Hindenburg had appointed Hitler as Chancellor of the German Reich. They also found that Carlos' reputation and success in reshaping and modernizing the Argentinean navy had preceded their arrival. The German newspapers had been full of reports how this German/Argentinean genius had accomplished tasks which heretofore had been considered impossible.

A few months before their arrival, on Sunday, 13 January 1935, Hitler had reintroduced compulsory military service for the German youth. After Hindenburg's death, the German Parliament had bestowed dictatorial powers upon Hitler, who wasted no time preparing for the eventual war. A German counterpart of Carlos' predicted, "You'll see, the day is not too far when we all will be called upon to do our share for the new fatherland."

It was a correct prediction, although not exactly in the vein of Carlos' thinking. Upon his return to Brazil, Carlos formally retired from the military. So did Hans, who settled down for good with his wife and two kids in San Bernardo. At least that is what he thought. Both he and Carlos had a surprise coming. Events in Germany changed all that in 1936.

Hitler had several points on his agenda. In March of that year, German troops entered the Rhineland/Ruhr territory. Immediately following that came the repudiation of the Locarno Pact. The order of "full steam ahead" came for the now open rearmament of Germany.

In June, Mussolini proclaimed the resurrection of the ancient Roman Empire after having swallowed up Ethiopia. When the Spanish Civil War broke out in July, Germany and Italy eagerly supplied "voluntary" troops, weapons and armored equipment to the Spanish Fascista Fuerza. I should add here, to keep the record straight, that a great number of members of troop contingents sent to Spain had actually volunteered.

The first steps were taken in October between Italy and Germany for closer collaboration, economically and militarily. An agreement was formally sealed on the twenty-fifth of the month. One month later, Germany signed the anti-Comintern Pact with the goal of stemming Marxism and counteracting Marxist propaganda.

Then came the search for "outstanding" German individuals. A search team went outside German boundaries to persuade Germans living outside Germany to become active on German soil. The drain of scientists, who had been persecuted and left the country to find recognition somewhere else, was felt. Commanders of the armed forces took over the task of searching for military contenders fitting the description "outstanding."

Grossadmiral Raeder had a bulging file on his desk which included the profile of Carlos. He sent a personal emissary to Brazil, advising Carlos by cable. Carlos had a pretty good idea what the reason for this high-level visit would be. He contacted his friend in Chile, notifying him of the situation at hand.

The visitor from Kiel, German naval headquarters, was Commodore Von Schrader, who later during World War II was to become the commanding admiral in charge of the Norwegian west coast naval operations.

Yes, Carlos was interested in assisting with the upgrading of the German navy, under certain conditions: that he retain his dual German/Argentinean citizenship; Hans Baer would be accepted on his team; his wife would retain her citizenship; he would be able to leave Germany any time; and he would personally pick the members of his team and report through Von Schrader to Raeder.

A cable was sent to the admiral of the fleet, who readily accepted all conditions without change. (This was very unusual for a dictatorial state; they really must have needed Carlos badly.)

The two made their contributions, quickly upgrading the somewhat run-down German Navy. Documents from archives prove that the two friends outdid themselves in comparison with their past performance for the Argentinean and Chilean governments.

As soon as the war began, they planned and coordinated the conversion of hundreds of merchant ships into war vessels. In 1940, almost one out of three patrol boats and one out of four minesweepers had served other purposes in peacetime.

When we invaded and overran Denmark and Norway, it soon became evident that the Norwegian west coast would be critically important for us. Its fortifications and unhampered navigation along the coast had to be assured.

Admiral Raeder had to decide who would be best suited to meet that challenge. His trusted emissary, who had been instrumental in rounding up a number of skilled military men from other countries, Commodore Von Schrader, was called in. Raeder did not need Hitler's approval for military appointments. Right to the day when Hitler committed suicide at his underground Reichschancellary in Berlin, he put greater trust in the German Navy than in any other branch of the armed forces. Raeder promoted Von Schrader from commodore to rear admiral, Dr. Carlos Mayer-Pantin from captain to commodore, and Hans Baer from commander to captain.

Von Schrader took his headquarters in Bergen. He would be in charge and responsible for all naval operations between Mandal in the South and Aalesund north of Bergen. Mayer-Pantin, as area naval commander, occupied headquarters in Stavanger, with full navigational and administrative responsibilities between Haugesund, north of Stavanger, and Flekkefjord south of Egersund. Hans Baer became his administrative assistant and chief of staff. This was a reversal of ranks in comparison to the Chilean assignment, but it worked well since they were perfectly compatible individuals.

Mayer-Pantin left no doubt who was in charge. And yet I have seen him listening intently to the opinions of Baer, Brinkman, his technical advisor and Wunderlich, his aide. By nature of their expertise and tasks, these officers bore influences on his final decisions.

He was of imposing stature. Tall, slim, well-groomed, with a light walk and refined manners, he communicated courteously with everyone. When someone stepped out of line, he felt quite uncomfortable and shied away from directly addressing the person in question. A tactful man, he had a way of conveying his displeasure by sending signals.

Principles of conduct, procedures and regulations were explained by Lieutenant Wunderlich, his aide, to every officer who had been newly appointed to his corps. A pamphlet would back up Wunderlich's orientation.

In the mornings, for instance, every officer was expected to be at his command post or desk by 0830 hours. We opened the casino at 0715 hours for breakfast, allowing officers plenty of time to leave by then. Mayer-Pantin would arrive at around 0820 hours for his breakfast.

One day, a newly assigned sublieutenant was finishing his breakfast in the dining room, when Mayer-Pantin arrived on the scene. The Commodore looked at the man with piercing eyes, his brows quizzically moving upward. When he hardly acknowledged the man's friendly, "Good morning, Commodore, sir," and went straight to his seat, I knew something was brewing.

The following morning, the sublieutenant sat there again. Obviously, he had not taken the hint from the previous day; neither did he seem to have studied his orientation manual. This time, Mayer-Pantin deliberately looked at his watch, saying nothing and took his seat.

When the sublieutenant left five minutes later, having saluted smartly, the Commodore called me over and asked, "Born, what is the lieutenant's name, and what is he doing here?"

I quoted the man's name and said somewhat lamely and quite unnecessarily, "He had breakfast, Herr Kapitaen." Then, starting my brain going in defense of the poor chap, I made matters worse by adding, "Maybe he did not have a chance to read all of the regulations, sir." (Poor thinking; I could have bitten my tongue off!)

"Nonsense!" he countered. "You know them, don't you, even though they do not apply to you."

"Jawohl, Herr Kapitaen," I said, "together with my chief-steward's regulations."

"You see," he continued. "What we don't want around here is incompetence and people who cannot read. You had better tell him what the score is, before I do."

Can you imagine the little ordinary seaman (private) telling the lieutenant what the score is? An order is an order, though. I wrote a brief message on a sheet of paper addressed to the officer, asking him to see me briefly regarding a sensitive matter after luncheon service that day. I inserted the message in his napkin folder.

We withdrew to the salon a few minutes after luncheon time. Though my heart was pumping double-time during the conversation, I must have hit the right note. He thanked me twice for my assistance before he left. I knew I had made a friend.

Sometimes, our senses play tricks on us. Mayer-Pantin was not exempted from this, though I remember only one incident. Having lived in Brazil for years, he had become accustomed to having a bowl of rice with his otherwise frugal breakfast every morning. Never at loss for an answer, Heinz Marzi replied to the Commodore's question one day, that the rice was regularly shipped in from Brazil. That was not quite true, but obviously pleased the Commodore.

One morning when Heinz and I were covering breakfast service, Mayer-Pantin called Heinz over and inquired, "Marzi, what happened to the rice? It is not as fluffy as usual and does not taste the same either."

Heinz's wheels turned instantly. "I beg the Commodore's pardon. The delivery of Brazilian rice has been delayed this time. We hope to have it available again soon."

That was not correct. We never switched labels and Erich Eye, as I said before, never spoiled a dish, certainly not rice.

And so it happened. Two days later, Heinz made me serve the rice with the statement, "Your Brazilian rice, Herr Kapitaen." Waiting for him to taste it, I stepped aside, anxiously awaiting his verdict.

After a few seconds, he looked at me and commented, "Tell Marzi, he did not have to tell me that this is my Brazilian rice again. I tasted that immediately." Quite relieved, I went back to my observation post.

Later on, I was to experience dozens of cases where people's imaginations played tricks on them. For example, in the late 1950s, I was responsible for the service in a hotel dining room and a cocktail bar in Ottawa, Ontario. Our bartenders had instructions to use less expensive liquor for mixing drinks, unless a customer would specify. One of our steady customers always ordered an extra dry Martini, made with Gordon's Gin. One day, he called

Marcel, the waiter, back to his table and asked: "Is this Gordon's Gin?" It was. But Marcel immediately answered, "Gordie, the bartender, must have made a mistake. I will exchange this for you right away, sir."

He took the Martini back to the bar. The bartender quickly replaced the customer's sip by adding some more gin, then placed the glass, unobserved, in the refrigerator, while Marcel said loudly, "With Gordon's Gin."

He picked up the adjusted drink with his next order. Serving it to the patron, he made the remark, "Sorry about the mistake, sir," and stood by. The man sipped at the glass, then said, "What a difference in taste. That's Gordon's Gin."

With food it is a bit different, but it also applies to a large degree. The truth is, once the palate has been soaked with one or two drinks, it becomes very difficult to tell similar products apart. Canadian Brandy, German Weinbrant and French Cognac seem to taste alike.

Korvettenkapitaen (Commander) Brinkman

Commander Brinkman, next in line of command after Captain Baer, served as technical advisor and liaison officer between naval headquarters in Stavanger and the Abwehr (Counterintelligence). Technically, Admiral Canaris, chief of the Abwehr, was Brinkman's boss. The same Canaris, who was highly regarded by his adversaries because of his fair play, his opposition to the political Nazi machine, and his collaboration with a number of high-ranking military officers–including the famous General Rommel–in their ill-fated attempts to remove Hitler from the scene in July 1944.

Brinkman had served as one of the youngest lieutenants in World War I, followed by an illustrious business career. Before the great Wall Street crash, he disposed of all stocks that became worthless, while holding on to those which started resoaring in the early thirties.

By 1932, he owned several merchant ships, founded a shipping company two months before Hitler became Chancellor in 1933, and shortly afterwards married a German socialite from the Hollsten Bier empire.

In my book, he was the best-mannered of them all. Immaculately dressed, about five feet eleven inches tall, slim, with elegant movements and grayish hair that flowed in waves down to his collar line (totally unmilitaristic), he gave one the impression of a friendly business tycoon. When Mayer-Pantin would introduce him to a visitor as unser Korvettenkapitaen Brinkman (our Commander Brinkman) I heard Brinkman at several occasions adding to the introduction, in an emphasizing manner, "With one N."

When I knew him a few months, I asked him one day about this. He explained, looking me straight in the eye, "That is easy, Born. My grandfather was English; and I have no reason to deny my Anglo-Saxon origin." He certainly was not intimidated by any Nazi propaganda!

When the war had ended, I discovered that Brinkman was not the only democratic-minded German naval officer who, not by choice, had to wear the uniform of a dictatorship. There was another good reason for having him aboard. Because of his family tie in with the Hamburg brewery, the officers casino never ran out of Hollsten beer. He had a standing order with the brewery and arranged for the transportation of X number of crates to be sent every eight to ten days or so with a merchant ship that happened to steam in our direction. In spite of the great demand, we never ran out of it. It is one of the leading beer brews in Germany, together with Dortmunder Pils, Henninger (from Frankfort on the Main), Wickueler (from my hometown Wuppertal) and Beck's Bier from Luehbeck.

In 1944, Brinkman was instrumental in my assignment to temporarily serve as administrative assistant at Navy Counterintelligence in Stavanger.

Korvettenkapitaen (Commander) Schubert

When I first met him in 1941 as a member of Mayer-Pantin's officer corps, he had not been promoted yet from lieutenant commander to commander. Right from the beginning, he struck me as a very unusual man. The kind one would trust immediately, a no-nonsense, straightforward man. Even seeing the man without uniform, with his six-foot tall, heavy frame, weather-beaten and tough-looking face, with deep wrinkles from years of exposure to sun and saltwater, one could only assume him to be a sailor or a farmer.

When moving about, he seemed to swing with the waves but somewhat exaggerated, even for a man having spent thirty years at sea. When walking, his hip would swing forward, then the leg would follow, on each side. His walk was a mystery to me, until one day I found out that he had two artificial legs.

As a teenager, he had helped his dad fish in the North Sea, mostly for cod and at times salmon. That was in the early twenties. It was a hard life, bringing in just about enough for the six-member family to keep afloat.

Later, he joined the mercantile marine and served on a dozen ships in as many years. Then in 1934, he joined the newly-created North German Harbor Patrol and Coast Guard. The Coast Guard division controlled the coastline between Emden in the west, near the Netherlands and Husum in the north, near Denmark. The area is generally referred to as *Die deutsche Bucht* (the German Bay), though it is much larger than an ordinary bay.

One day in November 1937, as so often before, harbor patrol in Bremen received several distress signals from boats out at sea. They could not find shelter fast enough and got caught in an unpredictable twin storm. At the time, weather forecasts were not nearly as comprehensive and precise as nowadays. Schubert went out, joined by other patrol boats in the area and soon reached the meridian where two steamers fought with the elements. He had been appointed to direct the rescue operation and lost no time in organizing the attempt. The crew of one of the two steamers had to be rescued, since the ship was obviously not seaworthy anymore and about to sink. These men had to be taken off that vessel, or sink with her.

Schubert aligned the patrol boats along the steamer, went aboard with eight men and arranged for the transfer of the crew. In spite of the ocean's violent action, the evacuation progressed better than could have been expected under the adverse circumstances.

Then it happened! Schubert and the ship's captain were the last ones to leave the deck, which, at that time, was tilted port-side about sixty degrees to the sea. There was not enough time left to slip down the ropes into the boat. They decided to jump. The captain landed flat on the patrol boat, the impact partially offset by two life belts. Schubert was not so lucky.

While he jumped, the ship trembled convulsively and jerked. Her deck tipped vertically to the sea at a ninety degree angle, just at the moment when Schubert hit the water. That in itself would not have caused a problem, but the ship's sudden additional tilt had created a tremendous wake, hurling the patrol boat's starboard belly against the momentarily vertical deck of the ship. For a few seconds, Schubert's lower body became pinned in between, before he could be dragged into the patrol boat. The pain was so excruciating that Schubert lost consciousness several times before reaching the hospital. His legs had been crushed to splinters. One had to be amputated above the knee, the other below.

"I can tell you," he said when he described the incident to me, "when I knew what had happened, I wanted to die. Only the encouragement of my family and friends got me over the hump. But it took quite a while until I felt there was still something left in this world to look forward to."

He took physiotherapy, learned to use crutches, and developed an amazing suppleness in moving around. Three months after the accident, one prosthesis was fitted to the left leg. Two months after that, the second to the right.

When he had amazed his therapists with his "juggling on crutches," as he called it, he astonished them even more with the use of his artificial legs. One week after the fitting of the second prosthesis, he refused to have anything to do with "these long chopsticks" anymore. His humor must have contributed greatly to his progressive recovery.

One day in 1943 at the casino, while he celebrated his promotion to commander, he started a fictitious argument with a fellow officer, unbuckled his right prosthesis and pretended to threaten his comrade with it, using it like a dagger.

Another time, a talent show was held in search of people who could help entertain the troops. The audition for officers was held at the casino a few weeks ahead of the scheduled show. Eighteen of our corps officers showed up, one of them Schubert. Some sang; others told funny stories and jokes. Two of them acted as jugglers, promptly smashing some of our kitchen china in the process (for which they had to pay later). Three had previously practiced and rehearsed an acrobatic act just for their own fun. It included jumping off the mezzanine floor over the balustrade onto the lobby floor without breaking any bones. Schubert was listed last. While watching all the others doing their thing, I wondered what he would come up with.

Before his turn came, he had asked to have a bare round table ready. Finally, it was his turn. Without batting an eyelid, he fished a harmonica out of his pocket, mounted himself with a tremendous swing onto the round table, and started playing an Irish song, while appropriately dancing an Irish jig to it. The audience roared with laughter and gave him a standing ovation. His performance crowned an entertaining evening like a great cup of coffee after a good meal.

The day after the amateur rehearsal, Schubert's clowning was still on our minds. After having been absent on a variety of other assignments, Heinz was still in charge when I returned. We were all having dinner in the kitchen. The old team from the previous year was intact, with the exception of Otto Januszeit, the other steward, who had been transferred. His replacement was a cute but rather dumb young chick, who had problems standing on her feet and thinking at the same time.

Upon my return, I had asked Heinz what she was doing here. "A good question," was his reply. "She doesn't know dishes, cannot carry plates, and knows nothing about service. Knowing the situation, you can imagine I was anxious to get rid of this klutz, shortly after she appeared. But I was told in no uncertain terms that the girl stays and 'to make the best of it.' I have a hunch there is somebody influential who appreciates her services, whatever they are, more than we do. Sorry."

I knew, of course, that Schubert had been commissioned to take responsibility for the flawless deployment of harbor affairs and also to protect the coastline against enemy intruders. The appointment was made based on his courageous and also illustrious past, as a man of action. There was nothing he would not undertake. What influenced Mayer-Pantin's decision most was Schubert's ability to get along with people of adverse behavior, as well as his exemplary tenacity never to give up on anything or anybody.

When he had studied Schubert's file, he knew this was the man who could keep the coastline straight, so to speak. Particularly impressive was Schubert's determination to rehabilitate himself by hook or by crook. After his convalescence in 1938, he reapplied for German Coast Guard duty. He had been given a comfortable desk job, but that was not his idea of active duty. He made a stab at it four times, then the Commission gave in just to "get him off our backs." The same thing happened to the draft board at the end of 1939. In February 1940, the multiple-times volunteer was put in naval uniform. After a lot of pulling back and forth and some influence peddling, Schubert won all those battles.

Admiral Von Schrader had suggested that Mayer-Pantin have a look at Schubert's file, as well as those of a number of other suitable applicants who were to make up the commandant's officer corps in Stavanger.

By providing Schubert's file, Von Schrader had used most effective evidence to assist Mayer-Pantin in making a selection, more so than giving him an outright order. Mayer-Pantin knew a good prospect when he saw one. A better choice for the task at hand could not be made.

As we sat around the table enjoying the dessert Erich Eye had prepared for us, Heinz remarked, "Commandeer Schubert is not only a good administrator and organizer, he also refuses to give up any of that hands-on experience he has."

"What do you mean by that?" I asked. Heinz looked at Karen, one of our two Norwegian kitchen assistants and said, "You tell Siegfried."

"Well, Siegfried," Karen explained in her lovely Norwegian accent, but otherwise flawless German, "the man is really something; he has to be admired!"

That statement stunned me. I knew that Karen, like many other Norwegian civilians who worked for us was not exactly thrilled to see her country occupied. These people worked for us merely as a matter of economics and survival. Karen was a fine lady in her forties, who cooperated well as our kitchen assistant. But I never interpreted her attitude–or that of any other Norwegian civilian–as pro-German. That would have meant kidding myself.

"You see," Karen went on, "during the winter of 1940-41, we had a lot of bad storms. On several occasions, fishing trawlers got into trouble. Who went out with his crews and boats to rescue them? Korvettenkapitaen Schubert! We all owe him; he saved a lot of lives."

"That is true," interjected Solvay, the other kitchen assistant. He added bluntly, "Don't kid yourselves, none of us are crazy about you people, but Captain Schubert is held in high esteem because he saves lives rather than wastes them." I could not quarrel with that philosophy.

Now I had an explanation for seeing Schubert moving about the civilian population as if he was one of them. No aides, no guards! At one time I had to wait for a boat ride to bring me out of the fjord to Kvitsøy for a rehearsal with the B Band. Reporting to his administrative building on Skagenkaien, Schubert came out of his office to show me around the harbor area. There were only the two of us walking about, looking at different facilities, going in and out of buildings and sneaking through narrow thoroughfares. Schubert acted totally unconcerned. Now I understood the reason. The buddy system for soldiers going downtown had been increased from a minimum of two to four immediately after the sailor on harbor patrol had been found floating beside Fiskepiren, at the beginning of June 1943. And here were the two of us, stomping around unprotected against assassins!

I heard the most astonishing statement regarding Schubert after the war, when I dealt with former members of the Norwegian Resistance. The term we had used for these people was "underground members." From the Norwegian point of view, they were considered freedom fighters. Not that it matters, but the latter term sounds to me as if it could be placed between the other two.

In any case, this man said to me, when Schubert's name came up, "Sigy, I tell you, Schubert could have walked into our secret headquarters during the war all by himself. We would not have hurt a hair on his head, but rather wined and dined him. We love the man who saved so many of our brothers. Why do you think we never activated any act of sabotage around the harbor under his command? He is one of our heroes, never mind the uniform he wears."

Needless to say, I was deeply touched by these remarks. They served as a prime example of the old adage that in the long-run people get what they deserve!

Oberstabsarzt Dr. Eckler

Commander Dr. Eckler was our area navy staff physician, in charge and responsible for health care of all naval personnel. In contrast to some sad experiences we had with doctors in uniform, he was a kind and considerate man, who exercised control over his colleagues' behavior. While it had become the order of the day in some military units that doctors turned into bad jokes, Eckler would not tolerate any of this.

At one point, an enlisted man had used the grievance procedure against an orderly in one of our satellite sick quarters, against the advice of his commanding officer. Nevertheless, the complaint verbally reached Dr. Eckler. An inquiry was launched immediately. When all the facts were in, the orderly in question received a reprimand he would never forget; his C.O. got a good slap on the wrist.

Dr. Eckler insisted on correct and sensitive behavior. On the other hand, he could be unorthodox when it came to caring for people. To give an example, one of Hitler's directives spelled out that at no time and under no circumstances would the military be allowed to use any of their military hospitals or sick quarters for the treatment of civilians.

At the time, Stavanger had only two small hospitals with probably not more than three hundred beds combined. When Schubert showed up at the pier with dozens of survivors of a storm at sea, Dr. Eckler promptly disregarded all directives and accommodated particularly the critically hurt at the Marine-Lazarett (naval hospital). Then he notified Commandant Mayer-Pantin and asked for special permission after the fact. Mayer-Pantin looked eye-to-eye with Schubert and Eckler in situations like these. Permission was always promptly granted in view of the fact that emergencies are out of the ordinary and have to be treated as such.

These were my kind of people! On certain occasions, one has to shoot first and ask questions later; particularly when lives can be saved by doing so. Come to think of it, we had a great number of men in the navy who did not fit the pattern of stereotypical Nazis. I am making no excuses, nor is it prejudice which makes me say that. A lot of us stood firmly behind Hitler, mostly for (wrong) ideological or simply nationalistic reasons. But make no mistake, not all those wearing combat uniforms were loyal to the idea and (so-called) ideals of national socialism. That specifically applied to many navy men, who had spent years in the mercantile marine. They had seen many foreign countries and, therefore, could not be indoctrinated with a hate others/master race propaganda.

Oberinspektor Pohlmann

Chief Inspector Pohlmann's actual service rank was the same as mine, able seaman. His duty rank, however, was equal to that of a lieutenant commander, his uniform jacket bearing three silver rings, two regular size and one narrower one in the center. Silver rings were used in the German Navy to distinguish an assignment, function or duty rank from the actual service rank of the person.

Fritz Pohlmann, who was about fifty years of age at the time, had an extensive background in the food business as a restaurateur, food broker, and marketing advisor for the North Sea fish store chain, just to mention a few. If you had learned the initial ropes of the hospitality industry like I did, you could talk turkey with him for hours and learn a lot. I sure did exploit that powerhouse of knowledge and experience, not only during my service at the officers casino, but also later in 1944 when assigned to naval headquarters, where he had his administrative office. He was another doer who spent as little time as possible in the office. In retrospect, I would categorize him as one of those individuals about whom the saying goes: "A busy executive is seldom in the office."

His assignment was to act as commanding officer for all food and beverage supplies and provisions, including warehouses located at the waterfront for convenient access for navy vessels and the mercantile fleet. Together with other inventive individuals, he always found ways and means to supplement the regular navy rations with extra portions not appearing on any supply list. He was a great man who gladly served others by his industriousness and looked after the welfare of naval personnel without lining his pockets. The moment we surrendered in 1945, he immediately participated in assisting a special task force with the sole purpose of rounding up extra food supplies.

Kapitaenleutnant Schmidt

Soon after my arrival in Stavanger to become promoted from first lieutenant to lieutenant commander, Schmidt was the no-nonsense officer, who had greeted us as newcomers at the Stabs and Wachkompanie. The unit's prime task was to protect military defense installations as well as those of interest to the Underground or Resistance, depending on which side of the fence one is standing. Targets for sabotage were ammunition and weapon depots, oil reservoirs, power stations and any other number of objects, the destruction of which would cause harm to us. That even included main food warehouses and, of course, vessels transporting huge food supplies. I described earlier the attack on one of these shortly before Christmas 1941.

Throughout the years, the company maintained an extra supply of manpower for emergency cases which would be utilized on a moment's notice. Over and above that, a number of sailors and functionaries were at hand. These people had specific backgrounds, allowing the Commander to draw on them for special assignments.

Schmidt was absolutely fair and highly regarded by all. When needed, however, he would not hesitate to detail a man to a hazardous task, as I was about to find out.

As naval officer casino chairman, he kept his finger on the pulse of the business, and made sure, right through the end of the war, that the organization was conducted in a correct and ethical fashion. Where his predecessor had failed miserably, and paid the consequences, he succeeded. He set up new guidelines and principles of operation which protected against pilfering, and also protected casino staff against interference from other officers. None of them were even allowed to peek their heads into the kitchen. The steward on duty had the right to politely ask the officer in question to leave. Abuse of personnel was not tolerated. That provided peace of mind for us.

One member of the Commandant's staff was a real troublemaker. Not only did he cause problems with Heinz, Otto and me, but he also sought almost constant confrontation with other officers. His popularity, therefore, was close to zero. Nobody seemed to have any use for the man. He stalked around like a peacock, looking for someone with whom to quarrel.

As planner of strategic defense installations, his duty rank was that of lieutenant commander; his service rank was that of an able seaman. Like Chief Inspector Pohlmann, he wore two regular-size silver rings around his jacket sleeves, with a small one in between.

He moved and behaved with an exaggerated air of importance, seeking attention, no matter how. He was another small fry who did not get enough attention at home and was trying to make up for it later in abundance.

After an accumulation of frustrating experiences with the man, Erich Eye and I had it up to our eyebrows with him. Something had to be done to teach him a lesson! We put our heads together and soon came up with a plan that should work.

A couple of evenings or so per week we served soup tureens, cold cuts, cheese and fruit for dinner, rather than a three or four-course meal. Cold cuts and cheese were rationed. Each person received a side plate with two hundred grams cold cuts and sixty-two and one half grams of cheese, according to regulated ration portions.

On the evening in question, we deliberately cut ninety-five grams of cheese for everyone, then shaved off a few grams from Engineer Walters' portion, making it look smaller than the other portions, which it indeed was.

The dining room was open for dinner from 1800 to 2000 hours. Walters arrived at about 1845 hours. He took his seat, while I took the silver-plated coffee server and walked over to him. The soup tureen was already on the table, as several other officers were having their dinner close by his seat.

Unfolding his napkin, Walters glanced around at the portion plates, noticing the difference in his cheese portion at the moment I poured him coffee. He looked up at me and said, "Born, you cannot tell me that this is sixty-two and one half grams of cheese! Do you want to shortchange me?"

I went to his left, picked up the side plate and apologized profusely. "I beg your pardon, Engineer, sir. We must have made a mistake, we will correct this immediately!"

Entering the kitchen, Erich Eye stood there, knife in hand, with a big smile, having listened to the exchange from the pantry. He lifted the cheese off the side plate, put it on the gram scale first, then removed another slice from it. Using the scale again, the piece now weighed exactly sixty-three grams.

Some of the other officers seated near Walters must have felt that I was up to something. As I reentered the dining room with the adjusted portion, they looked at me with expectant glances and curiosity. Hiding my anticipation of an outbreak, I put on a most purposeful walk and, having reached Walters, set the side plate above his bread and butter plate with the remark, "Here you are, Engineer, sir, exactly sixty-two and one half grams of cheese, as desired." The other officers noticed that the piece of cheese had shrunk even more. Pretending to be occupied with their own plates, most had difficulties suppressing chuckles.

Having placed the plate, I tried to leave the danger zone without delay. Nobody could be that fast! I had hardly made two steps, when Walters snapped, "Come back here! This is outrageous! Now it is even less than before. What are you trying to pull?"

As calmly as I could under the circumstances, I reiterated that he had demanded sixty-two and one half grams, with which I accommodated him. That was as far as I got. His face and neck turned red like a boiled lobster.

During the ensuing tirade, which lasted about two minutes, and included threats of court-martialing me, he lifted himself from the chair. As he stood in front of me shaking like a leaf in the wind, he reminded me of Adolf Hitler, who was a master at working himself into a lather during his speeches. Walters came close to a fit. Any moment I expected the corners of his mouth to form foam. I had learned firsthand why others around him avoided the man like the plague. Finally, when he had to take a deep breath–two minutes of uninterrupted talk can be exhausting–I saluted smartly, as if nothing unusual had happened and left the dining room like a weasel.

Returning to the kitchen, Erich Eye pretended to be surprised. "You are still alive," he quipped. "For now, at least," was my fast reply. I knew, of course, that a rather serious situation had developed, which could have negative consequences for me if I did not act decisively.

First, I got to the horn and called Lieutenant Commander Schmidt, the casino chairman. With a list of officers, who had been present at the table, I reported the incident without exaggerating anything, but emphasizing Walters' threat of a court-martial. Schmidt listened to me without interrupting once. When I had finished, he commended me for not delaying the report and for having made a list of witnesses. "Leave it to me, Born," he added, "and don't do anything until you hear from me."

When Heinz Marzi returned from his day off, I mentioned the incident to him rather matter-of-factly. But I could not fool him. "Don't tell me," he said, "that you are not ready to shit in your pants any moment."

I concurred that that was more or less the way I felt. But what was done could not be undone. I tried hard to adopt the philosophy I had read about sometime somewhere, explaining how useless worrying really is: "Worrying means paying interest on trouble which is not due yet."

The next morning at breakfast service, Schmidt instructed me to "be handy this evening for a meeting of the minds with Walters." This was fine with me, as I was eager to get this stink bomb out of the way, sooner rather than later.

At 1915 hours, Schmidt and Walters entered the dining room together. That did not look too good to me, but the conclusion I drew from that was wrong. Around 2000 hours the service bell for the salon rang. I went in. Schmidt and Walters were sitting at a settee table in one corner of the room, apparently chatting amiably. Schmidt said, "Sigy, (he never called me by the nickname my peers used for me) we would like to talk to you now, if you are not too busy. Bring Engineer Walters here a Scotch whiskey from our special stock, which the Tommies lost in the Atlantic the other day. I would like to have a Weinbrant; and catch something for yourself."

I repeated the order in military fashion: "One Black and White Scotch, one Dudardin, and I will have a Kuemmel (a colorless liqueur with a caraway flavor), if I may, sir."

As I arrived with the order, Schmidt told me to sit with them. Walters' face looked embarrassed, an expression I had never seen on him.

"Engineer Walters has something to say to you," Schmidt said as I sat down. My heart jumped to my throat. The atmosphere seemed to be deceivingly peaceful.

"I want you to know," began Walters with a surprisingly subdued voice, "that I have withdrawn my decision to have you disciplined. In this case, I don't even have to wait the usual forty-eight hours to reconsider. I probably wasn't quite fair. Lieutenant Commander Schmidt suggested I apologize, Born, for having treated you harshly. I herewith formally comply and hope we can forget the whole matter." Thud! The heavy rock I had carried around on my shoulders hit the floor.

"Of course, Herr Engineer," was my reply, adding to my voice the tone of forgiveness and proper respect.

"You see," Walters explained, "I have been under a great strain lately, which made me quite edgy. But, I really have no excuse for having jumped on you the way I did." Then with a smile which I had never seen on him either, he added, "Next time I know better than to ask for sixty-two and one half grams cheese, when I already have a larger portion."

The ice was broken! We sat for another twenty minutes or so and chatted about matters that normally would not have been for the ears of an able seaman.

Mankievicz And Von Der Knesebrecht

Both were first lieutenants and had top reputations in their respective fields of expertise: Mankievicz as hands-on expert for convoy guidance; Von der Knesebrecht in the area of protection, defense and camouflage.

They were also the only lower-rank officers who actively participated in some during-and-after-lunch discussions, as well as in situation room briefings. To the chagrin of some other officers, they never held back from expressing their opinions no matter how controversial or sensitive the issue at hand. Their analytical-mindedness and general intellect had proved to be correct in numerous dangerous situations. Cases were cited when ships and navy personnel had been saved by their applied tactics, who would otherwise have found themselves on the bottom of the ocean.

They could have been brothers in looks and behavior. Their tasks interlocked to a high degree. That in itself necessitated that these two individuals think alike. Lieutenant Commander Wunderlich, Mayer-Pantin's aide, referred to them as "the Duo" and explained to me one day what he meant by this.

Rear Admiral Von Schrader got caught one day with his speedboat and two other German ships which had somehow strayed off the course of the convoy, inside the rear end of a British convoy that was not supposed to be there either. Von der Knesebrecht, close to the Admiral's speedboat, instantly but calmly, as if this was quite a natural situation, contacted Mankievicz outside the British convoy. It took them only a few minutes to establish the positions of the different ships–including those of the British–and agreed on a plan of action. Von Schrader, who had a knack for surrounding himself with the best human material he could find (and who had "stolen" these two tacticians away from other operational areas) concurred without hesitation.

The plan worked so well that Von Schrader, with his speedboat, the gun boat and a cruiser were not only successful in disassociating themselves from the British convoy, but also in causing some embarrassing damage to it before vanishing into nowhere. The Admiral received the German Cross in Gold for that feat. Von der Knesebrecht and Mankievicz were awarded the Iron Cross First Class.

Shortly after the event, Admiral Von Schrader designated Mankievicz to assist Commodore Mayer-Pantin with matters of convoy guidance within the navigational sphere between the town of Haugesund, north of Stavanger, and Flekkefjord, south of Egersund. That was before my arrival in Stavanger in December 1941.

In February 1942, partly as a consequence of our inability to prevent Norwegian soldiers serving with the British forces, to spend their Christmas and New Year's holidays unnoticed in their mother country, Von der Knesebrecht was detailed to strengthen our vigilance, naval protection and defense installations.

The two had a way of operating within the expected framework; yet, they carried out exactly what they felt had to be done without, in most instances, checking with headquarters. Commodore Mayer-Pantin had practically extended a carte blanche, allowing them to use full discretionary powers as they would see fit. This made it easier for them to achieve results. Besides, due to the nature of their assignments, nobody on the upper level of authority—except the commandant, of course—was keen to take any responsibility for possibly negative outcomes of decision-making processes.

During tactical status discussions, some of which took place at the casino, the Duo spoke with one voice whenever it seemed necessary. It delighted me to hear them arguing their points calmly but with determination. At times their view was contrary to that of Mayer-Pantin who, nevertheless, not only heard them out but, at times, even overruled himself and the advice of other officers. This was a rather unusual situation within the spectrum of armed forces, to say the least.

The second half of 1943 saw Germany with only one battleship left: the *Tirpitz*. All the other battleships we used had fallen prey to the Allies: the *Bismarck*, *Deutschland*, *Graf Spee*, *Scheer*, *Bluecher* and *Scharnhorst*.

Grossadmiral Doenitz, Raeder's successor, decided the *Tirpitz* must be preserved. She had been exposed to several attacks within the Skattegat and the Skagerrak, though luckily without major affliction. She had to be steered to Norwegian waters, which seemed to be more secure for the navy than any other theater.

That, however, was a miscalculation. At the time the assumption was made, the navy high command in Oslo did not anticipate that our hands would soon be full. Numerous Norwegian resistance groups who had entrenched themselves in different mountainous strategic posts kept us busy by sending coded messages about our naval movements to the British.

Doenitz had communicated to Von Schrader the necessity of finding a safe refuge for the *Tirpitz*. Who would be better qualified to establish one than Von der Knesebrecht?

Von Schrader, without formally pulling rank, asked Mayer-Pantin to avail Von der Knesebrecht for this task, who instantly put his full attention to this top priority matter. But as usual he did not jump to any conclusions. He thoroughly familiarized himself with the charting patterns of the *Tirpitz*, her degree of vulnerability and any other factors contributing to a full analysis. Then he screened the safety factor most suitable geographically to serve as a safe haven for the battleship. He came up with the harbor of Narvik, situated barely north of the sixty-eighth latitude, in the northern part of Nordland County.

Unfortunately, that location was not safe for too long. Intelligence reports indicated that the Allies—particularly the British, still sulking because of their hair-breadth defeat in May 1940—were determined to take the boast away from us that we had one functional battleship left. The *Tirpitz*, with her mother ship, *Admiral Hipper*, and two escort ships, had to be moved fast! Our naval antiaircraft batteries along the northern coast of Norway were put on high alert until further notice.

It was already October, the time of year when the northern icecap starts moving further south, making navigation difficult. The plan was to move the entire convoy further north to the innermost inlet of Kafjorden, near the Eskimo settlement called Kafjord. It was obvious that this goal could not be reached without the help of several icebreakers.

One day before the arrival of the icebreakers, the Royal Air Force attempted to spoil Von der Knesebrecht's plan. At the start of dawn, they visited with three waves of bomber squadrons accompanied by Mustangs. All hell broke lose, but we were well-prepared. Already before the *Tirpitz* had been moved to Narvik, the surrounding terrain had been spiked with a number of naval batteries, whose function was to quickly fog in the ships and the harbor whenever an attack seemed imminent. It worked well. The best German Naval artillery units were stationed in that theater.

Damage was minimal. Three factors were responsible for the light damage to material and minimal loss of life: the fogging in of the harbor area; the persistent artillery resistance, forcing bomber personnel to release bombs harmlessly over the Ofotfjorden; and the gentlemen-like reluctance of the Brits to carry and release *Bombenteppiche* (carpets of bombs), which they were using to bomb German cities. The safety of the Norwegian population had to be considered. They were much more sympathetic to the British than to us and would not have taken carpet bombings for the sake of destroying the *Tirpitz*.

In the meantime, Von der Knesebrecht and his team searched for a comparatively safe and practical way to get the *Tirpitz* to her new destination. This was easier said than done! It had been relatively simple to navigate the ship through the Skagerrak and the Norskerenna along the western coast of Norway, then to guide her through the vast Vestfjorden waterway into Ofotfjorden and finally find her a resting place in Narvik Harbor.

Bringing her further north one more latitude was going to be a real challenge for more reasons than one. Because of her considerable tonnage, Von der Knesebrecht excluded the idea to simply lead her through the Tjeldsundet, not far west of Narvik, and then out to sea north of Harstad. That meant the voyage had to be made first in a southwestern direction back through Vestfjorden, an extra seventy nautical miles. Next, she would have to sail around the southern tip of the Lofoten Islands, turning north-northeast, cruising along fairly close to the shoreline until reaching Lopphavet. From there, she would have to steam easterly through Stjerroysundet into Altafjorden.

But we knew our navigational movements could not be veiled or disguised. The British received hourly updating of every move our ships made, no matter how small the vessel. No doubt, a big battleship like the *Tirpitz* would stick out like a sore thumb.

Norwegians collaborating with the British played a decisive role in this game of hide and seek. They kept the British up-to-date right along the entire Norwegian coast, particularly around Bordø, Narvik and the Lofoten Islands. Almost daily visits by the Royal Air Force provided evidence of how effective these Norwegian watchdogs were. There were a number of innocent-looking trawlers and fishing boats equipped with powerful transmitters. They sent their own observations directly and also transmitted coded messages which they received from agents in the mountains. Much later did we find out how well-knit this net of listening posts was!

Last, but not least, the other major handicap we had were the thick ice floats, ice drifts and icebergs. At least two icebreakers were needed to carve a path wide enough for a small convoy to pass through. In deep winter, any passage cut by the icebreakers would have to be used immediately by ships forming a close line, or everything would freeze up again. I have seen three-feet-deep ice refreeze within twelve minutes!

Von der Knesebrecht had taken these and other factors into consideration. He had requisitioned three icebreakers. The next day, two icebreakers threw anchors outside Vestfjorden, awaiting the arrival of the *Tirpitz*. The convoy left as planned, with Von der Knesebrecht acting as commanding officer at the helm of the *Admiral Hipper*. Strangely enough, with the exception of a couple of light skirmishes caused by a few British planes which apparently had been sent to observe the convoy, the *Tirpitz* and escort completed the four hundred-nautical-mile voyage in two days. Anchors were thrown while Von der Knesebrecht devised an intricate defense system for the protection of Germany's last battleship. I was destined to become part of this defense system in the Spring of 1944.

Eberhard Wunderlich

First Lieutenant Wunderlich, who received his promotion to lieutenant commander in 1942, acted as adjutant and aide-de-camp to Mayer-Pantin. As personal assistant and confidential secretary, one of his major functions was to assure quick paper flow of incoming mail. That included the screening and forwarding of confidential, secret, and top-secret documents to staff officers belonging to the limited need-to-know circle.

He had an inexhaustible drive to get things done. The way he went about it, however, was in the form of persuasion. He had earned the respect of subordinates and superiors alike at an early stage of his appointment. Great self-confidence must have been deeply implanted in his personality. He never hesitated to attack any difficult task with a deceiving ease that clearly baffled his less efficient peers.

As a former private and confidential secretary of a German industrialist, he had learned how to delegate responsibility, coupled with just about enough authority to enable others to make their productive contribution to an organization as expected. His communication skills were outstanding. In no time he would know people better than they would know themselves. Encouraging others to perform to their maximum potential was one of his prime goals. When I doubted my ability to handle a new assignment, he would say, "You can do it like that," snapping his fingers together.

While he comprehended the most technical and strategic matters with ease, he did not take for granted that everybody else would be able to do the same. He analyzed complex subjects and technical jargon, broke them into segments, and interpreted to others the contents of the subject matter in a simple, easy-to-understand mode.

No matter how busy things got at Headquarters, whenever I entered his office his desk always looked organized, almost bare. Besides being an experienced administrator, he had skills that others lacked.

Speed-reading was one of them. It took me a while to discover how he possibly could be so well-informed about the contents of early morning reports by 1000 hours. Incoming reports arrived only one hour earlier in the day.

Reading a newspaper was even more of a cinch for him. Asking one day how he did this, he replied, "Easy Bornchen." This was an expression of friendliness and fondness, which I appreciated much more than when some of my comrades called me milk-face or baby-face. "You can do that too. Read the headlines. Decide which are of interest to you. Then read the subheadings, if any, and the first three and last two sentences of each paragraph. That's really all you have to study to comprehend the content."

It was good advice which I implemented right away. I am sure it saved me a lot of time that otherwise would have been wasted. Twenty-two years later, a Canadian philosophy professor made an identical statement. At that moment, I had to think about Wunderlich. One simply does not forget people who have an impact on one's life.

One Friday, when I was with headquarters for about three weeks, he called me to his office in the afternoon. "At ease," he said, "and sit down." I wondered if something was wrong. I had been at his residence a few times while serving as steward in 1941, and again as chief steward in 1943. He shared with three other officers a four-bedroom house close to the officers casino, right around the corner from Ny Olavskleiv on Molle Gata. But at headquarters there simply was no time for socializing!

"Captain Baer and Lieutenant Commander Schmidt did not pull strings to get you back from the Arctic so you can take it easy here," he began, pulling my leg. "There are greater challenges awaiting you than just putting in time in the general office shuffling papers. We plan to utilize the flexibility you have shown during previous assignments. We will get you involved to assist at the *Geheimregistratur* (secret registry department), the convoy reporting service and sooner or later at the *Gekados Registratur* (top secret department), which is the administrative branch of our naval intelligence."

He pointed to an old Underwood typewriter at the left side of his desk, which had been "rescued" together with a number of crates of Black and White Scotch Whiskey that I mentioned before. "I want you to take this thing to your residence tonight," he continued. "Practice on that oldie as much as possible over the weekend. Come Monday, I want to see some results. In your upcoming assignments, you will have to type out notes and some reports for security reasons."

Moving the monster in front of him, he slid a piece of paper in the carriage and started hammering on the keys like a newspaper reporter, using two fingers, but with amazing speed. I thought he just depressed the keys indiscriminately. I was wrong. When he showed me the extracted sheet, it said: "This is Friday, 11 August 1944. As you can see, there is not much to it, Bornchen. Playing the piano is more difficult, even though your ear has been musically trained. A pair of eyes and a pair of fingers is all you need." He had taken less than a minute to type that out. Then he sent me on my way.

When I left for the day, carrying a briefcase in one hand and the typewriter jammed under the other arm, I thought to myself, "I need this like a hole in the head! What do I need typing for? Once out of uniform, I won't be using it ever. Well, an order is an order."

How wrong I was! It came in darn handy later on when menus had to be typed and a typist was not always around. Wunderlich had made a comparison between typing and playing the piano. That stuck with me. Whenever I withdraw to do some typing, I refer to it as playing the piano.

I hammered around on the thing all weekend. My roommate, Victor Boschetto, a great comrade from Innsbruck, Austria, announced about 1400 hours on Saturday, "By gosh, do you ever let this thing cool off? Look how the smoke curls to the ceiling! I thought your fingers had it by now.

"First you drive me nuts practicing without end on your blasted mandolin. Now this. I've had it." he said with exaggerated displeasure. Putting on his highly polished oxfords, he added, "I am going out to see my girlfriend four hours ahead of time."

"Are you sure you want to do this?" I asked. "Maybe you should announce yourself first and give her a chance to get rid of your competitor before you arrive?"

"Dirty dog!" he replied. "I might never come back."

"Promises, promises," I quipped. "Too good to be true." The last part he very likely missed, since he slammed the door, causing the walls to vibrate.

By Monday morning, I had mastered the unbelievable speed of typing twenty words a minute. Since that was not going to be fast enough for Wunderlich—or anybody else, including myself—I left the typewriter at my quarters.

I had hardly taken my usual seat at the reception desk, when Wunderlich rang for me. A file in hand bearing his name, I entered his office. The messenger who delivered files to different departments had not shown up yet. Besides, while still a civilian, somebody had given me sound advice, of which I took notice. "Always take something in your hand, when you go from Point A to B, even if you don't need it. Don't get caught in a hotel hall empty-handed. Have at least a dust cloth with you. That way you look busy if you are not doing anything." My American teacher used to call this "polishing apples." He was right, of course. These apples only look better, until one eats them.

On the other hand, the slogan can be a good one. The efficient waiter or waitress, for instance, is the one who always takes something with him or her when leaving the kitchen or the dining room. (Some professional advice here.)

"Where is your machine?" Wunderlich asked, when I entered his office. When I told him I had left it at home and the reason why, he agreed but picked up his phone and told the orderly on duty to bring over the next best typewriter available. When the soldier arrived, Wunderlich remarked, "Siegfried here is eager to demonstrate his newly-acquired skill. Put it on my desk."

That came unexpected. My anxiety rose. When I tried to slide the sheet of paper into the carriage, my hand shook like a leaf. Having participated in a number of concerts as a former member of the Wuppertaler Mandolinen Orchester, my stage fright had disappeared. Now I suddenly had it again! Once I had typed the first sentences, however, I had regained my confidence. I strummed the thing like the pupil who has practiced his piano lessons well.

"You can keep the old Underwood until you have managed forty to forty-five words per minute," Wunderlich suggested. That goal I reached after a couple of weeks–not bad for a woody woodpecker.

Another Friday came along. Around 1100 hours, when I had delivered the ten o'clock incoming mail to his office, Wunderlich asked me to sit down again. "Now what?" I thought. "Another assignment?"

"You know what?" he began. "I realize you have spent a lot of your free time practicing on the Underwood. It is a nice day outside. How would you like to be compensated for some of that extra time by taking off around noon and, at the same time, doing me a favor?"

"Whatever it is, Herr Kapitaenleutnant," I answered quickly, "consider it done."

"Fine," he carried on. "I have read your file, of course. Your achievements as a soldier are so-so, at best. On the other hand, you are supposed to be a hotshot, literally speaking, when it comes to target shooting. You twice won the first prize, free beer for one week, the traditional reward. Once with the Karabiner (rifle) and once with a pistol. So, I must be talking to the right guy." "Gosh," it flashed through my mind, "is he going to ask me to assassinate somebody?" "Here," he took his Mauser out of his holster and laid it in front of me. "Take my gun or, if you prefer, you can use your own Walthers. Here are my house keys. You know my residence at Molle Gata. Make yourself a good luncheon first. Then go in the backyard and try to get rid of those field rats that are pestering my comrades and me. If you use your weapon, the ammunition will be replaced. Do we have a deal?"

I agreed, taking his pistol just in case. As a precaution against his setting too high expectations, I stopped at the door, turned around and said, before saluting, "I may not be as good at shooting rats as with other targets."

From headquarters to Molle Gata was an easy fifteen-minute walk. As I had to pass the officers casino at the end of Ny Olavskleiv, I briefly dropped in to say hello and pick up a golf cap and a pair of plastic sunglasses. The guys, hearing about my "assignment," had a good chuckle. The new chief steward who knew about my having completed two tours of duty at the casino, had a good sense of humor. He promised me three bottles of Holsten beer per rat, not knowing about my reputation as a marksman. "Great," I replied. "Prepare yourself for a depletion of your beer stock." With that I walked out the door, turned left around the corner into Molle Gata, and arrived at my destination three minutes later.

Entering the kitchen from the side entrance, two of the other three residents, Dr. Eckler and Commodore Schubert, our harbor captain, appeared from the lobby. I saluted and reported the assignment bestowed upon me. "Splendid!" Schubert exclaimed enthusiastically. "Not only will we get rid of some of those stinking rats, we also might get a decently-prepared luncheon today, wouldn't we, Born?"

That was not included in the deal, but how could I refuse? "Of course, that stands to reason, Commodore, sir." I replied. Having removed my jacket, I invaded the refrigerator to inventory its contents. I took a sizable leg of veal, from which I cut three slices, and prepared a combination Wiener Schnitzel/Holstein Schnitzel. (Escallope of veal, Vienna/Holstein style.)

Instead of hard-boiled eggs on top of the Schnitzel, crossed with anchovies, I fried an egg sunny side up, and placed it on the meat. The anchovies I placed on a side dish, garnished with raw tomato and fine-chopped onions. Cream mashed potatoes and a tossed salad completed the course. Nobody wanted soup or dessert. Dr. Eckler and Commander Schubert had a beer with their meal, but I confined myself to a seltzer water. I did not want my steady hand influenced by alcohol.

It was close to 1300 hours when we left the table. "No need to wash dishes," Schubert remarked. "We'll do them tonight. Don't forget to serve yourself a couple of drinks after you've closed the 'shooting range.' And thanks for that great luncheon! Wish we could have that more often."

I could not help asking, "Sir, I understand you have two orderlies coming by to clean your house when needed. I thought they would cook for you gentlemen, at least occasionally."

"They are keeping the house in good order, but none of them can cook. Today is different, anyway. We are working here with confidential papers and cannot leave, not even around the corner to the officers casino."

Going to the dining area, I took a comfortable armchair, a pillow, a sturdy cord, and a detective story I had seen on a shelf during one of my previous visits. Then I carried everything to the backyard.

One glance was enough to show me that the rodents I was after hid in two places. Close to the base of the building to one side was a crevice, ending in a sizable hole; about three meters away from the wall, to the left, was a small chicken coop. It had more than sufficient spacing to allow several creatures to leave and enter at the same time.

I positioned the chair twelve feet away in case of ricochets, facing the two targets in such a way that my view could see both at one glance. Drawing a line between the chair and the targets would have completed an approximate thirty-degree angle. I used the cord to fasten the pillow on the right armrest, since I am right-handed and wanted to use this arrangement as a support when shooting.

Sitting down, I put on the light plastic sunglasses, unfolded the book and held it in my left hand. I unhooked the safety catch on the Walthers gun with my right thumb and allowed the arm to rest on the cushioned arm of the chair, holding the gun firmly in-hand. Then I began to read, holding the book at an appropriate height so that the two targets appeared just above the rim of the book.

The sun shone brightly but did not disturb my eyes, since I was facing north. I had chased the few chickens into the coop, clearing the area for the intended action. Everything was quiet except for the muffled sounds of the chickens.

A half-hour went by without anything happening. I had read about twenty pages and felt so comfortable in that chair that I became sleepy. Just at the moment when I wrestled with myself to stay awake, I saw a movement inside the hole in the base of the building.

A rat peeked out, sniffing, looking left and looking right as if to see whether the coast was clear. It came out a few tiny steps and started nibbling at something which I could not make out from my position. As I straightened my arm and took aim, a second one came out of the hole. I shot the first, but was not quick enough to hit the second before it vanished back into the hole. I got up and walked over to the rat. It was dead all right. Catching it from the side, the 7.65 mm bullet head almost severed the head from the body.

It was another twenty minutes before the next rat appeared. I had the pistol notch already aligned with the wall hole and squeezed the trigger, hitting the rodent halfway out of the hole. Number two.

During the next half-hour nothing happened. Could that be it? Maybe; maybe not. There was a small unlocked shed right beside the chicken coop. I went in and found what I was looking for—some old rags and turpentine. Tearing one rag apart, I soaked it with turpentine, rolled it up, stuffed it lightly into the hole, and lit it. It became an instant fireball, creating plenty of smoke to be uncomfortable for any creature.

Sure enough, after about fifteen seconds, three rats squeezed by the fireball, one by one, shrieking and obviously disoriented, sufficiently long for me to hit them. I missed one, though, and needed a fourth bullet to finish the job.

The sound of the last shot had hardly passed when Commander Schubert appeared at one window, shouting, "Are you missing that often, or are you executing a whole family?" Leaning his upper body out of the window and cocking his head, he added in astonishment, "My dear man, I have never seen that many rats in one pile! Schmidt would not believe it. Better leave some evidence. Wait a minute."

After two minutes, he reappeared with a cord, which he threw to me suggesting, "Maybe you should bind these rats together and leave them in a conspicuous spot."

"By golly," I thought, "he is quite serious! What a sense of humor. I only hope this will not bounce back into my face."

"Make it look like a clothesline," he shouted.

I attached the tails of the rats, one by one, to the cord, leaving about three inches between two. Then I strung up the cord, one end fastened to the outside door handle of the exterior door, the other end to the guardrail of the platform. It looked like a clothesline all right! Schubert laughed his head off. When he noticed my dubious look, he assured me, "Don't worry. I'll take the responsibility for this prank. We have to have some fun once in a while."

Going back inside the house, I brushed my hands, fingernails and forearms for what seemed to be an hour, like a surgeon before and after surgery. Then I cleaned and oiled my gun. Next I took a refreshing shower, had another bite to eat and wrote a "report" to Wunderlich. It was brief and said, "Lieutenant Commander, sir, order carried out. Rats removed. Six bullets used. Able Seaman Born."

After showing the note to Schubert, I placed it on a side table near an armchair in the living room. It was only 1515 hours when I left the house. Turning around from Molle Gata into Ny Olavskleiv, I strolled down to the harbor, went to a billiards room which I frequented whenever time permitted and played a couple of games with some Norwegians. The place was out of bounds for us, but the Norwegians got used to this oddball German who would drop in twice a week or so, hang his belt and jacket on a wall hook, and play French billiards with them.

When I returned to my quarters, I had the feeling of self-satisfaction, having finished a "productive" day. I was not too sure, however, how Wunderlich would like his new clothesline.

Dietrich Marquart

First Lieutenant Marquart had under his command naval artillery units that were sprinkled over several islands in close proximity to Stavanger. His reputation was that of a "Prussian roughneck," not to be tangled with under any circumstances. Rumors had it that he would exercise a man on boot hill for an hour, with full combat outfit just because the soldier had one unbuttoned button on his jacket. Soldiers were plainly scared of the man.

When I had met him first in 1941 at the officers casino, he did not strike me to be much different than most other officers. He even seemed to be somewhat reserved. But then, the environment could not be compared with boot camp.

During the second half of 1943, some Germans were not so sure anymore who would win the war. Few, of course, dared to discuss the military situation. Our army and motorized divisions had sustained a devastating defeat during the battle of Stalingrad. It became obvious we were sliding downhill, at least temporarily.

The German high command had decided that the average German soldier, no matter to what branch of the armed forces he belonged, needed hardening and upgrading. More pep talks were held by commanding officers than ever, and military staff training and upgrading was ordered right across the board. It was true that many of us–particularly in the navy–had hardly used a rifle, participated in war games, or had any hand-to-hand combat experience. That was where Marquart came in.

He arrived at our base, bringing with him an equally experienced upgrader and trainer, a drill sergeant who right from the outset successfully antagonized everyone including our own master sergeant. He lasted exactly six weeks, then was unceremoniously transferred to Germany. As soon as he had left, we had a ball celebrating his transfer. If he landed at the front, we mused, his muscles would have to be much bigger and reflexes faster than his mouth in order to survive.

In the meantime, Marquart was told by Commander Schmidt to tone down. In mid-August 1943, about two weeks after I had met Werner Boes, Schmidt called me over to his on-base small residence, which was situated right beside the administration barrack. "Sit down," he said, as soon as I had entered his lounge room. He went through the archway which led to the kitchen, took a couple of Holsten beers out of the refrigerator, and returned with two beer glasses in the other hand. My eyebrows raised, which he noticed right away. We were not allowed to have any alcoholic beverages before the evening.

"It's all right," he assured me, "nobody is watching. Karl Rust is going on annual leave soon. You know, we picked him to be Lieutenant Marquart's orderly. He is short, unassuming and a good-natured fellow who carried out his duties to Marquart's satisfaction. ('He also is the sharpest card player in the company,' flashed through my mind.) I want you to replace him. You know the entire officer corps and get along well with everybody, not counting the incident with Engineer Walters two years ago."

"I shall do my best, Herr Kapitaenleutnant," I replied. We chatted a few more minutes, finishing our beer. Then he got up and said, "Let's see Marquart now. He should be in his quarters. By the way, the reason your name is not on the list for military upgrading is this assignment. This will be followed by several other details until November, when you will be reassigned to the officers casino."

We walked over to the administration building, where Marquart had his quarters, went in, and Schmidt told him the reason for the visit. Mildly surprised, I took Marquart's outstretched hand, squeezing it like a lemon. In this case–I guess, to prove a point–I put some extra effort in it, though I had been told before that my handshake was vicious. I pretended not to notice when I saw the astonished quick wince on his face before he withdrew his hand.

It was arranged that I should meet with Karl Rust two days before he would commence his furlough, so as to be made familiar with daily duties and routines. It seemed to be an easy task. If I kept up-to-date, it should not take more than three hours per day. Cooking was not involved. Twice a week I would have to go to town, once to the laundry, the other day for doing some other chores.

The day before Karl left, Marquart summoned me over to his quarters. "I want to give you a few pointers," he declared. "I have trouble getting up in the morning. Since I have to be on the exercise grounds by 0745 it is imperative that you get me out of bed, by hook or by crook, at the latest by 0645 hours. Remember that! Breakfast is at 0705 hours, which you will fetch from the company kitchen in time. After I have left, clear up the mess here and clean both rooms.

"You will get a special daytime pass twice per week. Rust explained that to you. Occasionally, I shall call upon you in the evening, should I have visitors to entertain. Otherwise you are free to do what you want, unless the sergeant-at-arms needs you to temporarily replace somebody. Clear?"

"Absolutely, sir," I replied. "I'll make sure you have sufficient time to prepare yourself in the morning."

This being summer, I did not have to worry about the space heater Marquart had. In winter, it had to be cleaned out early in the morning, around 0545 hours, set, and lit.

I tried to give some thought to how I could best get Marquart up in the morning, and devised a plan that should be foolproof, although somewhat dangerous.

The first morning came. I entered the room on the first day quietly; on the second I slammed the door right against the wall. There were no door stoppers. He just grunted and continued to sleep. Approaching his bed, I shook one shoulder; another grunt. Then I simply took his bedspread and stripped it off to his ankles, shouting, "It is time to get up, sir."

He halfway opened his eyes and moaned, "Leave me alone, you damn dog."

Since that had not produced any results, I thought "You have to resort to drastic measures."

The door was about four steps away from the bed. I opened it quietly, tiptoed to his bed, a large salad bowl full of water in hand, and emptied quickly the contents over his head and shoulders. Dashing out the door, trying to close it in the process, I heard the heavy thud of a boot hitting the door panel, mixed with Marquart's loud curses. It was now 0645 hours. "*Befehl ausgefuehrt* (Order carried out)," I murmured to myself, satisfied with the achievement.

As I walked over to the company kitchen, however, I began to have second thoughts, mulling over the possible consequences of my action. I talked myself into believing that not much could happen; I just followed instructions. But I wasn't too sure.

I told Hans Steiner, the man in charge of food preparation and the mess hall, what happened. He threw up his hands. "He will just about kill you when you return," he commented. "This may be as good a time as any to desert," the joker added.

Balancing the breakfast tray with steaming coffee in my left hand, returning to his quarters, I cautiously opened Marquart's door and saw his reflection in the wall mirror, shaving. "Is it safe to come in?" I asked sheepishly.

"Of course. Why not?" was his counter-question. Then he turned to me, smiling broadly, "You have nerve and a hell of a way of waking somebody up! Don't dare tell anybody that you got away with it. It ruins my reputation."

"Of course not, sir," I assured. "Maybe one day, when I write my memoirs, it will appear." (That took me forty-five years.)

Another first was coming. He quite politely apologized for having treated me so roughly. He also thanked me for having made sure he would be out there on that whetstone, as he called it. Needless to say, I did not have to repeat the last step of the wake-up procedure. All it took was touching him lightly on one shoulder and saying in a normal tone of voice, "Lieutenant, sir, get up. It is 0615 hours." He would make a defending gesture with one hand, remove the bedspread and roll out of bed. No more "back talk."

My comrades, who would ask me how things were going with the "lion tamer," did not quite believe me when I answered, "Fine, no problem," until one day when one chap came up to my quarters one evening, asking for help. He had done miserably during training exercises and misunderstood an order. That had caused some confusion among the group and angered Marquart. The man was listed to report for punitive exercises after dinner hours the next day.

"You are looking after the man," he said, "and have told us you have no problem with him. Is there anything you can do or think of? The man is hard like granite. He doesn't care if we collapse and I am really scared."

"I am not a miracle worker," I said. "But let me see whether I can think of something. I will let you know by dinner-time tomorrow." I marked down his barrack code and room number. The rest of the evening I spent mulling over that situation. I did not want to become too brave, but on the other hand, I felt sorry for the guy. Finally, an idea had settled in my mind. Activating one of my philosophies, I reminded myself that unusual problems require unusual solutions.

The following morning, after Marquart had finished his breakfast and left, I took his appointment book out of a drawer. One of my tasks was to follow up on his appointments, military and private, sometimes making arrangements on his behalf and bringing these to his attention at appropriate times.

Nothing was entered for that day. Chances were he had not looked at it, as he relied on me. I walked over to the phone and dialed his girlfriend's number at her place of work. I had met her a few times. She seemed to be the kind of woman one could count on. I was correct. When I had explained the situation to her, she immediately agreed with my suggestion to set up a phony rendezvous at 1900 hours that evening at her place. I made an entry in his appointment book and placed it in the drawer.

Marquart habitually changed his boots before driving with Schmidt to the officers casino for luncheon. As he came in, I casually reminded him of his rendezvous tonight. He jerked his head around and asked, "What rendezvous?"

"With Sonja, Herr Oberleutnant, tonight," I replied. He looked kind of dumbfounded for a moment, then said, "I have no time tonight. I must straighten out one of your pals who loused up a few things yesterday."

"You cannot possibly be serious," I said. "Stand up Sonja? She may not like that, Herr Oberleutnant." I shoved the appointment book under his nose, while he put on his second boot.

Glancing at it, he said, "That is not my handwriting."

I quickly lied. "You told me to make a note about this some time ago. Why don't you call Sonja?"

He did. Replacing the receiver back on the cradle, he decided to postpone the punitive exercises to the next evening.

"Go the rest of the way," I told myself, trying to talk him out of it altogether. I emphasized how sorry and scared the poor guy was. Unexpectedly, he consented easily.

"You tell him," he ordered, "under the condition that he does not foul up things again. Since you deserve the credit for that cancellation, you might as well tell him so. That will boost your ego and at the same time will increase the admiration your pals have for your not being afraid of me. I know. I know," he added, seeing my astonished face. "They all think I eat fire for breakfast. Schmidt couldn't think of anybody else in the Company who wouldn't be scared to take on this detail." It was quite a pleasant surprise for me to hear him say this. He was human after all!

When I gave my comrade the good news shortly before dinner, he cried like a baby for happiness. The news must have flashed through the base like a bush fire. Within ten minutes a whole bunch of chaps entered his quarters, insisting that right after dinner a party be held celebrating the event. Several of them asked me, "How in hell did you fix that?" but I was determined not to leak any details and took the fifth amendment, as you American readers would say. As for me, I had the satisfaction that now they believed me when I had said, "Fine, no problem," in answer to their question of how things went with the "lion tamer." I felt very good about the turn of events. Of course, Marquart never found out about the conspiracy between Sonja and me.

THE ADMIRAL

The First Visit

Rear Admiral Von Schrader was the commanding naval officer of the Norwegian west coast. The first time I met him was in March 1942. It had taken the Abwehr two full months to complete its investigation, in reference to the "embarrassing situation" which had made it possible for Norwegians serving with the British forces, to spend the Christmas and New Year's holidays with their families at home, right under our noses, undetected. Commanding officers from all strategic western coastal areas were summoned to Stavanger. The purpose of this meeting was to study and discuss the report and the appendixed recommendations made for possible future prevention of such incidences.

As soon as word was out, the admiral's room was reinspected and made ready for his occupancy. Heinz Marzi told me, "You will look after the Admiral, Siegfried. You had better give it all you've got, because he doesn't want to deal with people who produce mediocre results. *Sei auf Draht*." (A military expression for "be on the ball," but literally meaning "be on the wire.")

I was mentally prepared for that assignment since it was barely three months ago during our arrival at the casino, that we were told that Otto or I would have to look after "the old man." I also remembered the chaos he could create among the officer corps, since most members were scared stiff of him.

When I first saw him, I could not understand how such a little, five foot five somewhat stocky man could be feared that much by so many. (Have we not all made the mistake of underestimating short people?) But he was a strict disciplinarian and a stickler for details, leaving no room for variations. His early morning bathwater, I was told, had to be thirty-seven degrees Celsius on the nose.

While carrying his two pieces of luggage to his room, he explained when he wanted to be awakened and what his bath temperature had to be, not knowing I had been briefed in advance. Then he asked me about the usual breakfast time.

"Under normal circumstances, all officers are free to come and go between 0715 and 0830 hours," I answered not too diplomatically. "But with you here, sir, Commodore Mayer-Pantin will likely set a firm time." Realizing what I had said, I hurriedly added, "After consultation with you, of course, Herr Admiral!"

"Who else has access to this room?" he asked.

"Only the chief steward, Heinz Marzi, and I, sir."

"O.K., keep it that way; no housekeeper during my stay here. You look after my clothing, making sure all my decorations are pinned on straight. Prepare the bath in the morning, 0715 sharp, clean up after me, and shine my shoes. I want them highly polished. Makes no difference how you do it, but I have to see my reflection in them." He looked down at my oxfords. "Like yours," he added. I was tempted but did not dare tell him about the definitive answer for shining shoes, which that chap in Kiel had demonstrated to me.

As I listened to the way he talked, I found his choice of words quite good, but his diction was staccato-like, propelling out words like bullets from an automatic weapon. The dialect was unmistakably that of a *Berliner Grossschnauze* (Berlin big-mouth). As an apology to my Berliner friends and in fairness to them, their behavior seems to indicate that they have to have the upper hand. On the other side of the coin, they are not afraid of the devil.

Once I knew them, I found them quite reliable and not at all capable of stepping over dead bodies in order to reach their goals. At times, I found them equally sentimental to the Rhinelanders.

Since I was not present during the two-day meetings that took place, I cannot report on them. However, by the behavior of the officer corps, I could tell they were no picnic. On both mornings, while Von Schrader had his bath, officers would come to see me in droves, inquiring "What is the admiral's mood today?" I could well understand that they were walking around with some kind of collective guilt feelings. They all were involved with security measures in some shape or form, though the ultimate responsibility for the safety of the coast fell on the shoulders of those making up the high command.

When the conference was over, it seemed a threatening cloud had been removed. While everyone suffered from some kind of mass tension psychosis during the Admiral's presence a big change in the overall atmosphere took place immediately after he had left the scene. It had changed from doom to joyfulness.

Even Von der Knesebrecht, who did not avoid wild horses, voiced some concern when he chatted with me about those tension-filled days. He came to the pantry after this was over and chatted with me informally, as he did from time to time. "Boy," he said, "am I ever glad to still have my head screwed onto my body." He very likely was not the only one who felt that way. But I could well understand his remark, since his major task was to protect, defend, and camouflage our naval forces.

The Inspection Tour

After my return from the Arctic in August 1944, Wunderlich called me to his office. "The Commandant wants to talk to you right now," he announced. "It's about a one-week free trip, but Commodore Mayer-Pantin will explain the details to you," putting me in suspense. Never on the defensive, I was curious but not worried.

When we entered the Commodore's office, a young-looking major from the army jerked himself out of a chair and introduced himself as the coordinator for military inspection tours. He was officially stationed at Hitler's supreme headquarters and, like his boss, sported the same (to my taste) ridiculous-looking *Fliegenschneuzer* (slang for the type of mustache, which was grown only underneath the nostrils, meaning fly-mustache).

Mayer-Pantin explained that Admiral Von Schrader was going to hold an inspection tour along most of the Norwegian coastline and had requested my presence aboard as steward. "This time," he continued, "the inspection tour will be out of the ordinary. The express boat *Stavanger II* will be used. Invited guests are high-ranking officers of the armed forces, secret service, and other arms of political circles. Have a look at this list. That will give you an idea. He handed me a watermarked sheet, headed with the logo of the Fuehrer's *Hauptquartier* (Hitler's Supreme Headquarters). I stared at it. It looked like a draft made from "Who is Who."

It read: General Jodl, supreme commander of all German forces in Norway; Reichskommissar Terboven, high commissioner of Norway; Wernher Von Braun, chief designer and advisor for the V-One and V-Two rocket projects; Adolf Axmann, deputy of Baldur Von Schierach, leader of the German Hitler Youth; Vidkun Quisling, leader of the Norwegian Nazi party (whose name became synonymous with "traitor" in the eyes of all those opposing Nazism). In 1933, he had founded the Nasjonal Samling (National Unity) party and in 1940 encouraged Hitler to invade Norway. While I was still in Norway, he was sentenced to death on my twenty-third birthday, 17 September 1945, and executed at Akershus Castle in Oslo on 24 October of the same year; Von Gallant, former air marshal and now inspector general of the German Luftwaffe, a most outstanding fighter pilot, whom Hitler grounded personally for fear of losing the man. Von Gallant had over two hundred shutdowns to his credit; Admiral Hans G. Friedeburg, who later in May 1945, was given authority by Gross Admiral Karl Doenitz to offer to Montgomery the surrender of the German forces in northern Germany, Schleswig-Holstein, Denmark and Holland; Colonel Gerhart Wiese, coordinator for German intelligence services. The same man who in 1936 served as Heydrich's aide and became involved in the passing on to Stalin the "phony" insurrection papers. (See "Destroy the Enemies of the People" *The Phony Insurrection, Blitz-History 1919-1941.*)

Alfred Rosenberg, Hitler's race ideologist, himself a half-Jew from Hungary. He stirred up hate against Jews, whom he stamped as the "inferior race," while displaying Germanic races as superior to others; Julius Streicher, Rosenberg's pal, publisher of *Der Stuermer*, the hate-all-Jews newspaper, and whose only mandate was to depict Jews as antisocial elements and former exploiters of the German people. The total insensitivity of that propaganda newspaper is unsurpassed in history; Adolf Eichmann, chief administrator and overseer of the procurement of Jews to solve the Jewish question. He was considered to be the arch henchman, responsible for the systematic extermination of millions of Jews in concentration camps. (Brought to Israel by Nazi hunters from South America, Buenos Aires, in May 1960, he was found guilty of war crimes against humanity, sentenced to death and hanged in May 1967.)

The last three men struck me as particularly sinister individuals. They had found each other! There were fifteen more names on the list: four administrative members from the military high command of the armed forces; two members of military intelligence; two representatives of the Abwehr, whose names were fictitious, I was informed later; two military strategists, acting as liaisons between the OKW (*Oberkommando der Wehrmacht*–High Command of the Armed Forces) and Hitler's supreme headquarters; two members of the military clergy; two political indoctrinators, representing Dr. Goebbels; one representative of the justice department in Berlin. None of their names, however, rang a bell with me.

When I was finished reading, Mayer-Pantin added, "By the way, Admiral Von Schrader specifically asked for you to serve as steward during the trip which will last about one week." I must have made an impression with the old man, I thought. "I know that is a lot of people to serve for one person. But the Admiral doesn't want to have anybody else around.

"You are to report to Commanding Officer Fribert tomorrow to draw food provisions. The ship's cook has drafted a list. I know I can depend on you." He got up from his chair to indicate the end of the meeting. I saluted him and his visitor and proceeded to the door. "And remember," he added, before I reached it, "any conversation you might overhear during the voyage must stay with you alone!"

Harald Fribert was an unusual man, to say the least. He had served twelve years with the merchant marine when drafted in 1940. Because of his previous experience and his excellent navigational skills, his promotions from petty officer second class to commanding officer came fast. However, he had been demoted several times. A totally independent kind of guy, he had some difficulties following orders. When he disagreed with a method, he just disregarded instructions and went ahead as he saw fit. He also went AWOL a few times.

Not to embarrass the admiral, one day prior to my reporting to Fribert, he had been hastily promoted for the third time from chief petty officer to commanding officer, a jump of five ranks. Such was his reputation as a seafaring expert that even when demoted the *Stavanger II* remained under his command.

I got to know him well during the trip. He was the epitome of a *Kumpel* (military expression for a great pal), and as reliable as anybody could be. If you had him at your side, it was like having a guardian angel. Never stressing authority, he practiced teamwork at its best, to such a degree that his men would think of him as belonging to the crew.

When I reported to the tall, lanky, and dark-skinned man, he shook my hand with the same firmness I did. I immediately had the impression I was dealing with a man who calls a spade a spade—my kind of person.

He let me have a look at the provision list. We made a few minor changes, knowing how many would participate in the voyage and also to make sure we would not run short of food supplies. This was something I always followed later in life during my years as food and beverage service executive.

We had four crewmen with us to carry the food supplies to the pier. It did not surprise me a bit that Fribert had removed his jacket and helped load the lorry and unload the stuff at the pier. His men seemed to be used to it. The whole way of communicating with each other was based on overall cooperation and friendliness, totally unmilitaristic but clearly infectious as far as I was concerned.

Before the war, the *Stavanger II* had been used for short fjord trips and could accommodate about sixty passengers. She would cruise through one of Ryfylke's most beautiful island areas, a day's trip, starting in the morning and returning late at night.

The German Navy converted her to a speedboat, equipped her with a three hundred-horsepower diesel motor, capable of doing forty plus knots per hour. A fine boat she was. Even after having spent only a week aboard, I felt very much attracted to her. Later on I took every opportunity I had to visit her and the crew whenever she had thrown anchor at Skagenkaien or, at times, at Strandkaien, on the starboard side when entering Stavanger Harbor inlet.

The voyage took us from Stavanger, north to Haugesund and Bergen, where the Admiral had his headquarters, then via Aalesund and Kristiansund to Trondheim. But we made altogether twenty-one stops; ten on the way to Trondheim and eleven on the return trip. It was certainly one of the most scenic voyages I ever made; simply unforgettable!

We visited the Ryfylke Islands, Hardangerfjorden, Sognefjorden, Nordfjord, Storfjorden, and the islands of Smøla, Hitra and Frøya west of Trondheim, as well as a number of out ports along the way.

Naturally, I was curious what this inspection tour was all about. From bits and pieces of conversations I overheard during serving breakfasts, luncheons and dinners, the purpose of this voyage became clear. In 1943, our armed forces had suffered terrible defeats at Stalingrad, where General Paulus surrendered his entire army to the Soviets rather than let them die to the last man. Hitler promptly sentenced Paulus to death in absentia, who in retaliation let himself be used by the Soviets as a mouthpiece, calling for the surrender of other commanding officers and their troops to end this senseless slaughter.

Field Marshal Erwin Rommel, probably the most popular German military leader Germany had at the time, could not stem the persistent attack of the Allied Forces in Africa. El Alamein fell. From then on in, everything seemed to go downhill. In July of that year, the Allies invaded Sicily and overthrew Mussolini. The systematic eradication of German cities by British and American bomber squads demanded its toll, not only in human lives, but also as far as the morale of the German populace went.

By August 1944, even the most useful idiot who had dutifully believed the propaganda of Dr. Goebbels for years knew that something had not worked as the Fuehrer had planned.

Goebbels, however, kept twiddling about the new *Wunderwaffen* (miracle weapons) which would turn the war around again in our favor. Since fools never die, some actually believed in this baloney until the Allies literally knocked at their doors!

After the ill-fated attempt on Hitler's life on 20 July 1944, military and political hard-liners were determined to fight to the last man. Hitler himself proclaimed a policy of *verbrannte Erde* ("burnt earth," meaning the accomplishment of total destruction of everything in sight, before surrendering to the enemy).

Some of Hitler's cronies advised the search for a geographical area which, in case of extreme emergency, could be used as the last fortress of the third Reich. What could be better suited than Norway? Nobody remembered who first had suggested that country, but it already had served as a natural fortress for us, with her tremendous coastline and rugged mountains. It could be successfully defended against attacks from the west, as it remained an extremely hard nut to crack. There was no danger from the east, since Sweden would continue to be true to her neutrality.

And so the group aboard the *Stavanger II* was given the mandate to assess the situation and make appropriate recommendations in due time.

I had met two members of the group before: Adolf Axmann, Deputy Fuehrer of the Hitler Youth, in 1941 during a mass meeting in Düsseldorf; and Colonel Gerhart Wiesel, who in 1943 described events to me that led to the liquidation of Marshal Tukhachevski and the murder of many Russian Army leaders and most political commissars by Stalin. (See *Blitz-History 1919-1941.*)

In between meals the two of them occasionally engaged me in conversation. Axmann, when drilling me about the Hitler Youth, looked sort of shocked when I told him point-blank that I thoroughly disliked it, but I added that I enjoyed being in the navy.

Wiesel and I had more in common. He filled me in on a few more episodes which he was free to talk about. I did not take notes, but they would fill a nice pamphlet of cloak-and-dagger stories.

When he heard I was going to be detailed to naval intelligence soon, he commented, "I am sure you will enjoy that kind of work and find it most interesting, that is, as long as you don't have to be a cat's paw like those field operators. Don't be surprised, though, when reports you receive are often quite different from what is openly said." I was about to find out what he meant by that!

THE MISSING GUARD

The Missing Guard

The protection of all waterways and surrounding areas as well as strategic targets was the navy's job. At the end of May 1943, my name appeared on the guard schedule. That was about two weeks before I was due to leave on my annual furlough. Based on my request, I was placed ahead of schedule for my leave. A comrade of mine was bombed out on 19 May while on vacation. He lived in one part of Wuppertal and I figured, quite correctly, that the other part in which I lived would soon be on the Allies' schedule.

The daily harbor patrol schedule covered the hours between 1800 and 0600. Twelve guards would arrive at 1730 hours at their overnight quarters located on Breigata. Four would be on patrol for two hours, then four hours off. The four would march together from their quarters to the centrally-located pier of a total of ten quays that had to be patrolled. At the beginning of the patrol they would congregate at Steinkarkaien (*kaien* is the Norwegian word for quay), then split up. Two would patrol west along the periphery of Kjeringholmen, Boreviga, Ryfylkekaien, Skansekaien and Skagenkaien, while the other two guards would pass along Ostervagkaien, Jorenholmskaien, Fiskepiren and end up at Bekkhuskaien.

This whole patrol bit was a matter of routine. At first, the timing of these patrols was changed frequently. But soon, this was given up. Nothing ever happened to give cause for concern until my second day of guard duty. The group of four to whom I belonged, was scheduled from 2200 to 2400 hours, and from 0400 to 0600 hours.

When we got ready to meet the previous team at 0400 hours, one man was missing. Nobody seemed to take that seriously. The missing man's partner suggested that his chum probably had already proceeded to the guard quarters. But that was not the case.

The four of us had waited this time at the point of assembly, expecting different orders from the sergeant-at-arms. He divided us so that each man would have to search in a different section of the patrol areas, which included some nearby side streets. I was assigned to a rectangular area south of Fiskepiren, framed by Klubbgata to the west, Pedersgata to the south, Lansgata to the east, and Verksgata to the north and, of course, Fiskepiren itself. The territory could easily be covered within a leisurely twenty minutes.

I decided to have a look at Fiskepiren first, before combing through some side streets. Fiskepiren quay was a rather narrow landing, that stuck out its tongue at Stromstein Straight. I kept myself in the center until, after thirty steps or so, I reached a tin hut, that was used as a toolshed. Its size was about twelve by nine meters, and four meters high.

I had approached the shed slightly from the left, constantly looking around. Then I proceeded to the back of it and around to the other side. Suddenly, my heart pumped overtime. In the approximate center of the wall, a German .42 Carbine was leaning with its front sight against the wall of the hut. A German steel helmet rested on the floor, to the right side of the rifle butt.

Walking around the entire edge of Fiskepiren, I called out my comrade's name but no reply came. Since there was not a set procedure to be followed for such a situation, I first patrolled through some of the neighboring side streets, continually calling out my chum's name. Of course, some people woke up in the process. Seeing me walking around at dawn with rifle fixed, apparently without aim, they shouted down in a clearly irritated mood, condemning this crazy German for the noisy wake-up call. In spite of the unpleasant, if not peculiar situation. I found a comical side to it. Though they clearly must have seen my rifle and steel helmet, they thought I had nipped at the flatman.

When I had completed my unsuccessful search covering more than the usual periphery of the search area, I walked to the point of assembly at Steinkarkaien. The quay was deserted.

I habitually carried a police whistle with me which I now used, blowing three times an SOS in each direction: north, west, south and east. The sound carried well, even across the harbor to old Stavanger, as I found out the next day when talking to a chap who had had a detail in one of our supply houses.

Within eight minutes, everybody arrived. I reported my findings to the sergeant-at-arms. Together we went to the shed on Fiskepiren. The sergeant made a few notes. Then we collected the rifle and the helmet, which I had left exactly as I had found them earlier. In cases of suspected foul play, we had the same instructions as police: do not touch a thing until higher authority arrives.

By now, two hours later, several navy divers were sent out to look for the body while swarms of army MPs made incursions throughout the harbor area and beyond. Orders went out to immediately interrogate any suspected Norwegians collaborating with the Allies. These raids were carried out by experienced field operators of counterintelligence.

Finally, at approximately 1600 hours on the day the search began, one diver found the body of the missing comrade. His uniform had entangled itself between the wooden beams of a frame which ran along one side of the submerged pier.

An army ambulance, which had been standing by from the beginning of the search, brought the body to the military coroner's domain. In cases such as this, the armed forces worked closely together; in other respects, they jealously used to guard their territorial and functional rights. Nothing new, really. Even among company commanders it was quite common to protect their interests just like in the world of private business enterprise.

I have seen cases where inventory figures of weapons and ammunition, for instance, were falsified for the sake of building up supplies, regardless of need. However, I do not claim this to be one of the reasons for Germany having lost the war.

As soon as the body was found and raised, speculation began of what had happened. The actual cause of death would have to be established first: coronary, suicide, accidental, or murder. A number of theories came to light: since the body was submerged in water, a normal coronary attack could not have taken place before the body hit the water. Suicide seemed to be more than unlikely. Why take off the steel helmet, which would have hastened the process of drowning. The placing of the helmet beside the rifle butt certainly was a mystery. Accidental death? Maybe. But assuming while relieving himself he fell into the water, why remove the helmet? And why not urinate against the wall of the shed? Murder? Could be. But would the assassin not have thrown the rifle and the helmet over the pier to delay discovery of the act? A number of unanswered questions remained.

The coroner did not discover any evidence strong enough to indicate violence to the body or from the condition of the deceased's uniform. A slight bump above the right side temple did not prepare the coroner to attribute to an impact by an instrument while the helmet was on. If it took place after the helmet was removed, the swelling would have been much larger, causing internal head bleeding, which was not the case.

When pressed for his personal opinion, the coroner offered a likely theory: the man accidentally fell into the bay water while standing, for some reason or other, at the edge of the ledge of the pier. Supporting this theory was the fact that, according to the man's file, he could not swim.

You may find this to be strange but, contrary to popular beliefs, over two-thirds of naval and mercantile marine personnel could not swim at the time! These figures have improved by now, but not as much as one might expect from seafaring people.

After some lengthy discussions, military authorities decided to treat the incident in dual fashion. Officially declared as murder by the Underground, it would be put on file as "accidental death." The official version could be used to continue interrogations of suspects. Over forty suspected activists were detained for one full week without shedding any light on the matter in question, nor could any pending actions of sabotage be uncovered.

The dead man was married and had three children of grade-school age. Lieutenant Commander Schmidt had the sad task of notifying his relatives. The cause of death was not mentioned, but in the letter of condolence emphasis was placed on the fact that he had fallen for the fatherland, with honor and courage, killed in the line of duty.

Three days after his untimely death, my comrade received a military burial, with me as a member of the honor guard providing the firing of the salute. Death had struck close by. It was not going to be the last time. Soon I would experience the terror of bombings, where thousands of civilians around me would die.

My buddy was put to rest in Stavanger, at Eiganes Gravelund, north of Alexander Kiellands Gate. After the war, the Allies gave me permission to visit my comrade's grave once more before we disbanded our own submarine collection and minesweeper task force base on the Island of Buøy, a few miles off Stavanger.

A HELL OF A FURLOUGH

Getting Ready

Bertold Reiner, my fellow Wuppertaler and soccer player, sent a telegram from home while on leave. The cable arrived on a Friday, 21 May 1943. The message was brief: "Have been completely bombed out on the nineteenth. Request additional leave to assist parents."

Hans Holtzmann from the base administration office told me about it before official announcements were made. Lieutenant Commander Schmidt had immediately granted Bertold another eight days. Something inside me started ticking. Bertold's parents lived in one of two major parts of Wuppertal. What could possibly prevent the Brits and "Amies" from destroying the other part where my parents resided? The same treatment would sooner or later be bestowed upon that population. I discussed this with Hans and, of course, the "mother of the company," the sergeant major. He saw from my file that I was listed for my next (the second) annual leave in September of that year.

"Sergeant Major," I said, "I know I am not due yet for my annual leave. But I have the stony feeling that it won't be long before my parents will face the same fate. If I am at home when it happens, I at least can help them to overcome."

"I'll tell you something," he replied. "To give a square deal to all, we have to compromise. Nobody knows whether your feelings are correct, but I understand your anxiety. Since we are short of harbor patrol manpower, you have to finish your tour of duty first; two weeks, from 31 May through 13 June. We will send you off on the fifteenth. By the eighteenth or nineteenth, you will arrive in Germany. I'll arrange this matter with Lieutenant Commander Schmidt; don't worry." The conversation was ended.

When returning from my harbor patrol duty, I contacted the quartermaster to draw a few new socks and some underwear in exchange for old and rather used ones. The chap in charge of the company canteen had all kinds of connections. So I asked the quartermaster if it was in order to ask the canteen operator to fix me up with a barrel of herring. That could be obtained from Norwegian black marketeers in exchange for Schnapps and tobacco. Since I hardly ever drank and smoked very little, I had accumulated a humble but useful stock. Exchanging that for the barrel of herring took only a day.

Since my navy pay as able seaman lasted just about long enough from pay to pay without enjoying any extravaganzas, I could not afford to buy my mom a Norwegian fur coat. At least, I wanted to bring something home which all could enjoy.

I got a mild shock, though. The barrel weighed over fifty pounds. That on top of my regular gear was quite awkward to tug around.

The navy truck arrived at noon on Tuesday, the fifteenth, already half-full of comrades who, like myself, were headed for home. The trip to the railway station lasted only twelve minutes. At the moment we reached the station the holiday train was being installed. About two hundred soldiers from the armed forces eagerly boarded the train, the usual onlookers noisily wishing *Hals und Beinbruch* (break a leg). A number of Norwegians looked us over, pretending to be curious. I found out in 1944 that all railway stations, ports, and aerodromes were regularly observed by Allied sympathizers, who promptly reported any move we made. In this case, they had an easy task categorizing us as going on furlough by the kind of baggage we carried and the lack of weapons.

The train started moving at 1320 hours. I had to get a window seat. Like the previous year, I wanted to enjoy the wonderful scenery again which a railway journey in Norway offers. I heard from surrounding conversation pieces that most of my buddies were concerned about increasing bombing attacks on German cities. It put a great additional burden on the mind of soldiers who, more often than not, would not know what the next day would bring. Now they also had to worry about their loved ones at home whom they were supposed to protect and defend!

The Trip To Oslo

The journey brought us in a southern direction via Sandness, Bryne and Egersund to Flekkefjord. From there, if my recollection is correct, we had to transfer to navy transport trucks, since the railway tracks ended. German army engineers and construction pioneers (foot soldiers) were busy since 1941, drilling and blasting through a number of huge rocks and mountains, in the attempt to lay railway tracks that would connect Flekkefjord with Kristiansund. That goal was finally reached in February 1944. When my last furlough took place in March 1944, I could stay right in the train from Stavanger to Oslo.

Going by transport truck/busses was not less interesting or less scenic, but it could easily raise the hair on the back of one's head. Looking out the window on one side, one would see high mountains and on the other side precipices that made one dizzy by just looking at them.

In order to complicate matters even further, the roads were made of gravel and were very narrow. Several straight stretches and mountain windings would not allow two motor vehicles to pass each other. I can tell you, most naval personnel did not fear the mighty ocean (in spite of their inability to swim), but they came close to wetting their pants in these mountains. The increase in tension became evident by the mounting body odor, which developed into a stench, defying the most insensitive nostrils.

At the time, deodorant soap or spray had not been invented. Some jokers, in order to hide their own fears would bring out switchblade-knives, asking some co-travelers politely, "May I be permitted to cut the air here?" The answer to the silly question was usually not so polite!

We did arrive safely in Kristiansund, where we were herded into one of these transit bases, which the German armed forces did not only maintain in Germany but also in all occupied countries. We had dinner and hit the sack.

After an early breakfast the following morning, we continued our trip by rail, proceeding steadily in a northeasterly direction, passing major towns such as Arendal, Larvik Sandefjord, Tønsberg, Horten, Drammen (where the beer was made which we consumed on Haon during our basic military training), Asker and Sandvika to Oslo.

I had a pair of opera binoculars with me, which were strong enough to see distant objects clearly. Since I loved nature, I made liberal use of them while traveling. When I stepped out of the train onto the platforms, I took them out. As we left the central station, stopping briefly to be grouped, I focused my glasses to the north, zeroing in on Holmenkollen, one of the finest ski slope areas in Scandinavia, and an all-year resort.

At this time of the year, the mountain did not carry any snow. One would have to go to Trondheim and north of there to find snow-covered ground in June. But I could see some activity on Holmenkollen, though from this distance and vantage point, it looked like a bunch of ants running busily back and forth on an anthill, rather than people moving about.

Interlude
The Holmenkollen Meeting

In late November 1942, I had the privilege and somewhat dubious pleasure of spending a four-day weekend on Holmenkollen. All Norwegian area commanders, deputies and aides were called to a high-level military gathering. Military Intelligence had strongly recommended each commander take security precautions on his own, not necessarily based on any concrete information. But one could bet the Underground (Underground to us; Resistance to the Norwegians) would get wind of this meeting and, if possible, arrange a few unpleasant surprises for us. What an opportunity; that many military commanders under one roof. A great target!

Secret agents from the military Abwehr and the *Sicherheitsdienst* (Civilian Security Service) had already laid the groundwork two days prior to the event. They had arrested and interrogated anybody who appeared to be a security risk. For that reason alone, the upcoming meeting could not be kept secret.

Dr. Carlos Mayer-Pantin, our naval area commandant, picked a couple of riot police method-trained chaps as bodyguards for himself: Captain Baer and (at the time First Lieutenant) Wunderlich, his aide. The latter called me up and said, "Look, Bornchen, we have another special assignment for you. The Commodore will fill you in later. Pack a few things for a few days. which we will spend in Oslo. Report to me at 1100 hours tomorrow, Thursday, 26 November."

When I arrived in the morning, as instructed, I was briefed about the four-day meeting and my role in it. Officially, I was one of the bodyguards, but my role as protector was in a different mode from the other two. I would find out soon enough.

Mayer-Pantin had requisitioned a second limousine for the trip. He occupied his own with Captain Baer, one bodyguard and his driver. We occupied the other car, Wunderlich, the other bodyguard, the driver, and I.

There was some light snow on the ground, but not enough to encumber the trip. Extra caution, however, was in order. Snow tires had not been invented yet. But the ingenious auto mechanic, who had our navy truck specially equipped when Heinz Marzi and I went on that bartering trip across Rogaland in May had come through again. His workshop had turned out conical metal studs with spiked ends, which he had inserted in all tires of the two cars. As we were about to experience, without these, we would have gotten stuck on our return trip, very likely more than once.

Upon arrival at Holmenkollen, the two bodyguards and I were introduced to the man in charge of security. He received us in his suite at the main building of the hotel, which functioned as the nerve center of the security operation.

Though in civilian clothes, graying hair left no doubt about his military background. He introduced himself as Colonel Entdecker, MGD (Military Secret Service, similar to OSS and MI-Six), and coordinated all security aspects between the three military intelligence branches and counterintelligence.

"What an appropriate name the man has," I thought. His name Entdecker means "discoverer" in German.

"We want to be sure, gentlemen," he began somewhat formally, "that nothing unpleasant happens during this conference. Abwehr has already taken numerous precautions during the last several days by interrogating a number of suspects. Some are being retained in protective custody, until after the meeting."

He turned to the two bodyguards. "You will receive civilian clothes," he explained, "and accompany your commandant and his entourage at all times." Turning to me, he continued. "And you will be outfitted with a tuxedo, acting as maitre d'hotel. But there is more than that. In conjunction with the banquet chef, who is one of ours, the two of you will make darn sure nobody gets poisoned. All preparation and service personnel, most of whom are Norwegian civilians, have been carefully screened, but one never knows!

"To be on the safe side, you are going to taste a sample of each course before it is served." (As if this was an ordinary request, I did not drop an eyelid. But it flashed through my mind, "By gosh, just like in the Middle Ages when food tasters had to poison themselves to save their masters and when messengers of bad news got shot!")

"You must act as normal as possible. I am sure you have tasted food many times before?"

"Yes, sir," I replied cheerfully, "though not under these circumstances. What if I poison myself?"

"We have a group of medical experts standing by who would take over and apply antidotes." What a relief, I tried to kid myself, keeping up my positive thinking.

The question of other security precautions came up. The colonel explained that, on the outside, a low profile would be maintained. Only a handful of uniformed personnel would formally guard the buildings. Besides, several contingents of agents would be inconspicuously sprinkled over the entire mountain area. In between meals I could spend my time as I wished.

Always eager to learn more about different types of hotel operations, I snooped around, observing front-of-the-house procedures, with which I was not nearly as familiar as with the food and beverage division.

On Sunday, 29 November, the third day of the meeting, I managed to talk to Eklund, the general manager of Holmenkollen. His services had been maintained by request of Vidkun Quisling, the Norwegian Nazi leader, since he considered Eklund one of his loyal followers. The Germans agreed, with the stipulation that two other key positions be filled by persons who had proven their loyalty to them. (Eklund would play a fundamentally different role from the one Quisling expected. But that is another story altogether.)

The Colonel had arranged for me the meeting with Eklund. Eklund came out of his office when I was announced and politely ushered me to his office with a formal arm movement. As soon as I had sat down, he selected another armchair beside mine, rather than sitting behind his desk. I immediately felt closer to him than I would have felt if the desk had divided us. That experience was a first for me. It taught me that a desk can be like a dividing wall. I did not forget this and later on in life when I became an executive myself, made liberal use of moving away from behind the desk and sitting with my visitors, which often resulted in good human relations. As my Indian friends say, "You live and learn."

We conversed in German. Eklund was quite fluent. At one point during the conversation he groped for the word *Empfangshalle* (reception hall). We had done away with that term some time ago and uniformly replaced it around Europe with the French word reception. As I was about to help him find that definition, I distinctly heard him using the English term "reception." It was followed by an embarrassing look on his face, like the look of a boy who got caught stealing apples. I immediately came to his rescue and said quickly, "If it is easier for you, Mr. Eklund, we can continue in English since I cannot speak your language."

With a surprised look but visibly relieved, he replied, "Your government does not allow us to address you in the language of your enemies."

"I know," I replied. "But, first of all, I offer this to you, which is equally disapproved of by my superiors. Second, if you do not have any listening devices planted in your hotel, who is to know?" His facial expression did not change to indicate that I had indirectly hit on a nerve, which would come to light much later.

He gave me a tour through all departments. A pneumatic tube system had been installed recently which, as he explained, had considerably increased the speed with which messages could be passed between departments.

Eklund had brought in from Sweden another innovation, a system that worked on electric impulses, allowing the front desk personnel to wake up hotel guests without the use of a telephone.

Years later, Conrad Hilton adopted and improved the system for use in his American hotels. It was developed into an electronic communication system located at the front desk. It included a room status indicator which would tell the room clerk at a glance whether each room was occupied, vacated to be made up, or changed for reoccupancy. In conjunction with the executive housekeeper, the front desk personnel would also be advised, by a color-coded signal where chambermaids were engaged in making up rooms. These electronic communication systems provided an excellent steppingstone for the computerized systems in use today.

Otherwise, there were no surprises. In the back of the house, the professional term referring to food and beverage preparation and service, table service personnel was not allowed to enter food production areas, but rather picked up their food orders at different wickers between kitchens and dining rooms like in all European countries. For several reasons, this arrangement is superior to that used on the North American continent, particularly from the point of view of control. I hasten to add that in other respects, the organizational structure of the hospitality field is exemplary here.

At the end of his guided tour through the facilities, Eklund offered to show me the different ski slopes. I took a rain check for the next day when the meeting would wind down after luncheon. I thanked him for his time and got ready for the next "food tasting session," hoping for no ill affects.

The next morning I awoke with the pleasant thought that this food nibbling assignment would be over soon. The assistant chef for the banquets, one of our plants who knew about my role, had pulled my leg before each meal. He told everybody who cared to listen how a guy like I could stay so slim while eating like a wolf. The truth is, I ate less proportionally while nibbling than if I sat down for luncheon or dinner. To be used as a guinea pig for the protection of others did not help one bit, of course.

Since not everyone in the kitchen could be observed at all times, the whole procedure came darn close to comparing it with Russian Roulette: I did not know what would hit me when!

Early afternoon Eklund went with me to visit some slopes. The layout was marvelous! There was something for everyone: short jumps, high jumps, gentle slopes for beginners and vicious-looking giant slaloms. One area was cordoned off in preparation for the upcoming winter ski competition to take place between the middle of December and early January. Obviously, a downhill obstacle run was put in readiness.

Eklund offered to borrow skis for me. I had never been once on those "wooden boards" and must have looked kind of dubious on such an event. Not wanting to appear chicken, I agreed after some hesitation, proclaiming my ignorance of the sport. "Don't worry,"

Eklund declared, "we'll get a ski instructor to show you the fundamentals before we send you downhill." He was kidding, knowing it took quite a few hours of training before one could even move on those boards.

The basic training workout tired me out. But at the end of two hours, I heard myself declaring that I was now ready to glide down the hill. Olof, the instructor, agreed to my chagrin. Selecting a gradual and easy slope, we went down in (I had the feeling) slow motion, ending up at the bottom of the slope with an almost elegant curve. I felt exhilarated and proud. Though there was some brush and a few trees on the way down, I had not veered off course once and had avoided these natural obstacles. By the end of the day I had accepted an open invitation by Eklund to return to Holmenkollen anytime.

Early Tuesday morning we departed for our return trip to Stavanger. It was then, during some icy sections in the mountains, that we recognized the blessing of the metal studs which in all probability protected us from serious injury, if they did not save our lives.

Mayer-Pantin did not forget the mechanic responsible for the safety feature. He awarded the man a personal commendation and granted him additional leave of absence.

The Oslo Adventure

I pocketed my binoculars and followed the group on its way to the travel transit base. Arriving there, we were told that our group had originally been scheduled to be transported via ferry from Oslo to Frederickshavn, Denmark. But we had to be rerouted, which would mean a one-day stay in Oslo. A reason for the change of plan was not given.

The base was bursting. After dinner, we each received an extra (generous) Kr 20 pocket money for the one-day delay. That was equivalent to almost six days' pay, since we regularly drew Kr 32 every ten days. We also received a pass until 0100 hours, two hours longer than the usual 1100 hour deadline.

One chap from the army, who was stationed in Sandvika, west of Oslo, started talking about "that marvelous whorehouse we have here in Oslo." Suddenly, everyone pointed their ears. What people have least of, they usually talk about most. With us, girls and sex were conversation pieces number one and two.

Several pals bombarded with questions the guy who had made the statement. There was not one city or an occupied area where one Bordello existed. The man from Sandvika explained, "The place has been in operation for about one year now and is located not too far from here. It is strictly supervised by the military. The girls, all French, have weekly health checkups. You cannot get the clap there; I guarantee it!"

Our curiosity rose. It did not take longer than a few minutes for twenty-some guys to elect the chap from Sandvika to be our guide. If nothing else, it seemed worthwhile to have a look at the place.

We collected our passes and left for our destination shortly after 2100 hours. There was plenty of time, we were told by our leader, since the place would stay open until 0200 hours for those who had extended one-day passes.

When reaching the street in question–too sensitive to mention its name here–we already saw a long line from a distance. "By golly," one soldier worried, "it looks as if we'll have to wait for hours to get in."

"Not to worry," was the leader's reply. "The guards all know me. I am a regular here. Besides, the girls all have time limits, and there are over thirty of them."

The line was about twenty steps long. Anton, our guide, motioned us to follow. He marched to the front of the line with determination, as if this was routine. Some in the line started yelling, "What is this? Do you need a cane? The end of the line is down there."

"We know that," our leader replied, "but we all have appointments; sorry guys."

With this he shook hands with one of the two guards stationed at the entrance, who immediately opened the outside double doors leading into the lobby, which was fancier than any hotel I had ever seen—wooden wall panels, chandeliers, wine-red carpets, sparkling mirrors on the walls, the works.

We checked our weapons and belts with the checkroom attendants, who were soldiers. A chap beside me murmured, relieved, "At least we don't have to tip these birds here. I wonder how long my money will last here in this fancy whorehouse."

The second set of doors led directly into the main room which gave the impression of an oversized but well-appointed living room. Furniture, velvet-covered walls, window drapes, all matched in good taste. Some lady decorators must have lent their hands by advising management well to achieve an air of elegance, yet combining it with a homelike atmosphere.

The only displeasing factor was the air. Without the benefit of a decent air-exchange, and this being summer, a lot of perspiring bodies congregating in a confined space made it smelly and heavy. A variety of different perfumes worn by the girls sitting and cruising about did not help the situation either. A cloud of tobacco smoke circulated around steadily. The smell was not much better than in a sportsmen's locker room, with a bunch of sweaty socks piled up in one corner. It took me several minutes to dare breathe normally. There was no choice.

I counted only eight empty seats in this room, though there was an archway leading to another somewhat smaller room. I jokingly asked Anton, who stood beside me, whether those of us who would not find any seats could sit on the floor with girls in our laps. But he did not bite and said only, "Just wait a few minutes."

It was then that I noticed three soldiers wearing identity stickers, going from table to table, after which most soldiers would retreat with their girls to the back of the room. A few others would just leave through the door we had just entered. Anton, seeing the quizzical look on my face, explained, "Some of these guys have overstayed their welcome here. They either have to pick a girl and go upstairs, or they have to leave. Your entrance ticket is time-stamped for that reason. This is a business like any other; money has to change hands."

He turned around and said, "Each of you owe me Kr 1. I gave these two guards outside Kr 20." By the time he had collected his money, we split up and occupied the seats that had now become vacant.

I took a seat against the wall with a good view over the main room and part of the adjoining room beyond the archway. My table companions were mixed, so to say: a noncom from the air force, a stocky army gunner, and another navy man like myself, a leading seaman. That made me second-lowest in rank, but nobody was going to pull rank here anyway.

As I found out, the girls rotated as call girls and table servers. Several rumors had it that they were making such a pile of money that they could go home in a few years and retire. In any case, they were shapely and quite attractive, as one would expect in a place like this. Most of them were between twenty and thirty years of age and I must say, their overall manners were much better than one would expect.

A tall, shapely blond took our order. The place carried almost any drink one could think of, including mixed or stirred drinks most of my comrades had never heard of. In anticipation of drawing a blank, I ordered a grasshopper. Was I in for a surprise. The girl promptly returned with the drink as ordered, three parts each of green cream de menthe, white cream de cacao and forty percent cream, correctly shaken with ice and served in a European tulip-shaped champagne glass. It cost me a hefty Kr 4; hefty in comparison to all other drinks listed on the beverage list. Served me right, showoff!

Five minutes or so went by, then I noticed one of the "eunuchs" in uniform pointing four girls to our table. The noncom and I got up from our seats as the girls reached our table. Two unceremoniously placed themselves in the laps of the army gunner and the leading seaman. The other two took the only two empty seats beside the noncom and me.

Not to be outdone by me, the showoff, the noncom offered to buy the girls a drink, which was accepted without hesitation and without protest by the rest of us. As it turned out, the noncom was well-heeled from home. His parents sent him money on a regular basis to make military life more pleasant for him. Some have it made under any circumstances, but can money buy everything?

We chatted with the girls, making polite and somewhat awkward conversation, even though it mostly consisted of small talk. The girls pretended to be interested in us. They asked all kinds of questions about our personal lives.

The drinks were not finished yet when the stocky army gunner's ears had turned fire red from excitement. I had noticed him shifting from one butt to the other, obviously having difficulties keeping the girl balanced in his lap. Suddenly, he announced, "I don't know about you guys, but I cannot stand it anymore; I have to proceed to the next act." With this, he lifted the girl off his lap, and wormed himself out of the chair, heading toward the back of the room, dragging the girl with him.

The red-haired girl to my right glanced at me expectantly, but I pretended not to notice. A few minutes of embarrassing silence went by; then the other two couples got up simultaneously and left me alone with the redhead. "Now what?" I asked myself. I had no experience in dealing with situations like this, and almost regretted joining this expedition. It wasn't that I did not like my female companion; on the contrary, not only was she quite attractive, but she also had a pleasant personality. As our previous conversation indicated, she was a knowledgeable person which, in my book, was an important trait as well.

We finished our drinks and, pulling myself together, I asked her in a matter-of-fact voice, "Shall we?" My heartbeat seemed to double up, after that courageous invitation. Without answering, she quickly took my hand and we both got up. Stepping beside her in the direction of the archway, I motioned with my free hand to one of the "eunuchs" close by, indicating our departure. The table now could be sold again, who knew, for the umpteenth time.

Walking through the archway, we entered the second room which was smaller than the one we had left and had a completely different decor, but equally in good taste.

Two-thirds of the distance to the left of the room, close to a flight of stairs leading to the upper floors, an oak table was situated. Two stern-faced people sat behind it, a matronly woman in army dress and a bullish-looking sergeant, who reminded me of a lion tamer I once met in a circus in Wuppertal. My lady companion had pressed a card in my hand before we reached the table and said, "See you upstairs?" and left. It sounded like a half-question.

The matron looked up and asked me, "Straight sex?" I was perplexed, but only for a short moment. "Of course," I answered, "or is there anything else?"

She shrugged her shoulders, stretched out her hand and said, "Kr 8." I started to wonder what she would have charged if my answer had turned out differently.

Playing dumb, I fished for some bills in my side pocket, while remarking with exaggerated astonishment, "Up front, in advance, without having done anything yet?"

"That is just for allowing you upstairs, you sissy," the matron replied sarcastically, making a come-on movement with her right hand for me to fork over the money. "You pay more upstairs, for sure!"

While this was going on, the bully had not said a word. But now he raised his butt off the chair and threw a menacing look at me. I quickly moved away and grabbed the handle of the staircase.

Walking briskly, habitually mounting two steps in a stride like a mountain climber, I glanced at the card the girl had shoved in my hand. It read: "Marlene, second floor, 204." Underneath was a dotted line, at the end of which was today's date stamped right beside the German eagle, leaving no doubt who owned the joint.

The Germans are great for stamping documents and presenting logos. In their eyes, no piece of paper is a document, if it is not formally approved by bearing a stamp.

Room 204 was situated at the end of the corridor to my left. As I lifted my knuckles to knock at the door, it swung wide open. Then Marlene tugged me inside and closed the door behind us.

She wore a light wine-red velvet housecoat, belted above her hips, accentuating her marvelous figure. As she moved, her housecoat flipped aside, revealing the upper halves of her trim-looking breasts, above the wide-cleaved negligee. Her nipples pressed invitingly against the translucent material. What a sight! My motor started running in anticipation of things to come.

I had entered a small, but attractive living room. It was equipped with a settee, two armchairs, a low rectangular table (quite unusual at the time), a counter/buffet, displaying crystal glassware and a dual-shelved wall bookrack stacked with books. Upon closer inspection, it contained a good assortment of books printed in different languages. As downstairs, heavy drapes covered the window. A small sparkling chandelier hung from the ceiling.

I must have had an admiring look on my face when I saw all this at a glance, because she said with some pride in her voice, "This is my kingdom, for now," emphasizing the last two words. Then she added, "Make yourself comfortable, my boy."

I could not help wincing at these two last words. But who was I trying to kid? Here was a grown-up woman, in her late twenties; and here I was, milk-face, not quite twenty-one, trying to buy her sexual favors!

Suddenly, I felt uncomfortable to the point that I wished I had not made it upstairs. An inferiority complex? Name it what you will. But hearing her call me "boy" brought to realization the odd-couple type of situation. My desire to be intimate with this five-foot-nine-inch-tall woman left me almost as fast as it had stirred me up when I had entered her domain.

Instead of sitting down, I walked over to the bookrack. Its lower shelf displayed a photograph of a young girl, maybe ten, with a bright smile and blond, curly hair that looked natural.

"Who is this youngster?" I asked, turning around to look at Marlene, who had parked herself on the edge of the settee.

She looked down to the floor for just a moment, then replied, "My daughter; she is ten now."

Relieved to have found another subject, I walked over and sat beside her, embracing her lightly with one arm and asked, "Would you mind telling me a bit about yourself? Or don't we have enough time?"

"Why not?" she answered. "It does not happen often that anybody takes a personal interest in me, except for the obvious."

And so rather than proceeding to the bedroom, we sat and chatted while having a cup of coffee; real coffee, not the wartime customary *Ersatzkaffee* (substitute coffee, made from chicory).

While studying at the University of Brussels in her last year, she met Jean-Paul, a young marine biologist who had just accepted an assignment from the French government to assist in the study of marine life. The two fell madly in love.

Upon her final graduation, Marlene went to France, where the two got married in 1932. One year later, Jeannine was born. They had settled in Marseilles, close to his field of endeavor. Their income was moderate, but like so many others of their generation, Marlene and Paul decided to make ends meet without exaggerated expectations, and she devoted herself to the upbringing of their daughter. They were a happy, close-knit family.

In 1935, Jean-Paul met another young man, Jacques Cousteau, destined to become internationally famous for his adventurous oceanographic and marine life discoveries. Jean-Paul's work became less confined to the Mediterranean Sea. It took him to the Bay of Biscay and even beyond, out to the Atlantic Ocean. Whenever that happened, Marlene and Jeannine stayed with Marlene's sister, who resided in Bordeaux.

The family did not have to change its lifestyle much after Germany invaded France, since it resided inside the part of France which was left unoccupied by the Germans. Everything seemed to work out fine.

Then, in June 1941, an ill-fated accident occurred. Jean-Paul did not return from a diving expedition off of Belle Île. While swimming about inside a shipwreck, his diving gear got caught between a maze of iron and steel. Both the pulling and the oxygen tubes were severed. Two other divers were sent down to bring Jean-Paul to the surface, but he could not be revived. A coroner determined Jean-Paul had died from a heart attack, possibly caused by shock.

Shortly after the tragedy, Marlene took Jeannine and moved in with her sister in Bordeaux, who had offered a permanent home for the two. Marlene, however, wanted to stand on her own feet. Everyday she looked for work, but the job market was poor and the fact that she did not have any work experience went against her. The situation became dimmer and dimmer.

Then, one day in October, while attending a class reunion with her sister, she met a woman her age who shared her fate, having lost her husband. After some soul searching, this woman had joined a group of others who were under contract with the German military to entertain the troops.

The picture this woman painted was not a dark one, as one would expect, leaving the (moral) questions of this profession aside. On balance, there were more advantages than disadvantages in this closely supervised activity. The danger of catching an infectious disease was minimized, as intercourse without the use of condoms was not allowed. And weekly health checkups practically guaranteed that if something should go wrong the infliction would be detected in its infancy.

"I am in my second year here now," Marlene concluded. "We are treated fairly and well. Food and accommodations are more than acceptable. The remuneration is so good that I have been able to provide for my girl more than sufficiently; and my bank account is growing."

She took a deep breath and, looking straight at me, added with a smile, "I know you were embarrassed when I called you 'boy' fifteen minutes ago. It slipped out. Frankly, at times I feel uneasy when I meet young clients like you."

I broke in. "Let's shake hands on that one," I said, equally relieved that no harm had been done. For a moment, we held our hands. Then, as if on command, we both got up and gave each other a heart-warming embrace, like brother and sister.

"I must go now," I said. "I have taken enough of your time." Taking out my folded wallet, she quickly cupped her hand over mine. With a denying gesture shaking her head from side to side, she said softly, "No, please no. I couldn't. I am so grateful you listened to my story. That is more than enough compensation."

We walked together to the door and embraced again as before. Then she opened the door, a questionable look on her face. Lifting her eyebrows, she asked, "Will I see you again?" Her voice heavy.

"You bet," I replied cheerfully, but barely suppressing my emotions. "Next time I pass through Oslo, I'll look you up."

Looking back while walking down the corridor, I saw her waving and heard her fading voice bidding, "Auf Wiedersehen." When I arrived at the end of the corridor, I turned once more, but she had closed the door. I had the distinct feeling we had struck an unknown chord with each other. Was it possible that two people from such different backgrounds could have built a real friendship in such a short time?

I had come up the stairs to my left, but the big sign pinned against the wall at eye level with an arrow pointing to the right and the word exit on it left no doubt where I had to go.

Arriving at the main floor landing, I looked in vain for a door. Instead, there was another sign with an arrow pointing down. I kept going until I reached what was obviously the basement floor, because the steps ended here. Walking through a narrow hall, filled with all kinds of piping and insulated wiring, I found an opening to the left.

Stepping though, I had entered a rectangular room which was almost bare, except for what looked like a restroom-like line to the left. A long water line ran along the entire wall, about five inches extended from it. Underneath, a mounted groove of corrugated iron allowed the water to be caught and channeled in a slanting position toward the far corner, where it would flow through a sloping pipe into a floor drain. A bunch of guys without pants and under shorts were lined up along the trough, washing their lower extremities under running water. Somehow, the sight struck me as very amusing, but not for long.

Immediately to the right of the entrance parked a six-foot table with two medical orderlies. One had kind of an account book in front of him, in which he entered my name, rank and dog tag number. He took the card Marlene had given me before we went upstairs, and added some information behind my name on the horizontal line. I had a quick glance and noticed the immaculate way with which he had recorded everything, including the time of the day. Even though I was accustomed to and had grown up with this German thoroughness, I remarked, "Very neat, Herr Unteroffizier."

He looked pleased, then pointed to the right wall, where about a dozen pairs of pants and shorts were hanging on hooks, and said, "Take off your pants and shorts. Wash your dirty prick and see the sergeant here."

"But, Herr Unteroffizier," I protested, stammering a bit, "I didn't do anything!"

"It makes no damn difference," he retorted, giving me a disbelieving glance. "You don't get out of here without having gone through the routine." There was no use arguing with him.

Stepping aside to shed my pants, I noticed two guys standing in front of the sergeant, who slightly moved around in his swivel chair, and closely inspected the penis of a soldier in front of him. I heard his remark, "What's wrong with that thing? Looks overworked to me. It sure needs an extra dose."

Without waiting for the soldier to reply, he took a gadget from a triple-glass cylinder, which, in all probability, contained a germicide, a forerunner of antibiotics. The thing he held in his hand looked like a syringe, but only at first glance. The body of the instrument was much larger. So was the extended piston rod and end ring. Instead of a needle, a tubule extended from the cylinder, the point of which was recessed and shaped in such manner that it fit and surrounded the head of the penis. The whole thing reminded me of a device which pastry chefs use for garnishing fancy cakes, except for the shape of the spray nozzle.

"Hold that pitiful-looking thing straight up," commanded the sergeant, and applied a douche to the man's organ by squeezing the piston. The man winced visibly, but the sergeant squeezed some more. The man let out a loud scream and started a dance I had never seen before. "Damn!" he cried, "that burns like hell." He limped over the rack in half-closed jackknife fashion, to retrieve his pants.

I went through the procedure as told. Passing by the corporal, he handed me a certificate, which proved when I was a customer and whose client I was. In the lower left-hand corner appeared a hot-line number. It was supposed to be used by the medical officer of my base, in case I would show any aftereffects. I added it to my pay book and walked out of the building.

Outside I teamed up with another couple of guys who were arguing with each other about who had shown greater endurance during their sexual encounters. I refused to get involved in the discussion. They would not have believed the truth anyway. It was nearly midnight when we walked through the gate of the base.

On the following morning, Thursday, the seventeenth, we were advised that, instead of going by ferry, we would be traveling through Sweden by train. Rules and regulations were hammered into our heads. When approaching a community, all windows had to be closed. At no time was anyone allowed to leave the train. Swedish soldiers, armed with machine pistols, were under orders to "shoot anything that moves." Our briefing lasted close to one hour. We were given another Kr 8 each and were told the special train would depart from Central Station at 2030 hours, as the trip through Sweden would take place overnight. "Report back here at 1900 hours to receive your travel documents," the transport coordinator ordered.

I was delighted to have some more time to spend in Oslo, as that did not happen too often. Oslo was, after all, the metropolis in Norway.

My substitute history and geography teacher, who had traveled widely and spent some time in a number of countries, had told us quite a bit about Scandinavia. He intertwined descriptions with his own experiences, which made us always look forward to his next hour of instruction. We appreciated his making this whole subject more interesting than would have been the case otherwise. After all, learning should be fun and should not be confined to throwing around boring dates, which, in my opinion, is one of several legitimate complaints students nowadays have.

I skipped my luncheon. Equipped with a street map of Oslo which the travel coordinator had lent me, I steered in the direction of Karl Johans Gate. One chap, who was equally eager to utilize the bit of time we had, joined me. The base was located at the upper end of Storgata, close to Haummanns Gata. We walked down Storgata, which runs in a southwesterly direction, and soon had reached Oslo Domkirke where Storgata ends. We went around the church to the right, entered Torgata's last block, and turned right into Karl Johans Gate.

Every city has its promenade. Some have even more than one. Rio de Janeiro and São Paulo in Brazil, Buenos Aires in Argentina, and American cities have more than one *avenida*, where young and old meet and, in pursuit of happiness, partake in the glitter of fancy stores, fine restaurants, cabarets, theaters and nightclubs.

Once the citizenry has chosen one street as its promenade, it automatically becomes sort of a sign board, by which the city's character is judged–not always correctly, though.

Copenhagen has its Stroget. In Paris, the Champs Elysee leads the line. In New York, its Fifth Avenue, and Bourbon Street in New Orleans. Toronto has its Yonge Street, unfortunately fast becoming infamous because of oversaturated vice activities. Düsseldorf declared the Ko (short for Konigsallee, or King's Avenue) as its number one promenade about a hundred years ago. And my own hometown, Wuppertal, bestowed this honor upon a comparatively short, but nevertheless, fine street, with the unglamorous name of *Poststrasse* (Post Office Street).

Here in Oslo, it is undoubtedly the Karl Johans Gate that is most representative of this marvelous city, though a number of other streets try to outdo each other, vying for some of the glory.

We had walked about two and one-half blocks down in a northwesterly direction, when I saw a sign on the second floor window of a stucco building which housed several offices. "International Berlitz School of Languages," read the sign in bold gold-plated letters. Opposite the street was a sidewalk cafe. Since I did not know how my companion, a bootsmann by rank, would react when I entered the school and conversed in the language of our enemy with those people inside, I suggested he wait for a few minutes at the cafe. He agreed without asking any questions and went across the street, gliding himself skillfully through the fairly heavy traffic. Not quite easy to do, since Karl Johans Gate was a wide street, even at that time. If I remember correctly, it had six lanes of traffic.

I entered the building and climbed the heavy oak stairs, holding onto the brass handrail. At the second landing, against the wall, was a sign split in the middle. On the left side, pointing to the appropriate direction with an arrow, the word "classrooms" was beautifully hand-painted in five languages: English, Norwegian, German, French and Spanish. I followed the arrow pointing to the other side, where the word "Director" stood alone. No translation was necessary since the difference in spelling is so negligible.

There was an empty space, followed by the word "Administration." It would have sufficed for three of the five languages; but *Forvaltning* and *Verwaltung* had been added for the natives and the unwelcome visitors, the Germans.

When I entered the office, a middle-aged man, with pitch-black oily hair pasted to his scalp, looked up from a file in front of him. His face looked serious, but its expression turned to concern when he saw my German uniform. He dropped his file on a desk, quickly walked over to me standing at the reception counter, and said in German, "Good day, sir. What can I do for you?" His accent was Latin, like a Spaniard, Italian or South American.

I asked to see the administrator, since I needed some information. At that moment, a woman stepped out of a side door. The man asked her in Spanish (my calculation was correct) whether she could look after me. She immediately walked over with a nice smile, opened the latched counter gate, and asked me in German to follow her to the room she had just vacated.

We had entered an office the type of which I had never seen anywhere before. Not only was it cozy like a living room, it also had an unmistakably international flavor. The office furniture was mixed, without clashing. Each piece must have come from a different country. The room was full of artifacts and boosted the impression of cosmopolitanism, containing Eskimo carvings, moose heads, leopard and tiger skins, the mane of a male lion, African hunter spears, a Mexican sombrero, photographs from the Kilimanjaro, the Amazon River, a Canadian mounted policeman at Parliament Hill, and a shrunken human head hanging from one corner of the ceiling. Talk about a cosmopolitan atmosphere! I wondered whether she had purposely omitted some items in her possession from Great Britain, France and the USA.

The woman offered me a Players cigarette, which I gratefully accepted. I had not seen these since early 1940. Sitting down, I came right to the point, knowing that my comrade was waiting for me across the street. Asking first if she preferred to carry on the conversation in German or English, she hesitated and opted for the latter.

I identified myself as a former student of the Berlitz School in Wuppertal and asked if she had a list of instructors at her disposal, although I did not expect it, since Berlitz had about sixty-some schools in operation around the globe.

To my astonishment, she answered in the affirmative but hinted at confidentiality. I told her I wanted to find out only if my former teacher, an American with the name of Stuerzinger was still instructing in Wuppertal, and if she had his home address, since I would like very much to get in touch with him.

She walked over to a shelf, retrieved a folder marked "Deutschland," opened it and went through several pages. "Sorry," she said, "I cannot find him listed in any of the eight schools we presently operate in your country. If his name should reappear anywhere, how can I contact you? I would be delighted to let you know."

Against regulations (it was not the first and certainly not the last time I would pay no attention to them) I gave her my postal code number, telling her also that I was stationed in Stavanger. Before leaving her office, I had another look around. "Quite a collection you have here," I commented. "Would you mind telling me your nationality? I cannot place you. Your English, German and Spanish do not reveal it. No accent."

"Of course not," she replied. "I was born on the Isle of Corsica in the Mediterranean, which belongs to France, as you may know. Since my father is Greek, I have dual citizenship. Having been stationed with Berlitz in several countries, I learned languages by direct exposure, the way we teach our students–total immersion without translations. That makes our method unique."

Based on my own experience, I could not quarrel with that statement. I thanked her for her time and left. The Latin chap in the outer office looked relieved when he saw me leaving, as if he had something to hide.

When I rejoined the sergeant across the street, he had just finished nursing an alcohol-free cooler. "Tastes great," he commented. "Have one. I'll take another one."

"I guess I owe you one for keeping you waiting." I replied. "Besides, I need something to cool off." Usually, daytime summer temperatures hover between seventeen and twenty-two degrees Celsius, but it had to be warmer today, with unusually high humidity.

We sat for a half-hour and chatted. I told him the reason for having visited Berlitz and described to him the kind of office the administrator maintained.

The drink was rather refreshing. I asked the waitress what it was, though it looked like a gin fizz, without the gin. I was close. It was the closest to a California lemonade, leaving out the rye whiskey–lemon juice, lime juice, a dash of Grenadine, and a tablespoon of powdered sugar. Not bad at all!

Leaving the cafe, we decided to stay in this, the southern side of the road, since the Storting (Norwegian Parliament) was only one and a half blocks away. It would be worthwhile looking at the building.

Coming closer, approaching the majestic-looking building complex from the front, we noticed several guards, placed at different areas, wearing the familiar but seldom seen Quisling uniform. Left and right of the main entrance were two sentries each on watch. They wore German Army uniforms with the broach chain-like shoulder slings, identifying them as military police. Obviously Vidkun Quisling, who in 1940 had talked Hitler into invading and occupying Norway, and subsequently became Hitler's puppet leader of Norway, was not feeling too secure in his own country.

This was no surprise to me, as most Norwegians hated his guts. I knew firsthand how much this man and his hordes were despised. Any time I attended a Norwegian cinema and Quisling's face appeared on the screen during the *Weekly Newsreel*, the audience would boo, hiss, scream, shout and raise fists, giving a hoot about the presence of Germans in uniforms.

The surrounding lawn was well-kept and a variety of flower beds displayed flowers, some of which would bloom into October. The greens keeper certainly knew what he was doing.

We went right around the complex, turning left into Rosenkrantz Gate, left again into Stortings Gata, turned again to enter Akkers Gata, until we reached the corner of Karl Johans Gate.

The area was swarming with civilian tourists and other pedestrians. Like everywhere, the tourists can be easily spotted by their cameras.

Nobody seemed to take any notice of us. That was typical. The Norwegians indicated their contempt for us by simply ignoring our presence. I was used to that. None of my Norwegian acquaintances in Stavanger would openly give me the time of the day when we met on the street. Their reason for doing so was different. They did not want to draw the suspicion of the Norwegian Resistance, as though they were German sympathizers.

Debating briefly whether to visit the Storting Gallery, which was open for visitors, we voted against it; the bootsmann for the simple reason that he did not see any German soldiers going in. My reason was different. For me, it would not be any fun listening to a rubber-stamp parliament. After the *Reichstagsbrand* (the burning of the lower house building of Parliament) in February 1933 (which was fixed, as I described earlier), it was easy for Hitler to exploit that tumultuous situation by stuffing the Reichstag with members of the Nazi party. Soon thereafter, real opposition existed only on paper. The Reichstag became nothing but a sounding board. There was no reason to believe that real debates were now going on at the Storting either!

To be frank, though, I had no ideas what a democratic framework of governing a country meant and how it functioned. Disregarding the ill-conceived actions of the former Weimar Republic of Germany, my country never went through a true democratic experience. The Germans only had monarchist autocracies as precedents.

I looked at my watch. It showed 1430 hours. We had plenty of time left to spend. We were at the halfway point of the street. Continuing our walk in the same direction, we passed a couple of impressive-looking hotels, which were located on the other side of the street mixed with several stores. Now we could see already a glimpse of the castle at the end of the street, looming behind the Karl Johans Monument. But first we passed the National Theater to our left, and Oslo University with its beautiful orchard extending to both sides of the street.

The castle is surrounded by a twin park. The southern segment is called Dronning Park, the northern area is the Castle Park. We walked around in this beautiful atmosphere for twenty-five minutes or so, then rested for a while on a park bench.

"Almost like home," the sergeant commented, "except there is no gambling casino around here. Not that it matters. My parents never had any loose change around to entertain such an idea." His home was in Baden-Baden, one of the finest spas and gambling resorts in Germany. I did not reply. What he did not seem to remember was, that Hitler outlawed any sort of "decadent activity," such as gambling, a long time ago.

Not to veer off and get lost, we stayed as close as possible to Karl Johans Gate. We both were interested in historical museums and had heard that there was one within the downtown core, the area between Radhus Gate to the south and Saint Olavs Gate to the north, a roughly ten-by-ten block square. Having left *Slottparken* (Castle Park), we asked several civilians, until an elderly man led us up Frederiks Gate, the first side street leading north off Karl Johans Gate when leaving the park.

With a twinkle in his eye, the old man said, "It is less than two blocks from here, but the displays are rather more limited now than a few years ago. Still, you might find them interesting." I wondered whether the Norwegians had been as smart as the Danes, who prevented their most precious artifacts from being looted by Goering's "art collectors," who were swarming all over occupied countries, confiscating art works for their master.

Walking up Frederiks Gate, we came to the second block in a few minutes which was (and still is) completely occupied by three university institutions in one building. The ethographical museum was closed, but the university's numismatic collection displayed a stunning variety of rare coins, paper money, and metals.

The university's collection of antiquities showed relics and customs of ancient times, including a Middle Ages collection from the periods prior to the 1600s. Small replicas of Viking ships were prominently laid out, but one of the greatest treasure collections of valuable articles of gold and silver, which my teacher had mentioned one day was conspicuously absent.

After the war, former members of the Resistance movement revealed to me that a group of intellectuals including historians, anthropologists, geologists and other scientists had worked out a plan of action in case of an invasion. A list of most valuable artifacts was drafted. These items were immediately withdrawn from museums and art galleries and relocated and concealed in unlikely hiding places. The plan was well-executed within twenty-four hours of the German invasion.

Unfortunately, the Norwegian Government was not that fast. The Storting needed forty-eight hours to mobilize after Germany invaded the country. Consequently, Norway's defenses became subdued in a matter of weeks, even in and around Narvik, where the British had established a bridgehead.

Today, Norway could be overwhelmed in equally short time, even with an ongoing alert and with the support of Northern European defense forces as a whole. While German forces at the time had to confine themselves to invading from the south and the west, Soviet, Polish and East German conventional forces, combined with amphibious and airborne units, could accomplish such a task just as easily. Chances are, Sweden's neutrality would be disregarded, which would make it even easier to swallow up territory. Neutrality does not guarantee peace. For the sake of the Scandinavian people, whom I learned to respect and to love, I sincerely hope this possibility remains hypothetical.

We spent three-fourths of an hour looking at the exhibitions and left. It was close to 1630 hours when we began our walk back down Karl Johans Gate. Having skipped luncheon, we were hungry and selected a restaurant diagonally located from the Storting to have an early dinner. The place called itself *Det Jazzhus*, indicating that there would be some live music. The sergeant had told me he liked jazz (phonetically, the Germans pronounce it *yuts*). So, why not add some of it with a meal on an empty stomach?

The restaurant was already packed when we entered. The atmosphere struck me as *gemutlich* (cozy) as in Germany. It was dignified enough without being stuffy. Tables were covered with checkered tablecloths. In the center of each table, a crystal glass rested with colorful flowers. The clientele was mixed as far as age went, and more German uniforms were visible than I would have expected.

There were no booths, but the longest wall to our left when entering the establishment ended up being covered by dark brown leather settees, in front of which were placed rectangular tables, providing sufficient space in between for the service personnel to properly serve food and beverages to patrons.

The headwaiter talked to an elderly couple who sat alone at one of the tables. The table was for six, like most. Cruising over to us, the headwaiter said in faultless German, "Follow me, please."

As we approached the table, the man got up with a smile and, with an easy-to-understand hand movement, said politely, "Good day. Please be seated." When we sat down, he asked, "Do you speak Norwegian?" I had learned enough from Heinz Marzi to understand the question.

"No, sorry," I answered, then asked in turn, "do you speak German?" The answer was negative. I switched to English, "Do you speak English?" The couple looked at each other sheepishly. I added quickly, "It's all right. I'll translate for my friend here." I avoided the word "comrade" to soft-pedal the whole thing. I was well aware that some Norwegians and Danes had been jailed for several days for having addressed Germans in that language. The sergeant did not drop an eyelid.

The service personnel was mixed, waitresses and waiters. I saw that eight were on duty. A couple of busboys were busy removing soiled dishes from the dining room and resetting tables for the next sitting.

The couple had assisted us in selecting from the menu. We went for a typical Norwegian three-course dinner. My glance followed the shapely figure of the waitress when she left our table to place the order.

The room was rectangular-shaped, except for two protruding walls. One enhanced the kitchen facilities, the other shorter one separated the restroom doors from view.

In one corner of an elevated platform stood a Steinway Grand. To its right, further in front of the stage were two music note stands. Behind these was a complete percussion ensemble. A man in his thirties had just appeared from a back room and started fiddling around with the snare drum. I could hear him reducing the tension on the skin. The light snare he applied deepened somewhat, until he had obtained the desirable level.

A few minutes later, while our first course was being served, three other guys appeared from the background and joined the drummer on stage. One carried a string bass, the other two saxes, alto and baritone. In the typically relaxed fashion of real jazzmen, they arranged their note stands and instruments, casually without hurry. The third, obviously the pianist, had placed himself at the grand piano and quickly leaped with his fingers chromatically over the white and black keys. Then he hit a few full chords. With an approving nod, he got up, and the four of them put their heads together for a few moments. Music sheets were passed around.

The saxophonist stepped up two steps. Close to the front edge of the stage was one stand-up microphone. I looked for amplifiers, but did not see any. But as the man bid us a good evening, I could hear his voice clearly from two directions: from the stage and from overhead, where a loudspeaker hung from the ceiling, opposite the stage.

He addressed the crowd in Norwegian and German. He indicated that, among others, a number of German tunes would be played during the early dinner hour concert, "for our German visitors," he added, smiling. Also, requests were welcome and would be promptly fulfilled. "If we don't know the tune, we want you to hum it, and we will fill in the spaces," he added good-humoredly. The audience applauded enthusiastically. Now I had an explanation why the band called itself the Goodwill Band.

The band started with *Strike Up The Band*. Then followed a funny variation of *Turkish March* by Mozart. It was, of course, a jazzed-up version, where the drummer played around on his precessions and on a string bass with two ordinary HB pencils. His clowning brought the house down! Years later, in 1967, a Stockholm audience appreciated a similar presentation of that tune with Benny Goodman's Orchestra, mostly consisting of British musicians, including a drummer with the unlikely name of Bobby Orr.

The pianist demonstrated unusual versatility. At times, he would step over the keys lightly like an elf, then he would change into stride piano style–a combination Erroll Garner and Art Tatum.

On one tune, the sax player played an alto solo, alternately competing with the bassist, back and forth. The pianist would suddenly break in as if fed up to be left out, and the four of them would go into a lengthy contrapuntal recital, combining two melodies into one. The crowd really went wild after that!

The band continued with a couple of tunes by Ernst Fischer, then a contemporary German composer. His music nowadays would be considered a fusion between classical music and jazz, like some composed by John Williams, former conductor of the Boston Pops Orchestra.

Next, the band tore into Ellington, Gershwin, Porter, Berlin and Kern. The sax player cautiously announced these tunes as "Broadway melodies."

Halfway through dinner, I went up and asked the sax player to play *Stardust*, by Hoagy Carmichael. It awoke memories in me, as it was one of the first American compositions I had ever heard when my father had bought a radio in 1936.

To the musically trained ear, it was obvious that the quartet had played together for a while. There was a certain discipline and knowledgeable anticipation among them when improvising. The apparent spontaneity of improvisation was carefully measured and held within a framework, never leaving the uninitiated listener behind. The applause was given accordingly. I was delighted to see that a first-rate jazz group was appreciated for its talent, rather than misused as background music for noisy half-drunks who could not care less.

The combo's enthusiasm was obvious and infectious to the audience. The four loved what they were doing. Making a living that way seemed to be secondary. These were real professional musicians, refusing to sellout to commercialism.

The band had just broken off for an intermission when the sergeant looked at his watch and announced it was time to get moving. It was 1830 hours. We barely had a half-hour to report back to the base. Too bad I could not stay all evening and listen to the band.

We paid our bill, said good night to the elderly couple, who responded light-heartedly with "See you later" and left. It was exactly 1900 hours when we checked in at the transit base.

We were told to have a substantial dinner, as there would be nothing to eat before we would reach Göteborg, halfway through Sweden. "Verdammt," slipped out of the sergeant's mouth. "First we miss out on luncheon, and now our bellies are too full to have dinner here." We packed a couple of open-faced sandwiches from the canteen with two bottles of *Seltzer Wasser* (club soda), although there was no way to cool them down during the trip.

The convoy of military busses left promptly at 2000 hours and arrived at the central station fifteen minutes later. The train was already waiting for us. Without any delay, it began moving as soon as everybody had boarded. We had selected to board a railway car to the center of the train. I talked the sergeant into this, since I had the silly idea it was safer in case of a frontal collision. That the train simply could derail never entered my mind.

Heading Home

The compartment was filled, but walking through the entire train later showed that nobody had to squat on the floor or lean against hallway windows. On my first furlough home in 1942, I was not so lucky to have a seat. I spent most of the time literally sleeping standing up.

With the exception of the first car which was half-occupied, all seats were filled. The officer in charge of this transport seemed to know exactly what he was doing. When I entered Sweden the following year under diplomatic cover, I was told the Swedish transportation commission did not allow overselling of seats. How they ever kept track of capacities at a time when nobody had heard of computers remains a mystery to me.

The air distance between Oslo and Halden at the Swedish border is 110 kilometers, an extra fourteen kilometers by rail. Moving in a southerly direction, we passed the towns of Kolbotn, Ski, As, Drobak, Cestby, Son, Moss, Rigge, Rade, Fredrikstad, Sarpsborg, and entered Halden Station just about when the sun set. Several stretches of the trip lead us along Oslofjorden. Like in 1942 when I went bartering across Rogaland County with Heinz Marzi, I was reminded of the endless beauty this country had to offer. It was breathtaking.

Sprinkled over the train, I had seen a number of *Heeresbegleitpersonal* (accompanying military travel personnel). They were held in readiness in cases of accidents, sabotage or outbreak of serious illness. But the train had hardly stopped in Halden, when a swarm of grim-faced SS men entered the train. Our leading officer conferred with one of them and I saw lists changing hands. After a few minutes, our travel leader ordered everybody out of the train with the instruction to leave our luggage.

A monocled SS officer briefly addressed us to explain a few things. Most of this we had been told in Oslo, but he had something interesting to add, with a cynical smirk on his face: "Make no mistake. We are here for your protection, but also to make sure none of you get lost! We shoot fast. So do the Swedes who are posted around railway stations." I did not have the vaguest idea that a shooting incident would happen before my return from furlough.

Two other SS men stepped forward and alternately read our names, while a handful of other SS men combed through the train. "What the hell are these guys looking for?" asked one man close by me. I tried to be funny. "You know," I replied, "they have orders to look for secret weapons we are not supposed to have. I wouldn't be surprised if they include in their search my barrel of herrings." Some started to chuckle but stopped immediately when they saw one SS man in front of us casting dirty looks at us.

It was around 2300 hours when the train began moving again. We made another stop after twenty kilometers, at Halden, where Swedish MPs stood by with machine pistols. Our official transport leader submitted papers to a Swedish major. The short stretch we had just left behind was kind of no man's land. Looking out the window to the left, there was Norwegian territory, while the ground to the right belonged to Sweden.

As soon as we left Halden the train picked up speed. We were now firmly on Swedish grounds. Windows had to be kept closed as we passed a number of communities. Then we entered the first city, Uddevalla. All communities were brightly lighted, reminding us that we were in a neutral country. This was a welcome change, since we had not seen any city lights for almost four years. Blackouts were in effect across Germany and in all other European countries we had occupied. The British were used to blackouts too. They had endured tremendous bombings in 1940, during the time Winston Churchill called the Battle of Britain. I had often wondered about the benefit of blackouts. On the one hand, it was somewhat more difficult for the enemy to hit targets. On the other hand, it did invite an excuse for indiscriminate bombings on either side!

When we arrived in Göteborg and the train stopped, it was about 0130 hours. The train had managed the distance of 230 kilometers in less than two hours. We were reminded again to keep the windows shut and stay away from the doors, which were manned by our protectors anyway.

The train was switched to a dead-end rail, where Red Cross personnel entered and distributed Swedish platters and hot coffee. I asked whether I could get hold of a newspaper. I had seen a kiosk on the next platform, which displayed almost any newspaper one could think of.

"Any newspaper will do," I said to the woman. She answered in German, with that typically Swedish singsong voice: "Maybe I can sneak some in, after I pick up my next food load. It is somewhat risky to do so under the noses of your bloodhounds (obviously referring to our SS escort) but I will try."

Fifteen minutes later she returned. With a twinkle in her eye, she dug from underneath a pile of food and chocolate bars, three newspapers: the *Stockholm Dagesblade, Die Zuricher Abendzeitung*, and the *Manchester Guardian*. "In case you understand more than one language," she commented, "I brought you a variety." She took a risk indeed! But then, who would dare to arrest her here?

It was almost 0230 hours when the train started rolling again. After a while, everybody quieted down. The food had made me sleepy. "Just as well," I thought and settled for some relaxation and a handful of sleep. Our destination was Trelleborg but that was far in the south of Sweden, another four hundred-plus kilometers to go. Soon I had fallen asleep.

I awoke from a jolt caused by sudden braking. The train came to a stop outside Halmstad. A red signal indicated to us to yield. We had nearly covered half the distance between Göteborg and Trelleborg, 190 kilometers. While I slept, we had passed major cities such as Mölndal, Kungsbacke, Varberg, and Falkenberg.

The wait lasted twenty minutes. When entering Halmstad Station, the usual exchange of papers took place again. Heavily-armed soldiers were stationed on each side of the train. Suddenly, we heard shouting followed by a single shot. Looking through the window, we saw one Swedish soldier gesticulating wildly right underneath our window. It turned out he had let go a warning shot, because one of my comrades in the previous car obviously could not hide his curiosity and had dared to stick his neck out the window. Others pulled him back quickly. The SS interrogated him right on the spot and threatened cancellation of his furlough if he tried that stunt again.

When we left Halmstad, I was wide awake. I unfolded my three newspapers, one by one, and read the headlines. Though the Swedish and Norwegian languages are closely related, my knowledge of Norwegian was too limited to make sense, not even from the headlines.

The Swiss newspaper was another matter. It reported heavy German losses on the Eastern Front. The commentary page predicted it would be only a matter of time and the Germans would be in for a shattering defeat at and around Stalingrad. The Swiss must have known something we did not. They were quite right, though. The defeat at Stalingrad clearly signaled, at least to some of us who could still think for themselves, the beginning of the end. We had bitten off more than we could chew!

The *Manchester Guardian* described, among others, the successful hit of one V-One platform at Peenemünde, from which some of our rockets were launched. The paper also reported that cities such as Hamburg, Cologne, Düsseldorf and Aachen had been bombed.

Without quoting details or naming its sources of information, the paper claimed that huge amounts of cash in British and American bogus currency had been discovered. Most of the counterfeit money was so good, the source claimed, that the British Treasury Department had to be consulted.

The fake money did not surprise me. Through an acquaintance of mine who served at the foreign office in Berlin at the time, I knew that a considerable number of German agents had been flown to Northern Ireland and channeled to England, equipped with all kinds of "manufactured" currencies. There was a dual purpose for this move: to supply agents with sufficient cash to move about anywhere in Great Britain, and to dump as much counterfeit money as possible on the open market, laundered or not, in order to cause havoc with the British pound. The latter plan did not work though, in spite of the fact that some businesses, strictly for profitable reasons, partook in money-laundering activities.

By the time I put the newspapers aside, we had passed Aengelholm, Helsingborg and Landskrona. We now approached Malmö. I took the Swedish newspaper to find someone who could understand the language. When I entered the second car from mine, moving to the tail of the train, one member of the SS "honor guard" stopped me by directly stepping into my way. "Let's see what you have there," he demanded harshly, practically ripping the paper from my hand.

"Just a newspaper," I replied meekly, adding foolishly, "I'm trying to find somebody who speaks Swedish."

"You have to be out of your mind," he barked at me. "You should know better than to read foreign newspapers."

I looked at the man's arm sleeves and shoulder tops, but could not make out his rank. So I said, "But Colonel, sir, Sweden is neutral." Visibly flattered and mollified to have been addressed by a much higher rank, he replied, "That's true, but we cannot trust anybody. The whole world is against us! Get rid of that paper."

"Of course," I said obligingly, but could not resist the temptation to add, without sounding too argumentative, "but I don't think the Swedes are that bad, when they allow us to pass through their country."

I turned to backtrack to my compartment, but first made sure he saw me entering the washroom. I folded the paper twice, opened my uniform jacket, and stuffed the newspaper halfway in my trousers. Jackknifing it, I closed the jacket again and used the belt to hold the newspaper in place. "A good thing," I mused, "that I did not walk around with the *Manchester Guardian* instead. I would not have got off that easily." It was forbidden under heavy penalty to read foreign propaganda, listen to broadcasts on the radio and, worse still, to spread that news.

As I left the washroom, the train came to a stop. We had entered Malmö Central Station. This time the stationmaster had joined the travel paper exchange ceremony. Everything seemed to be to his satisfaction. After ten minutes, the train slowly set itself in motion, but only about two kilometers. "What now," I thought. "Simple. The horse needed water." Five minutes, and we were on our last stretch. Only about fifty kilometers to go to Trelleborg.

While we brought the end piece of our trip through Sweden behind us, the sun rose. My watch showed precisely 0745 hours when the train came to a full stop at Trelleborg, not inside the roofed station, but on a track running horizontally with the dock and ending at a ferry landing.

To the left of the track, away from the dock, was a three-meter-high fence with barbed wire. To the right, heavily armed Swedish soldiers built a human chain, right down to the ferry landing. Our travel leader had left the train. A few minutes later we heard his voice through crackling loudspeakers: "Attention men! You will leave the train now, lining up with your gear to the right of the railway car you occupied. One guide is being assigned to each car group, who will lead you in orderly fashion to ferry pier B."

Now came the unpleasant part of the trip, running about with all that gear. It would be fun here and again everywhere in Germany, changing transportation. I wormed myself out of the car, cursing quietly under my breath at the herring barrel which was not only heavy, but also awkward to carry.

Like during a military exercise, everybody was outside within two minutes, standing, gaping and yawning for lack of sleep, or too much of it. The line started moving from the front of the train. Soon we all had reached the pier in question. Two hundred meters ahead, on pier A, a bunch of soldiers returning from furlough, who had just disembarked from the ferry, were waiting to be herded into the train we had vacated.

I noticed with satisfaction that we were allowed to embark the ferry without our protectors. Even though I never had any personal confrontation with any of them, the SS, with their black uniforms and skulls on their caps, and the SA, the brownshirts, always gave me the creeps. How could I have any use for them? Still in my teens, I had witnessed their brutality when they indiscriminately used their clubs on bystanders, who did not lift their arms in the Nazi salute when they marched by with their banners!

The ferry we had boarded was operated by the HAPAG, the Hamburg-America Line, but supervised by the German Navy now. The few civilians on board were either Swedish or German diplomats. They also were the only ones who crossed the Baltic with their automobiles. There were some businessmen as well, but I had no illusion that most of them were under some kind of cover or other.

Breakfast was second to none. It reminded me of the naval officer casino and the marvelous cuisine Chef Erich Eye would prepare. To this day, I have not forgotten that man! Preparing breakfast is invariably more time-consuming than luncheon and dinner, yet the two cooks aboard cranked it out for an estimated three hundred people like a piece of cake!

The ferry's route was to shuttle between Trelleborg and Stralsund in Germany. The distance between the two cities is about the same as between Göteborg and Malmö, 280 kilometers.

We had cast off around 0830 hours. Always curious about ships and boats, I got hold of the engineer, asking him a few questions. The ferry could squeeze out a maximum speed of about twenty-two knots, but would float with an average of eighteen. I did some quick arithmetic. One knot equaled one nautical mile, or 1.15 statute mile. Two hundred eighty kilometers are equal to 175 statute miles. With an average of eighteen nautical miles per hour, we should reach our destination within nine hours, barring any complications.

The voyage passed without incident. We tied up at Stralsund Harbor at 1650 hours. My calculation had been close. We had made good time. I bade my travel companions good-bye and hired a baggage carrier who had offered his services to transport my gear to the railway station. The next train would leave for Rostock and Hamburg at 1830 hours. The one after that was scheduled for 2200 hours.

The Furlough Begins

The transit base in Stralsund, where I was officially to report for the commencement of my furlough, was listed in my travel papers. It was located at quite a distance; too far to walk. A few steps away from where I stood was a taxi stand. There was no taxi to be seen, nor a telephone to call one. Only hotels had direct lines with taxi companies.

Across the street, double doors of a tall office building spit out people in droves. A man in his fifties with a *borsenjobber* (a funny phrase coined by a friend of mine indicating a black stiff-rimmed Borsalino-type hat, often worn by stock exchange brokers at the time) came across the street in my direction and steered toward the taxi stand. I asked him whether taxis were available. "Not on a regular basis," was his answer, "but I have a standing order."

He offered me to share the taxi with him, as my destination base was close to his home. His taxi arrived within minutes and we took off. I was surprised to see any taxi in operation, since everything was rationed, including gasoline. Asking the driver about this, he explained that he received a number of gasoline coupons each day, which would keep his vehicle moving several short fares. "But we also have here a black market, where one can purchase gas for a higher price. One has to have connections."

He hinted that a friend of his could buy unlimited supplies from a mobile army corps. I could not believe my ears! Field Marshal Rommel in Africa faced defeat by the Allies because of lack of gas and spare parts for trucks, tanks and lagoon vehicles. And here we had a crafty schemer, siphoning off gas at black market prices. What surprised me most was that these people had the gall to risk their lives for profit. This kind of behavior, if discovered, was punishable by death!

The man who had offered to share the taxi with me was an industrial consultant. Before the war, he had advised industrial conglomerates on matters of marketing. He had been drafted into government service as an efficiency expert and coordinator of specialized war production output.

With the expectation of Doenitz taking over as admiral of the fleet from Raeder soon, he was now involved in preparatory work regarding the development of radar devices to be used to equip our new U-boat fleet. At the same time, while increasing our ability to detect positions of enemy ships, he was given the task of pumping the brains of technicians, with the purpose of finding more effective ways to silence our own naval ships' movements. His mandate necessitated his commuting off and on between Kiel, Peenemünde and Stralsund.

I listened to his descriptions with fascination and would have loved to hear more. In any case, several months later I heard and read news reports testifying that the efforts of his team had been rewarded by reaching most of the goals.

When he arrived at his residence, he instructed the taxi driver to drive me to the base, wait, and return to the station. He paid for the whole fare. When I mildly protested, he firmly shook my hand, waving his other hand in a generous gesture and said, "Look, that is the least I can do for you people who keep our navy alive and moving. I can't take part in the action myself. To be honest, I'm glad I don't have to put my head in the noose, though the bombings we have to endure now can get on anybody's nerves."

When we were in motion again, I thought about the man's last remark. I had not seen anything so far that showed destroyed factories or any other buildings.

Arriving at the transit base I luckily did not find a long lineup of comrades waiting for their travel papers to be stamped. A leading seaman took my papers, glanced at them briefly, stamped them with the base ID, added the date and his signature and said, "Your official leave begins tonight at midnight. When returning from home, you are to report to Kiel Naval Base no later than Saturday, 10 July. Have a good time." He returned my documents and I left hastily, aware of the taxi running outside.

Stepping outside the base, a number of soldiers had invaded the taxi driver. I saw him shaking his head sideways. When he saw me, he pointed in my direction and said something I could not hear. The gang turned to me. One of them asked, "How the devil did you get hold of a taxi? I thought taxis became extinct."

"Not for privileged people," I answered lightly. Then I asked them where they were headed. Most of them just wanted to go downtown. I quickly conferred with the driver, suggesting he take a few of the chaps.

"For the full fare, of course," I assured. "It will help you buy some extra gas from your corrupt operator/friend. I guess we all have to make a living." I mildly excused his action. He agreed to take four. A flip of a coin decided who these four would be. Flipping coins seems to be an international solution in cases of indecision.

Entering the taxi, I looked at my watch. "We had better speed a bit," I suggested, thinking I could call the shots, since I was the host. We had only forty minutes left to reach the station. And I was not willing to shorten my vacation by missing that 1830 hour train.

We arrived at 1818 hours. Luckily, the police were busy with other matters than catching speeding taxis. I thanked the driver and rushed out of the cab. Presenting my baggage ticket at the counter, I looked for a porter. No one was to be seen. I swung the naval sack on my back like a rucksack–one cannot do anything else with this clumsy gear–took the briefcase with my waiter's tools in one hand, the barrel of herrings in the other, and started a forced march to the gate of the departing train. Sure enough, the blasted train stood on the last track.

The railway man at the gate saw me coming, puffing and steaming, and waved for me to go through, without producing papers. "Must be coming from Norway," he commented smilingly, seeing my barrel plainly marked. I did not bother to reply, since the stationmaster already was lifting his whistle to his lips to set the train in motion. It was 1829 hours, sharp. The punctuality of German trains arriving and departing on the dot had not changed!

One traveler who had seen me coming, reopened his compartment door and assisted with my load. As soon as I dragged the door shut behind me, the train started to roll.

I parked myself on the only vacant seat, a fisherman to my left, a navy wave to the right. She had returned my salute with what I thought was a triumphant-looking smirk on her face. As a petty officer, she had the upper hand and wanted me to know it. It proved to be another example that at times we misread signals, as she became quite sociable later on. I had drawn the wrong conclusion. Still, it became evident from part of the conversations we had that she indeed had had some disappointing experiences with some enlisted men.

Since my arrival by boat, I did not have a chance to buy a newspaper. Across the aisle, a man had unfolded the *Hamburger Abendblatt*, the front page facing me. I could read the main headline with ease. "The English bombard Hamburg for the third time; also used incendiary bombs. Other cities also hit. At least three thousand civilians dead!"

The man's glance met mine. He had noticed me reading the headline. "Isn't that awful? These damn English!" he said.

I had to hold myself back not to become argumentative with the man. Sure, it was more than sad that innocent civilians had to take quite a load of this war. But it seemed that we got some of our own medicine back which we had dished out to the British in 1940. We had conveniently forgotten the indiscriminate bombings we had imposed on them, even though Goebbels' propaganda came out with hogwash, claiming we only attacked military targets. Another thing we should not have been too surprised about that most Germans screamed, "Yes," when Hitler repeatedly asked if we wanted total war. It of course was meant to be for the enemy only. Now we had it!

My travel documents indicated I could go to Hamburg, then transfer to any train from there, taking one of two alternative routes southward to Wuppertal. The distance between Stralsund and Hamburg is 180 miles, or 288 kilometers. The train I had boarded was a *Schnellzug* (fast train), making an average speed of seventy kilometers per hour. It was scheduled to arrive in Hamburg at 2240 hours.

The navy wave and I had a few courtesy chats. She was attached to the signal corps in Sweenemunde, in charge of wave teleprinters. After a while, the conversation petered out. With the exception of the man with the newspaper, nobody in the compartment was inclined to converse. The atmosphere appeared to be gloomy. I leaned my head back to snooze a little.

After what I thought was a few minutes, I felt an elbow in my ribs. The fisherman woke me up with a friendly "we are almost there" wake-up call. It was 2235 hours. The train was on time. If I was lucky, I could switch over to the overnight express train to Wuppertal, unless it had been taken off the schedule.

The train entered on platform five. Stepping out with my gear, I found myself standing right in front of the departure schedule. The express train was still in operation. It would depart at 2415 hours and arrive in Wuppertal at 0600 hours.

I had been at Hamburg Central Station a couple of times before, but something seemed to be different now. The moment I felt an unusual draft, I knew what had changed: the huge station had turned into a skeleton and four-fifths of its curved roof was gone, no doubt the result of bombings.

With one and a half hours to spend, I checked my gear again and inquired about the location of the two railway restaurants which were customary at all large city stations in Germany. One is for ordinary travelers; the other for first-class customers. "They are both bombed out," I was told. "There is a temporary snack bar at the north side of the building. If what they have doesn't appeal to you, there is a restaurant still in operation right across the street, beside the bombed-out Hotel Alder."

I gave up the idea, afraid I would have to pay black market prices (thinking about the Stralsund fuel situation) and the fact that I did not have any ration cards either. Besides, I was running low on cash. I had not exchanged any Norwegian kroner into German Reichsmark.

Curiosity let me step out of the station. From what I could see in the dark, there were a number of former buildings within range, the walls of which still reached to the sky. There was nothing inside those walls. Ruins and rubble dominated the scene.

I quickly returned inside and went to the telegraph counter. To my surprise, my telegram was accepted. It advised my parents of my arrival by express train. The telegram would be delivered by 0200 hours, I was assured. The charge for the six-word telegram was RM 1.50, a measly twenty-five pfennig per word (six cents at the time). That cheap and fast, I mused. Somebody must be on the ball, in spite of all these bombings. I was about to admire the efficiency and organizational talents of my countrymen some more before I would leave.

Observing the people milling around in the station, it was obvious that prosperity was running thin, if it ever had blessed some in the first place. Most men, though clean-looking, were poorly dressed. Many had shoes on their feet which had seen better times. Trousers were sagging. The men had lost weight.

A lot of people struck me as having enough problems of their own, rather than listening to somebody else's. Some seemed to be carrying the whole world on their shoulders. Sure, we were used to good news, as far as the war was concerned, and we recently had experienced several setbacks and even defeats in the East and in Africa. Not to be taken too lightly, but could these have such devastating affects on people? Soon I would find out the main reason for that negative mood swing.

The express train was set in around 1145 hours. Shortly before, I had picked up my gear and somewhat lackadaisically advanced to the platform, in contrast to my stormy attack in Stralsund. I caught a good window seat, not that I expected to see too much, and unfolded the *Frankfurter Allgemeine Zeitung*, which I had bought from an old chap who sold newspapers and pocket books by pulling a wheeled cart along the platform.

There was a report from Sweenemunde, announcing the erection of another V-One rocket launching platform and Wernher Von Braun's teamwork on the development of a new *Wunderwaffe* (miracle weapon), the V-Two, an advanced version of the V-One. The editorial page condemned the brutality with which the Amies and Tommies (Americans and English) bombarded German cities and directed their attacks solely at civilian populations. The article concluded with the statement that Germans would not be demoralized by those criminal acts; the usual war propaganda in which countries on all sides engage.

Everybody tells the story in the best possible light, even if it means distorting facts! Come to think of it, distorting facts is really what propaganda is all about in contrast to reporting them.

By the time we approached Bremen, the clouds had cleared and the moonlit sky, for the first time, let me see the devastating affect of the Allied's bombings. As we entered Bremen railway station, there was rubble all around us. But the swiftness with which railway tracks had been cleared after those attacks was short of being miraculous. Railway personnel were living up to their main slogan, "Wheels must be kept moving for victory!"

If the sight of Bremen was pitiful, it got progressively worse when we reached Osnabrück, Dortmund, Hagen and finally Wuppertal. The city of Wuppertal (*Wupper* is the name of the river; *tal* means valley in German) actually is made up of a chain of large towns, placed on each side of the river. Going from east to west, it starts with Oberbarmen, then Barmen, Elberfeld (where I was born), Sonnborn, Zoo and Vohwinkel as last point west. It also includes Solingen slightly to the south, where world-famous steel companies fabricate some of the best steel knives in the world and numerous razor blades.

Dawn set in as we came closer to Oberbarmen. No destruction could be seen. Suddenly, like a wall, before entering Barmen, the now all-too-familiar scene of building skeletons and mountains of rubble began. I was shocked! Obviously, it was possible to wipe out complete communities. Barmen had gone up in flames.

The train had stopped. Several civilians and a handful of soldiers disembarked, the latter group looking in disbelief at the ugly sites. Ten minutes later the train arrived in Elberfeld. Entering the station, I noticed with relief that it looked the same as when on furlough one year before.

Long before the train came to a full stop, I recognized my dad's head with his railway cap looming out of the crowd. He simply could not be overlooked with his height of six feet six inches. Jumping out of the train with my gear, we ran into each other's arms, slapped each other's backs, and cried and laughed at the same time, overcome by emotions. Who says two grown-up men in uniform must not cry?

Mom and Dad had received my telegram as promised by the employee in Hamburg. In contrast to North America, telephone and telegraph services in Germany are combined with that of the post office.

At Home

It was only a fifteen-minute walk from the station to Oberstrasse Fifteen, the apartment house where I had spent the first nineteen years of my life. Even though it was early in the morning, our immediate long-time neighbors were at hand to greet the sailor from Norway. A great homecoming it was!

Only one of my close friends had not been drafted yet. He had been declared unfit for military service since he suffered from epileptic seizures. Fritz Rethmeier served with the Rommel Panzer Corps in Africa and had not been heard from for months. Rolf Adams had joined the *Luftwaffe* (German Air Force) and had been reported missing in action while in Hungary. Harald Brühl was at the Eastern Front as an army medical orderly. The last letter his parents received from him indicated his "disgust for this rotten war."

During my first night home I got a taste of the tribulations civilians had to put up with. We were thrown out of bed twice by sirens warning against air attacks, and spent a couple of hours in the basement, which had been converted to an air raid shelter in early 1940. Even though Hermann Goering, Grand Air Marshal of the Luftwaffe, had made the statement guaranteeing that no enemy plane would ever reach German territory, arrangements had been made just the same to prepare the populace for air raids.

The next day was Sunday. Knowing that most relatives would be at home, I made my rounds. Everybody seemed to be subdued, in contrast to 1940 and 1941 when our Luftwaffe had the upper hand. These bombings by the Allies were getting on people's nerves.

On the ground floor of our apartment house was a bake shop. The baker also lived there with his family. The bake house was right behind the building.

Early Monday morning, my Mom asked me to get a few fresh rolls. The baker baked these overnight, together with bread. The store opened at 0700 hours each morning, except on Sundays. Nobody would ever consider buying bread or rolls that were not made the same day. In those days SERVICE was still spelled in capital letters. Businesses were not stifled by union regulations and the customer was king!

I entered the bake shop from inside the building and bade everybody in the store good morning. Mrs. Rudolph, the baker's wife, was perplexed. First, I stroll in without wearing my uniform, and now this disappointing address.

"Should you not say 'Heil Hitler'?" she asked. There were six people in the store, including a man in his forties, who gave himself away by his extremely short-cropped hair, harsh-boned thick-set features, the dumbbell look and the brown shirt he was wearing.

I pretended to be in thought for a moment, then looked straight at his nutcracker face and said, "That may be compulsory for the Gestapo, SS, SA, and party members, but not for members of the navy." For a few seconds it looked as if the big ape was going to jump over the counter. He thought better of it though and remarked with poor diction, sounding like he had gargled with pieces of glass, "It is people like you who stand in the way of victory. Be glad you are not a civilian."

I had just received my rolls and my change and decided to have the last word. Shaking my head from side to side, I replied to nobody in particular, "All muscle and no brains. If your contribution to the war effort is to denounce people who dare to think differently, then no wonder victory is slipping through our fingers." And with that I left.

The next few days were pleasant, though most of my co-workers and acquaintances had been called up. On the home front, war efforts had been intensified. More and more women had to "voluntarily" work in munitions factories to produce ammunition, grenades and land mines for the front lines. Only in extreme cases of hardship were they exempted.

There was some bad news. My nephew Georg was thirty-six years old, and normally would have been drafted immediately like most others of his age. But because of his key position at the largest German Bayer complex in Leverkusen near Cologne and war-related work, his induction had been postponed several times since 1939.

Before I was called up in 1941, we discussed war in general. He told me then that if he would ever lose a limb while at the front, he would take his own life; he would not be able to cope with that kind of a situation.

Georg had been drafted in March of this year and, after his basic training, had been unceremoniously moved to the Eastern Front. The way destiny sometimes works, he had to partake in a vicious battle on the tenth day after his arrival at that theater. Shrapnel hit his leg near the kneecap. The shrapnel came short of completely severing his leg apart, and he crawled for several kilometers with the lower part of his leg dangling like a thread. "When that blasted thing hit me," he told me later, "I knew exactly what the score was. But you would not believe how one can change one's mind in a hurry. I suddenly wanted to live more than ever before in my life."

When we met again after the war, he was quite exuberant. It seemed he had survived that stage of transition well. At times, he would put on his (by then three-fourths length) artificial leg; at other times he would use a crutch. But the way he moved reminded me of Commander Schubert, our harbor captain in Stavanger.

The nights were not so pleasant. We had to rush into the basement, a makeshift air raid shelter. The cellar vault had been reconstructed and arranged in such way that if one house were hit and its exits blocked by rubble, we could walk along a connecting tunnel to the next. That foresight saved the lives of numerous people in cities that had used the scheme.

Every time the air raid siren went, we got dressed quickly, took a few extra things with us, and proceeded to the basement. Upon the all-clear signal we would return to our apartments. Since my arrival on Saturday, this had happened once or twice a night, except on Sunday. Never on Sunday? Maybe the Tommies and Amies had a hangover from the day before.

The Attack

Thursday night arrived. A few minutes after midnight on Friday, the twenty-fifth, the siren blasted off again. We went downstairs almost routinely, believing we could return to our homes after an hour or so. Not this time! It was our turn. My foreboding turned to reality.

During my train ride to Wuppertal, I had met several people who had experienced serial bombings. Some said that the British, who usually attacked at night, would set *Weihnachtsbaume* (Christmas trees), which allowed them to see the ground before actually launching their bombings. I had never heard about that before and was curious how this would actually work.

Before proceeding downstairs to the basement, I glanced out the window on the fourth floor landing. Barely three minutes went by and I knew what this Christmas tree talk was all about. Depending on how one looks at that kind of situation, whether one is at the giving or the receiving end, the Tommies indeed had found an ingenious way of marking their targets.

While our flak *(Fliegerabwehrkanonen,* or antiaircraft guns) sent licking flames to the sky, a couple of British planes went to work and released four flares, sending bright light over the city. The flares descended until they hovered approximately three hundred meters above the ground. They all seemed to oscillate somewhat. One on the northeast and southeast of central Wuppertal, just about where the previous attack in May had ended, and one on the northwest and southwest of where we lived. These devices were attached to balloons and also equipped with parachutes, which regulated the descent. Once they were nicely in place, forming a large triangle, all the RAF (Royal Air Force) had to do was unload their bombs in between. And that is exactly what happened!

Most of the cellar area was used for storing coal for heating and sorting potatoes, an old European custom which is now dying out. Some families also stored preserves on shelves. The remaining area did not allow building any rec rooms. But because of these air raids, some old armchairs and a couple of small tables had been placed, so people could rest a bit. Nobody living in that apartment house had small children, which was good in a way, because there simply was not enough space for placing cots.

Five minutes after we had congregated in the basement, the bombarding began. Waves of bomber units released their loads on the city. Only by the sound of detonating bombs could one tell how close or far they hit from where we huddled. During the next forty minutes I got more than an idea of what our civilians at home had to endure. And I am not ashamed to admit that I probably was even more scared than anybody else! "What a lousy way to die," kept flashing through my mind. Little did I know that I would feel this way more than once.

What I hoped for most was that our basement exit door would not get blocked, though I knew about the underground escape provisions that had been made.

To survey the situation, I went up the basement steps halfway through the terrible attack. At the precise moment when I reached the ground floor landing and looked up between the staircase handrail, an incendiary bomb blasted through the roof, exposing itself to my eyes. The burning liquid of the bomb splashed on the handrail on the upper floor, and ran down the four floors like a fire-breathing dragon to where I stood.

All this did not take more than two seconds, during which I instantly lurched backward away from the rail and threw myself to the ground. A stench like burning acid penetrated my nose and my eyes started to itch. After only a moment I quickly withdrew down the basement steps to join the others. Meeting their suspense-filled eyes, I shrugged my shoulders and said matter-of-factly, "Our homes are burning. We cannot return."

About sixteen to eighteen persons hovered there, suddenly unusually calm. Then, while bombs continued to fall around us, we realized that everything we had worked for in our entire lives had been destroyed in minutes. We all cried!

The Aftermath

The next few days were awful. Hunting for food became obsession number one. Los Angeles-type smog hovered over the entire city. A corroded smell persisted. Buildings kept smoldering. The sun was out, but could not be seen. Fumes, vapor and haze had the upper hand. Several chemical plants had suffered direct hits, sending a veil of toxic clouds across the city sky. I suffered from severe conjunctivitis so bad that on the second day after the attack, I could hardly open my eyes.

As my father and I strolled through the rubble-filled streets, we saw pitiful scenes. People were still searching for relatives and friends who had been buried under great masses of stone fragments. Rescue commandos could not be everywhere at once. But the overall organization for providing relief was admirable. Mobile soup kitchens sprang up like mushrooms, thanks to the ever-present and never-failing Red Cross.

People were notified by information commandos where they could go to get basic needs such as clothing. One of the few undamaged buildings served as registration office for those who had been partially or totally bombed out. (Later statistics indicated that seventy-two percent of the city had been destroyed.)

Those who had suffered total loss of personal belongings and property received RM 600 per person to begin with and sufficient coupons to buy absolute necessities.

The few hospitals were bursting at their seams, hardly able to look after all seriously wounded. But something had to be done about my eyes, which seemed to get worse rather than better. I went to a first-aid station that had been set up nearby, staffed by two medical orderlies from the army. They flushed out my eyes with warm water from a large syringe, gave me some ointment and a few pills of antihistamine and sent me on my way again. At least that eased the awful itching a bit.

The aftermath for people who have experienced intensive bombings is difficult to describe, and possibly could fill an entire chapter. It is probably the worst shock treatment one can think of. I witnessed horrifying scenes of grief and sorrow, but one particular incident engraved itself in my mind.

Strolling around on the second day in search for food, we met a woman smack in the middle of what used to be downtown. When we came by, she turned to us with a lost yet happy smile on her face. She carried a bundle in her arms, which she stretched out to us, removed a cotton cloth and said, "Look, is this not wonderful? I found my baby!" The woman had gone mad. The baby in her arms was dead! I felt my heart would break apart. Describing it is totally insufficient.

On the fourth day, communication lines had been restored. Dad was able to get in touch with his uncle, who had inherited a sizable farm in Westphalia from his dad after all his brothers had left for the city in search of greener pastures. (Most did not find these pastures green after all, but were too proud to admit it.) Fritz Born, who was respectfully called Berge Born (Mountain Born) by his peers, hearing that we had been bombed out, agreed to take us in for a while.

We found an old suitcase in the basement, packed it with the few essentials we had, and prepared for next day's departure. A messenger came by in the afternoon and asked for our participation in a citizens meeting in the evening. The purpose of the gathering was to found a self-help group, with the goal of bringing life back to normal. We decided to attend to say good-bye to friends and neighbors.

The meeting was scheduled in a school building, which had partially survived the air attack. It was about 1900 hours when we arrived. A couple of hundred people were milling around in the schoolyard, talking about their ordeals.

Dad went inside the half-ruined building and explained to the program chief why we had come. When he returned, Mom and I were surrounded by neighbors, who heartily shook my hand. Some did not know I was on furlough.

Several people I did not know came swarming around the school building corner and joined us. They constantly were swearing at the damn English and the cursed Brits for "getting us into this mess."

I was not particularly sympathetic to the British myself at that moment. But when the complaining did not stop, and some of them wanted to pin me down for a comment, I just had to speak my mind.

"Sure," I agreed, "any destruction of property and the taking of human life is detestable. But, maybe we should refresh our memory. What we receive now is what hundreds of thousands of Britons had to endure when our Luftwaffe dished it out to them in 1940." I mentioned London, Brighton, Bristol, Plymouth, Birmingham and Coventry. "What we have here now," I continued, "is a quid pro quo situation. We have to swallow some of our own medicine. It is kind of strange that, with the exception of priests and maybe hangmen, nobody seems to worry about other people's deaths, unless the victims are close."

I did not have the courage, though, to go that extra step and accuse our own leaders for being, at least indirectly, responsible for the mess. Nevertheless, my remarks had sparked heated discussions. I left the group.

On the way to the railway station the next morning, Tuesday, the twenty-ninth, we passed by the main office building. It was only moderately damaged and seemed to be open for business. Going in, I was relieved to be told that the communication equipment for sending telegrams had been restored into service the previous night. I sent a telegram to my commander with the request for additional furlough. Then we went to one of the few undamaged drugstores and picked up some more antihistamine tablets to relieve my almost constant sneezing.

With typical German thoroughness, I reported to a military drop-in center, that had been provisionally set up. Even though I had papers from the Wuppertal city administration about having been bombed out, I needed something from a military source. I filled out a list of my losses, confined to two uniforms and a pair of boots that went up in flames, the stuff I had carried downstairs on several nights in a row, but not on the night of the attack. All I had rescued from the flames was an undershirt, one pair of shorts, a pair of naval trousers, a navy turtleneck sweater and my pair of nonregulation oxfords, without which I would not go anywhere.

The sergeant on duty scrawled his signature on the list, then made out a Certificate of Total Loss and an additional entry in the pay book and sent me on my way.

My great uncle's farm was situated near Paderborn, a distance of approximately 190 kilometers, less than 120 miles from Wuppertal. Yet, it took us nearly seven hours to arrive at our destination. Trains had to be changed several times, as some alternate routes were used. Come to think of it, one could call it a small miracle that rail transportation had not come to a complete halt with all that destruction. With greatest skill and determination, army engineers and civilian building crews had restored order.

The Berge Born family accepted us with open arms, even though none of those who had left the farm had kept in touch through the years. It seemed to be that country folks who lovingly cling to nature, have a different, less selfish approach to life than we city slickers.

To make myself a bit useful, I volunteered to assist with cutting grass to make hay for the use of forage. That lasted only two days, because my pollen attacks became worse. Since that time I suffer from so-called hay fever every year. Like clockwork, it starts the beginning of June and lasts until the second part of July. The possibility of choosing farming as a career had to be discarded.

Time went by. Soon, the second to last day of my regular furlough came. It was 8 July. In two days I had to report to Kiel. Finally in the evening, a reply cable arrived from my unit, advising that my furlough had been extended for two full weeks.

I spent most of my time enjoying the countryside and getting acquainted with a number of distant relatives. It turned out that two-thirds of the farming community—made up of two villages side-by-side—were related to each other. As so often is the case, country people do not move around, period, unless they have to leave their farms for economic reasons which, shamefully, is too often the case nowadays.

On the negative side of farm living, it causes much more inbreeding than in cities, where there is so much more choice of meeting future spouses. From a total population of three hundred people, children and all, I met twenty-seven families bearing my name. I became friendly with one of the village girls, (no, not that friendly!) but backed off after we met for the second time, when she told me that her parents wanted to get to know me. I was not ready to commit myself to a serious relationship. They hardly ever last during war years! I knew that from some of my comrades who were in the process of going through nasty divorces, that was not for me. Why mess up life at such an early stage? There would be loads of time for that later!

Counting on additional delays, I took the early train out of the village with the unusual name of Aue-Wingeshausen on Saturday, 24 July. As much as we all hate good-byes, I parted from my parents at least with the knowledge that they would not be in anymore danger for the time being.

My father had been temporarily stationed at a railway nearby the village but knew that he, sooner or later, would have to return to his regular assignment in Wuppertal. That was possible only by moving somewhat closer. There was no thinking about returning directly to Wuppertal, since it had been almost three-fourths destroyed. Accommodations were nonexistent, even though from the total population of three hundred eighty thousand, nearly one hundred forty thousand had left the city. But that still left two hundred forty thousand people sharing living space meant for about a hundred fifty thousand. A sad situation that can only be understood by experiencing it! It is inconceivable for the North Americans, whose countries were never touched by war.

By order of the State and the City, bombed-out families unable to leave the city had to be taken in by others who were fortunate enough to still have their own apartments. When one considers the severity of this state of affairs, one can only admire the way the German people at the time pulled together at one end of the string. A community spirit prevailed.

The railway schedule indicated three train changes. The first in Paderborn, the second in Osnabrück and, having passed Hannover and Bremen, in Hamburg. I had taken a slight risk in leaving the village on my last day of leave not knowing about any possible major delays, but luck was with me. The eleventh hour (2300 hours), literally speaking, had just started, when I checked in at Kiel. The original date to report back had been changed from Saturday, 10 July, to Saturday, 24 July, midnight. Looking at my watch I saw I had exactly fifty-four more minutes left of my furlough. Great timing!

RETURN TO SCANDINAVIA

The Light-Traveling GI

While I had traveled heavily-packed like a mule on the way home to spend my furlough, it was quite a different story when returning to my base in Stavanger.

When I reported to the staff sergeant at the German naval transit base in Kiel, for naval personnel destined to return to Norway and Denmark, he first gave me a blast because of the way I looked–no regulation navy cap, navy knot missing, hair too long, no boots in sight, wearing oxfords. I had never traveled that light while with the armed forces; just a leather case with one T-shirt, a pair of socks, shaving tools, a bar of soap, my wine bottle opener and service serviette, and my pay book. My overall appearance was slightly better than that of a hobo.

When the sergeant ran out of insults and out of breath, I quickly squeezed in five words, "I've been bombed out, Staff Sergeant, sir." I produced the two certificates from Wuppertal.

He immediately changed his tune. "That is different," he said. "Sit down, make a brief report, and fill out these supply requisitions." I noticed he had handed me two forms for two sets of uniforms. No set, however, included steel helmet, combat boots and gas mask. He explained, "You don't want to carry these around. They are too cumbersome. You can draw these heavyweights and other clothing when you return to your unit."

After he had signed, I got up and went across the yard to the supply building. I had about twenty comrades ahead of me, most of them army personnel. When my turn came, the quartermaster took one look at me, and drew a sour face. I thought, "Now you get hell again." But he looked down on the requisition. Under remarks appeared the entry "to fit well."

"Why?" he asked. "You look like a bum. Are you also deformed?"

"Not really," I answered, "but I might look that way in ill-fitting clothes. As you can see, my head is rather small. I don't want a cap which slips over my ears; otherwise I need an electric light inside for me to see."

For a moment it looked like he was going to burst out laughing, but he pulled himself together remembering his role to act tough at all times. Instead he asked, "Who do we have here, a prima donna with special privileges or a comic?"

"Neither nor, Herr Quartiermeister, just an average guy who would like to look human, even in uniform." The staff sergeant initialed the request because he felt that a functionary should look decent. End of argument.

I received pretty good material handed to me. That was more than usual. Ordinarily, the stuff was thrown at you with the remark, "Fits," to nip any protest in the bud. Remember Kiel? I saw my cap was a bit too small. I guess, I deserved that. But then, I was overdue for a haircut which, as I found out later, did the trick.

Always eager to pick a fight with the navy, two chaps from the Luftwaffe loudly speculated why "that milk-faced navy boy" got special treatment. In passing by, I told them, "You cannot see it, but I am blue-blooded; that's why," and hurriedly walked out with a grin.

Slowpoke Journey

The next day I picked up my report certification and marching papers. As I described earlier, when traveling to Germany, I traveled by train through Sweden. The route started in

Halden, at the Norwegian-Swedish border southward via Göteborg, Aengelholm, Helsingborg and Malmö to Trelleborg, when I took a ferry to Stralsund, Germany.

This time my papers instructed me to proceed to Flensburg, then northbound by rail through Denmark to Frederikshavn, then taking a ferry to Fredrikstad, Norway. I was kind of looking forward to another pleasant and interesting railway journey through Sweden. Strangely enough, though Sweden had stressed her strict neutrality right from the beginning of hostilities in Scandinavia, Swedish Foreign Minister Christian Guenther allowed German troops to pass through Sweden on their way to Norway and from Norway to Germany. When asking about that alternative, I was told, "That is temporarily restricted, because something happened."

Later, I found out what incident triggered the restriction. Previously, I briefly described the attempt of a German soldier to defect. German and Swedish diplomats could not agree whose bullets had killed the defector first, those of the German security officer, or the ones fired by the Swedish guard. The body of the man had been riddled with bullets which drilled into it simultaneously from the front and the back. An agreement was finally hammered out, arranging for the transfer of the soldier's body to Germany. One can imagine problems that faced the dead man's relatives, who unquestionably had to suffer for the traitorous action of the soldier.

About 160 soldiers gathered together the next morning, waiting to be transported to the Kiel railway station. Some would be going home on leave, others returning to the Eastern Front, where the military situation had started to get hot under the collar. Some returned from home to join their comrades in occupied countries in the west and south. Others, like myself, returned to Denmark and Norway.

To give you an idea about the numbers of occupying personnel in Norway alone, army, air force and navy combined counted nearly four hundred eighty thousand. Only as late as March 1944 was that figure to be reduced to three hundred twenty thousand.

The train covered the distance between Kiel and Flensburg in less than two hours. A special troop transport train awaited us in Flensburg to bring us over the border into Denmark.

To kill time, some of the guys started playing chess or card games. There is a German card game called skat, which we all knew well. It is similar to bridge, but only three players play at one time. The highest bidder plays against the other two, but must win or payout his opponents. To win, the player has to have sixty-one points minimum out of a total of one hundred twenty. If he loses, it could mean he either overestimated the value of his hand, or the cards of his opponents are so unfavorably stacked against him, that he can be beaten with his own trump suit.

The train crawled across the border into Denmark until we reached Farhus. Two growling voices shouted, "Everybody out; take your crap with you." Some complained loudly about the interruption; others who had fallen asleep cursed.

It was about 0100 hours. Near my compartment, two teams of card players had fought it out since the train had left Flensburg. As time went by, their voices got louder and louder, fired up by Schnapps. One Landser, whom I bumped into when entering the hallway said, "Damn shit, just now when I finally have a good hand." He resented breaking up the game, because he had lost heavily since leaving Flensburg.

As we all gathered outside, some rubbing their eyes, I noticed another train lined up for us practically ahead of ours. The regular-sized tracks ended here, being replaced by a narrow track used in Denmark.

Since I traveled lighter than anybody else, it was easy to quickly find a good spot to relax in the new train. The two watchdogs who had shouted at us to get out were still active making sure that the transfer took place in minimum time. As if on military maneuver, one had to move one's frame like lightning, even if nobody shot at moving targets.

I made myself comfortable, reading my Tom Shark yellow-back (a German detective with an English name, similar to Nick Carter, the New York private eye). This train moved even slower than the last. At times it moved so slow that one felt running beside it would be a cinch. The rumble and slow-swinging motions made me fall asleep as soon as I had laid the book aside.

The slow train dawdled along, passing a number of small communities, reached Redekra, Hovsburg, Overjerstal, Vojens, Vamdrup, Lunderskoev and Kolding. From there, via Fredericia, Boerkop, Vejle, Hedensted, Loesning, Horsens and Skanderborg to Aarhus.

I woke up and looked at my watch: 0745 hours. Unbelievable! Normally the whole trip from Farhus should not have taken longer than three hours. We had conquered the less than 160 kilometers in six and three-fourths hours. That meant we had crawled along at about twenty-four kilometers per hour. And there were no stops on the way. Well, if I thought this was slow, I had another thing coming!

Looking out the window I saw droves of military district police swarming all over. Something was not right! They immediately encircled the train. We were told to leave the train for a breakfast treat by the Red Cross in a building close by, then to report back by 0930 hours. It felt good to be able to stretch our feet a bit.

Leaving the station, we walked the short distance to the Red Cross barrack. It had been erected diagonally from the station across the street at the corner of Banegaros Pladsen and Park Alle, less than three short blocks.

It was obvious that something unusual was in the air. Danish civilians, who used to ignore the occupiers the same as their Norwegian cousins did, seemed to glance at us with a strangely quizzical look in their eyes as if to say, "Would you not rather leave us alone now?" I became very curious.

Surrounded by a throng of soldiers, I entered the Red Cross building. It looked quite tidy though crowded. The nice window curtains, decorations, and well-kept furniture signaled the presence of the female touch. I squeezed myself behind a corner table with another couple of sailors, two guys from the air force, and a red-bearded lieutenant commander, who must have been given permission to wear his ornament while on furlough. We soon understood why.

He was a successful U-boat Kommandant, having two British and one Canadian ship fatalities to his credit. Most recently, he had caused some havoc among a British convoy in the Skagerrak. After damaging three ships, he had run out of torpedoes. The ensuing chase by the British gave him a lot of headaches. They were close on his tail, bombarding him with deep water depth charges, one of which damaged his boat. After emptying a couple of decompression chambers filled with a number of bits and pieces and heavy oil to indicate a hit, he lay low for hours. He even was forced to dive deeper than the then allowable maximum 120 meters.

When he and his crew eventually reached Kristiansund, Norway, they could barely emerge and had almost completely run out of oxygen. He received a hero's welcome. Several correspondents interviewed him. Photographs were taken and articles about his venture appeared in German newspapers and those under German control in Norway and Denmark. He already was decorated with the Iron Crosses second and first class. A few days after the event, Admiral Von Schrader, Supreme Commander of the Norwegian west coast defense, awarded him the German Cross in Gold.

In the meantime, a motherly-type Red Cross waitress with a most pleasant smile and personality had served our breakfast and placed a large pot of coffee on the table. We dug in and continued an amiable conversation.

The air force sergeant was the only other one who had seen some action. He had attended several bombing missions while the Battle of Britain took place. Once, after returning from his target (Coventry) the fuselage of his plane got hit by antiaircraft fire. His flight lieutenant barely made it to the Straight of Dover where they belly-landed. Miraculously, a German patrol boat came by to rescue them before the big bird sank. They reached Antwerp without incident. The sergeant credited his superior for making it that far in the first place. The two of them had used everything available to plug two bad leaks, even their shirts and socks!

We had not paid any particular attention to the constant coming and going of soldiers. Suddenly both entrance doors were thrust wide open, and the booming voice of a chief petty officer shouted, "Attention! Be ready to present pay book and identity papers!" We had several civilians in the mess hall, most of them Danes who were employed by German military authorities.

The petty officer was accompanied by three army MPs and two other individuals, who could be easily identified by their leather coats as Gestapo agents. Again, it flashed through my mind that something had to be badly wrong here.

Sabotage

The group split up and went from table to table. The two Gestapo men interviewed the civilians, while the other four, divided by two, looked after those present in uniform.

When our turn came, the petty officer, accompanied by one army MP, smartly saluted our bearded companion and asked quite politely, seeing the high decoration on Lieutenant Commander Kretchmar's chest, "May I see your papers?" The question was directed at all of us. He looked at all the other papers first, then at mine. Looking up at me, he asked, "How come you have navy papers, but you don't look like a navy private to me?" Before I could answer, he addressed Commander Kretchmar, asking "Can you vouch for him?"

"Yes, I am glad to do this. He just returned from home, where he was completely bombed out. That is why he looks like a half-civilian. I know his unit in Stavanger and the area commandant. But before you leave Petty Officer Lange, tell us, what is going on here?"

"All I can tell you, Herr Kapitaenleutnant, is that we seem to be dealing with a Danish Underground movement we did not know existed. Yesterday morning, our airfield on the Isle of Samaoe, about forty kilometers southeast of here, was sabotaged. Two *Stukas* (dive fighter planes) were destroyed on the ground by heavy explosives and one transport plane was damaged. Almost simultaneously, they also managed to blow up two petrol storage tanks and one ammunition depot. Timing devices must have been used.

"Nobody can understand it. These installations were well-guarded. Yet, during the explosions we lost three airmen. The security warning system at the depot must have been deactivated from the inside, to allow the saboteurs access. Twelve navy security guards were detailed to protect the petrol storage tanks. The four navy guards on duty were murdered, stripped of their uniforms, and their papers taken. The other eight off-duty guards didn't hear a thing before the explosions.

"But that is not all. Late last night, one of our supply ships anchored in Aarhus Bay, was damaged by explosives. To top things off, in the wee hours of this morning, a weaving factory at the outskirts of Holme nearby, mysteriously burnt down. They used to make field exercise garments for our troops there, using Irish yarn. There must have been several sabotage groups involved in this malicious destruction. We had a hell of a twenty-four hours.

"Aarhus Harbor and Bay have been cordoned off and rails and roads are carefully screened. We've got to get these rascals!"

Turning to me, he concluded, "You see, Private Born, these missing naval uniforms as sure as hell have been used as a camouflage for moving about the harbor here. The way you are dressed, you could have been one of these guys having split up one sailor's uniform with another man. Continue your good journey." With that, he left our table.

When we were finished with breakfast, we surrendered our entitlement cards and left our waitress a good tip. Kretchmar suggested we stay together and occupy a compartment in the train when continuing our journey, and pick up the conversation where we had left off. We showed surprise since we knew some railway cars were reserved for officers only. When the air force sergeant said something to that effect, the commander said jokingly, "Why? Am I not good enough for you guys?" We hastily agreed to his proposal.

Denmark
Germany's *Musterprotektorat* (Model Protectorate)?

On 9 April 1940, we invaded Denmark and Norway at the same time. Norway's King Haakon VII told his ministers that he would have to abdicate if the Norwegian government should decide to accept German demands. The government backed its king by calling upon Norway's three million inhabitants to resist the invaders as long as possible. As a consequence, the Norwegian Army, in conjunction with British, French and Polish forces, inflicted over five thousand casualties upon our invading forces.

In contrast, Denmark's King Christian X, who, incidentally was King Haakon's brother, conceded to our demands almost immediately. He stated that his government would do everything possible to maintain peace and order in the country. He wished to spare his country further hardship and to eliminate any friction between our troops and the country.

Because of the Norwegian resistance to German occupation, an immediate campaign of terror was instituted against the Jews. Property was seized, civil rights were abolished, searches and arrests took place, and identity cards of Jews were stamped with the Star of David. Fortunately, because of the long frontier shared with its Scandinavian neighbor, about half of Norway's seventeen hundred Jews managed to escape to Sweden.

The initial acceptance of us by the Danes and their early willingness to allow us into their country, were the main reasons for Hitler referring to Denmark as the *Musterprotektorat.* While the capture and deportation of Jews in all other occupied countries was on top of Hitler's list of priorities, Denmark's eight thousand Jews remained unmolested.

There were two more reasons for the exceptional freedom for Danish Jews. One was the Nazi racial theory by Alfred Rosenberg, Hitler's special advisor in matters of racial origins. Himself being a Hungarian half-Jew, Rosenberg claimed that the Danes were pure Nordics like the Germans and direct descendants from the same stock. According to national socialist philosophy, the Kimbric peninsula Jutland was the birthplace of the Teutons and the Gottons, and the Danes were blood brothers of the Germans.

The other reason for the leniency toward the Danish Jews was established by research: the high degree of identification of the Danish population with their Jewish brethren. It seemed to be clear that the Danes would not play the willing underlings by assisting the

Germans in persecuting the Jews as was the case with the Poles, Austrians, Czechoslovaks, Hungarians and the Ukrainians. The Danes were absolutely forthright in their opposition to antisemitism.

The former German Ambassador to Denmark, Cecil Von Renthe-Fink became the first plenipotentiary after the occupation. He quite correctly assessed the Danish attitude toward antisemitism. The Gestapo, however, kept pushing foreign office officials in Berlin concerned with Jewish matters in Scandinavia. Renthe-Fink was told to do something about the embarrassing fact that eight thousand Jews were living freely in occupied Denmark. He pointed out that any tampering with the Danish Jews' civil rights could do immeasurable harm to the otherwise peaceful relations between the two countries.

In November 1942, he was replaced by Dr. Werner Best, former administrative chief of the Gestapo. But even his report, two months later, fully concurred with that of his predecessor. He pointed out the prompt fulfillment of heavy quotas of foodstuffs with which Denmark supplied Germany. We also would have to count on sabotaging Danish factories which were turning out much-needed marine diesel engines, parts of airplanes and armored vehicles. He warned the German foreign office to "forget about the Jews for a while."

Antisemitic elements, however–and there were many at that time in Germany–led by fanatical Gestapo and SS leaders, kept the pressure on Dr. Best.

Without the knowledge of the German foreign office, the Gestapo assigned the infamous Auschwitz Gestapo Colonel Rudolph Mildner to investigate the Danish Jews situation. Mildner drew the same conclusions. So strong were these signals that he flew to Berlin to convince the foreign minister, Joachim Von Ribbentrop, that the Danes would not tolerate persecution of the Jews. He even pointed out that some German soldiers might not be willing to cooperate in drastic measures against the Jews, since they had become infected by the practice of racial and religious tolerance in Denmark.

In the meantime, the Danes had received knowledge about the demeaning and inhumane treatment arrested Jews had suffered in Germany, Holland, Norway and other occupied countries. Would the Germans dare to treat Danish Jews the same? The counter-question to this was, what would prevent them from doing so? Now the answer was obvious. The Danes decided to stop behaving and fight the occupiers.

By March 1943, two Resistance organizations were in place: BOPA or *Borgerlige Partisaner* (roughly translated "middle class partisans"), led by Holger Danske, and the Lyngby Group which was founded by a Danish Jew, David Sompolinski. The head of this group was Aage Bertelsen.

These two organizations were destined to give General Von Hannecken, German military commander in Denmark, a thousand and one problems. Intelligence reports which went across my desk in 1944, clearly proved the ingenuity with which they outsmarted the Gestapo as well as German counterintelligence. I remember at one point having read a situation summary report for the Scandinavian theater, in which Von Hannecken commented about the BOPA and the Lyngby Group's field operators.

He used this description, "Even if one thinks one has these rascals, they still manage to slip through one's fingers!"

As a first major task, the Resistance set about organizing three escape routes from Denmark to Sweden for those who, for various reasons, suddenly might have to leave the country. That goal was quickly achieved. The general population supported the Resistance, except Danish pro-Nazis, most of whom were well-known. Equally well-known were the members of the Schalburg Corps, a number of Danish pro-Nazis who had volunteered to fight for us in Russia. Later on, in August of 1943, they were recalled from the Eastern Front to deal with workers groups, who had begun protests and strikes, affecting the shipyards of Copenhagen and Odense, then expanded into general strikes throughout the city.

The infusion of the Schalburg Corps infuriated the Danes greatly, since these traitors were not only pro-Nazis, but mostly consisted of criminals which had been released from Danish prisons at the very beginning of the occupation.

In May 1943, persistent rumors kept circulating regarding the sooner or later imminent arrests and deportation of all Danish Jews. Gekados files did not indicate immediate arrest orders at the time, but Dr. Werner Best was under constant pressure, as I said before. The whole question of the Danish Jews eventually came to a boiling point when Hitler called Dr. Best to Berlin in August. During that meeting, Hitler bluntly called the fact that Danish Jews were walking around free, "a disgrace." Again, Dr. Best referred to the possible consequences of drastic actions against the Jews. Hitler replied, "You should see yourself that the Danes resist us now in spite of our leniency toward the Jews. We have spoiled them, nothing else. If conditions get worse, we have to declare a military state of emergency, which means the reins of governing would have to be handed over to General Von Hannecken."

By the summer of 1943, more and more Danes began opposing us and not solely for idealistic reasons; another good reason came into focus. From non-German radio broadcasts—BBC London and Beromuenster, Switzerland—it seemed to be clear that the Allies were winning the war.

Signs Of Defeat

Since 31 January 1943, when the Soviets recaptured Stalingrad from the German forces, things went downhill for Germany. The defeats our forces suffered at El Alamein in spite of Field Marshal Rommel's gallant efforts can only be called catastrophic. The transparent victories of British forces over the Axis Powers (German and Italian mobile units) signaled a turnabout in favor of the Allies. Mussolini's conduct of operations in the North African theater was primarily blamed for the decisive military drawback of the Axis Powers.

Reverting back a bit, British Secret Archives reveal that in 1943, Winston Churchill did have a plan providing for assistance to train and reequip Mussolini's forces. The Great Old Man, with his sense of anticipation and correct judgment of military situations, felt Mussolini was ready to have second thoughts about his alliance with Germany.

It was an open secret even then that Il Duce seriously considered making overtures to the Allies, the aim of which was a separate peace treaty. Only Mussolini's lack of courage to face Hitler with that possibility prevented it from becoming a reality. It undoubtedly would have been a sensational major event.

In July, the Allies began to invade Sicily. On the twenty-fourth, party leaders Counts Ciano and Grandi outspokenly commented on the miserable performance of Italy's military reserves. Most other leaders supported them.

On the following day, 25 July, King Victor Emmanuel arrested Benito Mussolini, who became a hostage in his own country. This was a most unusual action. He was quickly transported to an isolated mountaintop under heavy guard. Before this action was taken, the Fascist Grand Council had met and voted nineteen to seven for a nonconfidence motion in the Duce and his government.

Some military and defense experts raised doubts that the terrain was safe enough from attack, though a close observation immediately after Mussolini's transfer to the mountaintop seemed to indicate otherwise. The doubters were told that the hideout could never be stormed, because of its limited platform on the mountaintop, coupled with the overall strategic superiority of its location. The possibility of an airlift was equally excluded since it would be impossible for any aircraft to land there, unless it could stop on a dime. They had not counted on the ingenuity of Otto Skorzeny.

Hitler called him the day following Mussolini's capture and gave him the assignment to rescue Il Duce from the claws of the Allies.

Since the murder of Austrian Chancellor Engelbert Dollfuss by SS gunmen on Wednesday, 25 July 1934, Skorzeny had been of exceptional usefulness to the Third Reich. Himself an Austrian, Skorzeny had lent a helping hand in giving the Austrian Nazis legal status in July 1936. He also set the stage for the union of Austria with Germany in 1938, arranging for Austrian Chancellor Kurt Schuschnigg to meet with Hitler in the mountain retreat of Bavaria. Schuschnigg was compelled to sign an agreement that cleared the way for the Anschluss with Germany. That was in February 1938. Exactly one month later, on Friday, 11 March 1938, Schuschnigg resigned and Artur Seyss-Inquart, Austria's Nazi leader took office to reign the Austrian government.

Skorzeny had some more accomplishments. On Monday, 1 April 1941, his regiment was withdrawn from the Western Front and rushed to Temesva in southwestern Romania and successfully invaded Yugoslavia. There were a number of other successful ventures which Skorzeny had carried out. He never let the Fuehrer down and would not do so in the future.

One day after Hitler's order, Skorzeny's commandos left Staaken airfield near Berlin to fly to R[illegible] The initial commando consisted of twelve officers and twenty-five men. They all could speak Italian fairly well and pretended to be members of Student's XI Parachute Corps by wearing Italian paratroops uniforms.

Mussolini's birthday was on 29 July. A number of contacts were made with generally well-informed individuals about Il Duce's place of confinement. But several rumors turned out to be just that. The Allies had counted on the possibility that the search for the disposed leader was on and likely spread some rumors which would lead nowhere. It seemed the Italians were just as puzzled as we were as to Mussolini's involuntary domicile.

Finally, on Saturday, 11 September, while an Allied radio broadcast stated that Mussolini had arrived in North Africa (which was a false alarm) Skorzeny found out Mussolini's real whereabouts.

Wasting no time, he went into action. The next day, Sunday, in a glider with five other men, he carried out a most daring parachute raid by "landing on a dime" on the plateau of the Mount Grosso, where Mussolini was held under heavy guard in the hotel. Against all odds, twelve gliders landed altogether. The entire operation of freeing Mussolini took only eight minutes!

Alberto Faiola, captain of the *Carabinieri*, knew the approaching Skorzeny and ordered his men not to shoot. Skorzeny swiftly entered the room where Mussolini was held. Seeing Skorzeny entering with a machine gun, the two guards inside had second thoughts. Holding up their hands, they backed away against the wall.

Skorzeny turned to Mussolini and smiled. "The Fuehrer has sent me to set you free," he simply said.

Skorzeny was more of an adventurer than anything else. As such, he downplayed the trickiest and most dangerous deeds. He was destined to cause a lot of confusion and frustration in 1944 behind the Allied fronts in France. That is another story. But freeing Mussolini was about the only good news we were about to hear until the bitter end of the war.

The ever increasing acts of sabotage by the Danes against our occupation became particularly evident in the month of July 1943, when I passed through Denmark. The civil courage of the Danes was also on the upswing. All one had to look at were newspapers, which printed all kinds of incidents. Following is a brief excerpt, covering the timespan of only eight days, from Tuesday, 13 July, through Tuesday, 20 July. (Interestingly enough, each one of these, together with others, appeared in files of the naval counterintelligence administration, were I served in 1944.)

On 13 July, one man got thirty days in jail for writing the French word *Victoire* on a German signboard. Six Danes were sentenced to thirty days in prison for having "molested and insulted" German officers and soldiers. A fifty-year-old man was arrested and sentenced to thirty days for insulting an attachment of German soldiers on the march.

On 18 July, a previous offender was sentenced to sixty days imprisonment. He had "bothered" a German soldier who escorted a Danish woman. On 19 July, an eighteen-year-old youngster received thirty days for insulting Germans on the march.

On 20 July, one man got thirty days for spreading a rumor that we had confiscated copper and sent it to Germany. Another man got forty days; while intoxicated, he had insulted and molested a German soldier. Another got two years in prison for libeling Hitler and the German people in a letter to the German local commander. Still another man got twenty days for extinguishing a cigarette on a sign board belonging to the Wehrmacht. A forty-year-old worker was sentenced to thirty days for addressing a German soldier in English.

I could see another good reason for the Danes spreading discontent and disillusionment with us. During three years under our occupation, from May 1940 through May 1943, they had lived better than any other occupied nation. As a matter of fact, they lived much better than the German civilian population!

Danes did not have to worry about the rationing of food and clothing. Restaurants, cafes and nightclubs did a brisk business. Other industries operated also in normal peacetime fashion. The Danes were better dressed than any other European nation except Sweden.

I remember my astonishment well when I noticed that American nylons, which had been imported via Sweden could be pulled from ordinary vending machines for Danish Kr 3 a pair. I spent an entire five-days pay on these nylons which I later on bartered with some comrades who tried to keep their girlfriends happy.

Suddenly in June 1943, all this changed. Using the defiance of the Danes as pretext, the German government decided to teach these thankless Danes a lesson. A food shortage was artificially created. The Danes took more of an affront at that than anything else.

In a secret broadcast in early July, a resistance leader made the observation that those who had more or less accepted the idea of collaboration with the Germans, would cease doing so "when our Jewish brothers are in danger or when food would become scarce."

He was correct. The Danes love to eat lavishly. One should see how the Danes consider dining an art and practice it! The quality of their cuisine is comparable to that of the French. The forced belt-tightening was going to return to us like a boomerang! But what nobody expected was that the ever increasing acts of defiance were only a prelude for worse things to come. We had made a foolish error in judgment.

Such was the situation on Monday, 26 July 1943, when the six of us walked the short distance back to the Aarhus railway station.

More Problems

When leaving the railway station the overall activity was heavy, Wehrpolizei and all. We knew more about the reasons when we returned, but the hectic atmosphere which awaited us was unusual.

One of my navy chums, who was in his forties, had a quizzical look on his face that never changed. Seeing this commotion, he raised his eyebrows even higher. Any moment I expected his *Kraetzchen* (German slang for the rectangular four-cornered navy cap) to disappear down his neck like a sinking stern of a ship. Turning to his comrade, who walked beside him, he remarked, "Hans, I think there is something more brewing than we heard at breakfast. What do you think?"

Hans looked at me, not quite as quizzical-looking as his mate. The four of us shrugged our shoulders. Lieutenant Commander Kretchmar said, "Who knows? We will see." Then he added, "You know what? Wait here, guys. I'll try to find out."

He walked over to a German major, who was standing close by a sign vertically sticking out from the side of the railway building. It carried the Danish and German inscriptions for Aarhus Tourist Board. The major was surrounded by several military personnel members needing information or, in some cases, having to report to him. The major was permanently posted here to act as transport coordinator and German counterpart of the Danish stationmaster.

Returning, Commander Kretchmar looked at me and said, "It seems your buddy here is correct. What we heard at breakfast was only the beginning of our problems, not the end. Near Hadsten, two-thirds of the distance to Randers north of here, the rail tracks have been blown up while we had breakfast. Our engineers are on the way to assess the damage. Work crews to clean up the rubble and repair the tracks have been sent out, but it might take several hours to restore the situation to normal. Colonel Metzger, the area commandant, will make an announcement in a few minutes."

A confection stand on wheels passed us and stopped a few feet ahead. A Dane in his fifties, rather stocky, with deep lines in his face, opened up the half side of his stand that had been folded down.

We walked over to have a closer look at his display. He smiled broadly and said, "Good merchandise, not expensive." He carried a couple of newspapers, the *Danske Dagebladen* and the *Hamburger Handelsblatt*, a Swedish magazine, ice cream bars, chocolates, Dutch tobacco which strangely enough was rationed in Holland, open-faced sandwiches and a variety of Danish pastries.

His prices were nominal all right. We all bought a few items. Commander Kretchmar, who was the only one who understood and spoke Norwegian and Danish, purchased the *Danske Dagebladen* just out of curiosity. I bought the *Hamburger Handelsblatt* to share with the others and, though we had just finished breakfast, I could not resist buying a few of my favorite Danish pastries.

We pooled money to purchase a dozen open-faced sandwiches for later in case of further delays. It was a smart move. As the Dane wrapped our sandwiches in translucent wax paper and accepted our Danish money, his smile broadened even more than when he had greeted us.

For a while I was afraid his deeply-lined face would crack, but he survived. I could not make out his behavior. He acted as if he just had made the deal of the year. Later, I knew why.

I took the pastries in a bag and jammed the newspaper under my arm. As I was about to turn, several loudspeakers started crackling with static. The booming voice of Colonel Metzger, the Area Commandant, announced. "Attention, attention! All men on leave to Germany report immediately on platform five, track nine. The train will depart to Flensburg in forty-five minutes, at 1000 hours."

There was a short pause. Then, the speakers crackled again. "Attention, attention! All those returning from leave and traveling northbound to Randers, Aalborg and Frederikshavn are to report to the Aarhus Tourist Board for distribution of one day's spending money. You will report here to continue your journey at 1600 hours."

After receiving our pocket money we checked our baggage at the luggage registration counter, then left the building to go for a walk. We had almost six hours to kill. It was too early yet to go for luncheon. The idea of doing some shopping was out. After an annual furlough one is bound to be strapped for cash. The Danish Kr 3.50 we had just received would barely suffice to pay for a good luncheon.

I went to the vendor, who by now had reached the station exit, and bought an Aarhus tourist map. Equipped with that, we went out to enjoy the sunshine and fresh air. It was quite warm, around twenty-six degrees Celsius, which is warm for the Scandinavian theater. There was hardly any humidity in the air.

This time we turned around the station building to the back and entered Jagergardsgade. We had a set plan of how to best spend our time. Visiting a museum or art gallery was first on the agenda, followed by some window-shopping for lack of funds, maybe taking a swim somewhere, and, of course, having a good luncheon before returning to the station.

The Aarhus Arts Museum was on the map but we could not find it. Commander Kretchmar asked an elderly Dane if there were museums in town and where they were located.

"There is only the old town on Viborgvej at the east end of town," he replied. "It is an interesting place where old houses, some of them over a hundred years old, have been preserved. The area includes old shops, the old post office and merchants' establishments. Our art museum, where you could see sculptures and fabulous paintings, was closed shortly after you people arrived."

We started speculating about this. Maybe it had been closed because of lack of funds? Lack of respect for those who were running Denmark now made me boldly offer another possibility. From time to time, we all had heard rumors that Hermann Goering was a lover of the arts and could not resist stripping museums of any pieces he considered fit for his own personal collection. Could it be the Danes, like the Norwegians, got wind of this in time to bury their treasures? If so, good for them!

Passing through the residential area, it should have been a familiar sight for me by now to see Danish women, most of them overweight, leaning on their window sills, sucking at big cigars or puffing pipes. But, no matter how often I saw this picture, I simply could not get accustomed to it.

We had now entered the business district. Recently imposed restrictive measures on the Danes by us did not seem to have impaired this community yet. Goods of all kinds were aplenty and stores were fairly busy that early in the day.

After several blocks we noticed a beach near Strandvejen. We rented swimming trunks and took a few dips. Even though it was early in the day, quite a few people had taken advantage of this bright day, seeking relief from the heat. This being a Monday, I wondered how many of these Danes, especially men, had skipped work.

A couple of hours later we had luncheon in a *vinhus* on Hans Broges Gade, near Sankt Pauls Kirke. Refreshed from the swim and the good walk, our appetite demanded a substantial meal. My companions knew my background and took full advantage of having a "gourmet" in their midst, leaving the selection of food and wine to me. The menu was great, with a large selection that made it difficult to choose. At that time, no restaurateur had ever heard of a limited menu selection, which now seems to be the order of the day. This is not surprising, though, with the cost of food and labor nowadays!

Judging from its content, Froken Thorland, the owner of the restaurant, must have had great connections. Nothing was missing, not even *Pate de Fois Gras* (goose liver paste). And the house wine was second to none, which is quite a statement from a Rhinelander. We felt like never leaving, but when the clock showed 1430 hours, the meeting had to be adjourned.

It took us just fifteen minutes to return to the railway station. The commander gave us his baggage ticket and went to travel information while we picked up our gear from the luggage registration counter.

When Kretchmar returned, he pointed to platform four, track five, where our train would be assembled. Albert, the air force corporal said, "If you don't mind, I would like to fill my thermos with coffee from the canteen here. Who knows when we next will get something to drink." We promised to wait for him before boarding the train.

Entering the train, we quickly occupied one compartment, threw our stuff in the luggage racks and made ourselves at home. Several officers who passed by glanced at us and lifted their eyebrows, seeing a naval officer fraternizing with noncoms. Commander Kretchmar did not seem to take any notice.

By now we felt quite comfortable with each other. I had a strong feeling I was in the company of people who wore uniforms not by choice but because they simply had to. Our conversation still evolved around recent events at the Eastern Front, at home, and in Denmark. But nobody made any politically fanatical statements.

At 1635 hours, the train began to move and soon we had left Aarhus. The train crawled through the countryside. It appeared to be even slower than when we had left Flensburg. Would we ever arrive at our destinations?

A couple of compartments behind us a group of soldiers were obviously playing skat. From the gibberish one could tell that these guys were not only playing cards, but also lifting their elbows. The more and more stammering voices indicated heavy consumption of Schnapps. Arguments became louder, and then we heard the same voice that had complained in Farhus about the interruption of the game, coming loud and clear, "I will help you, you swine. Now it is my turn for a change. I will let you bleed!" It sounded as if he was recovering his losses and more.

After one hour rumbling along the tracks, our conversation petered out. Commander Kretchmar said, "Maybe I will have a look at the newspaper." Turning to me, he asked, "What about you, Sigy?"

"Good idea," was my reply. "We may be able to finish reading the paper before we arrive at the next terminal in Randers. This is just as bad as a slow boat to China, as the Americans say. The whole stretch is only thirty-two kilometers, but I bet it will take another hour before we reach Langa, not to mention Randers."

With that, we both unfolded our newspapers. Several pages that seemed to have been stapled together slipped out and fluttered to the floor. We instinctively bent down, almost bumping our heads together. What we picked up was neither part of his *Danske Dagebladen* nor my *Hamburger Handelsblatt.* We looked at the two sets a few seconds, then glanced at each other, equally baffled. We each held a pamphlet in our hands, printed by the illegal Free Denmark.

They contained a summary of recent acts of sabotage that had been successfully directed and carried out against the hated occupiers. After each report, a comment was added to convince the reader of the justification for the deeds. Both brochures had the same content. The only difference was that Kretchmar's set was printed on yellowish onionskin paper in

Danish with German translations, while mine was typed on ordinary typewriter paper, Danish on the left and English on the right side.

The reports presented descriptive pictures yet in a matter-of-fact fashion. The comments had punch and the translations were quite good. Overall, a pretty good piece of work, I had to admit. A darn good reason for the vendor's broad smile, when he handed us the newspapers. He probably was speculating right now on our reactions to his trick.

To top it all off, somebody had used a thick pen and printed some words at the end of Commander Kretchmar's set. It said in Danish and German, "Learn German before the Germans leave." In contrast mine said, "Learn English before the English come." That really broke me up, so much so that I had to excuse myself and sprint to the washroom.

While I was away trying hard to regain my composure, the group discussed what to do about these flyers. When something like this happens, the decision for action is left to the highest-ranking member. Naturally, everybody ogled at Kretchmar. He asked their opinion, but nobody wanted to commit himself, not knowing what his reaction would be.

Having returned and survived my convulsive laughter, it was my turn. "I think it would be a waste of time," I commented. "We cannot prove that the vendor spiked these papers with illegal material. I suggest we do nothing."

Surprisingly, the Commander concurred and added, "I know we are not supposed to become infected with enemy propaganda, but it sure is interesting reading. Besides, it might not hurt us to have this information. We have to complete our tour of duty anyway."

I recognized a spark of democratic thinking on his part. I had not misjudged the man and did not feel so alone with my tendency for broad-mindedness, which stood in gross contrast to Nazi philosophy. It was not the first or the last time I had met people who were still able to think for themselves rather than having been indoctrinated from above.

Before we had a chance to look at our legitimate newspapers, Randers terminal came into view. We had passed the towns of Hinnerup, Hadsten, Laurbjerg and Langa. It was now 1855 hours. The thirty-two-kilometer trip had lasted over two hours!

Checking in at Randers, we were told three things. The train was slow because, in order to make sure that no further sabotage would succeed, a team of four had been detailed to drive ahead of the train with a railway track inspection handcart. Anything unusual had to be identified by them, allowing the train to stop in time. If they did not notice dynamite traps, for instance, they would be blown up. "What a suicide squad assignment!" I thought to myself.

The trip would continue in a few minutes, trying to reach Aalborg before dark. That seemed to be a joke. We had used up two hours and twenty minutes to leave thirty-two kilometers behind. Another sixty or so kilometers lay ahead to Aalborg. Dusk would set in at about 2140 hours. With our prior speed, we could not possibly make it to Aalborg before 2330 hours. Things did not jive, at least not according to *Schuermann's Rechenbuch* (a well-known German mathematician's book of mathematics).

And finally, different transportation arrangements would be made for the remainder of the distance between Aalborg and our final Danish destination, Frederikshavn. Because of this, some of us should be prepared to stay in Aalborg for a day or so.

We reboarded the train without delay. It took only a few minutes and the stationmaster's whistle sent us on our way. We praised our own foresight to stock up with sandwiches and pastries, which came in handy now. It was dinner time anyway. We divided everything evenly, including Albert's coffee which he had secured in Aalborg.

At approximately 2100 hours we stopped in the middle of nowhere. The inspection handcart stood in front of us. The four men assigned to it were busy installing dynamo-operated searchlights at the four platform corners. After ten minutes, we started to move again. Without any further delay, we arrived at the Aalborg terminal. The railway station is conveniently located in the downtown area at what is now called John F. Kennedy Plads, overlooking Kildeparken, Aalborg's first park that was laid out in 1802. As we came to a complete stop, we heard the clock of Sanskrit Ansgar Kirke close by striking twelve o'clock midnight. A sigh of relief was probably in order.

We had managed to cover the distance between Aarhus and Aalborg, about ninety-five kilometers, in seven and a half hours, at a record speed of slightly less than thirteen kilometers per hour!

Six trucks awaited us outside the station. The convoy went through Vesterbro North via Limfjordsbroen, the bridge that connects Aalborg with Norresundby over Limfjorden, to the reception base which was located near the northern end of Oestergade.

Since the six of us had Norway as our final destination and we felt like a team, our air force sergeant requested joint quarters for us, which was promptly granted. Sergeant Sudhof was now in charge of the group. Commander Kretchmar had reluctantly accepted assigned officers quarters for the night. But we agreed to continue our journey together until we had to part. The clock showed 0100 hours when we turned in. A new day had begun, Tuesday, 27 July 1943.

I woke up with heartburn early the next morning. The previous evening I had noticed kind of a floor pantry, like we have in hospitals. I found some milk which I smelled first, then heated it up before I drank it. That may sound strange nowadays, but in those days refrigerators were not always working too well. By the time the others were rudely awakened by the sergeant-at-arms, I was already fit to travel.

The base was equipped with a huge mess hall where we all—even officers, surprise, surprise—had to pick up our own food and beverage orders at four well-organized pick-up stations. It was one of the best breakfasts I ever had! What also caught my attention was the traffic flow, which clearly showed that the person who designed the facility must have been a food production and service expert, practical-minded as can be. What I saw, but did not realize at the time, was a cafeteria-style operation, only better than most of them in the 1980s. This one was fifty years ahead of its time.

Before we left the premises, I asked for the early morning cook in charge, who turned out to be a jovial-looking corporal. He had assisted a qualified hotel and restaurant design architect in the design of the operation and ran it. His duty rank, indicated by big horizontal stripes, was that of a sublieutenant.

I identified myself, including that I shared his background. He was visibly pleased when I praised the quality of food and the overall layout. "Yes," he said with pride, "I am lucky to have a well-trained staff who enjoys what they are doing. That includes a couple of Danish pastry chefs who fit in here perfectly. We are a pretty good team. If it wasn't for all these poor guys who suffer so much or even die at the front, this war could last another ten years." That remark sounded selfish at the first glance. But I am sure he simply wanted to express how satisfied and thankful he felt for the role he could play. I thanked him for having chatted with me and joined my comrades.

Returning to our reception building, we had to line up to receive new travel instructions. It had been decided that starting immediately, because of these numerous acts of sabotage, the customary mode of troop train travel between Aalborg and Frederikshavn was changed. To vastly reduce, if not eliminate, any further acts of sabotage against troop transport trains, as had recently occurred, the new plan dictated regular civilian trains be mixed with railcars carrying members of the occupying forces. The idea behind it was simple but ingenious. Troop transport railcars would be added, interspersed with regular scheduled passenger trains. Usually, the first two or three cars would be for civilians, then two or three cars for military personnel, two cars for civilians, two cars for the military again and at the end of the train another two to four railcars (depending on the length of the train) for civilians. That way, civilians could not be singled out from being blown up with us. A practical solution; maybe not fair, but that word does not count on either side during war. Let us not forget how many civilians lost their lives in Great Britain when we almost leveled entire cities, which is equally true of all those Germans who lost their lives due to carpet bombs used by the RAF and American bomber squads in 1943 and thereafter.

Since this new transportation arrangement needed new logistics to be worked out, a temporary shortage of railcars might occur for a while.

When the briefing was over, we dispersed to get ready for the transport busses that would leave shortly for Aalborg station. During the trip we discussed how we would feel if we could not be accommodated on the first train. Nobody really minded staying an extra day or so in Aalborg if need be. I was not too keen on leaving Aalborg sooner than necessary. The town was fairly familiar to me because of my trip home the previous year. I liked it and would not mind at all procrastinating my journey by spending a bit more time in an atmosphere of comparative abundance.

It was 1000 hours when we arrived at the railway station. A number of other comrades and quite a few civilians had already gathered at the platform where the train was being assembled. At the travel base we had heard some smart cookie giving some advice about what to do to increase the chance of being held back from the train. Just move to the extreme end of the line and see what happens. That is precisely what we did. As the train was ready to be boarded, first the civilians since they had to get used to being assigned certain cars, then the soldiers, it sure enough turned out that about thirty of us could not be accommodated. We were sent to the travel officer to have our names noted and subsequently received delay money for one day.

A Day Off

Our plan for the day was made. We had made some concessions to each other and agreed to first visit the Aalborg shipyard. Kretchmar, the other two sailors, and I suggested to the air force guys they probably could learn something from the navy. The shipyard is located only about two kilometers northeast of the railway station, a leisurely half-hour walk.

We took the Boulevarden north which runs out into Osteraagade. Within the next kilometer stretch we passed some solid Danish history. Kretchmar, who knew this town better than any one of us, acted as tour guide. He even knew the historical dates quite well.

"The first solid house is the old town hall, built in 1762," Kretchmar explained. I made a note of the inscription above the entrance and found it to bear King Frederik V's motto, "Wisdom and Firmness."

Almost right beside is a Renaissance five-story house with triple front gables. It was built by the merchant Jens Bang in 1624 and bears his name. But during the occupation, unlike now, the historic wine cellar was closed.

After one block we passed the Jorgen Olufsen House, built yet another eight years earlier, in 1616. The handicraft shop did a brisk business but the art gallery had been closed, maybe for the same reasons as those in Aarhus. Now there is also a wine bar, where one can taste some of the best wines from around the world.

Shortly before we reached the end of Osteraagade we saw the beautiful complex enhancing Aalborg Castle near the waterfront, with its *Slotspladsen* (castle square). Kretchmar pointed this out as the oldest building in Aalborg, erected before 1600. Later we were told it was built in the year 1539!

We would have loved visiting the building, but that was out of the question. It was formally used by our regional military commanders. Later reports, however, revealed that the building was used as a camouflage for the Gestapo and the SS. Confidential papers, which even included blueprints of the building, indicated that suspected Danish saboteurs, who had been picked up between Aarhus further south and Frederikshavn in the north, would be brought here through underground passages and thrown into dungeons for interrogations by the SS. The actual rounding up of suspects was usually carried out by the Gestapo, the SS being too conspicuous in their black uniforms.

Gaining entry to the shipyard area was not as easy as it would have been under ordinary circumstances. But with all these acts of sabotage, the harbor protection patrol and guards had been tripled. The on-water harbor patrol had doubled. Several of our war ships were tied up for overhaul. Civilians could not enter the area at all, and only the presence of Commander Kretchmar gave us access.

One minesweeper showed a gaping hole in its port side. Dockyard workers were in the process of patching her up by matching several metal sheets to the size of the hole and beginning to weld these together. Our sailor companion with the ever so quizzical look on his face turned to us and muttered, "I sure as hell wouldn't like to belong to this ship's crew. These guys are patching up the port side if I ever have seen a patch-up job! Too much welding, not enough riveting." I guess he knew what he was talking about. It sounded convincing.

From where we were standing, we could look across Limfjorden to Norresundby. Since it was another bright day, we could even make out the tip of our travel base located at the north end of Ostergade.

There was not much else to see. The two air force men started teasing the rest of us about how much they learned near the smelly water. It was time to withdraw from this educational outing.

Walking westward along the quay, it parted after one and a half kilometers. The sign at the mouth of the left fork told us we were entering *Strandvejen* (Beach Road). After another five hundred meters the road led underneath a viaduct, the bridge that connects Aalborg via Limfjorden with Norresundby.

Coming free of the viaduct, we could see, some three hundred meters ahead, an oversized *Schnappsflasche* (straight-shaped whisky bottle), indicating we were closing in on the home of the world-famous Aalborg Akvavit Distillery, where Denmark's distinctively clear and zesty gin is made.

Quite a crowd waited at the distillery to be taken on a tour of the plant, which would last about thirty-five minutes we were told. Since two tours were conducted simultaneously, we would have to wait twenty minutes until it was our turn.

During the next half-hour we saw several copper pot stills, which had been used for several generations. Our guide provided us with a capsule history of the science of distillation. It had undergone very little changes in methods, and those only during the last century. The basic procedure, however, had remained intact since 800 B.C.

The guide discussed the different spirits such as brandy, whiskey, gin, rum and liqueurs. He went a bit more into details regarding Akvavit, explaining it is categorized as a miscellaneous spirit which is basically distilled from sugar-containing products. We learned that proof describes the strength of an alcoholic beverage and the blending of whiskey with neutral spirits.

Finally, the guide said a few words about the therapeutic value of spirits. "With the exception of excessive use," he quoted, "there is absolutely no evidence that alcohol per se causes any disease. It is harmless to the body and even can function as a valuable medicine. Many European doctors use it to fight diseases of the liver, bladder and the heart. But badly informed reformists, most of whom have been incapable of handling it with restraint, want you to believe otherwise by bombarding you with mumbo jumbo."

The round trip ended in the hospitality lounge, where we were given a sample of Akvavit, and several coasters with an Akvavit crest. Bottles of Akvavit were on sale. Kretchmar bought one; the rest of us were too short on cash.

When we left the distillery yard, the St. Mary's Church clock, one block away from Kastetvej, struck 1300 hours. It was time to have luncheon. Besides the warming, Akvavit had done its share to stimulate the appetite. The air force sergeant suggested we walk right down the Tivoliland on Fyensgade, where several restaurants had reasonable prices competing for customers. He sold us on the idea easily, since we wanted to make the most of the few Danish kroners we had left for the day.

Taking on a brisk walk, we covered the two-kilometer distance in less than twenty-five minutes. Before we even entered the grounds, we noticed and admired the beautifully cultivated garden setting surrounding it. Again I was reminded of the contrast between the outwardly peaceful appearance of Scandinavia in comparison to the rest of Europe. Deep in my heart I wished for nothing more than to belong to those lucky ones who would survive this blasted war without being thrown to the wolves.

The complex could not have been opened long before we arrived, since a milling crowd of people were lining up at the gate. We gladly paid the more than reasonable admission fee of Kr 2 to the grounds.

We did not have to search long for something to eat. The first eatery stall to the right of the center road attracted our attention. Two pipe-smoking Danes, who looked like brothers, had just finished setting up for business. Standing behind two octane gas-operated deep fat fryers, they were feeding one with fish fillets the other with Rissoli potatoes. At one end of the open stand a battery of German and Swedish natural well water was displayed. The end of the opposite corner showed a wooden beer keg elevated at hip's height and empty beer glasses beside it upside-down on a steel grating. The belly of the keg proudly exhibited a circular emblem still used around the world by the Carlsberg Brewery of Copenhagen. A sign above, resting on top of the barrel, advertised "the best beer anywhere, right here" in Danish and German.

The Lieutenant Commander ordered, in his flawless Danish, six portions of fish, potato balls, bread and six glasses of beer. When the orders came up, we paid individually and took our food and beers to the back of the hut where picnic tables waited invitingly. Each of us had paid only Kr 3.25 for the whole works.

The food tasted great, but the beer was not so hot, not to blame Carlsberg. This beer was brewed for the civilian population and was not allowed to exceed two percent alcoholic content by volume, the same as in Norway.

There were a lot of families who had made themselves comfortable on the picnic ground. Some had brought their own food from home by the looks of paper wrappings on the tables. But one could not see one piece of paper on the ground anywhere, a European tidiness badly lacking in North America. To be fair, I have seen improvements taking place in some communities where people now take more pride in their surroundings, thanks to the efforts of educators.

We returned the beer glasses and started walking around the grounds. This amusement park, though much smaller than Tivoli Gardens in Copenhagen, offered a great variety of everything under the sun. Astonishing, since it was very difficult in these times to obtain some of the replacement parts for mechanical items and equipment. On the other hand, it was common knowledge that Denmark had a fairly active black market going because of her abundant agricultural resources.

Walking around, we noticed most of the freak shows had already opened up. There was another homunculus, the man without a head, whom I remembered well from our local fun fairs when I was a boy. I attended that show many times and never could figure out how this "thing" could live with a glass container, a candle burning inside, in place of a human head.

After an hour or so we stopped at a booth where one could test one's luck, the owner boldly announced his gambling stand as Little Las Vegas. It was a simple dice game. Participants could bet a small sum of money (maximum Kr 3) on any number between one and twelve. The name of the game, which I never saw played before or after anywhere else, was Over, Under, or Bull's-Eye. Bull's-Eye was number seven; under was one to six; over was eight to twelve. If one played number three and the dice showed three, one would receive double money back. Numbers one, two, four, five, and six would have half their money returned. Seven to twelve lost their money; the same in reverse over seven. When number seven came up with dice, those having bet on seven would get quadruple their money back.

We watched this for a while and then decided to get into the act, splitting gains and losses. Within the next half-hour, modest amounts were lost but winnings were considerable. While we had lost together forty kroner, the gains outweighed that almost six times. "That's it," I said after I hit the seven three times in five minutes or so. Only the sailor with the quizzical look kept staring at the dice fascinated for a while, until his chum woke him up.

Kretchmar had kept track of the losses, while the air force sergeant kept count of the wins. Making a quick count before leaving the grounds, we divided Kr 194. That was comparable to ten days of extra pay for each of us. We felt like gold diggers.

Leaving the grounds, we turned right, crossed Kjellerupsgade and ended up in a typical Danish pastry cafe on Jyllandsgade, near the police station. It was shortly before 1600 hours.

We looked at the pastry counter to make our own selection, as is customary in all European cafes. Besides the traditional Danish pastries, we noticed a variety of fancy cakes and tarts. We ordered and returned to our table.

When the waitress served us, we asked about the tremendous selection of pastries which not even I had seen before in one establishment. She told us that one of the two founding owners had worked as a pastry chef in different European countries before the war broke out and had opened this business in 1936. I would have loved to talk to the man, but he was not in.

The place was pleasant and cozy. As there were full-length wall mirrors at two opposite walls, it looked larger than it was. The teak tables and chairs were dainty and seemed to be made to order for a cafe-type operation, rather than for heavy meal service. For my taste, everything fit in to give the impression of quiet elegance. We could have entered a private country club. Those who designed and decorated this fine establishment had excellent taste.

When we got up from the table we hardly could move anymore. I had the feeling I would not be able to eat anything before the next day's breakfast.

Our street ended directly at the railway station. Kretchmar inquired when the next busses would leave for the base. "At 1700 hours," he was told. The last one for the day would depart at 2330 hours.

We had heard about a place on Jomfru Anegade, one kilometer north of the railway station which offered cabaret shows. To inquire when shows would be on, we went to a concrete pillar we had seen behind the station building in Kildeparken, which was used for various advertisements. There would be two shows, one at 2000 hours and one at 2230 hours.

The name of the place at the time was *Nytels Konsentrere* (Entertainment Center). It was the only one in the area. Today the entire street is made up of restaurants, discotheques (which are still going strong in Scandinavia), and even a jazz club for the enjoyment of knowledgeable jazz buffs. We decided to attend the 2000-hour show, as the later one was too closely shaved for us to return in time to the base. We had over two hours to kill until then.

The air force sergeant, whose father was a stonemason, had walked over to a classical sculpture close by while we looked at the mortar pillar. Returning to us, he awoke our interest with his enthusiastic comments and we ended up walking through the whole park. There was a large collection of sculptures by Thorvaldsen and Anne Marie Nielsen, which had been placed in beautiful surroundings.

Reaching the western edge of the park, we saw a procession of people streaming into the Catholic Ansgar Kirke. The church bells were ringing, inviting the flock to participate in the traditional Sunday evening divine service. It was 1800 hours. Knowing well that our uniforms would be conspicuous, we waited until everybody was inside. Then we entered the house of God quickly and placed ourselves, standing up, to one side and behind the last row of pews.

There were certain similarities between this church and the Stavanger Cathedral, which I had frequented several times since my arrival. Both buildings were of Gothic style, accentuating pointed arches and tall columns. This building had probably been completed not long after the Stavanger Cathedral was rebuilt following its destruction by fire in 1272, or somewhere around the year 1300.

Though I understood very little, the priest appeared to be quite articulate, as one could sense by the audience's appreciative acceptance. The congregation seemed to be spellbound. He confined his sermon to about twenty-five minutes. The entire service, including gospel singing, lasted forty minutes. When the eyes of the priest met us for the first time, he could not conceal surprise to see these German uniforms. Obviously, he did not see them often in his house.

After the service, we waited outside for the man of God. He shook hands with us like he did with members of his congregation. Kretchmar had made sure he would meet the priest before we did. Judging from their body language, the two exchanged a few friendly words, though the priest had had the courage to interject in his sermon the sadness of Denmark being occupied by foreign forces.

Kretchmar had commented favorably on the priest's service, and temporarily threw him off balance with the statement that not all Germans are bad and godless people. He also told the priest that most of us were not here out of our free will. It was not without any risk that one would make a statement like this to a citizen of a country which is occupied.

Leaving the churchyard, we went across Kong Christians Alle and sat down on a park bench behind the North Jutland Museum of Arts, regressing a bit.

It was twenty-five minutes before curtain time when we arrived at the Nytelse Konsentrere. Now that we had some extra cash in our pockets, and since this was likely the last entertainment we would have for some time, we went all out for it and bought loge tickets. The girl behind the glassed-in box office lifted her eyebrows with a mildly puzzled look. After all, the show would be in Danish. Why did these six oddballs in German uniforms buy the most expensive tickets for something they hardly understood?

Entering the main lobby, there were a number of pessimists lining up at the triple section cloakroom, checking raincoats, hats and even umbrellas, though the weather had been great all day. There was no rain in the forecast as Kretchmar had told us while listening to the Aalborg radio station daily weather report in the pastry cafe on Jyllandsgade.

It was interesting to stand around and observe these people, who seemed to be oblivious of the fact that there was a war going on. Most women were dressed in evening dresses and the men in well-fitting dark suits or tuxedos. "Besides the Swiss and Swedes, they must be the best-dressed people in Europe right now," I thought. Some of the men were dressed in striped pants and tailcoats, like members of the House of Lords. For a moment I felt like we were standing in the foyer of the theater in London rather than in Denmark. We looked at each other with astonishment and admitted feeling out of place. But this was not going to spoil our evening.

The program was second to none: jugglers from Italy; the Waller tightrope walkers from Germany; two Danish comics who, according to Kretchmar, were teasing each other, their own politicians and the visitors from the south (meaning us, the German occupiers). All this was done lightly, just about within the line of not getting arrested. Heaven knows how utterly humorless dictatorial politicians are!

Following came the internationally famous Swiss clown Adrian Wetter. I had seen him in Wuppertal with my dad in 1937. Part of his routine was the same, but it was as funny just the same. His clumsy movements and strange ideas of doing things had to get to you! Before he came on stage, a horizontal line had been drawn on the stage floor, symbolizing a border. He came in, carrying a wooden gate with a door in the center. The gate was about four feet long and three feet high.

At first he winked at the audience, then, seeing the line, walked up to it and scratched his head with his free hand. He gestured he had an idea, set down the gate aligned with the line, opened the door, stepped through, closed it and took the gate under his arm. Looking back at the line, his face lit up. Staring at the audience again, he said in sincere astonishment, "Not possible!" The audience broke up. (In retrospect, Red Skelton reminds me of Adrian Wetter a lot.)

Finally came a magician and a hypnotist. The two worked as a team and called themselves Fram and Tilbake which translates into Forward and Backward. The magician asked for two volunteers from the audience to observe and to participate in some of the illusions. A curvy blond and, we could not believe our eyes, a soldier in German army uniform went on stage. Fram did a few tricks with shawls, golf balls, birds and rabbits, while Tilbake stood by pretending to be amazed.

A trunk was now brought onstage. Fram pretended to take the girl's measurements and made some adjustments on the trunk, that looked as if it had been sliced in several places. While the girl rested on top of the trunk lid, Tilbake put her to sleep. Gradually her body became suspended about three feet above the trunk. The trunk was opened. The girl slowly descended until resting on the bottom of the trunk.

The two men sawed through the entire trunk height in two places, then swung the upper and the lower part of the trunk forty-five degrees back, supported by hinges. The woman's upper and lower extremities seemed to have been severed from the rest of the body! On command of Tilbake, she wiggled one foot and rolled her head in a circle, eyes closed.

Sounds of astonishment came from the audience. I am sure we all have seen similar illusions where a woman's body is supposed to have been cut in two. But three parts? It beats me!

When the trunk was restored in its original position, the back of the stage was thrown in violet darkness. Suddenly we were aware that Fram the magician had vanished into thin air. Tilbake got into action by calling out the girl's name. She seemed to answer from the trunk, but instead came onstage from the right wing, smiling and apparently in good health. At the same time, the lid of the trunk lifted and Fram stepped out.

Now it was the German soldier's turn. Tilbake explained to the audience that the soldier did not want to be hypnotized. Fram measured his new subject with a tape, adjusted the trunk and had the man step inside. The lid closed, he asked, "Are you lying comfortably?"

"Yes, very comfortable," came the reply.

Fram and Tilbake took a wide-bladed saw and, one standing in front of the other in the back of the trunk, started to saw. The blade sank deeper into the trunk. Suddenly, when it had reached the approximate center, one could clearly hear metal scraping over metal. The sound was so screeching that some members of the audience covered their ears with their hands. Bluish smoke squeezed out of the spaces between the lid and the body of the trunk. The two stopped sawing.

Tilbake talked to the soldier in the trunk calling, "Hans, are you still there?" No answer. Several seconds passed. Fram and Tilbake lifted the saw out of and away from the trunk. The moment they turned back to the trunk, its lid opened by itself and Hans, still in horizontally outstretched position, was hanging suspended in the air, apparently fast asleep. Tilbake took his feet, while Fram held Hans' head. Gradually, they laid him on the stage floor.

Then, Fram and Tilbake tried to figure out why they could not cut Hans apart. This time, Tilbake took a measuring tape and measured the trunk and Hans once more. Looking up at his partner, he said in Danish and then in German, "You took the wrong measurements. Our saw blade hit Hans' iron belt buckle. Nobody can saw that apart!" He had emphasized Hans' name, at which the man jumped up from the floor and saluted before he realized where he was. He had been hypnotized after all!

As a conclusion of the program, a seventeen-piece jazz orchestra appeared, playing a selection of tunes by Duke Ellington. They called the medley *Ellingtonia.* The band had been brought in from Sweden and boldly called itself the Jazzmasters. Boldly, I say, because jazz was out of bounds as far as the German government was concerned. There is a paradoxical part to this. A lot of Germans who, among others, were put in uniform to fight jazz, were devoted to it!

After a roaring four-minute applause, the band played Stan Kenton's *Opus in Pastels* and *Eager Beaver* as an encore. That was a beautiful crowning of a delightful day. When we left the building, it was 1115 hours. That gave us just about enough time to return to the station to catch the 1040 hour transport truck.

The Last Leg

After breakfast the following morning, we were transported back to the railway station. This time there was no chance of squeezing out another day off. They read the names of those who had been held over. We had to board the train first! I had to listen to a few remarks again from some of my pals, who complained about their heavy gear. They were wondering how I could get away with traveling with a toothbrush only. But the teasing stopped when they knew my story.

When I traveled, I had developed the habit of buying one or several newspapers before boarding a bus, a train, or a boat. From a newsstand on platform one, I had bought the early morning edition of the *Luebecker Nachrichten*, which I unfolded the moment I had a seat.

Three articles began on the front page. The first reported the improved accuracy of our unmanned V-Two flying rockets. Several had been sent to Britain the previous day, causing extensive damage in and around London. The rest of the report consisted of technical mumbo jumbo I did not understand.

The second article was a print from Dr. Goebbels' speech in which he praised our new miracle weapons, referring to the devastating V-Two rocket in particular. He played down the importance of our recent defeats on the Eastern Front, calling our retreats calculated tactics. This was pure bull, of course!

The third article was a real shocker! Hamburg had been flattened some more by the RAF. It was estimated that within the two-hour attack which wiped out over eighty percent of Hamburg, forty thousand people had lost their lives. The calculation of civilian casualties was quite correct. Including previous destructions, Hamburg now had the reputation of having been hardest hit of all German cities: eighty-four percent of the city was gone!

When would this madness ever end? How many more tears had to be shed?

The journey to Frederikshavn passed without incident. This agreement of having military personnel and Danish civilians traveling collectively within the same train was introduced on other railway stretches as well. It practically eliminated acts of railway sabotage. Selecting targets this way became impractical for the Resistance.

When we arrived in Frederikshavn, the ferry already awaited us. We boarded without delay and finished the 170-kilometer distance between Frederikshavn and Larvik, Norway in less than five hours, though the sea was fairly rough.

There was a moment of apprehension when we passed two floating mines, one of which passed by the ferry, floating about thirty meters from the boat. But nothing happened. The communications officer sent a message to the nearest German naval base to have these floating mines swept or blown up.

Disembarking in Larvik, we said good-bye to each other as we had to part. For me, the usual changing of busses and trains began. It was 0100 hours the next morning when I made a telephone call to my base, to pick me up from the station. I had arrived at my second home, Stavanger.

BASE DUTY

The Functionaries

The morning after I had returned to my base from annual leave, I was told to check in at the functionaries quarters. The occupants all had special assignments within the base and were thus exempted from regular day-to-day company duties of the other enlisted men.

For the time being, I was released from the officers mess service to be detailed for other duties. Obviously the chap who had replaced me at the casino when I left on my annual furlough was doing all right. As the saying goes, anybody can be replaced. Of course, it all depends how.

In this case, they did not seem to need me anymore. But I did not really look at the situation that way. Ordinary soldiers in the forces who had been given special assignments are often relieved from them, regardless of whether or not they had met expectations. The main reason for this policy is to avoid complacency or possible collusion, depending on the type of task.

Base assignments did not bother me. I had made frequent visits to the base during my casino detail, and knew everybody at the base belonging to the who's who club.

We had seven bunks in the functionaries quarters, three less than in each other barrack room. And I soon found out, I was in good company. Most of the men were considerably older and wiser than little ole me. I could learn a few things from these well-seasoned guys that would come in handy later in life. Regardless of their more versed backgrounds, they immediately accepted me as their equal.

Hans Holtzmann was the eldest and responsible for the upkeep, cleanliness, and tidiness of the room. When drafted, he left a successful grocery wholesale business in Vienna behind. The forty-two-year-old man was detailed as *Schreibstuben-Beaufsichtiger* (supervisor of administrative company personnel) and as such reported directly to the *Hauptfeldwebel* (master sergeant).

Fritz Ballzuweit was the company armorer, operating the ordinance shop. He worked as a physics instructor for several years, then became the sparring partner of Herbert Runge who, during the Berlin Olympiad in 1936, became the first Wuppertaler to bring home the gold medal for amateur heavyweight boxing. As a fellow-Wuppertaler, I was very shocked to see this great champion going down the drain because of booze and women before I got drafted in 1941.

Then we had Ernst Roland, who was a full-fledged doctor of law. Until the end of 1943, he somehow escaped the attention of military authorities for quick promotion to officers rank, as was customary for people with a university education. When not involved in defending navy personnel during court-martials and interpreting the law, he stood by to assist Fritz with inventories. Occasionally, he advised the commanding officer in delicate matters.

Franz Trust acted as company postal clerk. He was a good-humored fellow who actually liked it when his comrades jokingly called him *Postbeutel* (mailbag). In civilian life, he was (one can almost guess it) *Postdirektor* (Director of Postal Services) of the main post office and satellite operations in the city of Essen. When somebody pulled his leg, he knew how to get even. When mail was distributed, he would withhold to the last minute, letters or parcels for which the receiver was badly waiting. Basically a sensitive guy, he would promptly give letters addressed to the unknown soldier to those whom he knew did not have girlfriends or families.

Our company tailor shall remain nameless because he committed suicide after the end of the war. He would make sure that all uniforms were kept in good repair, including those of officers. But most of the work he did came from sailors wanting to have their pants widened, which he did willingly, even though it was against regulations. He was originally from Czechoslovakia, married, with five children, and had a most pleasant disposition. We were deeply shocked by his taking his own life.

Besides Fritz Ballzuweit and myself, we had a third Wuppertaler, Bertold Reiner, who by the age of sixteen had turned out to be a promising soccer player. He had electrician's journeyman papers, volunteered to join the navy and had been drafted about one month before me. For no apparent reason, he was detailed as orderly to the company master sergeant.

When I settled in, I asked the group leader what my assignment would be. He first shrugged his shoulders, then said, "We'll find something. Hans Holtzmann, your quarters eldest, has been given a half day off tomorrow. Since you are not fully familiar with the company, he will show you around, so that you have no excuse for getting lost. Then we will see what we can do with you."

He sounded like I was his greatest problem and he was not too pleased to have me on his hands. I found out Commander Schmidt, through the master sergeant, had impressed upon him the loyal services I had performed to the area commandant's officer corps, and that I was to be handled with some respect. No wonder he acted kind of lost. It clearly goes against the grain of the superior-underling relationship.

When Hans Holtzmann had completed his rounds with me the next day, the sergeant-at-arms for the week came to my room. He had received permission from the master sergeant to detail me for the following two or three weeks as company messenger during the normal day service hours.

The main task was to receive messages from outside for distribution inside the company, deliver these to the respective person in charge of the unit and generally assist the sergeant-at-arms in keeping control on the ground, including the issue of daytime and afternoon passes. If any internal quarrel among the men occurred, I was to act as mediator or, if needed, as MP. My shift would be from 0800 hours until 1700 hours. I was to report the next day. That sounded easy to me; easier than serving meals three times a day.

Back at my quarters the guys started teasing me about getting here last and getting the softest job. Since I did not volunteer for it, I had no guilt feelings and told them that anybody could change with me at anytime, "If you can swing it."

The following morning, after having had a fast breakfast, I reported shortly before the appointed hour to the sergeant-at-arms, spit and polished. Only then did I notice that this small barrack was not only used as a message center, but also as a stockade. The message room was about nine by seven meters. An equal-sized room right beside it was used as the communications room, where messages were first read then sorted for pick-up and distribution.

Behind these two side-by-side rooms were four individual cells, which were invariably occupied by chaps from other units who had been sentenced to three to five days confinement. Most of them had to do time either for insubordination or for minor AWOL.

Part of my duty was to keep an eye on these birds and to feed them three times daily. Each morning right after breakfast, the cells were opened. The occupants were then given pails and mops to clean their cells and the gangway running in front of them.

The first day went by without anything unusual happening. At the end of my tour I was pretty pooped, though, from all the running back and forth across the base.

Meet Werner Boes

Always having been a music nut, I was delighted to see a Philips radio positioned at the side of the message desk. On the second day, I switched it on and turned the dial to Radio Bremen, the German propaganda station broadcasting in English. It was not the craving for propaganda which made me do it, but the kind of swinging music the station played in between to attract English listeners. The second reason was to keep up with my knowledge of the language. I could do this openly, since only listening to foreign radio stations was forbidden.

William Joyce, better known as Lord How How, the British traitor who had left his country early in the war and offered his services to the German government as broadcaster on behalf of the Nazis, was rambling along, trying to tell his countrymen how much better national socialism is in comparison to capitalism. I did not have the slightest notion that one day I would hear and see him in person, spreading his poisonous propaganda around–and that at a time when the war was already winding down in November 1944.

He had stopped his charade. The German disc jockey played Duke Ellington's *Don't Get Around Much Any More.*

I went back and opened the four cells. The pails and mops had already been lined up by a company work crew. Just to start some conversation with the three inmates–after all, they were no criminals–I told them to do a good job and I would see to it that they would get good food in turn.

Returning to the front of the house, I left the connecting door open for better observation. If some of the inmates tried to escape, they would not get far. Even if they passed me (I was only armed with the traditional dagger), they would run into a stone wall at the front gate, the only point of entry to and exit from the base. Besides, they only had a few days to do time.

The music had stopped. "And now," the announcer said, "one of your favorites, Vera Lynn." As soon as Vera started singing, I heard the echo of a man's voice coming from the direction of the cell block. Were my ears playing tricks on me? Clearly somebody had unmistakably joined in the lyrics. "We'll meet again, don't know where, don't know when . . ."

I waited until the song was finished, reduced the volume and went to the back. The three were almost finished cleaning up.

"Who of you has that Richard Tauber voice?" I asked. Richard Tauber was a German-Jewish tenor, particularly well-known for his Franz Lehar song *Dein ist mein ganzes Herz.* He managed to slip through the Gestapo's fingers just before the curtain came down in 1938, together with the actor Adolf Wohlbrueck. They went to England into self-imposed exile and were welcomed there with open arms. Their careers continued almost uninterrupted. Tauber switched effortlessly into the English lyrics, *Yours Is My Heart's Desire*, while Wohlbrueck took up acting in British films as Anton Wallbrook.

I had posted my question in German, of course. "That was I," one of the three answered in faultless English, but with an American drawl. That was the second surprise of the day. And that is the way I met Werner Boes.

My curiosity awoke. So did his, as he later explained. He had answered my question in English without realizing it, glad to have found somebody who understood. I instinctively felt there was somebody who probably had an unusual background worthy of looking into. I asked him how much longer he had to stay behind bars. "Two more days," he replied quite casually.

"Would you mind if I visit you this evening, providing I get permission from the evening sergeant-at-arms?" I asked. "Why not?" he replied. "I am going nuts in this cage here anyway."

We had conversed in English. The two other chaps were standing by dumbfounded. It dawned on me that an explanation would be in order. "Just practicing my high school English a bit," I commented lamely. But it seemed to satisfy them. I remembered vividly that several Danes had been put in jail while I passed through Denmark only recently, simply because they had addressed some German soldiers and officers in English. The last thing I needed was to throw unnecessary suspicion on myself.

When I checked with the sergeant after dinner, he said, "I think we can do better than that. You can sign a temporary release for Werner Boes and take him anywhere within the base, but you take full responsibility for him. If he does not return by 2300 hours, you will have to occupy his cell instead." I signed the release.

First we went to the canteen for a couple of beers. It got rather noisy after a while, so we retreated to my quarters. The other six guys all had evening passes and were in downtown Stavanger.

While we sat in the canteen, I had given him a glimpse of my background. When the subject of music came up and I mentioned rather proudly that I had been the youngest member of a twenty-six piece mandolin orchestra, his eyes lit up. We had found something else in common. "I am leading a quartet," he said. "We entertain the boys when they return with their submarines. We also appear every fortnight in the *Marineheim* (home for enlisted navy men), which is located on Strandkaien at the harbor. Why don't you come out and visit us on Kvitsøy (an island northwest of Stavanger) when we hold our next rehearsal and practice session? We could use another addition to our combo."

"Sounds exciting and interesting," I replied, "but I don't think I will fit in since I only played classical music with that orchestra. As a matter of fact, until my dad bought a radio in 1937, I didn't even know that there was anything else but classical music."

"That, you may not know, Sigy, is an advantage," said Werner. "When you can read music, you can play any kind of music. We usually do play some light entertaining music in the afternoon, then progress to more rhythmical songs as the day goes by. I've been doing the arrangements for the group. Your instrument should fit in nicely for first voice, and if you practice chords you can at times alternate with Franz Boetcher, our guitarist."

He sounded convincing. "Sure, why not?" I would give it my best shot.

While he sold me on that venture. I studied his features. Werner was about five feet ten inches tall, weighed about 140 pounds, had dark hair, dark eyes that seemed to glow and were recessed. His prominent cheekbones looked similar to those of Kirk Douglas, the American actor. He underlined his statements with rapid hand movements which could indicate a certain restlessness.

I remembered I had not even asked him which instrument he and the rest of the gang played. "We are actually a rhythm group," he said. "I play the accordion; Franz Boetcher is our guitarist; Leo Baldreich walks the bass, and Theodor Paris is our drummer. Right now we are simply known as *Das Quartette* (The Quartet), but I have an idea. If you join, we'll have four members whose names start with a "B". We might call the group *Die B-Kapelle* (the B Band)."

The ensuing conversation shed light on Werner's background. He was born in Strassbourg in 1920, the son of a musical family. His mother was a refined cellist and his father was a conductor of symphony orchestras. His parents discovered early in life that Werner had inherited the love for music. At age three he took piano lessons. Mom and Dad did not have to push him to practice. He could not stay away from the piano; at times, he had to be dragged away from it.

At age six he became the protege of Gilbert de Froberville, a professor of music at the University of Toulouse. Among other things, he learned the fundamentals of composing and the discipline classical musicians need for interpreting the music of the masters in its framework of composition.

At age eight he appeared as solo pianist with several symphony orchestras in France, Germany and Belgium. Critics considered him to be one of the very rare young geniuses of the twentieth century.

Barely nine, he composed his first minuet in G-major, the orchestration arranged by his own father. At the end of 1929, the great Russian composer Aram Khachaturian invited Boes Senior and Junior to Leningrad to perform excerpts from his suite, *Gayne,* and Tschaikovsky's *Piano Concerto Number One*. The press reported, "This outstanding young pianist seems to be incapable of flaws; his timing is that of a seasoned master, his technique and rendition impeccable."

An American talent agent convinced Boes Senior that the American public deserved to be exposed to Werner's extraordinary talents. A concert tour, lasting about eighteen months, was arranged. It was like a whirlwind tour, covering every larger city and town across the US. Werner enjoyed every minute of it. He became enchanted with the way the American public adored "the boy," and he readily accepted the freewheeling democratic approach of the population. Daily life seemed to be so much less restricted than in Europe. It was his private tutor, though, who made sure things wouldn't get out of hand. He trained Werner and reinforced generally acceptable behavior, good manners, and even some etiquette. Werner wrote home to his mom and his two brothers with great enthusiasm about America.

In 1932, Boes Senior had established himself as European Guest Conductor, commuting between New York, Boston, and Philadelphia. He applied for immigrant status which was preferentially processed and granted within six months.

In the meantime, his other two sons, Hubert and Alphons, had expressed the wish to follow Dad, though Mom was not enthused about the idea. Dad sponsored his sons, while Mom promised to follow "sooner or later." Werner's two brothers, who were nine and ten years older than Werner, arrived by boat in New York on the day that Adolf Hitler became chancellor of the German Reich, on Monday, 30 January 1933.

It was a bad time to come to America. The Depression had thrown millions of Americans out of work. What chance of finding a job would immigrants have? But perseverance paid off. Hubert found employment as a grocery clerk on Manhattan's East Side, grateful to contribute no matter how small to the Boes' budget. Alphons landed a job in the garment industry which at the time was pretty much in the hands of enterprising Jewish entrepreneurs.

When 1935 rolled around, Werner's dad requested an intermission for Werner's concert appearances. Werner could not do without using a musical expression. When explaining this to me, he called it an *intermezzo*. No concerts were booked during July through October of that year. His dad had made arrangements for himself, as well, in order to spend some time with his son simply relaxing.

During that year, the big bands pressed their stamps on the development of jazz, changing a raw and unpolished type of Negroid musical expression to the level of professionalism and even sophistication. Orchestras such as Duke Ellington, Artie Shaw, Benny Goodman, William "Count" Basie in Kansas City, Tommy Dorsey, Chick Webb, and a host of other orchestras introduced most significant new elements into the world of jazz. With increasing prominence, jazz was played by large orchestras, thanks in part to the development of swing music. Other contributing factors were the gradual breakdown of racial lines, eliminating the terms *white jazz* and *Negro jazz*. The late Benny Goodman deserves most of the credit for having been the first white band leader who disregarded the color line by hiring the also late Teddy Wilson as pianist and the still strong-going Lionel Hampton as vibraphonist in 1935, three years before his famous 1938 Carnegie Hall concert.

Not to ignore the importance of small groups, generally referred to as combos, in the development of more refined jazz music presentations, the combos that sprang up at Fifty-second Street in New York, and later on at Forty-second and Forty-third all played important roles in the creative progression of this original American art form.

Because jazz is the kind of music that demands to be listened to, like classical music, it should not be expected to sweep the masses. It is for people who have ears. If it has to be explained, the student will never understand it.

In spite of its happy, syncopated, swinging, melodious and romantic sound, it can only be played by real professional musicians. It is complicated, but jazz musicians do not sell out to commercialism, no matter how hard it is for them to make a living. Paradoxically, it is the untalented rock and roll musician who is laughing all the way to the bank. The taste of the masses demands musical noises that makes a barbaric appeal to sexual desires.

After Werner's last concert in June, one of the string bass players in the New York Symphony Orchestra introduced himself to Werner as Delmar Kaplan. He had replaced a permanent member who had taken ill and was Tommy Dorsey's regular bassist. He expressed admiration for Werner's technical skill and rendition when playing highly structured compositions, then asked, "Have you ever thought about playing jazz?"

Werner answered he did not really know enough about that type of music. While his father stood by, Kaplan said, "Come out with your dad tomorrow afternoon to the Chicken Coop on Fifty-second Street. Six of us from Dorsey will do some friendly jamming there. I would like to introduce you to our swinging Bobby Van Eps, our pianist. You may not know it, but you classical musicians have a lot in common with us jazz buffs. One thing is the ability to read music."

Werner looked at his dad, who consented, although he may have later regretted it. The two went the next day, and that is when Werner had his first exposure to combo jazz.

"Occasionally, I had heard the odd tune on the radio," Werner told me, "but I had no idea that this music was so much fun and at the same time could be quite significant. Like classical tunes, it demands to be carried out by trained musicians. It allows very little room for amateurs.

"I knew right then and there that this was the kind of music I wanted to play. Later on my dad, who is very broad-minded by nature, went with a bunch of New York jazz musicians and me to New Orleans where it all started. It was quite something and most inspiring. I got thoroughly hooked on jazz there, though I can tell you, Sigy, I will never turn away from the Old Masters' music either."

Werner did not renew his concert tour. Instead he put all his efforts into learning to play a number of other instruments. Boes Senior reluctantly agreed to use some of the money which had amassed in Werner's trust fund for that purpose.

In less than one year, he proficiently mastered the trumpet, fluegelhorn, alto and tenor saxes, and even percussions. He had the best teachers anybody could ask for. Members of the then Benny Goodman Band were impressed with this young man who handled musical instruments as if having grown up with them. Notables such as Buck Clayton, Bobby Hackett, Johnny Hodges, Lester Young, and yes, Gene Krupa all had a hand in providing Werner with the relaxed polish of a true jazz artist.

Then in 1938, Werner became interested in yet another instrument, the accordion. As unlikely a jazz instrument as any can be, he realized it to be closest to the piano, his original baby. "It was the best choice I ever made," he told me. "Not only could I develop a similar technique to that which is necessary for mastering the piano, I also found it easy adjusting to a rhythmical style, not to mention the ability to improvise which is such an important part of jazz."

Having played side by side with the man for almost two years, I can attest to Werner's unique style. For the benefit of the jazz, I can easily describe Werner's interpretation on the accordion as most similar to the greatest accordionist alive today, the Dutch Virtuoso Art Van Damme. When I listen to his records, I hear Werner all over again.

There was great concern in some artists' circles regarding the unstable political situation in Europe. Many, including Werner's father, considered the appeasement moves of Daladier and Chamberlain in September/October of 1938 as more than dangerous. When the democratic forces in Spain were defeated in the spring of 1939, the handwriting on the wall seemed to become more pronounced. Boes Senior tried in vain to convince his wife to join the family, even though he and his sons were all doing fine in their new country of choice, economically and otherwise.

Finally, when emigration papers were all approved by the US government for his mother to join her loved ones, Werner complied with his dad's request to visit her in Strasbourg and return with her to the US.

Werner, who always felt attracted to the sea, booked a passage on the newly-built *Europa*. The steamship left New York harbor on Wednesday, 9 August 1939 and arrived in Bremerhaven seven days later, on the sixteenth. The remainder of the trip he completed by train. In the late evening of Thursday the seventeenth, after almost ten years of separation, Werner took his beloved mother in his arms.

His earliest mentor, Gilbert de Froberville, had kept in touch with his mother throughout the years, continuously taking an interest in Werner's progress. The professor had recently accepted a two-semester assignment as guest lecturer at the Conservatory in Frankfurt on the Main in Germany. Knowing of Werner's expected arrival, he had invited him for a reunion celebration on the first September weekend and to proudly present him to the student body as his former Wunderkind.

Werner arrived in Frankfurt on Thursday, 31 August. On the following day, World War II broke out. "I was a dummy," Werner told me. "Having traveled on my German passport, I should have known that Germany would be fenced off more than ever. Instead of immediately returning to Strasbourg which belonged to France, I stuck around in Frankfurt for a whole week."

During that time the German government made another final sweep through Frankfurt looking for leftover Jews and foreigners. De Froberville and Werner were sitting on the terrace of a cafe in the afternoon, reminiscing and discussing the future when a military patrol accompanied by Gestapo men combed through the crowd. They confiscated Werner's passport and the identity card he had obtained when crossing the French-German border. He was told to report to the local draft board immediately. His request to return to Strasbourg was denied.

"I was angry as hell," Werner stated. "Here I was, feeling more American than German, with a German passport, getting stuck in a country with a government that had just started an inferno of a war. You cannot imagine the feeling of desperation which overcame me. When would I ever see my relatives again?"

His physical examination put him in the fit-to-travel (A-One) category. He received his enlistment papers for service in the navy, but was put on hold until further notice. De Froberville was held responsible for Werner's whereabouts. He himself had to report to the *Kripo* (short for *Kriminalpolizei*, or crime police) once a week.

Being aware of Werner's fluency in English, the draft board detailed him to the signal corps branch of the navy. His induction took place in March 1940. After his basic military training he was assigned to serve on Stavanger's main communication center located on the island of Kvitsøy, our main listening post off the mainland.

The Combo

I attended the band's rehearsal, joined the group for a couple of tunes and became the new member. Werner made up the charts and the arrangements for the small group, which now had become a quintet. Alternating voice and playing chords between Franz and myself worked out better than I thought. Fronts of our music stands were changed from the Quartet to the B Band Quintet.

Franz Boetcher and I had found each other, so to say. We could switch roles any time we wanted. Even when soloing for eight or sixteen bars, it did not matter who voiced or worked the chords. However, it took a lot of practice on my part to get used to some of Werner's chord progressions. Tricky, but it fit well with the overall sound of the band.

Franz began picking the guitar at the age of four. The little boy would sit on the porch of his parents' ranch-style house, humming and accompanying with his guitar tunes he had heard on the radio. When in grade school, his music teacher identified the boy's potential and encouraged Franz's progress with deeds. He gave Franz private lessons without charging a dime. Soon, Franz became proficient in runs and chord progression.

His technical ability surpassed that of his teacher's in a few years. In 1934, when he turned twelve, he became fascinated with the guitar playing of the legendary Django Reinhardt who, even though having only three fingers available, accomplished unheard-of technical ability on his instrument. Reinhardt was the leader of the Hot Club de France at the time, and had just accepted, as a new member of the group, Stephane Grappelli, who played piano and violin. In later years, Grappelli became, and still is, the greatest jazz violinist in the world, still a swinger at eighty years of age!

Franz played classical guitar in high school. While I played with him, his sound struck me as sensitive and romantic. In certain ways, his technique was comparable to that of Joe Pass. After we played a couple of gigs together, I could not help complimenting him on his amazing manner of performance. With typical understatement of the true artist, he replied, "Sig, I should be able to manage at least fifty percent more versatility with five fingers than Django did with three." By trade, Franz was an electrician, but he could have made it as a professional musician any time, beating today's guitar pickers by a mile!

Leo Baldreich, our bassist, born in 1921, had become the youngest member of the Stuttgart Symphony Orchestra. He took a similar route as Werner's, joining five other members to jam in their free time, but in private since jazz was considered in Germany at the time "undesirable nigger music." His idol became Arvell Shaw, who had played the bass for twenty years with Louis Armstrong, then joined in later years Wild Bill Davison and the Jazz Giants. Like Werner's dad, Leo's father disapproved of his son's extracurricular activity, but gave in.

Leo could not be rocked by anything! In the afternoon, when we played concert-type entertaining music, he played the string bass as relaxed as anybody could without falling asleep. When we switched to jazz, he became a different person. One could see by his radiant smile and his lit-up eyes how much he really liked plucking the thing. Once in a while, he would pretend to have lost some notes. Squinting at the music sheet in front of him, he would suddenly stop, shake his head, turn the base a full 360 degrees, then jump in again after a couple of bars. The audience loved it!

On drums we had a guy by the name of Theodor Paris. He joined the listening post on Kvitsøy about the same time I arrived in Stavanger in December 1941. He hated his first name, so everybody called him Teddy instead. When Werner tried to put a band together, he volunteered to play percussion. Teddy's father, who was an all-round music enthusiast, had bought several Brunswick records in the late thirties. Among these were two Tommy Dorsey recordings, with Buddy Rich on drums. Teddy became an instant fan. "One day," he told himself, "I will be drumming like this guy." But it was not possible for him to practice. There was no money.

Werner asked him a few questions. "Can you dance?" He answered with "No." "Do you play any instrument?" The answer again was "No, but, I know I can learn to handle the sticks and the *Schaumschlaeger* (literally meaning foam whippers, meaning brushes)."

"How many beats to the bar?" Werner asked.

"Four," was the prompt reply.

"One last question," Werner said. "Do you have rhythm?"

"Sure, plenty of rhythm," was the response. "Just ask my girlfriend." That did it!

For months, the two went to the basement of the communication center and practiced, and practiced and practiced some more. By the time I joined, Teddy was as accomplished as any amateur-turned-professional could be. We did not have any tom-toms. But the snare drum, base drum, cymbals, and a high hat was all Teddy needed to be the driving force, keeping the rest of us moving. He had great sticks and laid on some tasty brushwork. Quite good, but of course not as good as the great and only Louis Bellson.

Teddy was a constant joker. At times when Werner unexpectedly changed the charts, he would ogle at the girls in the room, paying no attention to the group. Then he would sense that a change in program had taken place. Instead of a tango, we would change to a tune in up-tempo eight/four time. He would poke his drumsticks in my back and ask before the chart would reach him, "What's up, Sigy?" My usual answer would be, "Change to woods, Teddy," which would get him on track again.

We had a great time and a lot of laughs. Time and again we found some new ways to entertain the troops and keep everyone happy. Werner seemed to be able to shake charts out of his sleeves.

We did not suffer from overexposure, though, since our ordinary navy duty schedule made it impossible for us to play each week. Some guys would stop me on the street in downtown Stavanger asking when we would play again and where. I would tell them, of course, but also ask, "Why don't you go and hear the chaps from the army at the army-air force mess? They have an octet, with reeds and trumpet, the works. They are all professional musicians and play well."

"Ja, I guess they are O.K., but they don't play the kind of music you do, and they don't have that swinging sound." Obviously, it did not bother these chaps that the five of us consisted only of a rhythm group. Maybe there was a difference in approach? We played for fun. The army octet had to entertain. It was its detail.

Then I hit on an altogether different reason. Not only was our presentation different (we could not openly call it syncopated music, let alone jazz), but Werner had arranged tunes for us that were not available to anybody else.

We had worked out a cleverly conceived plan by which he received the latest original charts from Broadway. His father would send these to Stockholm, Sweden, where they were repacked and forwarded to Lars Hansen, who resided at Kongsteins Gate. Once a month, Werner would check with him for mail. Later on, in 1944, when I was detailed to serve at the commandant's headquarters, Lars, who was our factotum, would bring Werner's mail from home to headquarters and hand it over to me. It worked like a charm!

That way we never ran out of fresh material. Besides the arrangements, Werner even wrote some German lyrics to some American compositions. That helped to divert possible suspicion on the part of anybody that we were playing American music. Our competition from the army-air force became somewhat frustrated. They simply could not figure out from which rabbit hat we produced most of our repertoire.

In July 1944, when I returned from my stint in the Arctic Circle, I found the band had become a sextet. Shortly after my departure, Leading Seaman Helmuth Branteis joined the group. He was born in 1910, became an accomplished violinist, and called the great Stephane Grappelli his buddy, although he never met the man. Since he was the oldest member in age and higher in rank than the rest, who were all PFCs, he formally acted as conductor. He fronted the group, standing up with Werner at his side, who never sat down while he played the accordion. Werner, of course, remained the key member.

The other new member of the band was Friedel Binder. Born in 1922, he came close to Werner's accomplishments, attended the Conservatory in Frankfurt by the age of fourteen, and later continued his studies in Goettingen and Hannover. He looked barely seventeen even though he was twenty-two. The group had found another victim in my stead.

Friedel took on my role, becoming the group's milk-face. But, what a pianist he was! He had not received his two junior pianist awards for nothing. When soloing, he easily brought the house down with Mozart, George Gershwin, Cole Porter and Duke Ellington. His versatility seemed to be unlimited. He used full chords, stride piano, and ran scales like a rabbit. He was quite a guy, to say the least. His style was somewhat in between that of Monty Alexander and Dave McKenna.

Camouflaged Jazz

We took only a couple of breaks during concert time. Starting around 1600 hours, we stepped softly, usually with a cross section of music by Franz Lehar, Eric Coates, Strauss and Ernst Fischer. Proceeding with tunes by Gershwin, Porter and Kern brought us to the dinner break at 1830 hours. Picking up our instruments again around 1915 hours, we dug into jazzed-up versions of German dance music and included some tunes with Latin-American rhythms, tangos, rumbas, and sambas. A short break came between 2115 and 2130 hours.

Next on the menu was music by Miller, Ellington, Basie, Shaw and the Dorsey Brothers, which more or less dominated the remainder of the evening. To avoid any unnecessary problems, in case somebody would glance over our shoulders to have a look at our music sheets, English song titles were changed. *In the Mood* became *In Stimmung; Serenade in Blue* became *Serenade in Blau; Moonlight Serenade* was *Moondlicht Serenade; Little Brown Jug* was *Kleiner Brauner Krug. It Don't Mean A Thing* became *Es Spielt Keine Rolle; I Got Rhythm* was *Ich Habe Rhythmus;* and *Sentimental Journey* became the German lyrics receiving the rather long title *Komm, Wir Machen Eine Kleine Reise.*

American Patrol, the number one hit with the boys, caused a problem. We kicked a few titles around, but eventually agreed to put it on thick with that one. We called it *Deutsche Marine Patrouille*, or *German Navy Patrol.* What a laugh!

Most of the time we rounded off the evening somewhat sentimentally with favorite tunes like *Stormy Weather, Stardust, Good-Bye* and *Auf Wiedersehen.*

By the time I rejoined the group in July 1944, the band had established itself so well that it became more difficult to accommodate all the booking offers. Every commander in the area, down to Egersund and up to Haugesund, tried to improve their staff morale, using our services to divert the boys' attention away from warfare. Entire U-boat crews would book us when returning from weeks of isolation out there in the Atlantic. In August, most members of the army octet, who regularly performed at the army/air force mess, went on leave. While we appeared as relief band during those weeks, the major dining room hall became a fire trap.

From 1900 hours on, there was not one seat vacant for the rest of the evening. Many chaps were standing in the aisles, staring at the stage, clapping their hands, shouting for more and generally made it impossible for the service personnel to work in normal fashion. Food and drinks would be passed over the heads of the audience until reaching their destinies. Money was collected likewise, traveling from hand to hand.

On the first evening of our appearance, the mess sergeant in charge just kept shaking his head. Coming close to the stage he would comment, "I've never seen the like of it." That repeated itself for four weeks. He must have been relieved when our term was up. For us, it was very gratifying to experience such an overwhelming response. I cannot think of any audience that is more grateful and enthusiastic than men and women in uniform. That is particularly the case during wartime, when one does not know whether or not one will still be alive the next day.

Whenever we played, we had extended liberty from our commanders. The concert ended at midnight, unless we performed for U-boat crews, who often held out until the wee hours in the morning, before everybody staggered all over the place.

After the concert, the members of the band relaxed with the cooks and service personnel. At times, some of the officers joined us for a drink or two. Once in a while, when Werner had one too many, we had to be quick in separating him from the others. With the excuse, "He is feeling sick," we would take him under the armpits and walk him out of the room. Suddenly, he would start bursting out, "terrible, awful!" That would be followed by "I am a traitor! How can I wear such a slut uniform." One can imagine the reason for us separating him. If overheard by a fanatic, Werner would have been reported and either sent to a concentration camp or sentenced to death by a military tribunal.

His self-accusations were ridiculous. He had no choice but to wear that uniform. Minds work strangely in a stupor. But being separated from his family, having strong feelings for the US, and likely the factor that he had missed out on quickly leaving Germany when the war broke out, were all contributing factors.

The worst thing, however, was a human tragedy. In one of the pouches of music sheets which Werner received via Sweden, a letter from his dad gave him the message that both his brothers, Hubert and Alphons, had been drafted, one to the marines, the other to the air force. His dad had also volunteered to serve!

When Werner described this to me, he emphasized, "That, Sigy, really hit me between the eyes. I should be with them, not here! And I cannot help feeling blue when I've had a couple of drinks. I just have to shout it out."

Like every band, we had a few girls who would hang around, wait for us to get off the stage, and have a little celebration with us. There were not always enough girls for each member of the band. That does not seem to present a problem anymore today, with all the groupies floating around. Though we never did fight about girls, it sometimes created some tension when the same guys were lucky more often than others.

I remember one day, when Teddy got shortchanged the third time in a row. We were sitting together with a few girls, enjoying their complimentary remarks about our music. Teddy noisily assembled and packed his percussions. Then he stalked off the stage like a sentry in front of Buckingham Palace, marched by without giving us a glance and left the room, slamming the door. It did not take much to sense that something was bugging Teddy. Werner and I got up simultaneously and ran after him.

We caught up with him before he had reached the end of the corridor. "What's wrong, Teddy?" Werner asked.

With an exasperated look on his face, Teddy exploded, "You have the nerve to ask what is wrong? This is bloody well the third time I got shafted. You guys drop your instruments like hot potatoes when the concert is finished, while I have to struggle for hours (a slight exaggeration) with all my metal pieces. You grab the cutest girls in the meantime and once in a blue moon I get one of the leftover chicks but nothing most of the time. I quit!"

We did not want to lose this great drummer of ours and made it a point from then on to assist with the disassembling and packing of his percussion accessories.

THE TERBOVEN VISIT

The Reassignment

In October 1943, Heinz Marzi's transfer to Trondheim became pending. Dr. Carlos Mayer-Pantin, through my company commander, Lieutenant Commander Schmidt, appointed me as Heinz's successor.

On Friday, the twenty-ninth, Schmidt gave me the good news. "Listen," he said, "Heinz will leave for Trondheim on 15 November. There is plenty of time for him to break you in. We know he taught you well in 1941-42, but some additional training in administrative and overall organizational matters doesn't do any harm. Get yourself new uniforms again and report to Heinz on Monday. Your duty rank will be that of a noncom, indicating that by the silver bar which the company tailor will sew on your left arm sleeve. Your pay will almost double for this detail. Congratulations." He shook my hand. "Any questions?"

"Just one," I said. "Will this assignment interfere with my annual leave due in March of next year?"

"No reason for that," he replied. "We'll find a way to bridge that time. Why do you ask?"

I knew I could be quite frank with this man. "I would like to see for myself how my parents are doing now after we were bombed out in June of this year. I would also like to discuss with my dad what I think is going to happen before this war is over."

"I have an idea what you are driving at," Schmidt retorted. It seemed he had lowered his voice, though nobody was around to listen in on our conversation. "Marquart told me about the chat you two had when you were his orderly."

"Now the devil is loose," I thought. Loudly I said, "That conversation was off-the-cuff and off-the-record, Herr Kapitaenleutnant." I was dismayed.

"So is this one," Schmidt assured. "I am just curious to find out why you think we cannot win the war anymore. Let's discuss this over a drink right here. You don't have to be worried. It will stay in this room."

I told him as much as I thought would be fairly safe, citing the numerous defeats we had suffered since the beginning of the year. Then I described to him my observations while I returned from home, coming through Denmark, the increasing attacks on our fortifications by the Danish Resistance, using the term "Underground." I even included in my descriptions the leaflets from the Resistance, which the newspaper vendor in Aarhus had so nicely inserted in Lieutenant Commander Kretchmar's and my newspapers.

What I did not dare tell Schmidt was that I regularly listened to foreign broadcasts, including that of the BBC. I knew about the intensive evacuation proceedings that had recently taken place along the British southern coast, providing war exercise terrain to be used by the British, Canadian, American and French free forces in preparation for the invasion of Western Europe.

When I had finished with my theory of how the invasion of Europe would take place, ending in a meeting between the Soviet and Western armed forces somewhere in Germany, Schmidt just shook his head and said, "I hope you are dead wrong, if only for the reason that all previous war efforts and human sacrifices would have been made in vain."

I knew Schmidt, like many other naval officers, was not enthused about Nazism and what it stood for. But he felt, like all of us, that we had to serve Germany as we saw fit, regardless of our personal approval or condemnation of the political system which represented our country.

In the afternoon, I received my new uniform sets. The same quartermaster who had outfitted Otto and me in 1941 was still in charge. "Getting the best brand-new uniforms seems to be a permanent feature with you," he commented smilingly.

It was not that I received an extra set, but when serving at the base I had one naval antiaircraft uniform, one blue navy sailor's uniform, and one white canvas drill uniform. For service at the casino I was entitled to three navy sets.

"Special people, special treatment, Staff Sergeant, sir," I replied. "You should be familiar with that," I added, equally smiling.

When I reported the following Monday to Heinz, he greeted me with a big hello, like a brother. "It's really great to see you, Sigy, as my successor," he emphasized. Looking at my silver beam, he commented, "You look taller now than when I saw you a few weeks ago."

"Yes," I replied, "that silver beam makes a great difference. It's like that silver lining in the clouds." He knew that phrase from his time as a beachcomber in San Francisco.

The new environment was not really new to me. On the contrary, it was more familiar to me than anything else before and in between. Heinz put me right to work, concentrating on areas of overall organization and administrative procedures. He demonstrated and explained the reasons for certain actions. He let me ask all the questions I possibly could think of and, generally speaking, closed some loopholes of knowledge that had not been covered during my previous service at the casino.

The second day during breakfast time, our commandant, Commodore Mayer-Pantin, gave me a welcome back handshake. He indicated that Schmidt and Heinz Marzi had supported my reassignment, which put me in a happy mood.

In 1942, when my co-steward was transferred, even though he had more experience, I felt kind of uncomfortable. Later on, over a few glasses of his favorite German gin, I had expressed my surprise to Heinz. I had nailed him on that occurrence, since I could not see anything I did better than Otto. Heinz insisted, though, to my embarrassment, that I had shown more personal interest and enthusiasm for my assignment. Somehow, that explanation did not make me feel any better. On the other hand, in spite of the fact that Heinz and I were so completely different, he the bold charge-taking macho-type and I the milk-faced tenderfoot, we were on the same wavelength when it came to dispensing hospitality.

By the end of the first week I had become comfortable with all newly-learned procedures, ready to take on the new challenge.

On Wednesday, 10 November, I was supposed to be off duty after luncheon service. A couple of my chums from the base who were also off had suggested we spend the rest of the day together and whoop it up a bit. Under the guise of having a cute girl lined up for me, I agreed. The real reason for this arrangement was to pump me for new information regarding my recent reassignment.

It was around 1500 hours, when I was all ready to go. Immaculately dressed, spit and polished, oxfords shining like mirrors, I left my quarters on the mezzanine floor and went down the fancy spiral staircase for the umpteenth time without leaving a trace of a fingerprint on the handrail. My appreciation for these beautiful surroundings had not been diminished one iota since I first became overwhelmed with them in December 1941. Again I told myself how fortunate I really was to have this privilege.

When I entered the pantry between the kitchen and dining room, I saw Heinz talking to someone on the telephone. As I swished by, I heard Heinz saying, "One moment please,

Commandant, sir." Solway, one of our kitchen assistants, was just wishing me a nice day off when Heinz caught up with me in the middle of the kitchen.

"Hold it!" he said. "Get to the phone. The Commandant wants to talk to you."

I returned to the pantry, picked up the receiver from the wall board, and identified myself.

The Call

"Mayer-Pantin here," I heard his unmistakably firm but controlled voice. "What are you doing right now?" he asked. I told him. "Hmm," he uttered, sounding almost apologetic, "you will have to change your plans."

Then he told me to report to the *Reichsminister's Gebaeude* (building of the then top Norwegian Nazi administrator) at the corner of Kirkegata and (now called Haakon VII Gate), at 1800 hours sharp. He had cleared this with my commander and casino chairman.

Reichsminister Terboven would be hosting a formal dinner for commanding officers of the three armed forces in Norway, the SS, the SD (*Sicherheitsdienst*, or Security Service), the Gestapo (*Gacheime Staats Polizei*, or Secret State Police) and the Abwehr (Counterintelligence Service). The dinner would be followed by lengthy meetings. Sixty-two guests were expected to participate. "SS Standarten Fuehrer Kardialgi, Terboven's closest aide and bodyguard, is going to screen each person who enters the second floor. He knows who you are. The security guard on the ground floor, whom you will have to pass, has your name on the service personnel list." After I had repeated the order, he hung up.

"Better get some rest," Heinz suggested, after I told him what my orders were. "These high-level meetings don't happen often, but when they do, they take some time." I reminded Heinz that I was well aware of this, since I had spent an entire week at Holmenkollen in Oslo as "food taster" at the end of November 1942.

He retorted, "If it takes that long, don't bother to come back here. I will be gone and somebody else will be running the show."

Then it dawned on me that I needed special liberty if I had to be out nearly all night. I never needed any special passes during my previous service as steward with the casino. We were exempted from limited leave during the day or on evenings. But this was different. I called Schmidt at the base. "You don't need one," he said decisively. "We know where you are; don't worry!"

After a couple of hours of rest, I made the usual simple preparations for catering work. I emptied my briefcase of some oddities and packed it with just two clean service serviettes, my universal bottle opener, the wine waiter's corkscrew, toothbrush and toothpaste, and a pair of socks, which I used only when my feet got sore.

This afternoon had been a bit foggy but not enough for me to ask for transportation. Walking from the northern end of Ny Olavskleiv, where the casino was located, to the southern tip of Kirkegata took less than twenty minutes.

I left around 1720 hours and walked without hurry down Ny Olavskleiv. Opposite the naval headquarters building, where the Atlantic Hotel is now located, one has a good look at Stavanger Harbor inlet. From where I walked, I counted only two vessels tied up along Strandkaien to my left view, and six ships to the immediate right, nearby Skagen. I could not see far enough to see any vessels tied up further out down Skansekaien.

When I arrived at the building, I did not see any security guards at the entrance. That was strange, since the Germans always took elaborate security precautions before and during top level meetings such as this one, particularly in occupied countries. Entering the lobby, I saw one civilian behind the reception desk. One SS officer stood close by, while one chap from the Luftwaffe had placed himself at the bottom of a flight of stairs behind a lectern, which showed the rim of a black waste-book.

The passenger elevator door was closed. A sign to one side said *Ausser Betrieb* in German and *I uorden* in Norwegian, meaning out of order. A grim-looking civilian in a shabby leather coat and large-brimmed felt hat loitered nearby, puffing intensively on a cigarette, as if determined to finish it fast. I had seen the same type in Denmark while passing through on the way back to Norway. Their calling cards invariably were shabby raincoats or leather coats, wide-brimmed hats, cigarette in mouth, and sickly-looking skin from lack of fresh air—Gestapo agents!

To the left and right of the lobby, several doors led to different businesses that had been rented out. One of them included a portrait studio which I had visited only recently to have my picture taken. The doors here were used by employees and deliveries of light goods.

As I came nearer to the desk, the SS officer stepped forward and with a movement of his right hand said, "Pay book." I handed it to him. He glanced at it, looked at me and said, "See the sergeant," pointing in the direction where the air force man stood.

I had just made one step when the SS man called me back. "Stop. Show me your briefcase first." I swirled around and opened the flap of the briefcase at the same time, holding it so that the light from the front desk lamps would show the inside. He reached in and withdrew his hand with the wine waiter's corkscrew in it.

"What the devil is this?" he asked. For a moment I was tempted to tell him that it was one of the new miracle weapons, but quickly changed my mind. With very few exceptions, members of the SS and the Gestapo were political fanatics, and fanatics do not have any sense of humor!

When I told him what it was, he shook his head. "Never seen anything like that. Does it work?"

"It sure does, sir," I replied. "If you have time later on, come upstairs and I'll give you a demonstration which, of course, will include the tasting of wine." The suspicious look did not leave his face, as if he was searching for some hidden trick. He did not reply, but instead let me go.

Next stop, at the lectern, I mentioned my name to the air force sergeant as instructed. He looked at his list in front of him. I saw him crossing off a line on top of the first page. Obviously names of expected guests and hired personnel were kept in alphabetical order. Then he looked at my left arm sleeve, "It says here chief steward. What is that silver strip doing under your degree of rank?"

I explained to him that my service rank was that of able seaman, but my duty rank as chief steward put me even with his rank. His politeness increased. He stepped aside from behind the lectern, made an inviting gesture with his left hand indicating I could pass, and said a bit apologetically, "Just curious. Kardialgi expects you on the second floor. See you later."

The Party

I saluted smartly, one of the few things I could do well as a soldier, besides sharpshooting. "At ease," said Kardialgi. He took me to a corner of the small reception room for a briefing.

"The sous chef from the Victoria Hotel is in charge of food preparation," he explained. "He has two cooks at his side from the army and two kitchen helpers from the Grand Hotel responsible for dishing up the food for the service personnel. Also they will clean soiled dishes and pots and pans afterwards.

"You take responsibility for the service with two waitresses from the Victoria Hotel, one man from the air force, and a second one from the army.

"There will be a reception in the main reception hall with cocktails and appetizer wines, beginning at 1830 hours. A five-course dinner will follow at 1945 hours in the dining room, which nicely accommodates the sixty-some invited guests. While you serve dinner with the other service personnel, the reception hall is going to be cleaned up and prepared again for the major evening meeting. You will have to stay until everybody else has left, including the food preparation and service personnel."

Kardialgi seemed to be a nice enough guy, SS man or not. Though his German was flawless, his diction hinted that it was not his first language. He was singing the language much more than any one of us, with curves going up and down, similar to the way the Swedes speak. I had met a few at the beginning of the year through a Norwegian friend of mine who was their host.

I went to the kitchen and introduced myself to all those I had not met. It had rather small aisles, causing danger to the food preparation personnel, who had to dance around each other, carefully avoiding bumping.

It seemed the facility was not originally built to hold that much cooking equipment. There was not a thing missing–flattop ovens with warming compartments underneath, open flame broilers, baking oven, roasting oven, a big grill, a small mixing machine, baker's scale, meat slicer, meat saw, triple-compartment bain marie to keep food warm, and a holding station at the pick-up counter for roast beef or Chateau Briand. In one corner, several chafing dishes for service personnel to finish food at dining room tables, were lined up and ready to be used.

One of the two waitresses and the man from the air force were chatting, the girl leaning against an ice cream cabinet, holding a menu in her hand. I asked the chef for more copies, and congregated all service personnel in one corner of the reception hall. We discussed the sequence of serving the five courses and any other procedures that had to be adhered to. Official banquet service, particularly in the military, entailed more uniform techniques in serving guests than used otherwise. One of them was the principle that once a server had entered the dining room with his or her oval platter for serving a course, the server could not leave the room before having served all portions from the platter.

Service personnel would enter and leave the dining facility in military fashion upon signal by the person in charge. The two Norwegian waitresses were accustomed to most of these procedures, as they had been borrowed by us for functions such as this several times before. When questions had petered out, I prearranged some signals with them in order to minimize unnecessary talking. Then we all prepared ourselves for the reception service at 1830 hours which would precede the dinner.

On the way back to the kitchen, I asked the two waitresses if they had ever heard the name Kardialgi, and if it had a meaning. They had not, but the name meant "heartburn" in Norwegian. I had to laugh. What a fitting description for a bodyguard. By nature of his assignment, he at times would indeed cause some would-be assassins heartburn by spoiling an attempt on Terboven's life.

The reception went by without incident. The head count was fifty-three. That would leave eleven guests for each server, plus the nine I would look after. I turned to the dining room to check on the table settings. Everything was in order. Two wine glasses rested upside down at the tip of each dinner knife. There would be white wine with the fish course and a red wine with the main course.

One of the army cooks had spent several years in Japan before the war. In order to get away from the almost traditional German appetizer, Bismarck herring, he had suggested to the chef, with the approval of Kardialgi, that *No-Numaki* would be an appropriate hors d'oeuvre preceding the other courses. This *zensai*, as the Japanese call their appetizers, is less exotic than its name indicates. It appeared in German on the menu as chicken livers wrapped in bacon.

The next course was French onion soup, followed by the entree (symbolically meaning the beginning of the meal, but it is a light course served immediately before the main course). Ours consisted of poached North Atlantic salmon in butter sauce.

Oriental pepper steak with Chinese-style mushrooms and peas, called *Mo-Ku, Wan-Tau,* with sweet potatoes and eggplant made up the main course.

The meal was topped off with *Irmik Helvasi* dessert, or Turkish farina nut pudding, served with cognac and coffee.

Although Kardialgi had left it at my discretion to what degree I would participate in the actual service during dinner, I decided to commence myself with the service of each course to Terboven and the four guests seated immediately to his right and his left, and divide the remainder of guests among my four colleagues.

That fell on fruitful grounds, since they appreciated it. Stations became smaller than what would have been the case if I solely acted as the conductor of the orchestra, the maitre d'hotel. The main reason for my making this decision was, of course, to provide the best service possible for these dignitaries. I also was fully aware that, if anything went wrong, my head would be on one of those service platters as a trophy.

At 1945 hours sharp, the dinner service commenced with typical military precision. The first two courses ran like a clock. When we returned with the used onion soup dishes to the kitchen, I saw one army cook wearing cook's helper gloves, remove the platters, on which the salmon course would be served from the chafing dishes.

He withdrew the bottom one from a pile and placed nine portions of salmon for me in the wide center cavity of the platter, using the smaller surrounding cavities to place accompaniments as the menu required. In one end cavity he set a sauce boat containing the melted butter sauce and encircled it with lemon wedges. I was ready to go and so were the other servers.

Placing my service tools, oval soup spoon and dinner fork, handily on the platter, I lifted it by the outer rim with my right hand, and placed my left white-gloved hand, with a fresh service serviette doubly folded underneath and in the center of the platter. "That should suffice," I thought.

We had poured the white wine, of course, before we left the banquet room to pick up the fish course. As required by etiquette, we marched in line into the room. Since there was no guest of honor, I always started the service with Terboven as the highest ranking person. Then I continued to his left, with General Jodl, commanding officer of all German forces in Norway, Air Marshall Oberhausen, Vice Admiral Born (no relation) from naval headquarters in Oslo, and our Commodore Mayer-Pantin.

Halfway through serving these five people, I noticed the platter becoming unusually warm; at least, so it seemed. I started to swear under my breath for not having used a second service napkin for better protection. When I started with Rear Admiral Von Schrader to Terboven's right, I winced from pain. Neither could I leave the room to adjust the situation, nor hasten up the service. I was in a real box! "Blasted idiot!" I cursed at myself, while trying hard to keep a straight face. To make matters worse, Admiral Von Schrader, who was a deliberate man, took his time selecting from the platter before I served out what he wanted. The two next to him were no better. Tears of pain came to my eyes, accompanied by the fear that some would float down onto the platter. Brigadier Dehnert, fourth to Terboven's right, looked up at me as I bent forward with the platter and asked, "Is there something wrong, sailor? Your face is twitching."

"Yes, Brigadier, sir," I replied. "That blasted platter is burning my palm!" He was kind enough to make quick selections and I left the room with long strides, pretending to make haste slowly, one of many slogans I had learned in the food business. Never mind that the other servers were not yet finished with serving out their portions!

Once outside, I placed the platter, not particularly cautiously, on the outer rim of a huge plant base, and started dancing from one foot to the other, probably looking close to a North American Indian rain dance.

Once back in the kitchen, one of the two army cooks who had just passed a first-aid course, welcomed me as his first victim. The cook-turned-medical orderly cautiously removed my glove. Part of the palm skin stuck inside. I was looking at raw flesh. What an ugly sight! Little did I know that, less than one year hence I would see serious wounds and mutilations almost defying description.

He walked over to the pot wash sink with me and to my surprise, held my hand and wrist under the wide-open cold water tap for two full minutes. At the time, that procedure was discouraged by medical doctors, believing this would make matters worse. Now, we know better.

Next, he cautiously dried my hand, touching it lightly with a clean woolen cloth. Then he applied a generous amount of first-aid cream to the palm and burn powder to the wrist, wrapped three thin layers of bandage around the wrist and hand, and then manipulated my hand into a wider-sized new glove. During the entire time, I moaned and groaned. I had a rather low pain tolerance level and did not care less that a soldier was not supposed to show pain. On the other hand, there was no way of quitting this assignment. The show had to go on.

The remainder of the dinner service took place without any incidents, painful for me but otherwise a cinch.

When dinner was over, we were given a chance to clear the dining room while guests stretched their legs a bit. We had to cross the conference hall with the soiled dishes to reach the kitchen. That task took only twelve minutes to complete.

We all helped to get the dishes and pots and pans done in a jiffy before we sat down for our dinner in an anteroom off the pantry.

It was close to 2300 hours when the meeting ended. A few guests lingered around for a while and had a nightcap. At midnight, Kardialgi announced, "You can tidy up now and clean everything. The dance is over." He seemed to have a sense of humor, rarely present among his peers.

Finally, at 0130 hours we were finished. The place looked as if it had not been used at all. Kardialgi, who had designated one of his underlings to drive Terboven to his temporary residence, had stayed behind with Brigadier Wendel, deputy city commander of the army, who insisted upon being included in the clean-up crew. He clowned around with a push broom, complaining it would not go where he wanted it. What a few drinks can do! With some it unfortunately works the other way around. Generally, alcohol brings the real person to the surface.

We asked Kardialgi for permission to stay for a while and have a few drinks. Only under the condition that he and Wendel could join us, was his answer. Putting two six-foot long tables together, we had sufficient space for all of us to gather around.

While the tables were set up and drinks brought out, I asked Kardialgi about the inconspicuous, or even lack, of security precautions outside the building.

"We learned from bad experience," he replied. "It is imperative that meetings such as this be kept hush-hush as much as possible. Obvious security precautions only alert the enemy to target in on us. The entire food preparation and service personnel, including yourself, as you know, have been notified at the last possible moment, so that not even accidental leaks could occur. A lot of mistakes have been made in the past. The substantial increase in acts of sabotage in Denmark during this summer, for instance, have partially been our own fault."

I told him that I got quite a taste of some of these when I traveled through Denmark towards the end of July. I knew well what he was talking about, but wondered whether he recognized the real reasons for the Danes' sudden defiance. As far as the protection of military installations and energy resources were concerned, they simply could not take place inconspicuously.

We all sat down, and as so often with army, air force and navy personnel, the conversation either circles around women, booze, or both. Since we had four women in our midst, two each from the Grand Hotel and Victoria Hotel, it soon became limited to booze. I have never been able to pin down why navy men seem to have the reputation for being the greatest boozers from the three armed forces. One of the two army cooks challenged me to drink them under the table. Under ordinary circumstances I would not have accepted that contest of skill, but my painful hand needed some kind of a narcosis. Why not have a few of my favorite maraschino cherry liqueurs and have it two ways, kill the pain, and win the contest?

Around 0330 hours, two chaps from the army and the air force steward challenged Kardialgi to a billiards game. That would be fun to watch. So, we all proceeded to the fourth floor where a non-pocket, French billiards table was taking the center of the game room. Drawing pins, the air force guy had to team up with Kardialgi. After four games, the army chaps gave up. The SS and the air force had beaten the army every time. The two victors were looking for some other victims to fleece.

By now I felt a burning sensation but little pain, though I was still comparatively sober. Brigadier Wendel and I took over from the losers. We both agreed we could not possibly do worse than the other team. Once one is on the bottom, as my great mentor and friend Chris Delahunty taught me years later, there is only one way to go—up.

Nobody knew that I had become quite proficient in this French billiards game by the time I was fifteen, thanks to my dad's training. In this case, though, I had to slide the cue over the thumb, like pocket billiard players do in North America. European players, in contrast, slide the cue tip through the bent index finger, which provides for more stability and accuracy in guiding the play ball.

To make it more interesting, the stake was Kr 5 per game per person. Both my partner and I had maintained a fairly good equilibrium. We played a number of combinations that caused our opponents to sadly shake their heads, while the onlookers commented with "ahs" and "ohs." We won five to zero, Kr 25 for a one-and a-half-hour effort. Not bad. It equaled eight days pay.

Returning to the second floor, we had two more rounds of drinks and then called it a day, or night, in this case.

The Day After

Briefcase in hand, I left the Terboven Building. As soon as I had walked a few steps I knew I had gassed up too much. The surrounding buildings seemed to sway and there were at least three times the number of ships tied up at the harbor than I had seen the previous evening.

As I entered Ny Olavskleiv, walking along the right-hand sidewalk, I looked up the fairly steep street. An army MP patrol swung around the corner from Lokkeveien, where our navy truck compound was located, into Ny Olavskleiv, marching in my direction. It was too late to turn around. They were walking on the other sidewalk but certainly must have seen me coming from below. I kept moving and did not look in their direction, pretending not to notice them, wishing that for once the ostrich position would work. How foolish can one get?

I was almost even with the three men on the other sidewalk, when I heard a shout, "Are you blind, you stupid bloke?" Turning sideways, I looked surprised and carefully crossed the street, walking as straight as I could manage. Reaching them, a sergeant, a corporal and one private, I sat my briefcase down to salute with my right hand. My left was still in the glove, but it looked like a mess as some blood had soaked through.

"Where do you come from?" the sergeant demanded. Before I could open my mouth, he continued, "You are completely drunk and stink like a pig! Your papers."

I reached into my pay book. A few seconds passed, then he asked where I came from. The corporal beside him sized me up incredulously and shook his head, refusing to believe what he saw.

I decided to give the vaguest answer I could. Pointing with my right thumb over my shoulder, I provided the meaningless answer. "I come from down there." The sergeant started to get into a fit. I never felt more relaxed and could not care less what these birds would say or do. The Germans boldly refer to this state as a "kiss my arse mood." The sergeant had called me stupid. Why not give a demonstration and prove him right?

The next couple of minutes or so I had to swallow verbal insults. He started by calling me the greatest heap of unmilitary shit he had ever seen, and ended up suggesting I should be hung up by the balls to dry out. Finally, he threatened court-martial procedures against me. What a great beginning to a new day. He scribbled some notes into a black pocket book.

When he had to gasp for air, I quickly threw in the remark that I had been on special assignment and was not allowed to give any details, not even after the event, and that I had my quarters at the naval officers casino, located at the end of the street. That perplexed him momentarily, but then he said that my commander would get a report which could not be overlooked, and dismissed me with a friendly "Get lost."

Nobody had seen me coming through the front door of the casino. I heard movements behind the big double door leading to the dining room. Both stewards were setting up for breakfast. It was almost 0600 hours when I crawled into bed, although afterwards I could not even remember how I managed that feat.

I was suddenly awakened by a loud bang. My bed was shaking. "Get up you good-for-nothing." I heard Heinz's booming voice. "If you can booze all night, then you can also get up in the morning!"

Peeping between my tired eyelids, my watch showed 0715 hours. The bed seemed to rotate as in an aftershock. Heinz had deliberately thrown the door against the end of my bed.

"You have to be kidding, Heinz, I've just had about an hour sleep."

"Whose fault is that?" he queried, stepping to the side of the bed and quickly withdrawing the quilt. "Move, or else!" he emphasized. I regretted having told him how I got First Lieutenant Marquart out of bed about three months earlier. Since I did not want Heinz to go to the next stage and give me the water bucket treatment, I peeled myself out of bed.

"You stink like a pig," he commented. (Didn't I hear that very recently?) "Wash up and brush your clappers. Your breath can peel the paper off the walls." Then he explained, "You have to drive with Erich Apfel to pick up beer from *To Bryggeri*. We are completely out except for a few bottles of Hollsten beer."

Erich and I left with the navy truck at 0800 hours. Ten minutes later, we pulled into the yard of the brewery. Nine other trucks from different army and air force bases were ahead of us, waiting to be loaded.

"You know what," I said to Erich and the driver, "remain out here while I go in and have our requisition verified."

The brewery had two processing offices; one for the civilian population, and one for the military. I entered the one plainly marked "Military Personnel Dispatch" and lined up at the first counter with the sign "Approvals." The second bore the letters "Loading." Applicants had to move from one to the other.

About fifteen people were standing in line. One corporal stood behind each counter and a staff sergeant sat further back at a desk, perusing and approving requisitions.

I had barely joined the end of the line when the two men directly in front of me turned around and one said, "You must have lifted the elbow quite a bit this early in the morning," lifting his eyebrows quizzically.

"That did not quite hit the target," I replied cheerfully. "I am a leftover from last evening."

Five minutes went by, then the sergeant behind the desk asked loudly, "Who is poisoning the air here so much? The stink in this store can make one vomit!"

I quickly stepped beside the row. Standing at attention, I said, pretending to be embarrassed, "I think it is I, Sergeant, sir," offering no additional explanation.

"Step forward, you pig, and get out of here fast!" He motioned to the two corporals to process my papers. I was getting a bit tired of being called a pig, but in this case it had a definite advantage.

Erich and the driver rolled their eyes when I reappeared with the loading papers in my hand. We moved to one of the two loading platforms which had just been vacated. The other waiting drivers jumped out of their trucks as if on command and started to protest. "If you don't like it, see the sergeant in charge inside. We have an emergency," I explained and turned my back to them. "I wonder what kind that could be," one man queried loudly but I did not pay any attention to him.

Loading the truck took only fifteen minutes. We returned to the casino before the clock struck 0900 hours. "That was faster than ever," Heinz commented. "When you have taken over for me, you had better go more often yourself rather than sending someone else. Nobody can refuse you in your condition." I had no intention whatsoever of repeating my disgraceful performance, which had only embarrassed others and myself.

I assisted Erich Apfel with taking inventory and prepared the dining room for luncheon service. Heinz commented on my "sailor's walk" and would not let me get into the act of helping with the service. "You would only narcotize half the officers corps," he said. "I wonder what would happen if anybody close to you struck a match?"

There are a number of ways to sober up, people insist. Some gulp down coffee by the gallon, followed by a cold shower. Others, like Heinz Marzi, take an antidote, such as a finger of straight gin with club soda as a chaser. I tried all that during the day, but nothing helped. Even after a good luncheon I still felt the same.

Finally, after a substantial dinner in the evening, I became myself again. It had been the second time in my life that I was heavily intoxicated, or to put it bluntly, silly drunk. The first time, if you remember, was in December 1941, on the island of Haon. Each time, I felt just awful, to say the least.

Before I turned in that day, I made a resolution: Never again! It was the only resolution I ever made, but I have kept it to this day. My late father would call it "being rescued from the devil alcohol."

ARCTIC ADVENTURE

My Last Annual Furlough

After the Terboven disaster, I took over for Heinz Marzi as chief steward on Monday, 15 November, as planned. The situation was somewhat different than in 1941. There was no deficit to be wiped out. On the contrary, Heinz had long since established a steadily increasing surplus that was beneficial for everyone, including the officer casino staff.

Some additional service staff training had to be done, but that's all in the game and is a vital part in any organization. Erich Eye, the chef, and Hermann Behrens were still preparing the food. Karen and Solway, the Norwegian kitchen assistants, had almost become steady fixtures of the casino. They were happy people who had contributed significantly to the good service of casino members, and were treated as full members of a team, the way it should be.

Members of the service staff, one male steward and two females from the German Red Cross, were kind of apprehensive when told there would be a change of leadership. But Erich and Hermann had removed their reservations before I arrived on the scene, telling them about my good sides and nothing about my bad ones.

Security measures had been substantially tightened around the Christmas and New Year's holidays. A repeat of previous years' capers, by which a great number of Norwegians serving with the British forces had fooled us by spending their holidays right under our noses, could not be confirmed this time. Maybe they were running out of tricks. There was no guarantee, though, that it had not taken place. We simply did not know. None of the additional lookout commandos who had been deployed right along the coastline reported anything unusual.

At the beginning of March 1944, my third, and as it turned out, my last, annual furlough was due. Lieutenant Commander Schmidt made arrangements to have me replaced at the casino for three weeks, as he had earlier promised. I was looking forward to seeing how my parents were doing now after they had left Uncle Fritz's farm. All I knew was that Mother's half-brother Otto had offered shelter in his own home in Leverkusen-Kueppersteg, a beautiful small town with a long name, situated a few kilometers east of Cologne. Father had to commute daily from there to Wuppertal, where he was stationed as a railway officer, but distances are so small in Europe when compared to North America. And even with the persistent continuation of city bombings, it did not cause any major problem.

When I picked up my marching papers from the base, the sergeant major mentioned that I was one of the first men on leave who did not have to transfer trains and transport trucks anymore between Stavanger and Oslo. Our army engineers, pioneers and Norwegian work crews had finally completed the last missing railway track between the two cities. This suited me well. Even though the bus trip through the mountains was always most enjoyable, I was not too keen on this hair-raising mode of traveling. The fatality of December 1941 when one truck went down part of the mountain during our trip from Haon to Stavanger smack in the middle of the mountains was enough for me! Some adventures are better avoided.

This time the trip was kind of awkward, but beautiful as always. Awkward, because we had to board three different ferries before arriving at Flensburg, Germany. The travel route led us from the border town of Halden southward through Sweden until Helringborg, then by ferry across the Oresund to Helsingør, Denmark's most eastern point. We continued by train to Copenhavn (Copenhagen), Ringsted, Slagelse and Korsor, then took a second ferry to Nyborg, a short train trip again to Faborg, at which point we boarded a third ferry to Gluecksburg, north of Flensburg.

Once there, my travel documents were stamped. I was told the pass-through base in Kiel had been bombed several times and on my return trip to inquire first where I should report back, since everything changed there daily.

That I could well believe. The destruction I had seen and personally experienced nine months ago was bad, but nothing in comparison to the sights that awaited me now. Only small villages had been spared from bombings. It was a miracle that traffic, or anything else, for that matter, was still moving at all! The entire country seemed to consist of one big pile of rubble.

Leverkusen-Kueppersteg, the small community where my parents resided now, had been spared so far, even though Cologne, the metropolis close by, had been visited by the RAF dozens of times. In Leverkusen itself, several houses had been destroyed. But there was evidence that these bomber pilots really did not have to bomb indiscriminately. They had so much experience by now, that they could pick out their targets exactly as they wanted.

The Cologne Cathedral was the landmark of the city for hundreds of years. That dome could not possibly be missed by anybody; it stuck out like a sore thumb. Yet, while not one surrounding building within four square kilometers escaped destruction, the dome was saved, only having a scratch here and there.

The Bayer IG Farbenindustrie complex in Leverkusen, the largest of its kind in Europe, did not even have a scratch, while most surrounding buildings were leveled by the USAF. Pilots had been instructed not to hit the complex, since that empire was built and had been owned by American industrialists.

From the nineteen days I spent at home I remember only three nights through which we could sleep. Enemy aircraft were busy bombing other cities than Cologne and surrounding communities. It's not too interesting to clobber the same target all the time.

Invariably, when the alarm sirens came on, I would not hear them. Nobody found that so strange. But two nights in a row, an 8.8-centimeter cannon, which had been practically placed behind my uncle's house, started to boom even before the air attack warning was given. When everybody huddled in the air raid shelter, they noticed me missing. The 8.8-centimeter big gun could not wake me up. Luckily, the town itself did not get attacked. Not knowing much about war tactics per se, I wondered, though, why the local antiaircraft battery commander had chosen to set up the big gun right behind a private house.

The deterioration of German war efforts had now become obvious, even to the feeble-minded. When I arrived on the scene, I had announced my furlough to be the last one before the war would be over. It was only natural that this war and its possible outcome would become the basis for discussion between my father and me. As I said before, though we had an excellent father-son relationship, politically we were at odds.

One night in the *Luftschutzbunker* (air-raid shelter), his doubts set in. As the bombs fell all over the neighborhood, he shook his head in sadness and asked, "Is this not awful? What are we going to do? I knew right from the beginning that you have been more than reluctant to wear this uniform. I ask you now, can we still win this war, my son?"

This was the time to be frank, if not bold. I repeated the theory I had offered to Lieutenant Marquart at the base during the summer of 1943 and again to Schmidt, my company commander and casino chairman, when reassigned in October of that year. I reiterated the numerous defeats Germany had suffered since the beginning of 1943. Adding to this, I quoted some acts of sabotage, which were carried out by the Danish Resistance. Then I went one step further than I had with Marquart and Schmidt. I admitted I had frequently listened to foreign news broadcasts, including the BBC in London, so as to get a more balanced picture of events.

"The British have evacuated a large number of communities along the south coast of England for exercising landing maneuvers," I continued. "That is all done in preparation for the invasion of Europe which, I am sure, will take place some time this year. British and American forces, accompanied by Canadian and French free forces will sweep over western Europe and finally meet with Soviet armed forces somewhere in Germany." I pretty well described to him what actually did happen, with the exception of the horseshoe landing in Sicily and Italy.

Dad indicated he would flee with Mom if that happened. The idea disturbed me. I pleaded with him not to make a mistake like that. It would mean jumping from the frying pan into the fire. "Stay right here," I suggested. "The bad Anglo-Saxons are not ten percent as bad as Goebbels and his propaganda machine claims. When we meet next time, the war will be over. Germany will survive better than you think. You will see!"

The Cologne opera house had been hit, but there was one building not too far from it where a makeshift concert hall remained intact. My cousin Otto Hofmeister, himself a well-known bass baritone singer, had been able to arrange for a couple of tickets for two opera performances. I saw *La Boheme* for the third time and *Carmen* for the fourth time. But it was nevertheless enjoyable and the only holiday pleasure one could expect from a country which lay in ruins. Somehow, I was not too sorry when the end of my furlough came along, although I felt more than sorry for those I left behind, particularly my parents and other relatives.

The return trip to Norway was without event. We were told to take the route via Berlin and Stettin, then a ferry to Sweden. Traffic through Denmark had almost come to a complete stop. The Resistance flexed its muscles everywhere. The pressure they applied by their various acts of sabotage was frustrating for German area commanders.

The Resistance had received more supplies from the British than ever before. We could not turn our backs anymore without running into opposition that really started to hurt. The point had been reached where a number of German soldiers just went through the motions of defending our occupation, knowing we continued to slide downhill. Morale was rock-bottom. Some were even resentful of harsh treatment that was dished out to suspects. Probably without realizing it the free-wheeling democratic way of the Danes had infected their way of thinking. My assumption was verified by a number of countrymen after the war, who had been stationed in Denmark.

I resumed my duties at the officers casino on Thursday, 27 March. Everything seemed to be in good order.

Attack The *Tirpitz*

Von der Knesebrecht, who had been promoted from lieutenant to lieutenant commander in 1943, had managed to safely guide the *Tirpitz*, the forty-two-thousand-ton Beast, as Churchill usually called it, from Narvik to Kafjorden, after the unsuccessful attack on the battleship by the RAF at Narvik Harbor. He knew the British would not rest in their attempt to sink the last battleship we had left at the time, so he acted accordingly. Taking all probabilities and possibilities into account, he convinced the appointed area commander of Kafjorden and vicinity that most unusual precautions must be taken so as to prevent the destruction of the ship. An impregnable spot had to be found. It would be costly but worthwhile if Germany wanted to hold on to her last battleship.

Because of the mountainous terrain surrounding the fjord, regular antiaircraft batteries could not be placed, except on the only plateau nearby Kafjord at the extreme inlet of the fjord. The elevation was only about two hundred meters, but allowed an excellent view on the fjord inlet, where the *Tirpitz*, her mother ship, the *Admiral Hipper*, and other escort ships had found refuge. Eleven fog-in batteries were erected between and around the mountain area.

Some of the best antiaircraft battery crews were withdrawn from other naval batteries, including those stationed in Narvik who already had proven themselves to be effective defense men. The battery on the plateau became known as the Fourth Naval Antiaircraft Battery. It consisted of four big 8.8-centimeter cannons, plus eight quadruple four-centimeter rapid guns. With the exception of the battery commander's quarters and an administrative barrack building, crew members' quarters and ammunition depots all had been built underground. The crew members' quarters were located directly underneath the gun installations, while the ammunition storage was kept inside and around the outer belly of the keg-shaped mountain.

With these stable and ingenious arrangements, the security of the *Tirpitz* seemed to be achieved, at least as far as air attacks were concerned. Was there anything missing? Not that the area commander could think of. But, Von der Knesebrecht did!

Having been given an almost unlimited free hand in his defense efforts by Admiral Von Schrader, he pushed for the installation of an intricate underwater chain-net system that would prevent any naval intrusion from outside the fjord. At first, the area commander was not convinced of its necessity because it would also inconvenience our own ship's movements. But the *Tirpitz* was not going to go anywhere anyway. It was a sitting duck, wherever it was, but more securely protected within this extreme inlet than anywhere else.

Von der Knesebrecht had several mines laid at the outer fjord inlet, some fixed, some floating. Further inward he erected an underwater fencing system, consisting of compartmental layers that could be moved shut and open in flexible fashion. Too elaborate? Not so, as it turned out.

The fourth battery and the fog-in batteries were in place by the time the *Tirpitz* arrived; the fjord defense system forty-eight hours after. The manpower requirement necessary to keep up this defense system was staggering and heretofore unheard of. Crew members of the *Tirpitz* accounted for twenty-five hundred men; the *Admiral Hipper* (the so-called mother ship of the *Tirpitz*) and two escort vessels had a crew of 685 men, the eleven fog-in batteries were manned by sixty-eight hundred men, and the fourth battery, after my arrival, had 184 men. Total combat force: 10,069 men.

That certainly was an excessive number of men and amount of material for the preservation of one battleship. It constituted about two percent of our total number of occupiers in the entire country!

But then, the *Tirpitz* was not an ordinary ship. The Beast always had been a constant, worrying threat to vital Allied convoys on their way to Murmansk or Archangel in Russia. Four British and two American battleships with destroyer escorts had to be kept in the eastern Atlantic and Scottish waters solely for the purpose of handling the monster if it emerged from any of the Norwegian fjords. Those ships were badly needed for offensive operations elsewhere. Something had to be done about the Beast. Midget submarines, or X-craft, were the only answer.

Von der Knesebrecht knew well why he was pushing for underwater protection. German intelligence sources had reported in January 1943 that the British were working feverishly on the construction of mini-subs, which could be sent, four-manned, to different strategic areas and most inconspicuously. A mini-sub could sneak into any harbor unobserved, plant explosives, and leave again without leaving a trace.

Our intelligence reports on the amazing miniature vessel were quite factual. By January, six crafts, X-Five to X-Ten, were ready for action. They comprised the Twelfth British Submarine Flotilla.

An X-craft was fifty-one feet six inches long, and five feet nine inches in diameter. It displaced approximately thirty tons in a submerged state. Its primary weapons were a pair of two-ton, delayed-action streamlined mines, or side cargoes secured on either side of the hull. The explosives were set and released by internal mechanisms to drop onto the seabed underneath the target. Limpets could be used as an alternative, but they were not nearly as effective against an armored hull.

It was a perfect submarine in miniature. Everything was scaled down: main-vent hand levers, valve wheels, high-pressure air bottles, battery cells, gauges, indicators and even the main periscope, which itself was a masterpiece of miniaturization, but also rather delicate and prone to faults. Ingenuity had no end. A London omnibus forty-two-horsepower diesel engine drove the craft on the surface and recharged the battery.

Inside, the craft was divided into three compartments. The battery was forward to the right; next came a wet-and-dry (W&D) driver's lock. It also housed a somewhat hazardous WC, a water closet in the form of a hand-pumped head. The control room was situated midship. The engine, with a main motor on the same shaft, was aft. Top speed on or below the surface was six knots, about seven nautical miles per hour.

The X-craft task force was put under the command of the best navigator/captain reservist Lieutenant Don Cameron, a quiet Scottish seaman who had learned his maritime trade in the merchant marine service before the war.

The six X-craft departed 11 and 12 September 1943, heading for the long passage to Kafjord, where the *Tirpitz* lay awaiting them. They were towed by full-sized submarines, and deliberately used a circuitous route, hoping to avoid shipping.

The *Tirpitz* had not anchored in Kafjord harbor for more than four days, when the RAF air attacks began. No dice! Any time they appeared in the vicinity, the entire theater was securely fogged in. There was no visible target to hit. We do not know whether the British became somewhat frustrated after more than several attempts to sink the Beast, or an alternative plan of action to sink the *Tirpitz* had been considered, regardless of whether or not the RAF would succeed.

In the wee hours of 22 September, the X-crafts, with the exception of craft X-Ten which had to endure a series of mechanical breakdowns, were lurking in front of the Kafjord opening mouth. Having wormed themselves (probably without realizing it) through a maze of mines we had laid at irregular points across the mouth of the fjord, they were waiting for us to open the underwater chain locks to allow passage for our own vessels.

Usually, our supply boats would advance to the mouth of the fjord, then wait for our escort ships to join them for the transfer of supplies. That included food supplies for all area military, and nonfood items and ammunition for the vessels and the fourth battery, plus fog drums by the hundreds for the eleven other batteries.

Cameron was nearing the outer nets protecting the inner fjord. It was 0445 hours. The booms were closed. For a moment, Cameron considered cutting a hole in the barrier, but he discarded the idea, seeing a couple of coasters (our escort boats) appearing from the fjord inlet. Good for him. What he did not know, of course, was that we had a number of nets and booms across the fjord. That included a double row of anti-torpedo nets with only a twenty-meter gap to seaward on the port bow of the *Tirpitz*.

On board the *Tirpitz*, life was proceeding as usual. The logbook entry at 0430 hours read, "Allowed two supply boats to meet supply ship at mouth of fjord." At 0500 hours, the log stated, "Called the hands. Set normal antiaircraft and anti-sabotage watch ashore and afloat. Boat-gate and anti-torpedo nets opened for boat and tug traffic. Hydrophone listening office closed down."

That turned out to be a bad mistake also showing some complacency. But it is easier to criticize than to understand that when nothing unusual happens, while dozens and dozens of alarm exercises take place, one does not take everything so serious anymore.

Cameron had correctly assumed it would be too risky to sneak into the fjord when the two boats had passed, since the different lock chambers were (without him knowing this) relocked immediately after our two boats had passed. There was only one way now to penetrate that sea fortress: by snorkeling in with the escort ships when they returned loaded with goods and materials.

And that is exactly what he did. The locks were only opened wide enough to allow one ship to pass at a time. So Cameron trailed the first and headed the second, underwater, of course. It worked all right!

Cameron looked at his watch. It was 0700 hours, sharp. They were on their way to carrying out one of the most important missions ever assigned by the British Admiralty!

About seven minutes later, bad luck had the X-Six craft run onto a rocky shoal. Momentarily, the mini-sub had to break surface. Now what? They had come up facing the *Tirpitz* about 120 feet at ten o'clock, and her mother ship, the *Admiral Hipper*, ninety feet at two o'clock.

A German petty officer on the *Admiral Hipper* sighted the shape and correctly identified it as a small submarine. But nobody, neither on the *Admiral Hipper* nor on the *Tirpitz*, paid any attention to his report. *Tirpitz* Commander Hans Meyer and his A-One Heinz Assmann, had been too thorough in preparing their twenty-five-hundred-man crew for all kinds of threats to the great ship. Too many exercises and false alarms had worked against Assmann's games. Maybe this was only a very large fish? No alarm was sounded.

Cameron had dived again quickly but was puzzled about the lack of reaction from the *Tirpitz*. He pressed on. Only minutes later, his midget sub ran smack into one of the anti-torpedo nets surrounding the *Tirpitz*. The gyro compass had been toppled before when they had hit the shoal. The X-Six just about managed now to pull herself free by having set the controls full blast astern. But now she was totally out of control and shot up to the surface.

The same German petty officer noticed her again and reported the sub the second time. Within seconds, the board patrol of the *Tirpitz* was notified. Heinz Assmann and several other crew members rushed to the railing and stared at the unfamiliar sight below, while Commander Mayer was called. They never had seen such a small U-boat before. Assmann told me later that he momentarily thought it could have been a German sub, maybe one of the miracle weapons Goebbels was constantly talking about. As far as navy men's uniforms were concerned, they could be hardly distinguished by nationalities, since they were so similar.

The sub was in such close proximity now that a hail of machine gun fire from the *Tirpitz* and even that from the *Admiral Hipper* could not do her any harm. Regaining control, Cameron took the X-Six under on one more dive, released the two enormous side cargo mines and allowed them to float to the bottom beneath the *Tirpitz*. The huge mines were equipped with timing devices, which would allow the X-craft to get out of danger in time, but not the battleship. Powerful plastic explosives that could have been transported inside the craft had not yet been invented at the time. Cameron and his men had no illusion, though. The aim of this venture clearly was to cripple the *Tirpitz* bad enough to prevent her seaworthiness for a long time, but there was no way of returning out to sea. It was indicated from the beginning of their assignment that a return trip would be more than remote. As planned in advance, they opened the tiny boat's vents and valves, sinking her, while they escaped through the top hatch, one by one.

In the meantime, Commander Meyer and his second in command Assmann knew that an act of sabotage was in progress. A quick decision had to be made. Should he risk sending down divers to investigate the situation? In preparation for this choice, a ladder rope had already been lowered. Meyer assumed correctly that in any case some kind of timing devices would be used. When he granted me an interview months later when I arrived on the scene, he said, "I felt that time was actually ticking away fast! No need or sense to endanger lives unnecessarily."

Cameron and his three companions were quickly plucked from the water and taken aboard the *Tirpitz*. Later, Cameron described the reception aboard as lukewarm. Meyer had his own kind of explanation. Sure, we were not enthused about their caper. What floored us was the way these guys came aboard nonchalantly. Cameron identified his crew as members of the Royal Navy; that they had carried out explicit instructions of the British Admiralty, calling it Mission Accomplished, then formally surrendered and kept their mouths shut during the entire ensuing interrogations. What nerve!

The four had been taken under deck for not longer than five minutes when several muffled explosions could be heard. But they hardly vibrated the planks of the ship. Something had not worked as well as the Brits had hoped for.

Von der Knesebrecht was notified, who arrived one day later on the scene with a couple of explosives experts. Normally, the amount of explosives used would have been appropriate to blow several huge holes through the vessel's walls. But under closer examination, proof was found that the material had become adversely affected by the salty sea, rendering it partially ineffective. However, though the *Tirpitz* was not mortally wounded, she would be inoperative during the coming winter, held in place for long-term repairs. Just about at the time that she would have been seaworthy again, in April 1944, she burned out one-third by incendiary bombs. Meyer called it an irony of fate, as good a description as any.

After the war I learned that the British knew about the misadventure of their mini-sub crew within twenty-four hours. Corrective action was taken only two days after the event. Attempts to attack the *Tirpitz* by air were reintroduced. German documents at the fourth battery revealed that between 24 September 1943 and 25 April 1944, the day of my arrival, fifty-four air attacks were made on the *Tirpitz* within a total of 212 days! That was an average of one every four days. Only the one described below was successful. Obviously, actual events were recorded with meticulous precision on both sides. I compared my figures with those in the war files of the British in September 1945. They claimed only one more attack than we had registered!

Somewhere between the sixth and the eighth of April, the Brits got lucky, which was unlucky for us, of course.

My comrades went through the warning stages three, two, and one for the umpteenth time. As usual, by the time stage one was declared (the most acute stage) the whole territory lay fogged in before the RAF appeared. But this time there was a difference. What is generally referred to as an end of winter north monsoon had swept into the fjord, but with the tendency to suppress the upper fog layer in such a way that the two top masts of the *Tirpitz* stuck out.

That was the scene for which the British had looked for a long time. Respecting the anti-aircraft fire of the fourth battery, they avoided attacking from the south, from which they would have to fly over the plateau of the artillery installation. Instead they came in two waves: one attacking directly from the north, flying over the island of Arnoy; the other approaching from the western direction over Vanna Island, then turning seventy-five degrees southward to equally attack the target from the north. This second wave had crossed Vannsundet and the northern end of Ullsejordon

In less than fourteen minutes the attack was over. The *Tirpitz* was an easy and helpless target. While the fighter planes and barracuda dive-bombers only had to aim their loads around the two top masts sticking out of the fog, our *Tirpitz* defense could not see a thing! The forty-centimeter guns could not be used. No target could be seen. The bombers flew high enough to remain out of reach for the fourth battery. The 8.8-centimeter gun crews gave it all they had but could not land one hit.

To make matters worse, two bombers had unloaded their leftover load upon the fourth battery, taking three of the four quadruple four-centimeter rapid machine guns out of commission. It was a black day indeed for the *Tirpitz* defense!

As a consequence of the attack, one-third of the *Tirpitz* burned out, 139 crew members lost their lives, together with seventeen from the fourth battery. The wounded counted close to three hundred, including several members of the mother ship, the *Admiral Hipper*. The *Tirpitz* was still afloat; but at what cost!

Bad Luck

That is what it looked like, and that is what it was. On 9 April 1944, Captain Baer and Lieutenant Commander Schmidt both came to the casino pantry after luncheon service. Judging from their solemn faces, something was up.

They came right to the point. Military men do not fiddle around. I had learned that a long time ago and could well understand it. I guess my own urge to call a spade a spade originates back to my time in uniform. It has its advantages, at least in the long run.

In spite of all the different charges I had had, my categorization as naval artillerist remained intact. In fact, I was one of fifteen which existed in the German Navy at the time. Captain Baer regretfully informed me that the order to transfer me to the fourth battery, stationed at the seventieth latitude for the protection of the *Tirpitz*, had been phoned in in the morning from Oslo. Marching papers would be made out immediately and sent by special courier to Stavanger within two days. The day of my departure was set for the fourteenth.

But he and Schmidt had to add something. This was actually my third transfer coming from Oslo headquarters. The other two times they had sent someone else instead, of which I did not have the slightest idea, but they were told that I had to be sent this time.

My replacement at the casino was a Berliner who was also expected to arrive from Oslo in two days. I should wait for the man's arrival and try to do my best to acquaint him with the duties, procedures, and responsibilities of a chief steward.

I had been looking forward to spending some more time at the casino, especially now that I had just returned from my third furlough and drew almost double my normal pay. Maybe I had been too lucky too often, and now it was my turn to get the shorter end of the stick.

When I told Erich Eye the news, he made a face which appeared in front of my eyes for some time to come. To make me feel better, I suppose, he suggested that this could be the lesser of two evils. "The lesser evil?" I said excitedly. "What the heck are you twiddling about?"

"Let me explain," he replied. "While you were at home last month, General Hueblein, der *Soldatenklau* (the soldier scrounger) swept through Norway. Sixty-six thousand men have received their transfers and will not be replaced as occupiers here. He cashed in on personnel from all branches of the armed forces. The fittest from the navy have been withdrawn for retraining as marines to serve with other infantry men at the front and to partially replace those killed in battle. Let's face it, we who are still here are the lucky ones."

I could not argue with that. As much as I disliked the idea of moving to the North Pole, it probably was better than being shot to pieces at the front. I had better keep my mouth shut! But I surely did not look forward to that transfer.

My replacement arrived from Oslo on Wednesday, the twelfth. That gave me only one day to orientate the man. That, however, was no problem. He was an old fox and had more experience than I had. With typical Berliner aplomb, he personified confidence, the type of person who nowadays calls every challenge a piece of cake. He seemed to be a very pleasant and likable chap, and I was glad they had appointed somebody who knew the ropes. Nothing is worse than to have the blind leading the blind.

On my last day of service, I was summoned to the salon for a good-bye handshake. Most of the officers were assembled to wish me a good journey and, of course, the traditional *Hals und Beinbruch* ("break a leg," although in German it means "break your neck and a leg," not so nice in comparison to the English version).

Inspector Pohlmann had a present for me, a pair of insulated, felt-covered *Knobelbecher* (German military slang for boots), usually not distributed to non-officers. I was elated. But there was more. Captain Baer and Lieutenant Commander Schmidt had a personal message from Commandant Mayer-Pantin, urging me to let them know how I would like it at the fourth battery, good or bad. Baer said, "If things get too tough up there, we will try to get you back."

I knew these men well. They were no hypocrites! Their suggestion to report my findings engraved itself in my mind.

In the late afternoon I went to the base by bus and said good-bye to my comrades. I also received three extra pairs of woolen long johns and a second thick scarf. All those transferred to the Arctic were entitled to these special additions. During the two years and four months of my commission in Stavanger, I had spent most of the time at the officers casino. Nevertheless, the guys at the base were sincerely sorry to see me leave. I felt that.

Pretending to be quite unconcerned about the whole thing, which I was not, I told the chaps that this was only going to be a short stint, and that I would be back in no time, just to cover up my apprehension. But who was I really kidding?

When I left on the fifteenth, the weather became balmy, almost like spring. Eighteen degrees Celsius (sixty-six Fahrenheit) at that time in Scandinavia is pretty good. "A good thing they did not send me off at the beginning or in the middle of winter," I thought, putting on my cap of positive thinking. I had heard that those living around that seventy-degree parallel had to put up with over seven months of winter and darkness, while enjoying only four months of cold spring. There was no fall and no summer.

I boarded the same train I had used exactly six weeks ago when beginning my trip home. The route was the same as before. But this time, occupied with my thoughts about the future, or rather lack of it, I did some brooding and did not pay the usual attention to the beautiful countryside. There were several comrades in the railway car I had selected, all of them destined to spend what likely would be their last annual furlough at home. But I kept to myself, as I did not feel like talking. As far as I could make out, I was the sole victim aboard to be transferred to the end of the world. That was going to change. By the time we arrived in Oslo, we had several dozens aboard with the same destination, who had been assembled from different naval bases. Not to be the only sucker made me feel a bit better already, but enthusiasm would be an exaggeration.

Once in Oslo, we were pooled with yet another number of men who had arrived before us from coastal antiaircraft units in the counties of Ostfold, Vestfold, and those situated within the Oslofjord coastline southeast and southwest of Oslo itself.

I would have loved to pay a visit to Marlene, my friend at the "house of pleasure." At least I would have loved to find out whether she was still there since my first visit in June 1943. But this time, there was no time off. A special transport train would be assembled and set in early the next morning.

The train left on the sixteenth as scheduled. We had 360 navy men aboard. The immediate goal was the city of Trondheim. When looking at the map, you can see Trondheim located at what would be considered the dividing line between the southern and the northern part of the country. Horizontally, the earth's mass is narrowest at that point. While it is about 450 kilometers wide in the center of the southern part, it is only forty kilometers wide between Verdalsora–seventy kilometers northeast of Trondheim–and the community of Vera, eastward near the Swedish border.

The train journey led through the scenic highlands of the Norwegian interior country. Soon we had passed through the county of Akershus, entering the southern tip of Lake Mjosa, the longest lake of its kind. It stretches from the small community of Minnesund in a northerly direction via the city of Gjovik to beautiful Lillehammer, at the northern end of the lake, a distance of about 105 kilometers. We had another 350 kilometers ahead of us before we would reach Trondheim.

Lillehammer is as beautiful as it had been described to me by a girl whose acquaintance I made when she had visited us at the casino some time ago. The train would stop here for fifteen minutes to take on water. When opening the window wider, I noticed that temperatures had dropped at least ten degrees Celsius. That was not so unusual. Inland temperatures of any land mass are always more extreme than those close by the sea, and Lillehammer is rather removed from the west coast. The warming affect of the Gulf Stream, which influences so much central European and also southern Scandinavian theaters, does not reach that far inside these countries.

We had hardly left Lillehammer when the train started to puff-puff heavily. We were climbing the mountain range of Gudbransdalen. The number of tiny communities we passed seemed to be thriving as winter resorts. Left and right of us were skiers appearing and disappearing, trying to outdo our speed.

There were no scheduled stops before Trondheim. But at Otta, the train stopped in the middle of nowhere. We started to wonder what happened and craned our necks out the window and asked loudly, without addressing anybody in particular, "What is going on? Did something happen?"

Eventually, the message was passed from car to car: The conductor of the train and his pal had decided to have a nice cup of coffee and a sandwich at a booth that catered to skiers passing by. Our travel leader got awfully upset about it, but that did not help. These easygoing Norwegians could not be rocked. Even when they were confronted about the delay, they quietly finished their late breakfast, then reboarded the train as if nothing had happened.

Talk about old world charm. Most of us did not mind that holdup at all, since we were less than eager to reach our destination in the first place. Outside, the temperature reading from an oversized thermometer board showed six degrees below Celsius. The mountain range had made another substantial difference.

When we arrived at the town of Dombas, having left a couple of kilometers behind us, another railway track led off to the right which we took. Since we left Akershus County, we had traveled constantly in a northwesterly direction. A continuation of the rail line would have brought us to Andalsnes. The new track led straight north to Trondheim. It was 1530 hours when we arrived there. Temperatures had dropped to twelve degrees below Celsius.

Ten trucks were waiting to rush us through the snow-covered streets to the corner of Sondregate and Dronningensgate, where our reception camp was located. It was the major base for all naval personnel traveling in northerly or easterly directions. It bustled with activity, more than ever, since all human replacements due to the attack on the *Tirpitz* had to be processed over and above the ordinary troop movements of enlisted men who would go on or return from furlough. The latter included some mountain climbers, who were on special assignment on behalf of counterintelligence. Their task was to smoke out Norwegians who observed our navigational movements and signaled results from high in the mountains to the British. The operation was done in unison with trawlers and fishermen's boats. That was all we knew at the time. What we did not know then was that these activities were not limited to these sources alone.

We were assigned living quarters, then had to line up for orientation. Because of the additional work load processing, the base commandant asked for volunteers to assist. His own manpower capacity had not increased and things had to be kept moving in military fashion, so to say.

A number of groups, including the one with which I came, were waiting to be shipped farther north. We were told that there was a bad clog-up of troop movements around Bodö, Narvik and Tromsö. Icebergs and ice floats were slowing navigation to a snake's pace and at times prevented any movement of boats and ships. It would take several days to unsnarl the knot. That was all right with me. I was in no hurry to freeze myself to death. Procrastination was not my style, and it certainly did not prevent things from happening as they were planned. But any delay was welcome in this case. Besides, I was sure that what lay ahead was not a pleasant future.

That was well substantiated when I talked to some men for the first time who had spent one year or longer within the Arctic Circle. They all seemed to have that faraway look gleaming in their eyes. Or was I mistaken?

On the second day we received holdover pay for three days. Together with my double pay I had received at the casino since November, I found myself with some money saved for the first time since I wore the uniform. During the last furlough I spent very little, as there was simply nothing to buy in Germany without ration cards.

Since I was sitting on my butt the greatest part of the day assisting with pencil work, I made sure I would retain my fitness by taking daily walks within four kilometers around the base, mostly in the evening after dinner. The four-men pass rule was still in force. For security reasons, it had been introduced a few months before. But that was no problem. I always found another three chaps who would be just as anxious as I was to walk and get fresh air in their lungs.

One evening, just as we had turned from Dronnigensgate into Nordregate, a beautiful sound of choir voices came our way. The nearest church was situated at the southern end of Nordregate, but the sound came from the opposite direction. We soon reached a courtyard and a building recessed from the sidewalk that looked like a school.

We went around one side, following the sound, and finally stopped in front of two double windows. The window transoms were partially open, allowing the sound to swell out. The windows were clear of ice. We clearly could see a mixed choir, obviously rehearsing since the song was frequently interrupted by a conductor. I counted twenty-two members, eleven men and eleven women. They all seemed to be in their thirties and forties. They maintained great harmony. One could hear they were not rehearsing for the first time.

One of my comrades had moved to the next window which overlooked the second part of the large room. "Look here," he said. "They even have a full-fledged orchestra lined up."

The choir had stopped. In a few seconds, both the orchestra and the choir joined in a medley of Irving Berlin tunes, *Let's Face The Music And Dance*, *It's A Lovely Day Today*, and *There's No Business Like Show Business*. How much I wished I could be part of it! Besides my love for nature, music was my life, and still is. The four of us would have loved to peep and listen longer, but is was getting too cold to hang around.

It was Wednesday, 19 April, when we finally could resume our trip. We had about a thousand kilometers ahead of us before we would arrive at our destination.

An Arduous Trek

We were sent by rail with the immediate destination of Bodö, the end of the rail line to the North. Narvik mines produced a tremendous amount of iron ore. But only a fraction of it was transported at the time down south along the Norwegian coast. It was more efficient and cheaper to send it by rail eastward and then southward through Sweden. The distance to the border from Narvik is only thirty kilometers, only a stone's throw. That custom, to the best of my knowledge, has been maintained to this day.

The trip along Trondheimsfjorden and then through the county of Nord-Tröndelag, passing along the dividing *Namdalen* led into the county of Nordland. The last leg of the stretch led around the northern coast of Skjerstadfjorden right into Bodö, where we arrived at nightfall. It was not bad timing, considering that snow-removing locomotives had to be called to our assistance twice, freeing the rails from snow and icy lumps.

We had to march about twenty-five minutes from the railway station to our overnight quarters. The mercury now showed nearly twenty degrees below Celsius, a sign of things to come.

I remember well that when we woke up the following morning, we had the dubious pleasure of looking at a landscape that can be described, at best, as desolate and solitary as can be. "My God," one man said, "I wouldn't want to be buried here!"

"That is only the beginning," another man commented. "The farther we come north, the worse it gets."

"From here," we were told, "you will be shipped by boat north off the Lofoten Islands to Harstad and Tromsö. That might take a while, as numerous ice floats have to be avoided." We were also given the good news that from here on in, the Tommies were very active with aircraft surveillance. Only two days ago, a troop transporter from Tromsö sailing south had been attacked by the RAF off Vesteralen Bank near Harstad and sank. Most of them had been on route home for their furlough.

We boarded around noon. The ship was equipped for about three hundred, but a lot of returnees to Harstad, Tromsö, and vicinity had to be taken on. I quickly dropped off my gear on the lower deck and rushed back to the upper deck. I did not want to miss the departure. As I leaned over the railing of the bow, I saw a ship tied up at the pier about two hundred feet ahead. The name *Altmark* was clearly readable. Asking a bootsmann close by, he explained that the former tanker had been used first as a supply ship for the battleship *Admiral Graf Spee*. At the beginning of the war it had been put to use as troop transporter, but since 1942 it served as a floating jail for British POWs.

Toward the end of the war, I met two former crew members of the *Altmark*, who indicated that crew members were often exchanged in order to avoid too much chumminess taking place between the two nationals.

My own guess is that confined space brings this about, coupled with the fact that, after all, the Anglo-Saxons and the Germans are carved from the same wood; therefore, they have a common bond. The only thing that divides them is the language, and that gap is closing fast.

When casting off, we had eight hundred plus men aboard. I thought right away about the situation described to me before I was drafted into the navy. When we had unloaded our gear it was obvious that we were packed like sardines in a can. All of us on the lower deck had to squeeze together right on the planks: up–down; up–down; nose–feet, nose–feet.

We had sailed about eighty nautical miles in a northwesterly direction toward the Lofoten Islands when the air attack alarm went off. We had been instructed that if there was an alarm, of which they had quite a few off Bordø and around Lofoten, only the ship's crew would be allowed to be on deck, taking their fighting positions. All others had to remain below deck, no matter what. My idea of surviving an air attack was, of course, to be on deck. I had heard too often that the engine crew, who had to stay below, were the first ones to drown. But an order is an order.

All I remember is that during the twenty-five minutes of alarm stage one, we felt like chickens squeezed into a coop that is much too small. If it was any consolation, my comrades were just as scared as I was, which was plain by their facial expressions and conversations.

After the clear signal, the voice of the second in command came over the intercom, advising we had to change course. Most of the waterways northwest of the Lofoten Islands were solidly frozen. Icebreakers had to be employed first.

So we steamed in a north-northeasterly direction through Vestifjorden, then entered Ofotfjorden and tied up at Narvik.

The remaining two hundred kilometers we could only manage piece by piece. It took three full days to reach Tromsö, only a hundred and fifty kilometers north of Narvik. We were accompanied by icebreakers, in whose paths we had to follow. Time and again, floating ice passed by us, occupied by polar bears. Most of us had never seen polar bears, so we looked at them with curiosity. Sometimes, though, I had to laugh. It seemed the bears were just as curious about us as we were about them. They seemed to wonder what we were up to, rather than the other way around! Further south, we had seen numerous whales, but not up here at the sixty-eighth parallel.

Before disembarking at Tromsö, we were warned not to touch any of the ship's railings or the plank ropes without gloves. The temperature had sunk to thirty degrees below zero Celsius! One chap, however, while disembarking, held himself at the fallreep rope with his bare hands. He screamed murder and when removing his hand looked at a bloody palm. The outer skin had come off! I could not help thinking about my burned hand during the

Terboven meeting. It had looked just about the same as the hand of this sailor. Extreme heat and cold seem to have the same affect.

Two things stayed fresh in my mind about Tromsö. Besides it being an island, some of the buildings looked as if they had been built on top of each other. At least that is the way it looked at the time. The city is also connected by bridge with the island of Kvaloya, with a majestic background of mountains that are fifty-five hundred feet high. It was a marvelous sight.

Two hundred seventy-two men were left, destined for Kafjord. One hundred thirty-nine crew members who lost their lives had to be replaced, seventeen to replace the men killed who were artillerists of the Naval Antiaircraft Division 710, and another forty-eight men to beef up the fourth battery, which usually took the brunt of air attacks. The remaining sixty-eight men were needed to make up for those who had been severely wounded out of the two hundred and ninety-plus. Their fitness classification had been downgraded to noncombat duties.

Two patrol boats had been removed from formal combat service, stripped of armor, weaponry and everything else not absolutely necessary. They were then converted into makeshift troop transporters. We were divided and had to board the two boats.

I did not like at all what I saw. These boats really had been stripped to the bone, with standing room only. There were no cabins; not even enough space to rest under deck.

Since the journey was expected to last only about five hours to Kafjord, it could be uncomfortable but a reasonable sacrifice under wartime military circumstances. But that was not all. Somebody evidently had no regard for human life, in this case, our lives. There was not one life craft or lifeboat aboard, nor were there any life belts! Nobody dared to ask any questions, though. It was small consolation that if something bad happened, the transport leader likely would drown with the rest of us.

We did not get too far, which was probably good. Sailing through Grotsundet north-northeast of Tromsö was easy. But, as soon as we entered Ullsfjorden to get out to sea and to get around Lyngstuva, the northern tip of Lyngen island, fast-moving pack ice floated in our direction. It came from the island of Arnoy, situated in front of the fjord's mouth in the north.

The oncoming rush of ice floats told us we would not even be able to come close to the mouth of Ullsfjorden, and it was too late to ask for the assistance of icebreakers. The onslaught of ice floats came totally unexpected. The military meteorological watch commander got clobbered later for that lack of information.

Both boats reversed course to a southerly direction. It would not lead us anywhere out of the fjord, but rather farther inward. Reaching our destination by sea had to be abandoned. Instead, we had to accomplish that by land.

As the saying goes, it never rains without pouring. We had just about backed up twelve nautical miles when the boat I was on ran into shore ice close to the town of Svensby. The bow of the former PT boat had engraved itself with a loud grating sound. We were stuck! The boat commander did not dare order the engines to take on reverse speed, for fear that the boat had sustained sufficient damage to sink if removed from the pincer.

SOS signals were given by both boats and immediately answered by military naval units in the area. The Tromsö area commandant advised us to abandon ship, and try to reach the nearby community of Svensby by foot. Never had I seen a disembarkation that fast! We almost fell over our own legs, which is not so unusual when trying to keep balance on ice. Now I knew how it felt to be shipwrecked. I did not have to read books about that anymore.

We had lined up for a head count in fairly respectable distance from the abandoned boat, but I was sure we were not yet on solid land. Including the ship's crew, we had 138 men.

Svensby was only five kilometers south of our position. That was easy to reach on foot. But food and other provisions had to be left behind; there was no means of transportation.

When we arrived in Svensby, two surprises awaited us. The area commandant had arranged for transportation to the eastern side of the island of Lyngen: twelve Russian-type sleighs. Horses and huskies would arrive later. The second pleasant surprise was the efforts made by the population of Svensby. Not only did they provide us with food and shelter, better than could be expected, they also had sent a messenger to Lyngseidet, nine kilometers away at the northeastern coast, to round up more sleighs and polar dogs.

There was actually a third surprise. We had been shipwrecked ridiculously close to our destination. Birtavarre, the small community at the inner end of Kafjord, was barely twenty-five kilometers away! The trick was, of course, to get across the island to the east, then cross Lyngen Fjord to enter Kafjord. A decision had to be made whether the risk to travel across Lyngen ice would not endanger our lives again, since the ice sheet was not equally thick in all places.

Our transport leader, who had learned a lesson in the meantime, talked with the village leader (Svensby was a community of about fifteen hundred inhabitants at the time), who advised not to take that risk. Rather, he suggested, we should trek by sleigh to Lyngseidet, then south to the end of Lyngenfjord around Oteren, then turn north like a sharp V along the eastern side of Lyngen, crossing Skibottsdalen, Manndalen, and finally Kafjorddalen to Birtavarre. However, the twenty-five-kilometer distance by air would quadruple with that route.

Many of us had found refuge in a school building. We kept several stoves going overnight while sleeping on the wooden floors. At around 0300 hours we were awakened by what I first thought were howling wolves, but it turned out to be the arrival of the additional huskies from Lyngseidet. We stopped complaining.

At 0500 hours the next morning we were thrown out. The decision had been made to go by land, which would take an estimated eleven hours. Though provisions were confined to a minimum, one could not expect the huskies to go faster than nine kilometers per hour without replacement dogs.

Before leaving, I had checked with an outside thermometer. The mercury had dipped to forty-eight degrees below Celsius (minus 54.6 Fahrenheit). Luckily, there was no wind, which would have made matters worse. In spite of the bitter cold, I was kind of looking forward to this adventurous trip, thinking about a book I had read in which the author, Jack London, had described his experience in the Arctic. Besides, this was not an ordinary way of transporting soldiers. As I said before, anything that varies from routine is always welcome by men in uniform.

Long before we reached the halfway point, the village of Oteren, I felt like I had frozen icicles along my body. I was not the only one. I heard some of my comrades cursing and swearing about "the blasted cold." When I looked at the horses and huskies, however, I felt more sorry for them. They seemed to be steaming out of all body openings.

We arrived at Oteren at noon, where the beasts and the humans were fed. Again, I was pleased with the arrangements made by these local people: Two large camps had been prepared, where we all could gather and rest for a while.

When we left around 1330 hours, another rest period was already announced to take place at Skibotn, twenty-two kilometers away. One chap had to be left there. He had rather suddenly developed high fever. One of the three amphibian planes from Kafjord which were attached to the *Tirpitz* was sent the same day to bring the sick man to the only naval hospital near Birtavarre. He suffered from diarrhea, exposed himself in the underbrush, and developed an inflammation. The naval physicians had a hard time diagnosing the problem.

In Skibotn, a couple of new husky teams and a number of fresh horses were awaiting us to replace the older mares. One hour of rest and we were on our way to conquer the remainder of the journey. When we crossed Manndalen (Mann Valley) two packs of wolves kept an eye on us. One ran parallel with us, while the other pack followed us like the Old West American Indians following a wagon train. They kept a respectable distance and would only come closer when darkness set in, but at that time of the year, the Arctic sun dips only slightly below the horizon.

It was 1945 hours when we finally arrived at Birtevarra. The forty-eight of us collected our gear and walked the three kilometers or so to the plateau overlooking Kafjord inlet, where the fourth battery of the Marine-Flak-Abteilung 710 with its fortification had been erected. It was Tuesday, 25 April 1944. The others were to be picked up the next day and sent to their new posts.

The Fourth Battery

The first shock hitting us upon our arrival was that our accommodations consisted of wooden Fin tents interspersed between antiaircraft guns. Each tent looked like an American-Indian teepee, with sufficient space in the upper center of the cone to allow a cannon oven pipe to stick out. We had been appointed to fortify the strength of the fourth battery. Underground facilities for artillery personnel were exhausted. Prefabricated barracks had been ordered from Sweden. In the meantime, Fin tents had to do.

Each tent had four double cots placed along the interior walls. The cannon stove in the center had to be kept going day and night, no wonder with that extreme cold, fifty degrees below Celsius or colder at night, while during the day it would warm up to about forty below Celsius.

We left our main gear at a supply barrack, had dinner at the battery mess hall, and then lined up for inspection by the battery commander, a lieutenant, whose name I wiped off my memory. He was a typical *Kommiskop* (military bloke), determined to make life tough for others. The dislike was mutual. I had absolutely no use for him, and he hated my guts because I did not fit in with his picture of what militarism and militaristic behavior should be. Needless to say, of course, he had the upper hand.

Instead of welcoming us, he immediately tore into a cynical outburst of what we could expect under his command. Anyone not following orders to the letter had better be prepared for harsh treatment. "You may have had a picnic where you came from," he declared, "but not here. Whoever does not comply gets his arse ripped open to his stand-up collar. Make a note of it!" That even beat some of the threats we had heard in boot camp on Haon. I knew we were in for something!

It took me several days to find sleep in those tents. We rotated duty to keep the oven going full-blast in order not to freeze to death. When I turned my face against the wall, I could feel a bit of warmth on my back, while my chest hair was covered with icicles. Turning around, the icicles would defrost, but my spine would feel like a big iron stick. Besides, on the average, two out of three nights the alarm sirens would throw us out. The Tommies loved to visit us.

Our artillery training began on the second day. Most of us newcomers had never received any training in handling four-by-four centimeter and 8.8-centimeter big guns. That in itself (though it was not any personal fault of ours) disgusted the commander without end. "How can they (referring to Oslo headquarters) send me human scrap like you to defend the *Tirpitz*," he fumed.

Two more 8.8 guns had been added since the attack on the *Tirpitz*. Also four more four-by-four centimeter guns. Each big gun needed ten men to handle it. Seven were needed at each four-by-four centimeter. We all learned fast how to operate these weapons. We had to, or else!

Overlooking the terrain from the plateau showed how well the *Tirpitz* was naturally shielded. From both sides of the Kafjord harbor and fjord inlet, mountains enhanced the territory, stretching back left and right of the fourth battery and leveling off several kilometers behind us, exposing Kafjorddalen (Kafjord Valley).

On the eastern side of our plateau, a permanently-frozen waterfall streaked down to a pond, our only water supply. Every morning a detail of twelve men were sent down the slope of the plateau to provide us with water for daily cooking and sanitary requirements. Steps had been carefully carved in the side of the plateau, which the men used to reach the pond. Ten men carried two pails each. The timing was of great importance. Each man had to follow his predecessor within four minutes; otherwise, the two-meter-thick sheet of ice on the pond would refreeze. Two men were stationed on the pond to maintain open ice. Whenever one of the carriers got out of tune, the ice had to be reopened.

Kafjord is about the narrowest fjord I ever saw in Norway. I understood why Von der Knesebrecht had selected the area as refuge for the *Tirpitz* and how he managed to equip the fjord inlet with the intricate underwater chain net system. He very likely could not have found a more secure hiding place. For the British to attack the monster battleship successfully in this position was only possible for reasons described.

On the third day after our arrival, Friday, the twenty-eighth, I was told in no uncertain terms to have my disgustingly long hair cut. I had frequented a Norwegian barber in Stavanger for years, who gave me what was called a short facon cut, which left some hair over the ears and on the upper neck.

I went to the battery barber and told him to go easy. He did, but that was not good enough for the commander. Under threat of getting stockade for two days, I had to have a second cut. What a catastrophe! Looking in the mirror, a head like a plucked chicken stared back at me; a real caricature of myself.

The whole situation was definitely not my cup of tea. I did not want to press the panic button at this early stage, but I knew sooner or later I would have to sit down and write to Stavanger, as had been suggested. I finally did on Tuesday, 9 May. Although I avoided whining, I told my former superiors the overall situation without holding anything back. I bluntly stressed the unfair treatment by the commander, which was of course not limited to me, and asked for a transfer.

As soon as the company mailman confirmed my letter having been sent without screening, which was frequently done in the military, I felt relaxed and took the approach of marking time.

Besides the daily training and defense exercises, we had to stand on guard each night, two at a time. The scheduling was done by the master sergeant, who was one of a few in the outfit to whom one could talk. He was reasonable and fair. He even arranged to have people who were somewhat compatible share guard duty.

That was not quite easy. I found out soon that, for no apparent reasons, some hated each other's guts. At times fights would break out without provocation. Some of these poor guys had not been on furlough for an entire year or longer. They hated to look at the same faces day after day and they developed the counterpart of a tropical frenzy, an Arctic one! I had heard about the existence of it, but did not believe it until I became a witness.

I shared my guard duty most of the time with Ernestus Tossati, a former Jesuit monk. He was of Italian extraction, but had been born in Austria. As a representative of the Society of Jesus, he saw it as his duty to defy Nazism. He had been arrested three times for inflammatory statements made against the state and in 1941 was encouraged to join the German armed forces as a chaplain. He politely declined. "I regret this now, Siegfried," he told me one night when we made our rounds through the compound. "Now I have to wear this uniform against my will anyway, and cannot even be of service to God."

I found him to be one of the noblest men I ever met, the epitome of goodness. We became good friends and when on guard duty spent most of the time crying on each other's shoulder. But, deep in my heart, I was convinced he suffered more from his fate than I did.

In that year, the days of the three ice saints fell on 13, 14, and 15 May. According to Nordic tradition and belief, these three days break the winter spell. They personified the last hurrah of winter against the approaching summer. For the last time, the mercury dropped to forty-six degrees below Celsius during the day (fifty-one below Fahrenheit). Ernestus and I had to stand watch all three nights, when the temperatures dropped to fifty-six below Celsius, or sixty-nine degrees below Fahrenheit.

There was no way to stand still more than a minute or so. The clear and crisp cold air even temporarily cleared up my chronic sinus congestion. Indeed, it was so bitter cold that when spitting out, the spittle would hit the ground in a frozen state! Unbelievable, but true. To make matters worse, whenever we were off watch, the sirens would go off, chasing us out to man battle stations. There was no thinking about sleep.

Eventually, on the eighteenth, the prefabricated pieces and building parts for erecting barracks arrived from Sweden. Brother, did we ever dig in to get the two double-barracks built! The whole job, accommodating eighty-some people, took less than two days to complete. We had no regrets vacating the Fin tents.

During the fourth week in May, I was called to see the sergeant major. I reported to the orderly room and was told to take a hot seat. After a few minutes, the sergeant came out of his office and ushered me in. I started to wonder what was up. He offered me a chair and came right to the point. "I have read your file, of course," he began, "and convinced the commander that we can make better use of your skills." My file was in front of him. "It says here that you have some administrative experience; that you are reliable, flexible and quite a marksman." He took a breath.

"You will be removed from the 8.8-centimeter gun and placed at the *Leitstand*, the positioning and guidance equipment that measures height and speed of enemy aircraft. As you know, based on these estimates, all 8.8-centimeter guns zero in on approaching targets. Maybe with your help, we can shoot down a few Tommies. You will have a permanent leading position on the equipment. Let's find out whether you can transfer your target practice shooting skills from handguns and rifles to cannons.

"Also," he continued, "I need assistance with paperwork here. Your daytime duty at the *Leitstand* will be about two hours, disregarding alarms of course. The rest of the time you will work here under my supervision." He smiled. "I know you will like this much better than the rough military life outside." (Darn right, I thought.)

Target practice turned out to be very satisfactory, even for the commander. It also took me only a couple of days to adjust to the pencil work requirements at the administrative office. I had never seen any personnel files before. Now I had free access to them, even mine. What I was most curious about was why this battery had such low-caliber-type corporals, all muscle and small brains. We had twelve, but only two of them seemed to be able to talk sensibly. The others were cursing and swearing at the men all day long. By their behavior, they added to the daily frustration of these artillerists. No wonder almost everyone hated everyone else to the point where they wanted to smash in each others faces like hitting fire alarm boxes!

With exception of the two I mentioned, the assessment in the files of the other noncoms reflected a mirror of their manners–hard-nosed, low intelligence level, loyal to the cause, totally obedient, carries out orders without asking questions, no scruples in pushing underlings to the limit. There were a few other traits listed, more or less undesirable as far as I was concerned. None of these descriptions surprised me in the least. But it was an almost opposite type of person to whom I was used to in Stavanger. Company Commander Schmidt had surrounded himself with real leaders, rather than with pushers, who also showed some human compassion. There was a substantial difference here!

Obviously, unit commanders were given some choice as to what type of person they would like to see in command. When I came to the bottom of an attached guide file, it dawned on me that I was looking at what we call in industry a job specification, a guide which suggested the type of person to look for in filling the slot. This was interesting reading. Under characteristics it quoted absolute loyalty, toughness, strong disciplinarian, continually expects more of others, good indoctrinator, and autocratic. It said nothing about leadership ability. What really blew my mind was the underlined statements. "Needs only near average intelligence to fulfill the requirements of his tasks." Unbelievable! It certainly highlighted this commander's mentality, if anything.

There were the usual regulations and criteria such as minimum and maximum height, previous preparatory training for advancement to corporal, and a few other statements bearing little importance to the mandate of that rank. All this was dated and signed by the battery commander and countersigned by the regional commandant. "Aha, they have found each other," went through my mind.

The first week in June changed two things. For the first time in the year we had a heat wave; the temperature went to twenty degrees below Celsius. A week before it still was around thirty-five to forty below, and for three days in a row, it dropped to sixty-eight below Celsius, in conjunction with a vicious windchill factor which, mostly throughout the year is low in the Arctic. The sun did not completely set anymore. It just hovered around the horizon, a fact I had not believed in the past. We all carry some ignorance around. It was true, one could read a newspaper at midnight!

For some of my pals this caused a problem. They could not find any sleep during the night, until we covered the barrack windows with blankets.

On Saturday afternoon and Sunday, 3 and 4 June, I was off duty. Since the cold had finally snapped, I decided to leave the battery grounds for the first time since my arrival. Generally, there was nowhere to go in the first place, but now I wanted to find out whether there was a suitable terrain in the vicinity where I could continue my pistol shooting target practice. In wise foresight, I had acquired quite a few extra rounds of 7.65 millimeter bullets from Hans Steiner in Stavanger.

Meet The Natives

I had left the grounds going in a southerly direction, where the mountain sloped gradually. There were some pine and spruce trees with plenty of underbrush. Soon I came to a circular opening. One tree was lying on the ground, appearing to have been chopped down by lightening not too long ago. It still looked alive.

One of the two battery cooks had supplied me with a bunch of empty vegetable cans, which I unpacked and lined up on the fallen tree. I practiced for about twenty minutes, but I could not shoot for longer than three minutes at a time without putting on my gloves again. I soon found out that shooting with a glove on is quite something else.

When returning the next day, I was equipped with an old glove. I had cut off the top of the glove where my index finger went through. That worked much better. Yet, after one round or so, I had to warm up my trigger finger by putting the exposed part into my mouth for about half a minute. I had to chuckle when I thought about having to do this when in real danger.

The third time I went out, I instinctively felt that I was being watched. Turning around a couple of times, however, I could not see anybody. After the second round of target shooting, I knew there was somebody watching me. I could feel eyes on my neck when I moved forward to rearrange the targets.

Having done so and returning to my shooting stand, I saw four Eskimos appearing from the bushy section behind the opening, watching me curiously. "Now what?" I thought. Their pose was not threatening, but to be on the safe side, I swiftly put my Walthers pistol in my holster underneath my jacket. Then I lifted my left arm, palm outward, hoping this gesture would indicate intended peacefulness. If it worked with American Indians, as I had read in translated Buffalo Bill stories, why not try it with these northern inhabitants?

To my relief, the one who seemed to be the eldest of the four (he looked like ninety) responded with the same gesture. Then he motioned to follow him and his companions. I joined the party, trying hard to appear unconcerned. I noticed one of the men was wearing something in a pelt over his shoulder, but I could not make out what it was.

Walking through the snow with them put me at a disadvantage. I had trouble keeping up with them in my military boots, even though I was wearing the felted pair from Inspector Pohlmann. These men wore large net snowshoes, with which one can walk much faster, as I later experienced.

We walked diagonally with and west of where my battery was located. After about twenty minutes, we arrived at what evidently was a settlement. There were several igloos. About fifteen Eskimos gathered around an open fire. A big pot on a fixture hung above the fire. One woman had just thrown something into the steaming pot and stirred with a large wooden stick close to the size of a paddle.

The eldest motioned to me to sit down near the fire, then put one hand on my shoulder, pressing gently. He quickly went into one of the igloos and returned with two other men, one of whom looked even older than the one I thought was the eldest. The three of them sat beside me, but the two newcomers sat only after they had greeted me in the same fashion as I had used at the shooting stand. My feeling was that they had not met anybody yet in German uniform, as they continued sizing up my clothes. There was no way to start a conversation. I tried German, English and Norwegian; no dice.

Ten minutes went by. In the meantime, a number of other Eskimos came out of their igloos and joined us by forming a large circle around the open fire. I counted now twenty-four altogether. Some women carried their babies with them in large colorful slings above their hips.

As if on command, three men got up and approached the big steaming kettle. Two had several large-sized wooden cups on wooden trays. Upon closer inspection, I saw the cups depicted beautiful carvings, showing the Arctic sun and landscapes of the North. The third man took the cups off the trays, one by one, and filled them with the steaming brew from the kettle. The mugs were passed around.

At first glance, the liquid resembled coffee. It was not as dark as a strong cup of coffee, but thicker and looked somewhat slimy. The smell, though, was just plain awful! I thought of the possible consequences if I refused to drink the stuff. After all, I could not risk insulting these people by rebuking their hospitality. So, as the men around me lifted their mugs to drink, I did the same. While frantically holding my breath, I took a couple of gulps. As soon as the liquid hit my stomach, I felt the impact. I was cold through and through, but this stuff almost immediately warmed me up.

When I resumed breathing, an overpowering aroma rose from my stomach and went through my nostrils. I was drinking whale liver oil, to which something undefined had been added to make the drink even thicker and heavier.

On my second visit to the camp, this time on my own, one of the men present, who probably did not belong to the same family, explained to me in halting English, that the additive consisted of chicory and a bit of flour. Although the stuff tastes like the pits, it surely coats the stomach walls for hours, beating whiskey any time!

When I talked to my comrades later about my encounter with these people, I was corrected by a chap who knew more about them. He explained that these people were called Lapps or Laplanders. "Eskimos," he said, "are those who live in Greenland, northeastern Siberia, Alaska and Canada." We live and learn.

Whenever possible, I monitored foreign broadcasts to get a balanced picture of war events, first on the island of Haon, then more extensively in Stavanger particularly during my service at the officers casino.

Here at the battery administration office, I had little opportunity because I was seldom alone in the room. But on Monday, 5 June, the day after I met the Lapps the second time, I entered the office about 1145 hours and everyone had already left for the luncheon break.

Switching to BBC long wave, which could be received quite clearly, I heard for the umpteenth time coded words and numbers, sent primarily for the information of secret agents, working underground in countries we had occupied.

There came a long pause. Then the fifth line of words and numbers were given through. Somehow, I had the urge to take a pencil to mark down the message, which was repeated once. It consisted of eleven segments, starting with one two-digit number and followed by ten words. I could not make heads nor tails out of the message, but secured it for safekeeping in one of my Berlitz books.

After the war, when I worked for Captain Cornish from MI-Six in Mandal, I dug up that piece of paper one day when we chatted in his quarters. He explained to me that the message had been coded and sent in reverse, the first segment being the last. It read, "Because of bad weather, Allied invasion postponed until 6 June, A.M."

On that day before noon, we were informed of the Allied invasion of the European mainland with the comment that they would be thrown back like at Dunkirk in 1940. I did not take this seriously. This was not 1940 anymore. Their modus operandi would be quite different now. In any case, any news which would shorten this bloody war was O.K. with me.

The Toothache

During the week, I developed a severe toothache. The previous year in Stavanger I had suffered swollen and bleeding gums from the initial stages of scurvy. Dr. Schoenfelder, our naval dentist, had to cut open part of my upper gums and work at some roots that had been affected by the disease. He explained that this can easily happen because of lack of vitamin C.

In any case, my toothache appeared in the same area. Now what? Who in this forsaken territory, would look after our teeth? I became worried. When I reported my pain to the sergeant major, he said, "That's no problem. We'll send you to the *Tirpitz*, our regional dental office." At first I thought he was pulling my leg. I had never heard of a ship with her own dental station. He was serious, of course. How silly of me to believe that ten thousand enlisted men would not have any dental care available!

I was given a daytime pass and walked the three kilometers from the fourth battery to Kafjorden Inlet, where the *Tirpitz* was tied up. There was no harbor, per se. With the exception of the *Tirpitz*, all other ships were anchored somewhat away from the pier.

It took me almost an hour to arrive at the inlet. Snow and ice-covered roads made walking difficult. Besides, I simply could not get used to walking in boots, though the pair from Pohlmann was much better than ordinary *Knobelbecher*.

There was a small communication booth at the pier. I presented my ID papers and was told to take a seat in the sizable waiting room. About twenty-some navy men were already waiting. Most of them had the same reason as mine for being there; others waited for passage to the *Admiral Hipper* or one of the escort ships.

From a side room whose door was ajar, I could hear the click-click-click of Morse equipment, sometimes drowned out by the sound of a voice using ordinary telephone wires.

After fifteen minutes, a white-haired master private (a rank not used by the Western Allies) came out of the signal room. He announced a boat was waiting for those destined to board the *Tirpitz*. I joined another twenty-five men and walked down twenty steps that led diagonally to the edge of the pier. We boarded a small motorboat, barely big enough to hold twenty men. This was no problem, I thought, since the *Tirpitz* could not be farther than half a kilometer away.

The boat operator, a petty officer second class explained we would approach the *Tirpitz* from port side, where we had to climb up a fallreep.

It took six minutes to get there. When I dragged myself up the rope ladder, I was not so sure whether I had joined the right branch of service. While I climbed the thirty-seven sprouts the rope ladder swung to and fro. Looking down, I thought for a moment I would get seasick from the height and the swinging until I finally reached the upper deck. I was tempted to ask one of the ship's doctors for pills against seasickness but then discarded the idea.

The nearer I came to the deck while climbing, the louder noises got. Now that I had reached the surface, the noise was unbelievably harsh. It seemed I had entered a town full of people working at a bunch of machines in a huge factory. I had to bend forward to understand the petty officer's instructions, who received us visitors at the railing. I was passed on to five more petty officers, before I eventually reached the between-decks that housed the dental office. This post-to-post guidance was necessary in order not to get lost. Indeed, this monstrous vessel was a small world in itself.

The oversized waiting room could handle at least eighty people. Later on, I counted eighty-eight seats, a good guess. Several doors were identified as treatment rooms, X-ray rooms, and surgery theaters. As I took a seat, one of the latter doors opened. A sailor, accompanied by an orderly, stumbled out as if half-drunk. Evidently, his sedation had not yet worn off. He was holding a thick wad of blood-soaked gauze in front of his mouth, and his face looked cheesy, as if he would faint any second. The orderly led him to a seat not far from mine. I heard him instructing the patient not to leave until further notice. The sight of the blood-soaked wad made me feel sick again.

Right beside me sat a young sailor who had made himself comfortable in his chair. Unconcerned, he read a pocket book. I mused that this was not likely his first visit.

The entrance door had opened and closed several times after I had appeared on the scene, admitting more and more patients. The room was almost filled now. Another orderly appeared. He started at the end of the line near where I sat and asked everybody for an ID. When he came to me, I inquired how long I might have to wait. He put on a quizzical look and asked, "Why? Are you going to a ball?" His voice did not sound angry, though. I decided to return his humor and replied, "Not right now, but I have to leave by Saturday to join a wedding reception." This was Tuesday. He laughed heartily and told me my turn would come within the next hour or so. I was not totally kidding about that wedding. One of my comrades at the battery was scheduled to undergo a *Ferntrauung* (long-distance wedding) on the upcoming Saturday at noon.

The entrance door opened again. A young sailor entered the room, saluted and glanced around. His eyes lit up when he saw the chap sitting beside me reading. He steered in our direction and said quite exuberantly, "My God, Hans, what are you doing here?"

Hans looked up, then jumped up from his chair and pumped the newcomer's arm like weighing a baseball bat in his hand. "Oskar," he replied, "what are you doing on this ship?"

Both sat down. From the ensuing conversation I learned that both were serving on the *Tirpitz*. One already was part of the crew for sixteen months; the other had been attached three and a half months ago. Yet this was the first time they met! Indeed, a world in itself, I thought. If anything, this was proof.

The Long-Distance Wedding

The wedding had been planned far in advance. Anton, the groom, would be formally wed by a naval chaplain at precisely 1200 hours on Saturday, 10 June, his bride's wedding taking place simultaneously in Germany. Congratulatory telegrams would be sent by relatives and friends, and timed to arrive around 1300 hours. The formal wedding reception had to be postponed, of course, until after the war.

One roommate of Anton's had made a round through the battery compound and collected money for the groom for what he called the greatest wedding gift he could think of. He did not elaborate what he had in mind. But we all gave generously, trusting in the collector's good taste.

The magazine and tools barrack was sizable enough to temporarily pile up all items in one spot, which we had done the day before. The resulting free space was to be used for the after wedding celebration, as a substitute for a reception. One room in the administration building had also been stripped naked. It was kind of an *Ad Akta* file room, which was also used for storing paper goods and some excess cutlery for the mess hall. Anton's friend did not divulge for what purpose this room would be used. "It's going to be a great surprise," was all he said.

A special rotating on-off watch plan had been worked out by the sergeant major, allowing all personnel to join the festivities at one point or another. Plenty of whiskey and beer had been lined up for the entire garrison to participate in this marvelous excuse to whoop it up. Because of my background, I was detailed to assist with arranging the celebration room. A couple of chaps were ordered to help run the pub. It was nothing fancy, certainly no mixed drinks or cocktails, but none of us wore tuxedos either!

As we were nearly finished with setting up, one joker commented, "I sure hope we are not doing all this for nothing. It would be nice if we could send a cable to the Tommies asking them to keep us in peace today so that we can consume the stuff rather than seeing it going up in flames."

One of our cooks, who had been trained in pastry making, prepared several fancy tarts and one multi-level, rectangular butter cream nut cake, Anton's favorite. A traditional Anglo-Saxon wedding cake, as we know it in English-speaking countries, is not part of the German tradition.

The chaplain arrived at 1100 hours by an amphibian plane flown by one of our navy pilots. With its ice landing gear, it landed right beside the *Tirpitz*. The chaplain was a jovial-looking man. He gave the impression that he enjoyed bouncing from unit to unit in the northern territorial range to perform these weddings. He was the only one available for that service north of the sixty-eighth parallel and, as he explained later, there were plenty of wedding requests, which kept him busy all right.

The ceremony took place outside between two 8.8-centimeter guns, a constant reminder of where we were. Temperatures were mild now, around twenty degrees below Celsius, but not mild enough to extend the ceremony beyond fifteen minutes. At the end of it, the chaplain unveiled a fancy shawl which he fastened around Anton's neck. Where the end pieces met in front of Anton's chest, right in the center, one could clearly see the German Eagle in black on a white background. Underneath, two hands appeared in reddish flesh colors, which met in a handshake, symbolizing the bond of two people. The colors were appropriately black, white, and red, representing the German flag colors at the time. It looked good on Anton.

We all shook hands with Anton and then retreated to the mess hall for our luncheon. Halfway through the meal, several good luck telegrams were read by the sergeant major, who added his own good wishes.

Those not on watch proceeded to the celebration room. The atmosphere was rather peaceful for a change. Some men even engaged in some joyful conversation, something many had not done for some time.

The other two bartenders and I stayed as sober as possible under the circumstances. "You don't have to abstain," I had told them, "but control your intake." They did.

After a while it dawned on me that I had not seen Anton's best man for some time. He cruised around quite a bit after the wedding ceremony, had left the room a few times, but now seemed to have vanished into thin air. I had the feeling he was brewing up something. His comrades knew him as a practical joker and a man who came up with all kinds of unusual ideas.

We were just about ready to dig into the pastries and cake, when the door opened and Anton's friend marched in with two girls hanging on his arms. With him were a couple of other chaps who carried a gramophone between them. A third man wrestled with a box of records.

"Now we can really start the party," Anton's friend announced. "I would have loved to round up a girl for each of you guys, but these two young chicks have to do."

Since there was not nearly enough room for more than about twenty guys to gather at one time, it was decided to make this a come-and-go affair. This way, each man had a chance to dance with one or the other girl. That went on for the rest of the afternoon. Strangely enough, no fight broke out. By the time we were set to have dinner, the girls were rather pooped but they took that with unusual patience. I did not know the whole story–yet.

After dinner we retreated to the celebration room once more. While I worked at the service bar, I observed a couple of chaps from the kitchen passing our door twice. They were loaded with covered food trays and steered in the direction of the administration building.

Whenever we ran low on beer, one of the bartenders left the room and brought in another case. I had worked out a rotation system by which one case of beer would be placed outside the barrack for about ten minutes then brought back inside for immediate consumption.

It was my turn to fetch a case. When I returned, I saw Anton's friend hovering in one corner of the room with a number of other guys, whispering to each other. Then they nodded their heads in agreements to whatever the issue was. I am not nosy by nature, so I did not ask any questions. If I had to be in on the secret, they would let me know, I figured.

Around 2100 hours most of the guys had begun losing their state of balance. The booze had affected their equilibrium. The girls were visibly relieved, and the groom was stalking around kind of lost and somewhat glassy-eyed. It was time to close the bar. The sergeant major, who was officially responsible for the party, concurred with my request. He rounded up a couple of fellows who were still cruising under their own steam to assist us with dismantling the bar and cleaning up the room.

Unobserved by most of us, Anton's friend had left the room with the two girls. Suddenly he reappeared and came over and asked me to follow him. "I have to show you something," he said simply and started to walk. He led me outside the building and crossed over to the administration building. Once inside, he steered toward the vacated file room. Before opening the door, he said to me, "I want you to see this and tell me if there is anything missing." I was puzzled.

The room was not naked anymore. There was a commode, two double bunks moved together, three comfortable chairs and a table which bore the trays I had seen passing by the other room. The commode was equipped with a variety of liqueurs and Schnapps. Twelve bottles of beer stolen from my pre-cooled supply were resting on the lowest shelf. Matching glasses were present too.

Upon closer inspection, I noticed the trays were nicely laid out and decorated with a variety of open-faced sandwiches, so popular in Germany and Scandinavia. Checkered tablecloths hung from the windows, which gave the room a cozy impression in contrast to the old cold look. To top it all off, Anton's friend had arranged for artificial flowers on the top of the commode, and a centerpiece in the center of the table. He had not missed a thing.

I must have looked perplexed. Before I could open my mouth, he explained, "The two girls will stay here overnight with Anton, who does not know yet but soon will find out. I have paid the girls generously to make sure Anton has a wedding night that is second to none! The three of them will be locked in here until tomorrow night. I know, I know," he added, when he saw me drawing a face expressing disgust. "I am not looking for your approval. I just want to know whether anything is missing."

"There is," I replied. "If they are locked in here that long, you had better provide chamber pots."

"That part is no problem," he asserted. "The noncom on night duty and his successor will check every hour on the hour. He will accompany Anton to the washroom when needed, and make sure he returns. The girls, of course, have no intention of flying the coop and breaching their contract with me." He sounded like a business agent. A contract, he called this. I was surely dealing with a real nut!

The next day at dinner time, Anton was released from prison and brought with a great hello by the conspirators to the mess hall. He hardly stopped smiling for the rest of the evening, a possible indication that he did not resent the trick his friends had pulled on him.

The other guys kept pulling his leg, accusing him of not having been willing to share some of all the fun he had.

"Why should I," he countered. "You paid for my entertainment. It was the greatest wedding present any groom could get. Thank you, boys. The girls really checked me out."

Almost two uneventful weeks went by with the usual alarms but no actual combat, except some of the guys started fighting amongst themselves again.

The Plane

On Friday, 23 June, I had just returned to the administration building to attend to some files when the alarm siren blared. I always had my combat gear ready even in the office, since these alarms were almost routine.

Within three minutes, we were battle-ready. As usual, I adjusted my detection scope to about 650 meters and waited for word from the radar screen operator directly underneath the *Leitstand* (guidance system). Stage two came, then after another minute, stage one. The radar communicator constantly sent situation reports to the battery commander and me, which we received through earphones. A single aircraft had been sighted steering in our direction. The plane's identity was not known. Since we were obviously dealing with one single plane, orders for the fog-in batteries were withheld.

I was instructed to estimate the plane's height and speed as a common procedure, but aim in front of the target for the purpose of giving two warning salvos for identification. In spite of the fact that the naval battery at Lyngstuva at the northern tip of Lyngen Island had already requested identification from the single aircraft without getting a response, we wanted to be on the safe side.

The *Leitstand* sergeant suggested it could be a German plane. The commander doubted that since it certainly would have identified itself earlier. It was probably a British spy plane making a reconnaissance flight over the territory. They were becoming bolder by the week anyway.

They had their field glasses trained in the direction from which the plane was expected to appear. Now it came in sight. I had to lower my scope range to about 230 meters to get the aircraft into focus. Aiming to have two 8.8-centimeter guns send off a salvo about forty to fifty meters ahead of the plane's flight corridor, the commander ordered to fire. No response. A second demand to identify was ignored. Immediately, the order to aim directly on target was given. I made a slight correction. The estimate, which the artillerists received through my throat microphone, must have been on the nose. The aircraft burst aflame into several parts, which one could see filtering down somewhere between the mountains.

Jubilation flared up from all corners of the plateau. "We shot him down; we got him," the men were shouting. The commander came over to me and shook my hand and said, "Excellent aim, Born. You might get the Iron Cross for this."

I felt as if the pit of my stomach was bursting. Never mind that it was an enemy plane. People had lost their lives because of my accuracy! No matter how my future actions would be judged, one thing was for sure, I was not going to aim dead-on anymore, unless we were under direct attack.

The real surprise for all of us came the next day. Kvaloysletta air base north of Tromsö sent out cablegrams to all naval air defense batteries north of the sixty-ninth parallel requesting information regarding one missing aircraft. We had shot down one of our own!

The resulting investigation cleared us, since the pilot and copilot of the aircraft had not identified themselves. (It was never established why not.) We were ordered to begin searching for aircraft parts and human remains in the surrounding mountains without delay.

The regional naval commander had requested assistance in the search from General Eduard Dietl who had his headquarters in Narvik and was German commander of two thousand mountain troops. The request was granted. Two teams would arrive on Sunday.

I was included in our first search team and received a taste of what it means to climb mountains with treacherous crevices and precipitous declivities. Sure, we were equipped with mountain boots, which helped. Each team had one experienced climber as a leader, but that did not decrease my fear of falling into nowhere or getting caught in an avalanche. I guess I had seen too many movies of this kind. Besides, my nerves were not the best anymore. After abstaining for almost two years, I even had begun smoking again.

On the second day of our search we reached a vista. A dozen civilians were busy there moving rocks and underbrush. It looked from where I stood as if they were wearing striped clothes. Two uniformed men stood by, machine pistols poised. That struck me as strange, but I soon found out what they were doing. These workers had been sent from Tromsö to help with the search and were political prisoners supervised by the SS.

In my simple-mindedness, I had started to talk to one of the men, asking if they had found anything so far. He swiftly put his hand against his mouth and muttered, "I am not allowed to speak." At that moment, one of the SS guards rushed over to me, having seen me standing close by the prisoner. He made a threatening gesture with his submachine gun and shouted at me, the surrounding mountains providing a clear echo, "You idiot! Don't you see these are political prisoners, ready to be sent to a concentration camp?"

That deserved some reply, machine gun or not. I was in a bloody mood anyway, blaming myself for the death I had caused. "Now I know, you damn ape," I shouted back. "Do you think I can read your rotten mind?"

He gaped at me with an unbelievable look on his coarse face. Clearly he had not expected any back talk from a navy private. Evidently lost for a reply, he shrugged his shoulders and turned around. I let out a sigh of relief. What I had done was just like playing with fire.

Our group leader/mountain climber had sprinted over. "Are you nuts?" he asked. "You are dealing with the SS."

"I know that," I replied without lowering my voice. "I am not playing dead in front of these blokes. It's high time these oppressors get a bit of their own medicine!" I was plain mad.

Since the plane was shot down, I had hardly eaten anything. My stomach seemed to be permanently twisted. Monday, the twenty-sixth, I reported sick and asked to see a doctor. I was withdrawn from the search commando. The sergeant major sent me and another man who had developed a bad cough to the naval hospital, which was located on the west side of the fjord inlet. Transportation was not available for anybody, unless one had to be moved on a stretcher.

The medical doctor on duty gave me a good checkup and decided I needed at least a one-week rest. My nerves seemed to be shot, and the anger I was carrying around had caused inflammation of the stomach walls. Put on medication, I decided in my own mind that I should try to take it easy, and have a good rest away from all that excitement. One thing I had forgotten, though, was that all ambulatory patients were required to move to an attached air-raid shelter during alarm. So what? It was better than taking up combat positions.

Delayed Good News

On the third day of my hospital stay the door opened and a familiar face looked inside the room, Lieutenant Commander Von der Knesebrecht. That visitor I had not counted on, but he was a very welcome one. My roommate was playing patient by himself, while I was reading a book about *Bewohner des Nordens* (Inhabitants of the North).

Before we had a chance to jump off our seats and salute, Von der Knesebrecht said quickly, "At ease, guys, you might overexert yourselves, and you know, Sigy, I don't put importance on formalities." That was him all right! He had not changed a bit, a real chum, for whom his men would walk through fire. He and Mankievicz, whom I mentioned earlier, were the two officers who undoubtedly inspired me most during my wartime service. They were real leaders, at least in my book. Harbor Captain Schubert was of course another one.

We had a long chat. It was then that he filled me in on the details of his special assignment to protect the *Tirpitz*. I found his descriptions fascinating, though he did blame himself for the attack by the mini-sub and the partial burn out of the *Tirpitz*. He could be more than fair with others but obviously not with himself.

He was on a territorial inspection tour and, of course, had heard about the aircraft shootdown. My roommate had left at that point. So Von der Knesebrecht commented, "Knowing you, it bugs you. But I am also sure your conscience would not be relieved if it had been an enemy plane. Try to get over this episode; you had no control over this event." Yes, he could read me like a book!

We had dinner in the common room. He left with the promise to take me on a guided tour before I returned to the fourth battery. He already had cleared that with the battery commander, who was more than mildly astonished that we knew each other.

A number of comrades visited me during the following days. As usual with soldiers, some tried pulling my leg by claiming I should not have left, since they had not shot down an aircraft after my departure. Others pretended to be jealous that I could take it easy "while we have to sweat it out on the exposed platform, ripe to be bombed to hell by the Tommies." I did not argue the point. Maybe I felt better already.

On Sunday, 2 July, Ludwig, the battery commander's orderly, appeared with a big smile on his face. "You have to be a lucky dog! Did you hear already?" he asked, emphasizing the "lucky dog" part. What the heck was Ludwig talking about? Was he ready to be admitted to the psychiatric ward?

"I didn't think you had," he answered his own question, seeing the baffled look I must have had. "Your return transfer came through. Strange," he added, "that you were not formally notified. I will have to check on this and let you know what the score is."

Needless to say, my heart jumped for joy. I had not received any reply to my letter from Stavanger and did not know what to think of it. Continuing on the note of positive thinking, I did talk myself into believing that no news may be good news. It was! But why had I not been notified? There must be a hidden reason. Ludwig certainly was not the authorized bearer of this news.

On Tuesday, the fourth, Ludwig reappeared. He had done some spying for me, which was fairly easy. His boss had placed a call to the area commandant that same Sunday afternoon requesting somebody else to be sent instead of me. The counter admiral promised to check into that situation. On Monday, Ludwig overheard the conversation that took place during that follow-up meeting at the battery commander's quarters while he pretended to be busy in an adjoining room.

The admiral was not the bearer of good news. He had contacted naval headquarters in Oslo, requesting to swap somebody else for me, but he was told, "Born must be sent personally." The two of them speculated without coming to any conclusion how Oslo could retransfer one man out of ten thousand, a comparatively astronomical figure.

Ludwig had left about one hour when the sergeant major appeared to give me the news. I pretended surprise but did not hold back my delight. He showed me the transfer papers that bore the code of my destination and the remark "southern Norway." The code was that of the Stabs and Wachkompanie in Stavanger, but only I knew this.

I informed the medical doctor, who arranged for my release on the sixth. When I returned to my room, Von der Knesebrecht was waiting for me. He took me on that promised tour the next day. He had a jeep-type vehicle equipped with a caterpillar track, which could not get stuck anywhere. It was quite something at the time.

Von der Knesebrecht and I visited two of the fog-in batteries, which included a demonstration. I was impressed. The way the system worked did not account for not holding the chain of fog patches together on the day of the attack on the *Tirpitz*. "The chance of that happening again," Von der Knesebrecht commented, "is about one million to one. The kind of suppressing wind we had on that day is practically unknown here. I guess luck was simply on the Tommies' side."

We made our last stop on the east side of Kafjord inlet, where the opening and closing of the intricate compartmental underwater chain system could be better observed than from the west side. The linkage was simultaneously operated from each side, chamber by chamber. To open all chain compartments, I was told, took approximately thirty-five minutes. It was quite a system.

In parting, Von der Knesebrecht wished me good luck. Sooner or later, he said, he probably would return to the south. How right he was, but under quite different circumstances and as one of a few who survived the German retreat. He handed me a note to take to Dr. Carlos Mayer-Pantin. It contained a summarized report, an up-to-date picture of the *Tirpitz* positioning.

Reporting back to the fourth battery the next day, I was told to report to my friend the commander. I knew he was upset for losing me, not because he liked me but because he wanted to further exploit whatever talents I had shown. I did not really blame him for that.

When I walked into his domain, I sensed his anger. He offered me a seat, though, then he tore into what bothered him. "What strings did you pull to get away from here?" he asked.

"If there had been any string-pulling, Herr Oberleutnant," I replied bravely, "it was done from the other end. Naturally, I kept in touch with my former superiors, as I had been encouraged to do when I left. You cannot seriously expect me to be thrilled with this detail here. The sooner I can leave, the better."

He shook his head in resignation. Then he made a last effort to scare me. "Based on the code number of your transfer here, it seems to be a pass-through unit for marine personnel processed for front action. They will not be able to keep you in Stavanger either."

"Wishful thinking," I thought, knowing how the man disliked me. Loudly I said, "It just so happens that this code number is the one used by the unit I came from, which is under the command of the area commandant in Stavanger."

He gave up, got up and informed me arrangements had to be made first for my return. It would cost the navy a few bucks to move me back. (Did I ever care about that!) In the meantime, the hospital doctor had recommended I be put on light duty. "You will be here a few more days, which likely will not kill you. In the mornings you will be trained on our radar screen; in the afternoons the sergeant major will keep you busy with paper shuffling."

Always eager to learn something else, I was glad to be assigned to radar observation during the last days of my service with the fourth battery. Who knew, it might come in handy one day.

The radar observation post was located directly underneath one of those 8.8-centimeter guns. That was not so pleasant but then, what is during war? Whenever the cannon fired, it felt like being temporarily lifted off the ground with my chair, just like it would be with an earthquake measuring 7.5 on the Richter scale. My trainer, a nice chap who formerly had been with the signal corps, noticed my dismay the first time the cannon blasted off. "How on earth can you stand that?" I asked.

"Not so difficult," was his answer. "I use Einstein's theory of relativity. Better to be shaken by our own guns, than dying in my boots by direct hits of British bombs." He had something there.

The last few days went by in no time. My comrades kept wondering how it was possible for me to get a retransfer to my old unit, but none of them expressed envy. On the contrary, they hardly stopped congratulating me on my good fortune. Most of them repeated over and over again how much they would like to accompany me on my way back to civilization.

My marching papers were made out for the thirteenth. I left on the fourteenth. For me, it was easy to say good-bye, not for my comrades. Some of them cried when they saw me leave. That almost made me feel like a heel, leaving them behind in this desolate environment.

Ernestus Tossati, my comrade and Jesuit friend with whom I had shared many hours on watch, stepped forward and gave me his blessings. Then we hugged and slapped each other's back.

I threw my gear into the back of the small truck and took my seat beside the driver. As the vehicle slowly turned to the camp exit, the boys kept waving at me and I returned the motion until they vanished from my view. Suddenly, I felt lonely. Destiny allowed me to meet one of them again after the war.

The trip to the north had taken eleven full days. The return trip to Stavanger only five. I arrived in Stavanger on the nineteenth.

When contacting Lieutenant Commander Schmidt by telephone, he instructed me to check into one of our provisions compounds downtown. Dead-tired from the journey, I retired at 2200 hours with a feeling of elation. I had returned to Stavanger, my second home.

AT HOME AGAIN

Headquarters Duties

The following morning I slept in. I prepared my own breakfast right beside the provisions master's office, where he maintained a small pantry. Everything I needed was there. "You use whatever you like," he said. "Schmidt has told me to give you a free hand. Call him after you have had breakfast, but take your time."

Around 1100 hours I gave Schmidt a ring. "Listen," he said. "don't bother to come out to the company base. Report to the sergeant-at-arms at naval headquarters. You are going to work for the commodore's administrative officers staff beginning today. Good luck, and say hello to Lieutenant Commander Wunderlich for me." He hung up.

I took my time. It was shortly after noon when I had my things together. As I walked with my *Seesack* on my back toward the end exit of the long provision shed, the sergeant operating the *Marineheim* stopped me. I sat down my briefcase and mandolin and saluted. He knew me well as a member of the B Band, but had taken a long look at me first. "By Jove!" he exclaimed. "I hardly recognized you, Sigy. What happened?" he asked, looking at my short-cropped hair. "Did you get scalped by the Indians? Where is that civilized haircut you used to have?"

I was not crazy about his remarks but could not really blame him for them. He did not mean any harm. It just came out that way.

"You are asking too many questions at one time, Petty Officer," I replied, somewhat surlily. "Do you think I like the way I look? I could choke the scabby dog who did this to me."

He wanted to hear more about my northern adventure, as he called it. So we walked together to the provisions master's office. Both of them wanted to hear my story. While I gave them sort of a summary, the radio played subdued. Suddenly it stopped in the middle of a tune. We interrupted our chat and began pointing our ears. They now played a few bars of a Wagnerian tune, then the announcer came on with a special report from Hitler's headquarters, reporting an assassination attempt on Hitler's life. The Fuehrer had been miraculously saved, which was described as Providence. The guilty ones, no doubt, would soon be punished. End of report.

We looked at each other for a short while. Finally, the petty officer said, "Thank God, the Fuehrer is safe." It did not sound too convincing to me, but I did not offer any comment. I indeed had wondered for some time how long it would take until someone in the officers corps would try to stop this madness by radical means.

The group involved in the attempt to remove Hitler from the scene included Field Marshal Rommel. Realization had set in that the war was lost for Germany. Efforts had to be made to change history in the hope that the Allies would go easier on Germany. However, allied files that were opened to the public in 1985, showed that Hitler's death would not have changed the position of the Allies. The Yalta Agreement demanded the absolute and unconditional surrender of Germany. Period!

I helped the petty officer load his truck. He had offered to drive me by headquarters and pick me up the following day from headquarters around noontime, so that I could formally report back to Schmidt. Since I was shown in the files as a member of the Kompanie, he still was my commandant.

It was 1400 hours by the time I walked into headquarters. With one exception, all personnel members were present. I was greeted with great commotion and comments, which included the super-modern hairstyle I had adopted. What hairstyle? I just had to get accustomed to it until the missing hair returned.

Lieutenant Commander Wunderlich took me to see Captain Baer, second in command to Mayer-Pantin. Baer was the one who had told me to keep in touch when I left Stavanger. I handed Von der Knesebrecht's report addressed to Dr. Carlos Mayer-Pantin to Captain Baer, and expressed my thanks and deep appreciation for having been retransferred. Between the three of them, Baer, Wunderlich and Schmidt, they had documented to Oslo the need for my return, which obviously had worked.

"You know, Born," Baer explained, "a coincidence came to our assistance. We have reasons to believe that our request was effectively received by the transfer committee anyway. But what probably helped the chairman of the committee to make up his mind is his name, Vice Admiral Born! He even remembered your having served dinner during the Terboven visit last year in November." I knew the other Born was not related to me, but at times even small common denominators can have far-reaching consequences. Call it luck, if you wish.

Having returned to Wunderlich's office, he disclosed to me I would be broken in gradually at headquarters, beginning as receptionist, then moving to other departments in due time. Anything was all right with me, I assured him. "Having survived my North Pole assignment, Herr Kapitaenleutnant," I said, "was an ordeal. Anything after that should be a cinch."

"That's the spirit, Bornchen. Delighted to have you back here with us where you belong," he replied. This was music to my ears.

Next day's news came fast. Already Stauffenberg, the officer who had placed his leather dispatch case with the bomb inside against one of the sturdy legs of the situation room table at Hitler's headquarters, and his closest co-conspirator, Olbricht, were dead.

One day after that, on 22 July, Hitler, who mistrusted almost everybody now, had appointed SS Master Himmler to take charge of the OKW (*Oberkommando der Wehrmacht*, or High Command of the armed forces). The handwriting was on the wall. It meant a total subordination of all armed forces under the hangman's assistant of Nazism.

It was customary for the sergeant-at-arms at headquarters to await the arrival of officers and administrative staff every morning inside the lobby. We would enter the lobby, salute him, and then proceed to our assigned departments.

On Tuesday, the twenty-fifth, I saluted as usual, hand at the service cap and said, "Good morning, Sergeant, sir."

"Not anymore," was his reply. I was flabbergasted.

"Why?" I asked. "I don't have to salute anymore?"

"Oh yes, you do," he clarified, "but from today on with outstretched arm! Direct orders from Hitler's headquarters."

"You have to be kidding, sir," I could not help remarking. "The internationally accepted salute of soldiers around the world is denied us now? That means Himmler is really running the show."

"I guess you are right, Born. We have no choice."

It turned out I was not the only one who was surprised and baffled about this turn of events. The others, including officers, had a problem buying it. Clearly, this was the most controversial order ever received from above. Suffice it to say that it took more than half the officers corps two full days of wrangling whether or not to comply. Eventually they gave in, notwithstanding their strong feelings against such an order.

The following weeks I served at the reception office, learned how to type with two fingers, killed a few rats at Wunderlich's residence, and generally was introduced progressively into administrative procedures in different departmental functions.

On Friday, 8 September, I received a transfer to the *Geheimregistratur* (Secret Department). My service there was then rather suddenly interrupted because of courier Bender's disappearance.

THE COURIER

Procedures

Naval regional commanders maintained a regular courier service between main bases. We had two carriers, one who would carry messages south of Stavanger down to Flekkefjord; the other in northerly direction to Haugesund and Bergen where Admiral Von Schrader had his headquarters.

Documents which these two couriers delivered consisted mainly of "Eyes Only" reports of various natures for area commanders. A few of the types of reports delivered were: troop movements, including transfers of military men on special missions; planned or new defense installations; changes in naval defense tactics; recoded code keys; actual developments on the Eastern Front, unscreened and not for general publication; loss of naval and merchant ships due to warfare or accidents; and acts of sabotage in Scandinavia and names of suspected and known Underground activists.

All these couriers knew, with very few exceptions, was the confidentiality of these documents but not their content. Still these people had top security clearance and received special training in Kiel, Germany, which included martial arts and tactics of diversion and elusion.

Whenever there was reason to believe that enemy agents had gotten wind of specific documents being sent and would attempt to apprehend them, two or three couriers would be sent to different destinations at the same time. That forced enemy agents to increase their manpower to shadow our couriers. To add to the confusion, different means of transportation would be used, not to mention the irregularity with which couriers were set in motion. None of them knew who carried what–real documents, doctored documents, bogus papers, or even newspapers! There would be a surprise waiting for those receiving any of this material by unauthorized means.

These measures were introduced early in 1943, after we lost one courier who had become too exposed as the bearer of important information. But it took us until the end of that year to realize that inconspicuousness cannot be achieved as long as couriers have to carry a steel-plated briefcase with locked chains around their wrists.

I had just served one week at the secret department after the rat extermination incident when Wunderlich came to my desk. "We have important matters to discuss," he said. "See me before you leave."

He seemed to have developed the habit of brewing up something special for me every Friday. Two weeks ago it was the typewriting exercises, last week the rat business, and now something else again.

When I entered his office around 1630 hours, he came right to the point. "Bender, who is our south-bound courier, has vanished into thin air," he began. "The last time we heard of him, he reported to Egersund base but never arrived in Flekkefjord. We have investigating teams out in the field right now.

"In the meantime, Winterhalter, our north-bound courier is going to pick up where Bender left off. The courier pool in Oslo is empty for the moment. We talked to Admiral Born who, as you know, assisted us in getting you back from the Arctic. Until we find Bender or another courier is assigned to us, we want you to service the north-bound route. Then," he added with a wide grin, "let's find out if you are nearly as good at avoiding the enemy as you are in shooting poor rats! Any questions?"

"I assume this is an order?" I queried. "For all I know, Bender could have been bumped off and I have to fill in the void. Not a pleasant thought, Herr Kapitaenleutnant." We knew each other well enough to tease without my taking offense to his statements or sounding disrespectful in turn.

"You know I am not kidding as far as your assignment is concerned," he continued. "You will receive your directives and documents this coming Sunday at noon. Get prepared to leave in the evening for Haugesund." With that, I was dismissed.

The Birthday Present

Sunday was 17 September 1944, my twenty-second birthday. My roommate, Victor Boschetto, had arranged a little birthday party behind my back, but when he heard about my new assignment when I came home on Friday, he advanced it one day. Some guys had pooled a few kroners and bought Wachholder Schnapps from the commissary and arranged for some open-faced sandwiches and, of course, Danish pastries, knowing how much I was hooked on them.

They also had booked a small back room within the downtown enclave in which we were residing. One guy brought a gramophone from the company base with some partially worn-out records. But what the heck, it was better than nothing. During wartime one learns to be easily contented.

One chap, who was a graphic artist in civilian life, had drawn me a birthday card. There was a caricature of me on the front sitting at a desk, surrounded by a pile of books. My receding forehead wrinkled up in what seemed to be deep thought. Underneath was a statement underlining the virtues of learning and aging. Then it said, "Today I reached the age of twenty-two." Inside the card the sentence completed, "but I am not one gram wiser than I was yesterday!" A fitting description of the way I felt.

When I reported to Wunderlich on Sunday, I mentioned to him I had forgotten on Friday that I was not trained in martial arts. "Makes no difference," he replied. "Nobody will attack you aboard ship. In Haugesund, a reception committee will accompany you to the base. Besides," he added, "we rely on your wits and your ability to move fast when getting crowded. If needed, use your handgun."

Our headquarters sergeant-at-arms, who was not exactly thrilled to have been called in on the Lord's Day, appeared with the briefcase, attached it to my left wrist with the chain and locked it. He explained the chain lock and the briefcase lock would be opened upon my arrival in Haugesund. Then he gave me the name and rank of the receiving officer to remember. "No notes," he added.

Wunderlich shook hands with me and made it clear that I must not lose the briefcase or I had better get lost also. He blinked one eye when he said that, but I knew he was not kidding. At the moment, though, I said aloud without realizing it, "I wonder, whether Bender somehow lost his?" I turned at the door, saluted, and left.

Outside the sergeant-at-arms told me the commander's driver would pick me up from my quarters around 2200 hours. The convoy would sail at about 2300 hours. He handed me my official marching papers.

The first thing I did when I arrived at my quarters was to have a closer look at my orders. I was expected to board minesweeper number 214. No indication of which other vessels would make up the convoy.

I did not feel too comfortable about the whole thing, but then I remembered what my first English teacher told us about Murphy's law. I tried to shrug off my strange foreboding, but it was no use. My palms started to sweat and, whatever it was, something inside commanded me to do something.

I left my quarters. I had no one to talk to. Victor Boschetto was working the afternoon shift at the convoy guidance office. Going downstairs to the lobby of the accommodation complex, I passed the communication desk. An idea struck me. Why not call Commander Schubert, our harbor captain?

The navy guard on watch assigned me one of the telephone booths and rang the number for me. Schubert answered himself. I was in luck. I told him about my new task and asked him if he could tell me which other ships were included in the convoy. "Normally not," he answered. Then, "Are you free to talk without anybody listening in?" I glanced over to the desk. The attendant was fiddling around with some papers. I assured the commander we had privacy.

"O.K., Sigy, I'll make an exception." Reading off a list, which he told me had been completed just a few minutes ago, he mentioned two patrol boats, one supply boat, one container ship, one oil tanker and two minesweepers. Then he asked me what my orders were. I told him I had to board minesweeper number 214, but would prefer to board the other one he had mentioned, number 456, since I knew her commander and most of the crew. Schubert pointed out that he could not change the order for me and if I switched ships on my own, he would have to disavow any knowledge of my action. He wished me *Hals und Beinbruch* (break a leg) and hung up.

I went back upstairs and hit the sack. I had not gone to sea for a while and, therefore, did not know how my system would react to the swing of the ship. A bit of sleep would not hurt.

I had trained myself a long time ago to automatically wake up at any predetermined time without an alarm clock. At 1900 hours I awoke, but more because my left wrist hurt from the chain than anything else. I went downstairs, took a shower, and had dinner. Then I packed my regular briefcase, which did not turn out to be easy with one arm already heavy with the document case. Luckily, all I needed was a razor with a fresh blade, toothbrush, fresh underwear, socks, and my board shoes. My usual two clean service serviettes, the universal bottle opener, and the corkscrew I left behind. I did not count on having to open and serve wine bottles on that voyage!

Gottlieb, the commandant's driver, arrived with his BMW at 2200 hours sharp. He was still the commodore's driver; the same chap who had picked up Otto and me from the naval base and drove us to the naval officers casino in December 1941. Most soldiers were not kept on duty in the same unit or formation longer than two years or so. Gottlieb was lucky!

We drove only five minutes. It would have been easy for me to walk three times the distance, but that chain on my left wrist was too much of an invitation for those who would have wanted to have a look at the documents.

I asked Gottlieb to wait a few minutes, as I wanted to first formally ascertain with the harbor police the structure of the convoy, playing dumb. The supply boat and the container ship, I was told, were waiting offshore to join the convoy at the point of departure. The two minesweepers and the two patrol boats were tied up at Strandkaien, opposite the harbor inlet from Skagenkaien. The oil tanker was being filled up from the oil reservoir tower. Looking at my orders, the sergeant made a couple of entries in his logbook. Returning my papers, he commented that I probably would have a nice voyage ahead of me since it would be clear with a calm sea and a moonlit sky. He was only partially right.

"We have to drive around the harbor inlet to Strandkaien," I said to Gottlieb when I hopped back into the car. Another four minutes and we had reached our destination. I bade Gottlieb good-bye without telling him I would board another ship than planned. I could keep secrets as well as anybody, if not better. Since he had stopped in front of minesweeper number 214, I let him drive off first, then set myself in motion to board number 456, which was the second-next ship, tied up between the two patrol boats. It was 2235 hours.

As I approached the ship I could see the two deck guards fairly well, though sunset was in progress. Coming closer to the gangplanks I identified myself and asked for permission to come aboard. One of them turned away from the railing and returned with an elderly midshipman who was one of the chaps that knew me as member of the B Band. I saluted and went aboard.

On the way to the commander's quarters we passed by several crew members who knew me also. They greeted me with a big hello as if I was a member of the crew. I immediately felt at home. Some of them had served previously on a U-boat with Midshipman Krueger. They had faced great danger many times, and could hardly be intimidated by more.

Former First Lieutenant Von der Knesebrecht, now Lieutenant Commander, our naval protection and defense expert, had worked out a plan to beef up the defense capability of vessels other than U-boats, battleships, destroyers, and cruisers. That included patrol boats and minesweepers. A rotating system was introduced, by which those who served on patrol boats and minesweepers received battle experience and specialized training on larger vessels as well as U-boats. Besides, like in the case of minesweeper number 456, former steady crew members of U-boats were permanently transferred. Not only did this beef up the defense capability of these smaller vessels, but it also served to prevent battle fatigue of navy personnel. I was going to soon find out how handy it was to have such experienced and warfare-tested daredevils aboard!

First Lieutenant Tuleweit, commander of the 456, greeted me at his cabin door as if I were a dignitary. When I mentioned something about red carpet treatment he laughed and replied, "No carpets here; just the usual decks and boards." He motioned me to an armchair which would have been fit to be used in any boardroom. Come to think of it, his cabin, not larger than any other, was furnished as elegantly as could be. I wondered whether he had a girlfriend somewhere who picked out the carpet, some of the furniture, and the cute curtains in front of the bull's-eyes.

I fished for my travel papers when Tuleweit commented, "What a pleasant coincidence that you have been ordered to sail with us on your first trip as a courier." He knew that Winterhalter had been put on the southward route but did not know I would be the replacement. "Or am I mistaken?" he asked when he saw me wincing a bit.

"Yes and no," I replied inconsequentially. "I am supposed to board minesweeper number 214, Lieutenant, sir," I said meekly. "But I was hoping you would take me on, since you know me from the officers casino, and I know some of your crew members."

"Sure, glad to have you with us, Sigy," he said assuring me. "Not that we expect anything to happen on this three-hour trip, but you are in good hands with us here. One thing, though, I have not seen your marching orders."

I asked him about the length of the trip. Since we had only about thirty-eight miles (or slightly more than thirty-two nautical miles) to conquer, three hours seemed to be much too long for me. Tuleweit explained, though, that they had to gauge their speed according to the slowest boat, so as to keep the convoy together. The container ship, the supply boat, and the oil tanker were all fully loaded and could only manage about eleven nautical miles per hour, half the speed of minesweepers and less than half of patrol boats.

Krueger reappeared and assigned a berth to me, located in the front section of the stern of the boat where the motion of the ocean would not upset my stomach too much. He did not want me to get seasick and vomit all over the place. As an extra precaution, he placed me in a lower bunk, closest to a WC. "We are now preparing to cast off," Krueger stated. "When the convoy is assembled, the off-duty crew would like you to join them."

Assembling the convoy lasted about twenty-five minutes. One minesweeper took the lead, while the other minesweeper and two patrol boats built a belly, taking the container ship, the oil tanker, and the supply boat between them. These three were not sufficiently armed to defend themselves. The other four could well look after themselves.

Minesweeper 456 was equipped with four quadruple four-centimeter shell rapid guns, which were quite effective antiaircraft weapons when used with precision and determination against low-flying aircraft. Two were mounted at the bow of the ship and one each fairly centered at starboard (the right side of the ship) and port side (the left). The turreted structures allowed the antiaircraft gunners to zero in on any approaching plane with the necessary speed and accuracy, revolving the structure horizontally and simultaneously adjusting the four gun barrels vertically.

At the stern (the end of the boat), one 8.8-centimeter battery gun nozzle loomed out of a camouflaged, cloth-bound linen cover. It was the first time I had seen a traditionally land-based, antiaircraft cannon mounted on a ship. This was quite unusual, since the recoil of this big gun is enormous for a small vessel such as a minesweeper.

The off-duty/stand by whistle went off. I left my own briefcase on the berth and followed some guys who started to walk with the typical swing of sailors to the mess hall. This ship did not have any ordinary seamen under seventeen, who normally have to divide mess hall duties. But this was not an ordinary vessel to begin with! Commander Tuleweit ran the show in as much a democratic fashion as possible in the military. All mess hall duties were shared among entry ordinary seamen and trained ones. At times, even able seamen chipped in.

After I had gone around and shook hands with everybody, we all sat down for a light supper. It was customary on Tuleweit's boat that, during each mealtime of the day, one leading seaman and one petty officer second class would join the crew. A willful separation of ranks was carefully avoided. This was no surprise to me. I had found out from other seafaring personnel, especially U-boat crews, that it invariably is the commander's behavior and his relationship with the crew that sets the tone and creates a feeling of unity or division.

Unexpectedly, the petty officer said a somber grace before we attended to the business of filling our stomachs. I got another surprise. I expected most of them to shovel it in. Not so. They all knew how to eat with forks and knives without switching over, the European way. The table neighbor to my right offered to cut meat, sausage, and cheese for me, as only my right arm was free. This was quite considerate. There was no dirty talk going on at the table either. I was impressed!

We had about twenty-some people around the table. Some of them had led the conversation to the subject of table service, knowing that I had served some time at the naval officers casino. Would I please observe the service and suggest hints for improvements? I felt a bit embarrassed, as I had not come here to comment on anything or teach. But they would not have any excuses. After the meal, pressed again, I made a few comments, most of them justifiably complimentary. I promised to return at a later date, when my left hand would be free, so I could give them a little demonstration.

"While we are out at sea," the petty officer explained to me, "we never drink Schnapps, beer, or wine." I was glad to see Tuleweit enforcing this common-sense rule as strictly as the American navy did. Some German commanders had loosened up this rule and had to pay consequences which, at times, were devastating to the ship and her crew!

It was 2445 hours when we vacated the table. The petty officer took me to meet the IA and other officers on board. A door close to the commander's cabin bore the name "Dr. Med. R.D. Schmucker, M.D. Surgeon" in gold-plated letters on a black background.

We knocked, went in, saluted, and I shook hands with a giant six-foot-five-inch-tall, white-haired gentleman in his fifties. His height reminded me of my dad, who had served as the fourth-tallest member of the Kaiser Wilhelm's guard between 1909 and 1911.

The overall physical appearance of Dr. Schmucker, including his British-looking handlebar mustache, fit the description Heinz Marzi had given Otto and me of Engineer Ross Sitwell. Sitwell directed and was the brain behind the four capers in the early twenties, South Africa, India, China and Brazil. I pulled myself back into the present. This man likely did not speak English but, based on his looks, he could have passed as a Britisher any time.

Dr. Schmucker went behind his desk, opened what looked like an appointment book, and asked me a couple of questions about my weight, height and age, how long I had served in the navy, and if I had had any major surgery. He explained in an apologetic tone of voice that since he was responsible for the well-being of all personnel aboard, he had to know basic information about each member.

He told me to step on the scale, which was placed next to a side door marked "Surgery Room." Making a note in his book, he commented that I could allow myself an extra twenty pounds for my height. "How is your appetite?" I was five feet, eleven inches and weighed 140 pounds.

"I can eat like a horse," I exaggerated, "but the navy has a knack for finding all kinds of special assignments for me such as this." I lifted my left arm high with the steel case. "Such as this, which keeps me under suspense and is not exactly conducive for putting on weight. But I like to walk on eggshells," I added, trying to be funny.

He laughed heartily. "For a skinny youngster, you have a good sense of humor," he retorted, as if to indicate that only heavyset people can have that trait. "That comes in damn handy in wartime." With that, he gave me a couple of pills for seasickness and we left the cabin. I thought, what a difference between this man and the bastard who examined me at the Muster Examination Board in 1940!

The sea was calm. I got permission from the petty officer to use the crew mess hall for writing a letter home. Since I had returned from the Arctic, different assignments had kept me quite busy.

I had just stepped over the base of a bulkhead, which is used on ships to divide compartments and ship's sections, when a loudspeaker above my head started crackling, followed by the voice of the navigator. He announced that we were passing the southern tip of Karmøy, a narrow, but thirty-four-kilometer-long island, whose northern extremity ended off Haugesund. A bit more than the halfway point had been covered.

The mess hall door came into sight. Suddenly the pealing noise of the air alarm siren attacked my eardrums, succeeded by the sonorous three long honks of the ship's horn. That indicated alarm stage three, before it would advance to stage two and, finally, to one. The voice of the A-One came loud and clear through the intercom over the loudspeaker system, "All crew members, except engine room personnel, take your battle stations on upper deck—on the double!"

Several guys who were off duty came streaming out of the mess hall, running to their bunks and lockers. I followed the crowd. One leading seaman looked at my head, then quickly ran to one corner of the room, lifted a few blankets out of the way, and picked up a steel helmet. "Put that on," he ordered, "and follow us." That was plain enough.

As if they had rehearsed this many times, the men split up into two groups, running toward two different sets of iron steps that led to the steerage. Then they again used separate staircases to reach the upper deck. Though I was younger than most of these guys, I had a hard time keeping up with their speed. No doubt, I needed more exercise, but did it have to be that way? It was a good thing I had put on my board shoes.

My former mentor at the officers casino, Heinz Marzi, had indoctrinated me to stick to certain principles: finish what you start; think before you act; and many others. Some of them were even funny, such as foresight is the mother of the porcelain crate. (It sounds funnier in German.)

Included in Heinz's advice was to adopt the habit of looking at the time when something out of the ordinary occurs. I had done so when alarm stage three was announced. Checking the time again after the entire crew had lined up on deck in four groups, I noticed it only had taken two minutes and twenty-five seconds. Not bad.

Lieutenant Tuleweit appeared on the navigation bridge and went through a check-off list with his key men. At that moment, the second-stage alarm signal was given. Several petty officers came down the bridge and gave instructions to the four groups. I saw Tuleweit pointing in my direction talking to his sublieutenant, who swished down the handrail like a weasel and gave me Tuleweit's message that I should make myself as inconspicuous as possible and not take any unnecessary risk. I almost had to laugh. What unnecessary risk, waving with the briefcase?

Everybody dispersed to designated areas. Within a minute, all four turrets were manned; crates of four-centimeter projectiles were ready to be used. The big 8.8-centimeter cannon was exposed. Without the canvas cover, it looked even more threatening. But that was nothing new to me. I had learned to use them with deadly effect during my stint with the fourth naval antiaircraft battery high up at Kafjord for the protection of our last battleship, the *Tirpitz*. These monsters could do quite a job, but they had the disadvantage in comparison to the four-by-fours, which could be maneuvered and changed to different directions much more quickly.

As soon as the nearest signal post on Karmøy had reported enemy planes in approaching mode, the petty officer in charge of communications requested identification and number of planes. That was easier said than done. Even to this point in war, September 1944, Germany was not up to speed on radar equipment. Our listening disks which looked like huge satellite dishes, had powerful ears but would only reflect senseless blips on console screens. Telescopes had to be used for actual identification when the object was already in sight. The fact that we were technically ahead of the Allies in the fields of torpedo weaponry, which was quite precise, and rocket development (V-Ones and V-Twos) was no consolation in cases of air raids.

When stage two of the warning system was activated, based on the likelihood that enemy aircraft were zeroing in on the position of the convoy, Tuleweit, who had been elected leader of the convoy, requested the employ of an air force squadron for our protection. Everything had been done on our part to be as well-prepared for the expected onslaught as could be. The antiaircraft teams were busy maneuvering their artillery weapons for maximum flexibility.

Because of my skinny frame, I always had trouble sitting on a chair for any length of time. Before rushing on deck, I had grabbed a pillow from my berth. I placed it on a small wooden crate right beside the funnel and sat down. Somebody had told me once that a ship's funnel is one of the last pieces to sink. Why not use it as a safety straw? Besides, I did not feel bad about not being able to make myself useful with that awkward briefcase. Furthermore, I would only be in the way.

On orders of Dr. Schmucker, several crew members were assisting the only official orderly aboard to move first-aid kits to designated areas for handy accessibility. Those people seemed to have thought of everything.

We did not have to wait long. Soon we heard a roaring sound which became louder by the second. Though it was a clear night, I almost wished one could see more having one of those deceptive thoughts we sometimes have that danger would be diminished if one could see the enemy. My wish was granted the moment it flashed through my mind. British aircraft had released these flares, with which I was so familiar from last year when they bombed our home out from under our seats. This time, they used only two: one ahead of the convoy, the other close at the tail. Now I really knew what we were in for!

It was light enough to read a newspaper. I pressed myself hard to the outer backward curvature of the funnel, since the piercing noise came from the bow of the ship. While diving Mustang fighter planes had their machine guns strafing the surface of the boat, our quadruple rapid gun crew spit bullets back into their paths. Close by where I was squatting, one strafing projectile hit the inside railing and ricocheted into the top of a bulk room head, creating the sound of splintering wood.

Following the Mustangs with my eyes as they had swished over, I counted nine. Several screams came from one of the patrol boats. "Some crew members must have been hurt," I thought. Turning around, I saw the top mast of the patrol boat having been shaved diagonally in half. With it, the rail of the captain's bridge had splintered in different places. Several crew members were carried under deck on stretchers.

A second group of Mustangs appeared from the same direction as the first one had come. The same scene repeated itself. This time we did not have any projectiles flip-flopping across the deck. Our artillerists seemed to enjoy giving those Tommies a real hard time, receiving their approach ahead of time by scattering their paths with a net of four-centimeter bullets, thus forcing the pilots to veer off course. One of the Mustangs, though, had come too close for comfort. Before the pilot could stray off, our boys had hit the fuselage of the plane, just about when it was five hundred feet from our starboard side. The plane began to jerk, released black smoke, tipped so much to one side I thought its left wing would hit our second mast while flying over the vessel, and then crashed into the container ship three hundred feet from our port side, at a forty-five-degree angle.

My comrades had started to cheer when the Mustang began to sway, but stopped instantly when seeing where it hit. All this took only seconds. At the moment of the impact, there were two great explosions and a huge toxic cloud formed, surrounding the container ship. The slight wind, which unfortunately blew in our direction, brought with it not only a yellowish bank of clouds, but also a sickening smell, comparable to a pile of rotten eggs.

I saw my comrades putting on their gas masks and I followed the example, though I had found it almost unbearable to wear during my basic training on Haon. The filter had been renewed only recently, but some of the foul smell nevertheless penetrated through.

Tuleweit gave orders to stop all engines on all ships. The convoy had to be held together. Too bad we did not even have one destroyer with us, not to mention a battleship for better protection.

In foresight, Tuleweit instructed the crew to lower some lifeboats in order to rescue from drowning some sailors who had jumped off the container ship. I thought the trial was over, but that proved to be wrong. We had hardly lowered two of our lifeboats when a third wave of Mustangs decided to pay us a visit. "Is this ever going to stop?" went through my mind. Events moved so fast that I did not realize the whole mess had started barely ten minutes before!

As soon as the container ship got hit by the aircraft, I saw the quartermaster stumbling on deck with a supply of brandy, the best medicine to revive people. His assistant followed suit, looking at Tuleweit on the bridge, who seemed to give him a prearranged signal.

The man sprinted forward to give one bottle to each artillery team handling the four-by-four centimeter guns ahead of the bridge. The quartermaster took another three, two for the front-aft teams and one for the gunners handling the 8.8-centimeter big gun at the stern of the ship. Not all of them had a chance to take a nip before the third attack began. It takes a few precious seconds to put on and take off a gas mask. Some sailors, though, had removed their steel helmets and, cigarette in mouth, crouched behind the gun shield to get ready for more action.

When the third attack began, we could see only one of the so-far unhurt patrol boats, which had sailed slightly ahead of the rest of the convoy. The toxic cloud allowed barely sufficient sight to fend off the attacking Mustangs. Again, we were lucky. We heard some bullets crossing the deck. One went through the signal room window and harmlessly lodged itself into the floor, right beside where the wireless operator sat. A second chap, who was in the room at the time, told us that his comrade did not move an inch. He just looked at the engraved projectile and, with good humor, commented about the poor aim.

As if I did not have any other worries, I tried to figure out whether the third attack was launched by a third group of planes or whether the first group was paying us a second visit, because we were dealing with nine Mustangs again. About one year ago, one of our ace fighter pilots had been sent by German Air Force headquarters to visit different airborne units, lifting somewhat sliding morale among members of the Luftwaffe. An air force pilot, whom I met during one of our concerts, had taken me and other interested members of the band to visit his base on that same day. The air commodore mentioned that a squadron of fighters in the RAF is generally divided into two or three groups of nine planes each.

The entire flak (aircraft defense guns/antiaircraft fire) on the four armed ships, the two minesweepers, and the two patrol boats, must have done a heck of a good job this time. The Mustangs could not even come close to any of us before they veered off and vanished.

The artillerists had reloaded their guns, of course, and Tuleweit instructed everybody to stand by. While two groups of detailed men jumped into lifeboats, the other boat crews were ordered to do the same, trying to rescue the men who had jumped overboard.

Believing the danger to be over, I picked myself up and went to the railing on port side. Ripping off my gas mask, I could see at least eight heads swimming above water. The toxic cloud had lifted a bit and the Christmas trees were still shedding enough light to see the surrounding edges. "Only a few more minutes," I thought, "and the all-clear signal will be given." Wrong again!

Like lightening, one of the two signal men dashed out of the communication room with a piece of paper in his hand, sprinted up the ladder leading to the commander's bridge, and handed to Tuleweit what obviously could only be a message. The latter's voice came over the intercom, "All men. Maintain alarm stage one; battle ready for bomber attack!" His A-One took a foghorn and warned our men who had gone overboard for the rescue attempt.

While walking back to my selected hiding place, I passed by where the quartermaster hovered over his provisions. His outstretched arm offered a half-full bottle of Dujardin brandy. "You look like a ghost," he commented. "Take a gulp."

"Thanks," I said, and took the bottle. "A ghost cannot be nearly as scared as I am. I must have wet my pants already. Before something worse happens, I better warm up my intestines." Having swallowed a huge gulp of the stuff, I returned the bottle and remarked, "What a hell of a birthday this is! I may not see the end of it. A moment ago I thought everything was over, but it seems to have been only an introduction to the dance to follow." I tried to use some grim humor. For a moment I fantasized what a terrifying feeling it must be to be condemned to death!

Having reached my hiding place, I could hear the more sonorous, deep sound of bomber aircraft, familiar to me from last year when I got bombed out at home.

These Mosquitoes were flying at much greater height than the Mustangs did, barely within reach of the four-by-fours. They must have been briefed by the Mustang squadron leader about the effectiveness of our air defense and just stayed at the periphery of our rapid guns' distance capability. There was not much we could do. We were an easy target. They only had to aim their bombs in the vicinity of the smoke cloud surrounding the hit container ship, while our flak's sight was restricted.

From below, it looked as if they were following some kind of zigzag pattern during the attack. The roar became louder now. Tuleweit gave orders to zero in and give it all we had. They kept on course, disregarding our persistent flak fire. The attack took place from the rear of the convoy. The height and distance estimator of the 8.8-centimeter gun reported to have counted sixteen aircraft.

I craned my neck to one side of the funnel and saw at that precise moment that all bombers I could see had released their load, which came raining down on the convoy. I hit the deck again, instinctively trying to cover my head with the steel briefcase.

There were several explosions almost simultaneously. The planes had passed overhead and I saw some of them curving as I followed their path. "Oh no!" I thought. "They will turn and hit us from the front now." I quickly crawled around to the aft position of the funnel. Doing so, I noticed the big hollow pipe tube of the 8.8-centimeter gun at the stern of the boat swinging around, now pointing over my head toward the bow of the ship, bracing for the second wave of attack. Damn! Why did I not pick up some cotton from the first-aid box when I passed by a few minutes ago? It would come in handy now for plugging my ears.

It was too late. The big gun started roaring. I had buried my face on the deck plank, briefcase in front, and stuck my index fingers into my ear canals as forcefully as I could. The noise was still deafening, and the deck planks vibrated vigorously against my chest.

Taking a peek, I saw the artillerists reloading the big thing with amazing swiftness. I was quite familiar with the 8.8-centimeter cannon, having returned only two months ago from the Arctic, where we had to use that weapon every day for the defense of the *Tirpitz*.

A second volley followed suit, then a third, succeeded by a thud. I clearly heard one man jubilantly shouting, "We caught the bloody dog!"

Looking sideways around the funnel to the frontal port side of the boat, I saw one Mosquito spit out black smoke, quiver briefly, and then go into a tailspin. I estimated the plane to be at two thousand-meter height, but was not sure. As it started its spiraling and slanting descent, it looked to me as if it had its course locked in on us! What else did we need? The other bombers had vanished.

As it closed in on us, its course seemed to change slightly to our port side toward the center of the convoy. I counted four more seconds, hoping the plane would hit water. No such luck! With a tremendous resounding blow, it landed smack in mid-ship of the oil tanker and carved itself into the body of the ship. The resulting explosion even shook our boat, three hundred meters away. A yellowish-white flaming mushroom reached for the sky. Several sailors jumped off the stern and the bow of the tanker, most of them with their clothing aflame! An inferno of burning oil rushed into the ocean. From the tanker came an unforgettable groaning and cracking sound. Then it split in two and started to sink fast, the center parts first, the bow and the stern last, taking with them a circular gorge current of water. It was a hair-raising and yet a fascinating sight!

Within minutes, the still lingering toxic smell from the sunken container ship was replaced by the intense scent of burning oil. During the third Mustang attack I had ripped off my gas mask. It did not prevent the rotten egg smell, stifled my breathing, and did not allow clear vision. Choosing between two evils, I decided to forget about the gas mask and put up with the oil odor which, at times, seemed to cauterize my lungs.

When the all-clear signal blared, we all went over to port side, where Tuleweit gave us assignments to assist with the rescue of those who had gone overboard. We were informed that everything depended on us, since we were the only ship left that could maneuver. Minesweeper number 214, one of the two patrol boats, the oil tanker, the supply boat and the container ship had all hit the bottom of the ocean. The second patrol boat had to throw anchor. It had sustained major engine room damage and was inoperative.

We were divided into teams. Some had to line up stretchers and carry the wounded to Dr. Schmucker's operating room. Two more lifeboats were lowered to the sea with sailors known to be experienced swimmers and familiar with rescue operations of this kind. I would have felt terrible being the only one on board not contributing to the rescue efforts. Tuleweit first did not want to hear anything about it, but then gave in when I kept complaining. I assisted Dr. Schmucker's orderly in making notes, as he made his initial assessment of the severity of each rescued person's wounds.

I placed myself on a stool right beside the hoisting winch, which was used for cranking the wounded aboard. Putting the briefcase on my knees, I used it instead as a clipboard to write on.

The whole rescue operation lasted over one hour. There were few light cases. Many survivors had suffered severe burns, some of them when they jumped off the container ship and later off the oil tanker. Others had to leave their sinking boats, jumping literally into the burning ocean, an awful decision to make!

Some had suffered injuries from bombshell fragments, severing or almost severing limbs. It was a bloody sight in the real sense of the word!

Altogether I counted sixty-four bodies that were brought under deck. Another nine did not make it that far. They were dead on arrival, when brought aboard. Their corpses were assembled at the stern of the upper deck, close to the 8.8-centimeter cannon, and covered with canvasses.

Those who were slightly wounded did not waste any time helping us look after the seriously wounded. There seemed to be a common bond among all of us because we realized, if we had not known it before, that we were literally all in the same boat. The feeling of belonging overcame me as it had when having been bombed out with my countrymen. Most of all, I gave homage to Providence for having saved my life for the second time in fifteen months!

When there was nothing else for me to do on deck, I started going below. What a mess! Not only had the toxic rotten egg smell succeeded in creeping inside the belly of the boat, it had mixed with the different smells of medication, including chloroform. Blood-soaked rags were piled up at the end of gangways, and a number of blood trails led in all directions.

Most members of the crew were waiting in the gangways for further instructions, their bunks being used for the wounded. I damned the shackles on my wrist that prevented me from making myself more useful.

It was agreed that the patrol boat should be taken in tow, rather than radioing for a rescue ship. There was no chaplain aboard. So it behooved Tuleweit to preside over the nine dead sailors naval warfare funeral. I had not known any of them, but as their bodies were sliding down the planks to the sea during the salute, my heart started to ache and I wept uncontrollably.

The patrol boat, in spite of her handicap, had saved the lives of eight who were shipwrecked, including that of the other patrol boat's commander. It was 0225 hours when she hoisted her anchor, and we began towing her behind us at about six knots speed. Another half-hour and Dr. Schmucker, after amputating a leg here and a hand or arm there, had finally patched up the last of his patients. Some of those who were ambulatory, I noticed, were wearing makeshift bandages. Not even halfway through with his treatments, Dr. Schmucker had ordered a couple of orderly helpers to rip bedclothes apart in strips. Due to lack of sufficient antibacterial medication, over thirty bottles of brandy had been used to clean the wounds.

Tuleweit called us together in the general mess hall to receive reports from team leaders and comment on our conduct during the endured crises. He was full of praise and so was Dr. Schmucker. I had my own thoughts also. When a hellish situation occurs, such as the one we had just experienced, panic is the order of the day. Not in our case. Events kept us so alert and busy that we hardly had time to be afraid. Regardless of exterior reactions of people, we are all afraid. Only some can hide fear better than others.

Outside Haugesund Harbor a tugboat took the patrol boat in tow to guide her safely into the local shipyard. It was now 0510 hours, Monday, 18 September 1944.

The Next Day

Before I disembarked, we all had a stiff drink and shook each other's hands. I felt close to these men. It was probably their persistence and courage which had saved my life! I had been condemned to be pinned down like a log to the planks, unable to contribute to the defense.

As I went down the plank of the fallreep, balancing the two briefcases in one hand, while holding myself steady with the other at the ropes, I heard a bunch of guys loudly bidding me their farewell. Tuleweit had extended to me a standing invitation to visit the ship when I signed off. It was a great feeling, like leaving a large but close family behind.

I was not surprised that no one from the naval base office met me at the harbor. First, my contact person likely did not count on my appearance, since I was to have boarded minesweeper number 214, which by now lay on the bottom of the ocean. Second, who gets greeted at 0540 hours in the morning, though it was a matter of procedure to pick up couriers and agents at their point of arrival.

Walking along the pier, I saw well-kept continental-style buildings. Glancing across the inlet, not even the warehouses on the other side looked dilapidated like those one finds so often in larger harbors. Come to think of it, through my excursions across the Norwegian coastline, I found the harbor fronts generally much better looking than in Germany, France, and England.

The kilometer-long jetty on the inner quay functioned as a mooring area for small boats. We were outnumbered. Some Norwegians seemed to have their summer vacations extended far into September. Good for them!

Turning away from the harbor, I passed Haraldsgaten, where fishermen were preparing to fill large tables with fresh-caught fish, mostly sole and cod, ready to be deboned and/or sold. I had not seen this done for at least a year in Stavanger where we, the occupying German forces, seemed to requisition more fish at times than the fishermen could catch. On several occasions toward the end of 1943, while I had to visit the navy dentist's office at Strandkaien in Stavanger, I saw long lines of Norwegians at a fish retail outlet. I had asked Werner's girlfriend about this, and her answer was that there simply was not enough fish to go around anymore. I felt deeply ashamed. Here was one of the greatest seafaring and fish-catching nations in the world, and its population had to line up for fish!

I watched the activity for a while, oblivious to quizzical looks which some cast at me, seeing the briefcase chained to my wrist. Wunderlich had given me a sketch, showing the immediate vicinity of the naval base which, strangely enough, was located away from the harbor but within walking distance. Turning down a couple of side streets, there was a farmers market complex, but the stalls were not open yet. It was too early.

After another five-minute walk, I recognized the building which had been described to me. Unlike our commandant's headquarters building in Stavanger, which was fairly well guarded particularly at night, there was not one sentry to be seen here.

Six steps led to the main entrance. I had hardly climbed these when the double doors swung wide open. A navy guard in battle dress without rank insignia quickly took me inside.

"I cannot believe it," he exclaimed. "Are you the missing courier?" he asked unnecessarily, considering the obvious briefcase and link chain.

"In the flesh," I replied, nonchalantly. "Neither missing nor dead," I added in a tone as if nothing could rock me. If he only knew what kind of a tenderfoot I really was!

He led me along a small ill-lit corridor and opened a door to our left with a mother-of-pearl sign, fancily adorned with the letters *Kommandierender Marineoffizier* (Commanding Naval Officer), but no name. I thought, "Good idea; ranks remain, people change."

Once inside, the guard, who turned out to be the sergeant-at-arms in charge of security, picked up the telephone but did not dial. After a few seconds, he snapped, "Connect me with the commanding officer." Then, obviously having listened to an unfavorable reply, he said, "Nonsense. Leave that up to me! This is important!" He hung up.

He turned around and indicated how concerned his commander was when he received the report about the attack on the convoy, "Because you are carrying damn important papers."

"I am going to brew some coffee now," he announced. "You probably can use some after your ordeal. And our commanding officer is one of those people one can deal with only after they have had some of this brew." He went through an open archway to an adjoining room, where he started fiddling around with a hot plate and water kettle.

Five minutes went by. I heard someone opening the main entrance door, after a key had been latched. The commander appeared in the door frame, a lieutenant-colonel, immaculately dressed. I jumped up, forgetting for the moment that metal-framed briefcase. During the raid on the convoy I had pulled and twisted the chain around my wrist many times, causing scrapings. The renewed jerk made me wince. The commander leisurely returned my salute and identified himself formally as Lehner, the receiver of the documents.

"At ease and sit down," he ordered. As he withdrew two keys from his uniform jacket and opened the chain lock first, the petty officer reappeared with hot, steaming coffee. The commander set the briefcase to one side on his desk. "This can wait until later," he declared. "Let's first hear your story." He motioned to the sergeant, who took a clipboard to take notes.

The commander told me to start from the beginning from the time I had received my orders in Stavanger. I could not possibly leave anything out, including the fact that I had boarded a ship to which I had not been assigned.

The debriefing took about three-quarters of an hour. I did not want to lose myself in too many details. But, any time I left something out, the fox of a commander urged me to elaborate. Like a bloodhound, he knew whenever I wanted to abridge.

When the conversation petered out, he instructed me to sign my statements. Ernst Roland, my legally-trained comrade and friend from the base, had taught me to create the habit of reading everything first or have the stenographer read back the account before signing anything. When I mentioned this, somewhat lamely, the commander asked when I intended to return to Stavanger, and if a cable should be sent to announce my return.

I asked for permission to rest for a day but not to send a cable, as I wanted to surprise everybody. He chuckled, agreed to play the game, and directed the sergeant to provide accommodations and meals for me. A woman naval service officer would transcribe my statements and present these to me in the afternoon for signature.

Arriving at the navy base around 0800 hours, I had a substantial breakfast and hit the sack. The daytime sergeant-at-arms made his cot available to me, for which I was grateful. Now I could sleep without interruptions.

It seemed I had rested only for a couple of hours when someone tapped me on my shoulder and said, "There is a cute-looking service officer at the gate who wants to talk to you." Glancing at my watch, it was close to 1600 hours. I had slept almost seven hours but did not feel rested.

I quickly got dressed and went to the guardhouse, where a chestnut-haired beauty awaited my arrival. She bore the rank of staff sergeant and returned my salute with a pleasant smile. Then she took the transcripts of my report out of her leather briefcase. We both sat down at a table and I read what now was becoming a formal document in its entirety. She had double-spaced everything, thirty-four pages in all, including the commander's additional questions. It dawned on me then, for the first time, how much conversation can take place within forty-five minutes.

I asked three minor changes be made for the purpose of making some meaning more clear. She entered these with a pen in the appropriate spaces between the lines. Her handwriting struck me as dainty yet determined and sophisticated.

On the bottom of the last page were two short lines, one for me to sign as the reporter, the other for her signature as witness. As she placed the papers in her briefcase, I offered to walk her to the front gate, which she accepted with a friendly, "Yes, thank you."

While we walked the thirty steps or so to the gate, I noticed, not to my surprise, that she drew a lot of attention from a number of off-duty sailors. She held herself erect with her height of five feet ten inches and slender build, and walked like a gazelle. Her hair was cut man-style in the back, but plenty of natural curls were framing her navy cap left and right.

We stopped at the gate where I thanked her for bringing the papers over for my signature. As I was about to salute, she said, "Since it is my understanding that you are not going to leave before tomorrow, my girls and I would like to invite you to dinner tonight at our base dormitory. We would like to hear more about your adventurous experience if you are not too tired."

I accepted without hesitation. The last thing I wanted to admit was being tired. She would pick me up with her captain's staff car at 1830 hours.

The sergeant, whose cot I had used, returned from his shift at 1800 hours after I had shaved and showered. When he heard about the invitation, his eyes almost popped out of his sockets. He exclaimed, "That is really a first! None of us ever got invited to the waves' domain. There are a lot of classy women out there, you know. I wouldn't be surprised if they give you a hero's welcome." I hoped not. I had nothing to brag about.

We drove like the devil to the northern part of Haugesund. That captain's driver must have won several races, the way she blitzed around. She wiggled through the narrow street downtown traffic, without ever applying the brakes. I glanced at the staff sergeant, lifting my eyebrows a bit. She noticed, smiled, and said, "Great driving, isn't it? She is our trump card when it comes to testing somebody's courage. You should see her flying one of our navy planes. That is really something!"

"Frankly," I commented, "I wouldn't mind observing that from the ground, rather than as a passenger."

"After what you have been through?" she replied. Not to destroy the image, I just shrugged my shoulders.

The mess hall was in much better shape than all the men's mess halls I had ever seen. Tables were covered with tablecloths and nicely set up with decorative centerpieces of flowers in season. Proof, again, that women indeed are different from men in many respects. *Vive la différence!*

Just like a guest of honor, I was seated between the captain and the petty officer. The captain was a matronly lady in her late forties, who, nevertheless did her best to make little ole me feel at ease. This is difficult, when one is far outranked by more than half the people in the room. Besides, they were all women. I was not used to being the cock of the walk, nor was I the type to ask for it.

After a delightful three-course dinner, the captain introduced me as "the young courageous navy private, whom we have invited today to tell us a bit more about his participation in the horrible event, which we only know from intercepted teletype messages." It was my turn to rise and shine.

Slightly embarrassed by part of her introduction, I began by stressing that there was nothing courageous about lying flat on deck and hiding behind a big funnel. "Full credit for the fact that I am alive to tell my story here goes to my comrades, commander and crew of minesweeper number 456," I continued. "Their devil-may-care approach saved my life and that of many others."

The attention in the room was intense. Like so often in my life, I felt pleasure in speaking my mind, even if it meant being controversial which, in that day and age, could mean skating on thin ice.

"You see, ladies," I commented with determination, "in my book, those who save lives are the real heroes, not those who destroy it!"

I had hardly finished the sentence when my heart jumped into my throat. But not to worry, as the enthusiastic applause testified, not only did I get away with speaking out, but I definitely was on the same wavelength as these members of our signal corps.

The rest of my story was easy to tell. Some waves seated closest to the head table had been selected to ask additional questions, which I answered as well as I could. But the question I had in mind did not come up. So I decided to ask it.

Turning to the captain beside me, I asked whether our signal for air support by the Luftwaffe had been received and transmitted. I knew well that we maintained four different air bases nearby, Flesland Airport south of Bergen, a provisional landing sight we had built in 1940 on the island of Stord, halfway between Haugesund and Bergen, Karmøy Air Base on the island of Karmøy south of Haugesund and, of course, the twin air bases of Sola and Forus slightly south and southwest of Stavanger. Altogether, at least on paper, we had nine squadrons at our disposal, but not one had come to our rescue!

The captain verified the receipt and transmittal of our SOS request to each of these destinations, but was told in each case they were deployed somewhere else. I thanked her for the information, but did not comment. There was no use pointing fingers. This was 1944. The time when the Luftwaffe had the upper hand had long since past. Our decaying war efforts became more and more obvious.

It was almost 2100 hours when I was ready to leave these hospitable ladies. I shook hands with every one of them. There were over 120. Now I did not only have a sore left wrist, but also a sore right arm. As a friend of mine used to say, things have to balance each other out. What a consolation!

This time, the staff sergeant drove me back to the male navy base herself. On the way, we stopped for a moment on an outlook, which affords a beautiful view over Haugesund Harbor. A whiff of her 4711 Koelnisch Wasser (world-famous Cologne perfume) went into my nostrils.

My motor started running. But then maybe it was just the hormones which needed attention. For just a moment, I had the crazy idea of making a pass at her. I almost immediately dismissed the thought. Unlike in the American and Canadian forces, male and female members of the German armed forces were not allowed to cross ranks, no matter where your heart lay. Her rank was three notches higher than mine. Besides, she was at least five years my senior. "Ridiculous!" you think? Not then!

She must have read my thoughts. Leaning over, she took my face in both hands and gave me a not so brotherly kiss smack on my mouth. Then she quickly withdrew back behind the steering wheel without taking her eyes off mine and said, "I really like you, Siegfried, but we have to be grownups about this situation. In war there can be friendship, but there is little sense in building a bond that cannot hold."

I had to agree with her. Not only was this a beautiful woman, she also had brains. She started the car and a few minutes later we arrived at my destination, stopping about ten steps away from the base entrance. This time I reached over and reciprocated, paying my dues. Then we both embraced. The warmth of her body nearly drove me nuts. Talk about torture! This was a case of overpowering compatible chemistry, and we both knew it.

"Promise to look me up next time you come to Haugesund," she begged. "Maybe we both can get a two-day pass and really spend some time together." I enthusiastically agreed, while my imagination and anticipation caused the wheels to turn in my head. I whistled all the way to the sergeant's quarters.

He had put up a foldable cot for me. "I thought this is easier than assigning you to the garrison for one night," he said. I thanked him for this gesture. Then a thought struck me. Since I had survived the ordeal, everybody I met had been extra kind. Did they feel sorry for me? Well, if so, why dwell on it? What counted was that my life had been spared, for which I was eternally grateful! And I had even met a woman here in Haugesund who seemed to care about me and awaited my return. How great could life be?

It was 2345 hours when I retired. My boat would cast off tomorrow around 0900 hours, leaving plenty of time for a good night's rest. At 0800 hours the next morning I was granted permission from the guard on duty to call the signal corps base. The switchboard operator instantly connected me with Leonore, my girl sergeant.

"I had an intuition you would call," she said with a voice of elation. "It's great to hear your voice once more before you leave. I do care about you."

"I know," I replied. "Same here. I will be lonely in Stavanger without you, Leonore–sergeant," I quickly added. Strange, I thought, how quickly people can become fond of each other.

I heard a lovely laugh after I had added the sergeant behind her name. "Forget the sergeant, Sigy, and forget about that talk I gave yesterday, referring to grownups."

We said *Auf Wiedersehen* (see you again) rather than good-bye. I kept the receiver at my ear until I heard the dial tone.

The Ghost

Reporting to the harbor commander at Haugesund Harbor at 0830 hours, I had another surprise coming. This time it was a nice one. The boat that would bring me back to Stavanger was the *Stavanger II*, the one Admiral Von Schrader had used for his inspection tour two years ago.

Harald Frieberg was still her commander. This time his rank as commanding officer was more befitting of his actual duties. He must have kept himself out of mischief for some time, I thought.

When boarding the boat, he greeted me at the end of the fallreep, obviously delighted to see me. I saluted him as smartly as I could, clearly addressing him as Commander, looking at his rank insignia, the gold rings on his arm sleeves. As I ascended from the boarding ladder, he put his arm around my shoulder like an old friend would do. "I've seen your astonished look, all right," he said. "But this time I got my rank back from 1941 without anybody having to pull strings. I have pretty well given up on booze, but not on girls," he emphasized.

"Have you ever noticed," he continued while we went under deck on the way to his cabin, "why more married men have girlfriends here than those who are bachelors?" I knew this, of course, from observing my comrades at the base, and the officers from the officers casino. But I had never tried to analyze that fact. Harald was not married, so what was he driving at?

"You see," he explained, "the married guys are so used to regular sex, they can't be without it. So they continue where they left off at home by chasing broads here. I am just one of those who put a dent in this picture. It sure beats masturbating by a long shot!" Brother, that was straight off the cuff! Not that I expected anything else from this man, but it nevertheless embarrassed me (although I could not quarrel with his point of view).

We cast off shortly after 0900 hours on what looked like a clear and crisp day. The boat was not in a hurry. There was no need to squeeze out the maximum forty to forty-five knots out of her. Even a slow fifteen knots would bring us to Stavanger by noon.

This was actually the third time I had boarded the boat. Harald left a stoker in the engine room (there were no stokers on this diesel-engine boat, of course) and assigned one leading seaman as combination navigator/outlook at the steering wheel. We congregated with the rest of the crew of fourteen in the glassed-in mid-ship area for a powwow, where the VIPs enjoyed their meals during the inspection tour.

As much as I wanted to get my mind off the immediate past, I did not mind answering a few questions from the crew. Harald's A-One, a sublieutenant, jokingly indicated that this would never have happened aboard his boat. "Next time, sail with us!" Easier said than done. Besides, it could have been worse, much worse!

We tied up at Strandkaien in Stavanger shortly after noon. Friebert did not want to hear anything about rushing to naval headquarters. "First, Sigy, we are going to invite you for luncheon at the *Marineheim*," he said. The mess was located on Nedre Strandgate. To get there, we only had to cross Strandkaien. I accepted.

As we entered the main mess hall, several customers said hello to me when we passed their tables. Some asked me when the B Band would hold its next gig. "In four days," I answered. That would be Saturday, 23 September, as Werner Boes had told us.

Until recently, a number of naval women service members had acted as waitresses to serve luncheon, coffee and cake in the afternoon, and dinner later in the day. That had been changed. They were needed somewhere else, we had been told, and they had been replaced by female personnel of the German Red Cross.

We had picked up a couple of menus at the door. After a few minutes, one girl came over to take the order. She was somewhat stout, but a good waitress who could pile up plates along her forearm better than I had ever learned. She originally came from Munich and had worked before her voluntary service with the Red Cross at the Hofbraeuhaus. Those waitresses were used to carrying four or even five one-liter steins filled with beer in each hand. Some of the elderly ones looked so strong-armed that you would not like to run into them in a dark alley.

It is only an eight-minute walk from the center of Nedre Strandgate, where the *Marineheim* was located at the time, to what is now called Haakon VII Gate, where we had our naval headquarters building, only about thirty steps southwest of the famous Stavanger Cathedral.

I put on my most ordinary air of self-satisfaction, quite happy with the way things were going, and walked into the main reception office, as if I had left a few minutes ago. The chap who had replaced me only recently when I was transferred to the secret department was busy making an entry in a waste-book. "Take a seat," he said, without looking up. "I will be with you in a minute."

That was not the procedure of greeting visitors according to the book. The person in front of him could have been an officer, in which case he was expected to jump up like having fire under his seat and salute.

When he did look up, he let out a big yell. "It's Sigy. I don't believe my eyes," he shouted. The three office doors along the wall opened simultaneously. Two guys who were sorting messages in the side room tumbled out like drunken sailors. Captain Seidel, having been attached to Mayer-Pantin to replace Captain Baer, after the latter's untimely death in August, stood in the doorway inquiring about the noise. And the three paper shufflers in the secret department streamed out and started shaking my hand vigorously. "Call the adjutant," the sergeant ordered to nobody in particular, "and tell him, we have an unlikely visitor."

Eberhart Wunderlich's office was right across the entrance hall from where we were. While this greeting ceremony was going on, we had left the door open. The noise must have swept like fire through the building. Everybody seemed to have vacated his office. They kept coming from all directions, even from the top secret department, which was never supposed to be left unguarded. Members of the Resistance could have had a field day, sweeping about the building and collecting classified information.

Wunderlich broke through the crowd while all my pals started asking questions at once! "I will do the debriefing," Wunderlich said jokingly. Then he shook hands with the ghost.

Once in his office, I gave him a rundown of the event. By now I could repeat it by heart to anybody who wanted to hear it. As soon as I was finished, he pressed a button at his desk. In seconds, the sergeant responsible for organizing the paper flow at headquarters knocked and came in. He saluted and gave me a nod.

"Have we started preparing another copy of the sensitive GKDOS papers 119?" he asked.

"We had started on them, sir," was the reply, "but I told the boys to put everything on hold when I heard about Born's unexpected return." It sounded like he was disappointed about the change of events and that I had turned into a nuisance.

"Good," Wunderlich commented. "Put the stuff through the shredder," he ordered. "Not the originals, of course," he added on second thought, dubious whether his first order had been understood. Anything was possible unless instructions were absolutely clear. The sergeant was dismissed.

"Before you go," Wunderlich said, "I have a question and a comment to make. Why were we not notified by Commander Lehner that he received the documents after all?"

"Herr Kapitaenleutnant," I replied, "I asked him not to send any cables. I wanted to surprise you here, for better or for worse. After all, how many times can one be dead and then resurrected?" I knew I could get away with that kind of talk without him taking offense. Besides, once one had survived danger like I had, everything else that happens later seems to be easier to bear. The Germans call this kind of an approach, a "kiss my arse mood." The progressive next step to that is the "devil-may-care attitude." It helps to build confidence.

"Your humor is not always in good taste," he retorted, "but you are partially right. This is my first encounter with a ghost. May it be the last!" He continued, "Now to my comment. Your reappearance causes another problem." I somehow sensed he was getting back at me for my staged smart aleck approach.

Drawing a file closer to his chest, he lifted and opened it. I could clearly see the type, "Able Seaman Siegfried Born, NHQ Courier (temporary), Marching Papers, 17.09.44."

"It states here you had orders to board minesweeper number 214. Against these orders you chose to board 456 instead. That is insubordination and punishable by court-martialing."

I felt as if all winds had suddenly left my sails. Now what? He couldn't be serious! I came miraculously through this disaster with my skin and earlobes intact, only to spend some time behind bars, or worse? "But Lieutenant Commander . . ." I started to stammer.

He cut me off. "Not another word," he said firmly, "there is no excuse for anybody to disregard orders." He pressed the call button for the sergeant again. Now my heart started pumping like crazy, and my armpits got wet. Could I possibly have misjudged the man for almost three years?

The sergeant reappeared. "I have here in my hand," Wunderlich began, "Born's marching papers from last Sunday." He handed the folder to the sergeant. "Look on page three and read aloud what it says under boarding." The sergeant read, "Born is under orders to proceed at an appropriate time to Stavanger Harbor and report with documents securely placed in the briefcase tied to his wrist (left or right) and locked, to the present commander of minesweeper number 214 no later than 2245 hours of above date."

"Stop!" Wunderlich commanded. "Somebody in the special assignment department has made a mistake that could have had bad consequences for Born here. Correct this immediately from minesweeper number 214 to 456."

A big rock fell off my shoulders before the sergeant had closed the door behind himself. Wunderlich turned to me and said, "Got you there for a moment, didn't I?" He sure had!

After my ill-fated first trip as courier on my birthday, the seventeenth, I made six more trips, all by boat, one each to Skudeneshavn on the isle of Karmøy, and Leirvik on the isle of Stord, and two voyages each to Haugesund and Bergen, headquarters of Admiral Von Schrader.

On the twenty-eighth, the newly sworn-in courier arrived from Germany. I introduced him to the northern courier route on the following day and resumed my duties at the secret department the second of October.

One of the first pieces of mail I opened on that Monday, classified as secret and confidential, was an order directed to all military units of the armed forces. I read the text with interest, but also understandably with some personal consternation. "Report until 10 October 1944, all English-speaking officers and soldiers available for special missions. These are to be directed to Friedenthal, near Berlin, in view of their incorporation in the commando units of Lieutenant-Colonel Otto Skorzeny."

On the lower left-hand side of the page was an explanation for the unit commander. Skorzeny had received yet another tricky assignment from Hitler. The code for it was *Operation Greif* (Operation Grab). Its goal was to cause confusion behind enemy lines of the invasion forces in western Europe. They would be trained in American and British behavior, including the use of slang, the way cigarette packs are opened and cigarettes shaken out of a pack, and a host of other various typical behavior patterns. They would be wearing Allied uniforms and operate behind enemy lines. Some of them would ride captured American and British tanks and jeeps, and redirect Allied advancing troops in wrong directions, either directly or by turning road signs around. No escapade would be too dangerous.

Even though Allied Intelligence did get hold of a copy of this directive within hours, as I saw in MI-Six files after the war, these German contingents caused, as planned, a lot of confusion for quite some time, to the chagrin of the invaders! At one point in time, rumors had it behind Allied lines that Skorzeny would try to capture Eisenhower right from under their noses. That never entered the plan, but had Skorzeny tried, the devil of a fellow, I suggest he would have succeeded.

When I studied the document, my apprehension rose, knowing I had to pass it on to Mayer-Pantin. If I was chosen to be sent, I certainly would be in hot soup. Sure, the assignment would be adventurous, but there was more involved here than ordinary wartime danger. This was a real suicide mission. Since wearing enemy uniforms was strictly against the Geneva Agreement, caught in the act, one could be shot on sight as a spy. This was not an engaging thought!

Having sorted out all incoming mail for the department, I asked the department head for permission to personally forward the interdepartmental folder to Wunderlich. He agreed without asking any questions.

I had put the new directive on top of the pile, when I handed it to the commandant's aide-de-camp. He took one glance, the speed reader he was, then looked at me with the usual twinkle in his eye. "What about it? Would you like to try something different?" he queried. "You like to live dangerously."

"I am not exactly weary of life, Herr Kapitaenleutnant," I retorted. "My goal is to survive this rotten war. Besides, I only speak little English, not enough for Skorzeny, I am sure."

"That's not what your file says," he countered. Then he put on his smile. "Don't worry," he carried on, "we need you here. You are not available for any other special missions, except our own here." He quickly had found the key word for an exit.

During the week of 9 October, one man from the convoy guidance department took ill and was scheduled for surgery. I was to replace him until further notice.

The department was operated by three men who divided the twenty-four hours per day, seven days per week service. My roommate, Victor Boschetto, was one of the three. When he heard about my assignment, he first started complaining. Now he would not only have to put up with me at the residence but also at work. Then he realized he had miscalculated the situation badly. Whenever he was on duty, I and the third man would be off and on rotation, vice versa.

"What a relief," he commented. "I'll see you less often than ever." We always kidded each other. In reality, we never got into each other's way and harmonized well, like good brothers.

The Phony Invasion

The convoy guidance service operated independently from our naval headquarters communication center. They had their own navy "cryptosystem" for coding and decoding incoming and outgoing messages. Our purpose was to keep close tap on the movement of naval convoys between Flekkefjord to the south and Haugesund to the north of Stavanger.

Our office was situated on the second floor to the rear and to the southwest end of the headquarters building. When looking out the window, we had a vantage view of the beautiful downtown pond then called Bredevannet, now renamed Breiavatnet. When on the afternoon shift, I caught myself many times dreaming of peace and tranquillity by taking in that scenery while the music of Edward Grieg from the radio would underline the picture.

On the right-hand wall when entering the room, a huge situation map depicting the coastal area between Haugesung and Flekkefjord, displayed a number of pinned-on flags, each one representing a moving vessel. The entire navigational theater was divided into thirty-centimeter squares, and subdivided again by five-centimeter squares. The large squares bore letters; the small squares numbers.

Each convoy leader reported the changing positions of the convoy every half-hour by referring to the respective letters and numbers. Convoys and ships names, as well as predetermined key words, were coded. Code changes took place irregularly throughout a ten-day period.

There was a sizable desk, large enough to spread out other navigational charts. One conference-call-type telephone connected the office with all coastal antiaircraft batteries and telescopic sub-lookouts. Whenever a message was sent by one of these posts, all phones would ring and everybody listened to the message.

Two more telephones rested side by side, one to make regular city or long-distance calls; the other had a direct line to the navigational officer on call. That standby task was rotated weekly among the commandant's officer corps members. Unusual messages or situations had to be reported to that officer at our own discretion.

There was a small filing cabinet containing operation details which were on hold for one reason or other. A wall safe behind a sailing ship oil painting on the opposite wall from the situation map was used for retaining information for transfer to the secret registration department the following day. It also contained our master code book, code changes, key ciphers, and key letters to be used by those authorized.

What I liked best about the place was a marvelous swivel chair stationed right beside our regular duty chair. The latter we used for performing our administrative work, while the swivel chair came particularly handy during the longest shift within the three-day cycle, from 1800 hours right through till 0800 hours the next morning.

Usually around 0200 hours incoming messages would trickle or almost phase out. I would replace the ordinary office chair with the swivel chair, turn the three-way lamp on low, put my feet on the edge of the desk, in un-German fashion, and lean back with a newspaper over my face. This was a great way to relax and snooze off intermittently until about 0600 hours, when the lines got busy again.

Nothing happened out of the ordinary during the first week. The convoys traced their assigned routes and distance away from the coast. Several British planes were sighted, but they maintained a respectable distance. One thing was quite obvious, though. Whenever a convoy left Stavanger, it would not take long to be under British observation. This close monitoring of our convoys had started in October 1943. Nobody had any other sensible explanation for this observance than the Resistance reporting our navigational moves. I was about to find out later that a source not counted on had a hand in the game.

During the second week, while I covered the afternoon shift from 1200 to 1800 hours, Wunderlich visited me, inquiring how I was doing. I thanked him for this easy assignment and added I could do this for the remainder of the war.

"Always the same wisecracker," he commented. "No deal. As soon as the other chap reappears, you will be out of here. This is no challenge for you. Remember, you are scheduled for service at the top secret department. We need you soon."

He left me with the suggestion that if a tricky situation should occur, to call him personally. On my following night shift I had that opportunity. I had just assumed my favorite relaxing position after an uneventful evening. Everything seemed to be in perfect order. Suddenly, the conference-call telephone rang. Picking it up without delay, I listened to the excited voice of a battery observer reporting the sighting of two submarines and a large convoy on the horizon, which was not supposed to be there. He had barely finished his statement when I distinctly heard artillery fire booming. Then the voice of an observer from a neighboring battery shouted something about an impending invasion of the coast.

I horned in with my code, advising that the messages would be immediately forwarded to highest authority and directed them to standby for further instructions.

It just so happened that Lieutenant Marquart was not only responsible for all battery operations in the vicinity, but also served as standby navigational officer during that week.

The reports sounded serious enough to awaken Mayer-Pantin, but I decided against that. Instead I called Wunderlich. He arrived within eight minutes. "I can't get hold of Marquart," he puffed, somewhat out of breath. They roomed together with two other officers on Molle Gata, where I had shot the rats nine weeks before.

"I have an idea where he is, Herr Kapitaenleutnant," I volunteered. Consulting my address booklet, I called Sonja, Marquart's girlfriend. She answered immediately.

"Is Dietrich with you?" I asked, not wanting to lose time.

She recognized my voice. "Yes, Sigy, he is."

"Then get him on the double to the phone. Kapitaenleutnant Wunderlich wants to talk to him." I handed the receiver to Wunderlich.

"Damn, Dietrich! The devil is loose here. Put on your pants and rush over to headquarters."

"I should have guessed where he was," Wunderlich commented. He was visibly annoyed. "I wish he had nearly as much in his brain as he has in his pants." I pretended not to have heard; but I had to hold my breath a bit not to burst out laughing.

After Wunderlich investigated closer, he said to me, "Your hunch was right not to call Mayer-Pantin. Now we can play down the whole episode as a simple error in judgment. This was a false alarm, luckily enough." Two convoys had accidentally come closer to the coast than coastal defense expected, kind of a misunderstanding in itself. There was no pending invasion. The two sighted submarines were our own. We could breathe normally again. In the future, though, Marquart did not leave his residence when on call.

Gekados—Top Secret

This department served as the administrative arm of the regional naval intelligence service. Its prime function was to identify the importance of incoming coded and uncoded messages, then comments and recommendations were passed on to selected individuals on a need-to-know basis.

Messages that contained recommendations by the area commandant for possible action were usually sealed and sent by messengers who carried out courier services. Internal documents were distributed personally by the Gekados administrative assistant, who handled the respective files.

Incoming reports were categorized. Those without specific markings had to be screened by us to determine who would have access. Others were plainly marked *Einschraenkend fuer K.O.* (restricted to C.O., or Commanding Officer). Some were marked *Nur fuer* (eyes only), followed by the name and rank of the receiver.

The screening of documents was done by two men who operated the department as a tandem. Each would consult with the other for document highlighting and to determine which staff officer should be informed of the content matter.

A message decoder was used for decoding messages, all of which arrived sealed. The decoder system itself was somewhat more sophisticated than the one used at the convoy guidance department. Messages sent by our commandant to naval bases or other military units were coded to print by us. Procedures entailed the use of an encoder, then teletyping by our centralized communication department. The whole process may sound a bit more complicated than it was, but actually worked quite satisfactorily. Roughly translated, we called it our naval "cryptosystem."

When assigned to Gekados at the beginning of November, after my security clearance was upgraded to the highest level of secrecy and security, my pay tripled. I was now going to carry out duties which normally would be performed by a midshipman, an officer candidate. That was O.K. with me. I received my silver beam again, which I had worn when acting as chief steward at the casino. Taking on more responsibility than usual sometimes does pay off. I was quite pleased with myself, having become part of headquarters, a CDM (central decision maker). This new assignment particularly promised to be most interesting.

The chap I was going to replace had received his transfer to Kiel, Germany, main naval communication center. He had three days for my orientation to familiarize me with general procedures of operation. It only took two days. I had made extensive notes during his training sessions, but was told they must not leave the premises.

On the third day, I was free to rummage around. The first thing I did was look for some files dealing with the two Resistance movements in Denmark. They had caused so many problems in July of last year when I returned from my annual furlough in Germany while passing through Denmark.

The file drawer D-E-F was more than half full of documents marked "D" for Denmark. Sure enough, there were all reports in order of occurrence. At the beginning of the first file, a brief explanation was made describing the two major Resistance organizations, referred to as the Danish Underground. There was a personal profile on the leader of BOPA (*Borgerlige Partisaner*, or middle-class partisans), Holger Danske. Following was an equally detailed profile of David Sompolinski, a Danish Jew and the founder of the Lyngby Group, as well as a profile on the group's leader, Aage Bertelsen.

A summarized report in the form of a comment was attached, where the ingenuity of these groups in outsmarting and outmaneuvering the Gestapo and German counterintelligence was admitted. The two groups were also credited with being instrumental in the fact that in 1943, from a total of eight thousand Danish Jews residing in Denmark, only 472 had been captured! Escape routes from Denmark to Sweden, set up by the two organizations with the active participation and assistance of the Danish population as a whole, had made this possible.

Next appeared a list of arrests of ordinary citizens who had defied our authority. It included those I had read about in the newspapers while passing through Denmark at the time. I could not read all cases, but I counted sixty-nine incidents between June and December alone! They were all arrests for minor offenses, ranging from molesting a German soldier to urinating against a German signboard. Forty-six suspected members of the Underground had been detained during the same period of time, but only two could be confirmed due to some of our collaborators blowing the whistle on them.

Several summarized reports followed:

A German named Duckwitz came from Germany to Denmark in 1928 to operate the German Kaiser's kaffee branches in Copenhagen, on behalf of the coffee chain stores in Germany. After the invasion, he was posted in the German embassy. He was considered too soft with the Danes, short of accusing the man of being a sympathizer. In July/August 1943, General Von Hannecken was appointed German military commander in Denmark. He had submitted a few apologetic self-accusing reports regarding the Danish Resistance. One of his statements was, "Even if one thinks one has these rascals, they still manage to slip through one's fingers."

Hand Hedtoft was known as the leader of the outlawed social democratic party and suspected of coordinating acts of sabotage. He later became Prime Minister. Toldstrup was another Resistance leader. It was suspected (correctly) that his primary concern was with air drops of weapons, ammunition, explosive devices and, occasionally, secret agents who had been trained in England. Speculation was that his headquarters were somewhere in Copenhagen. (That was incorrect. Instead he maintained his headquarters for a long time in Aalborg.)

August 1943 proved to be a busy month. Strikes broke out in the shipyards of Copenhagen and Odense. The German high command withdrew the Danish pro-Nazi Schalburg Corps from the Russian Front–traitors in the eyes of Danes–to deal with their countrymen. This developed into a general strike. At one point in time, a German officer fired on the crowd, and was beaten to death. The situation became progressively nastier.

Finally, in the wee hours of Sunday, 29 August, a state of emergency was declared. German soldiers were posted on all government buildings, rendering the Danish government impotent. Prominent Danes and high-ranking officers of the army and the navy were taken hostage.

By 1944, the situation had deteriorated so much that, in North Juitland, for instance, few German trains moved through undamaged.

In February, General Lindemann became the commanding officer of all German forces in Denmark. His mandate was to better utilize German military power and more effectively counteract terrorist acts. It turned out to be an impossible task!

On 6 June 1944, the BOPA organization successfully sabotaged the Globus Factory located outside Copenhagen. It had produced V-One and V-Two flying bombs used on Britain.

Finally, on Sunday, 2 July 1944, martial law was declared in Copenhagen. Later on, it spread to other large communities.

I had read enough for the time being, and replaced the folder in the file drawer and went for luncheon.

After luncheon, I picked up where I had left off. Curiosity got the better of me. I wanted to find out what really happened out there, rather than swallowing what we were formally told.

Running over the pages of several files, two items caught my particular attention. One was a brief assessment report on the Danish Underground. The other was titled *Die Bohr Affaere* (the Bohr Affair).

The Danish Underground

1. Composition: Danish Nationals.

2. Identification: Hardcore Underground members, loyal to the king of Denmark. Activity is concentrated on harassing German occupying forces, and sabotage and assassination of identifiable members of SS, Gestapo and other key personnel, including officers well-known for their lack of sensitivity toward the Danish population. (It sounded to me as if it were directly copied from an Underground manual.)

3. Numerical strength: Not known. Could be negligible. But their efforts are most effective because of fanatical leadership and widespread collaboration by ordinary Danes.

4. Force capability: Almost unlimited; operations are covert. Members well-trained in sabotage activities and guerrilla warfare. Foot troops and some naval experts involved. Heavily supplied by British MI-Six.

5. Air Force potential: Nil

6. Basic capability units: Quite able to identify German weaknesses based on classified information made available by their own and British intelligence sources. Often successful in counteracting our own administrative decisions and moves. Highly active and alert. Capable of carrying out sufficient acts of sabotage and assassinations to intimidate German effectiveness. Assisted by a number of Danish citizens who occupy influential positions in government, industry and agriculture. Greatly supported by Allied Intelligence, particularly British MI-Five, MI-Six, and American OSS.

7. Leaders of BOPA and the Lyngby Group believed to be making more crucial decisions with advice from Allied Intelligence.

8. Overall Objective: To cause German occupying forces constant hardship, undermine German morale, and eventually contribute to the downfall of the Third Reich.

On the bottom of the page was a brief comment: Occupying forces must be prepared to take counteraction and increase overall vigilance!

The document was dated 21 September 1944, and signed by General Lindemann himself.

What we had in our Gekados files under "the Bohr Affair" told only part of the story. Fortunately, I was able to compare this case after the war with information unavailable to us at the time but gathered by American OSS and British intelligence agents. For the sake of continuity and providing a more detailed picture, I have combined all materials:

Professor Dr. Niels Bohr was well-known in international scientists circles, but we knew very little about him. His brother, the famous mathematician Harold Bohr, was known to us. We almost dismissed Niels Bohr as a strange, absent-minded, if not confused professor, who tinkered around at Jacobsen House in Copenhagen, which the scientific foundation of Carlsberg Brewery had provided for him. He seemed to like reading detective stories and took an active interest in world politics. Otherwise, we did not comprehend his scientific formulas, nor did we see the significance of his ten-million-volt cyclotron. In hindsight, we far underestimated his brilliance and did not observe any of his achievements. The report called it great lack of foresight on our part, and was labeled as frustration point number one.

In July 1943, a number of circumstances too voluminous to mention here, brought the real value of Professor Bohr to the attention of the German foreign office.

The following month, a special agent of the Gestapo with the code name Regnif (finger spelled backward; same word in German and English) was flown to Copenhagen with the order to formally arrest Niels Bohr. Regnif must have been a typically thorough German, risking nothing without including everything in his calculations.

Since he knew as much as zero about physics and was told that Bohr now specialized in nuclear physics, he decided to request the assistance of a Nazi nuclear scientist. When interrogated later about this, he stated, "I wanted to be sure that Dr. Bohr would be asked questions of a scientific nature, including those pertaining to nuclear physics. I did not want him to have the better of me."

That led to a second point of frustration. By the time the requested Nazi scientist was available in October 1943, Niels Bohr was not available anymore. He seemed to have simply vanished into thin air!

Regnif's punishment for this terrible blunder was not mentioned. But the Gekados file closed with self-condemning comments regarding the failure to apprehend Dr. Bohr. It ended with a lecture to field operators for improving future tasks of this kind.

It often happens in the field of science that numerous scientists in different countries are working on similar projects, sometimes unaware of doing so, and how close they are in arriving at solutions to mutual problems.

In 1935 and 1938 respectively, the German science fiction writer Hans Dominick talked about atomic weight 500 and uranium 235. He came very close in his description of how the atom would be split. Readers like myself found his stories interesting but treated them as what they were, science fiction. Little did we know at the time how much food for thought Hans had provided German scientists, who further developed his theories and came very close to actually splitting the atom, but not close enough to develop the atomic bomb before the end of World War II.

MI-Six provided more specific information on Professor Bohr. Confined to the subject at hand, let me summarize:

The Allies were well aware of Dr. Bohr's intellect and expertise. Through British intermediaries, the US government invited him in 1942 to assist on a project in America. It was felt that specific information about the project did not have to be spelled out to Dr. Bohr, since he had many times in the past worked with almost every leading nuclear scientist in the world. The project in question later became known as the Manhattan Project, the development of the atomic bomb.

Bohr declined the invitation. First of all, he felt quite safe in Copenhagen—no wonder, since we practically ignored the man. Second, he would be more useful by continuing to keep an eye on our (German) scientific developments right on the spot. Thirdly, feedback from the Danish military attaché in Berlin clearly evaluated his reports as most useful. Last, but not least, in his unobtrusive way he lent a decisively efficient hand in enabling refugees to leave Denmark.

In October 1943, when our Gestapo began to arrest the eight thousand Jews living in Denmark—of which the Gestapo was able to capture only 472—the Allies became most concerned about Niels Bohr, even though they and the Resistance did not know about his forthcoming arrest by Special Agent Regnif. What caused the increased attention and anxiety was that Bohr either could be arrested because he had Jewish ancestors, or that he would be pressed into service for us.

On behalf of the US, Allied authorities sent Dr. Bohr a more urgent invitation, expressing their concern on his behalf and the possible consequences of disregarding their urgent appeal. This time he agreed without delay. While he destroyed and burned all incriminating documents and memoranda on movements of refugees, Dr. Linstrom-Lang, his friend and fellow scientist on his staff, planned to take Mrs. Bohr, their three sons, and their families to Sweden.

One of eight different escape routes was selected. It fell upon fisherman Christian Hansen to use his craft, which had only a small one-cylinder diesel engine, to carry out this task. He already had twice made successful trips with other Jewish refugees aboard.

The entire Bohr family, together with some other refugees, went aboard the *Soetjernen*. After an adventurous trip, including German patrol boats cruising close by, they eventually reached the middle of the sound, when a larger boat belonging to the Danish Resistance took over all passengers and brought them safely to Sweden.

Hansen, who had cursed at his boat's damn engine many times, nevertheless returned to Copenhagen rather proud that his boat had had such a distinguished passenger. His boat, whose name means the starlight in English, had not brought him any shame.

How to bring out Dr. Bohr from Sweden? On the surface, it was easy, but not so easy in practice. Stockholm airdrome was used, of course, by British aircraft as well as aircraft of the German Luftwaffe.

It was common practice for some time that a pair of Mosquito bombers would land in Stockholm every day and depart every night from Britain. A specially constructed seat in the bomb bay of each aircraft allowed two persons to be brought into or out of Sweden in that fashion.

After Dr. Bohr had settled a few urgent matters on his own in Sweden, he finally declared himself to be ready to be brought to Great Britain. The next evening he was stripped into a Mosquito bomb bay and flown to England. After several months, he agreed to be taken to the US, where he worked for about one and a half years on the atomic bomb project.

The man who had worked under our noses for three years and five months (and could have been of invaluable assistance to us) made a considerable contribution to enabling the US to finally defeat the Japanese.

The Norwegian Mind

Lars Hansen was our factotum at headquarters. He looked after minor building repairs, took charge of the late afternoon building cleaning crew, and occasionally helped with moving nonsensitive messages between departments. He was well-liked because of his great disposition. Nothing could rock him.

I had liked the man the moment I first met him. He was twelve years my senior, and developed into kind of a brotherly friend. I had met him the previous year when I occasionally accompanied Werner Boes to pick up a parcel full of music sheets. We had a few amiable conversations then, but more often after I became attached to headquarters.

Almost every day, and particularly during the afternoon hours, when things quieted down a bit, he would stroll in at the reception desk, or later at the secret department, to chat with me. We had exchanged many ideas and had made statements and comments, by which we knew fairly well what to expect from each other. Quite often the conversation would borderline on the political field, but mostly centered around human relations.

One day I expressed surprise to him when I had heard the audience at a local Norwegian cinema booing, screaming and shouting at Vidkun Quisling, whenever he appeared on the screen. (We had instated the man as the country's leader, after we occupied Norway.)

"Not too many of us care about this bugaboo, Sigy," he replied frankly. "You told me the other day why you did not join the Nazi party before you got drafted. I am telling you, we have only a small group of active Quislings in Norway. That man has betrayed us."

He watched me closely, but I pretended not to have heard the last remark. At least I knew where he stood, and I gave him a lot of credit for his outspokenness. It also was evident that he trusted me not to blow the whistle on him.

A factory was located on the south end of Stavanger which manufactured doorknobs, pommels for swords and uniform buttons for our forces and the Quisling Guard. It blew up early Saturday morning, 4 November, waking Victor and me. At first we thought an earth tremor had taken place, until we knew the cause.

The perpetrators must have used a lot of TNT. The entire building war destroyed, and the affect from the explosion could be felt twenty kilometers away. Within one hour, the regional army commander, who also functioned as city commandant, received instructions for MPs to cordon off five square kilometers around the block, and assemble all residents in a square nearby, which occasionally was used as a soccer field.

Next, the SD (*Sicherheitsdient*, or Security Service, a civilian police force) moved in to conduct initial interrogations of civilians right on the spot. All factory employees not residing in the cordoned off area were arrested at home and brought to the scene.

Nobody had heard or knew anything, of course. It drove the SD interrogators to frustration. "It would be better for everybody," the public was told, "if the culprit came forward. Otherwise, the Gestapo would take over soon and start shooting people at random until they have the information."

At that moment the city commandant retracted the remark with the courageous public statement, that nobody would shoot anybody under his nose, as he was the city commandant.

For no apparent reason, I did not sleep too well from Sunday to Monday. I rose earlier than usual and arrived at headquarters before 0800 hours. A sealed package was waiting for Gekados at the reception desk, my former domain. I picked it up, unlocked my office door, and opened the package.

It contained an updated situation report of recent Underground activities in Scandinavia, including the bombing of the only heavy-water plant in Northern Norway. The observation was made that the British would not have accomplished this feat without the active advice and assistance of the Resistance, which recently had become bolder in their attempt to make life more miserable for the occupiers.

Attached I found a list of names of suspected members of the Underground which were still at large but would be arrested if found. They were assumed to operate in or near the Stavanger region. The list was to be made available to field operatives of Marine Abwehr, naval counterintelligence service, for follow up.

I flew over the list a second time. Then I hit on two names that seemed familiar to me. At least the last names were. One was that of a dentist on Ny Olavskleiv, the other that of my barber on Erlands Gate. Could that be coincidence?

The dentist had one son and two daughters, all in their twenties. I had met the girls twice, as they were friendly with some officers living on Molle Gata. My barber was a fine gentleman, as far as I was concerned. I knew nothing about his family, but I liked the man.

Reading the report once and the list twice had taken me about fifteen minutes. Now I started to brood. A dilemma was facing me. I had to forward the report and the list to Commander Brinkman who, in turn, would have to notify our field operators about the list of suspects. I suddenly felt hot under the collar and opened the upper button of my uniform jacket. Drawn between duty and human consideration, I had to find a solution, if not at least a compromise, to this ballgame. Just not doing anything would not do. Inaction on my part would almost certainly condemn these people to death!

While we worked at our papers during the day, we usually kept our door open, as there was no exhaust system and the office was kind of boxed in in the center of the ground floor, void of any windows. The air got thick at times, particularly when my partner smoked his Briar pipe.

I looked up. Lars Hansen had appeared in the door frame. "Can I come in?" he inquired. He acted timid, seeming to have lost his cool, and visibly shaken. "Have you heard about the factory?" he asked, totally unnecessarily.

"Not only have I heard about it, I also heard it," I retorted. Then I added in exaggeration, "It almost threw me out of bed. What are you people trying to prove? Could you not find a more valuable target to blow up, like this building, for instance?" I tried some grim humor.

Lars had a rather strange look on his face, as if his thoughts were somewhere else. He was clearly worried. One of his cousins had worked at that factory and had been questioned vigorously over the weekend. Did I think there would be more arrests because of this incident?

"What I think does not matter, Lars," I commented. "But you can bet your bottom kroner that the Gestapo will continue digging and drilling until they find somebody who can be charged with this shenanigan. And you know, they are not easier with their interrogation methods than the SS, who would have been called into the act if that factory would have made actual war material."

I could not tell him anything else, but an idea struck me. Maybe I could help indirectly without feeling too bad about it one way or another. I put the report and the list in my desk drawer and got up. My colleague had not yet arrived.

"Do me a favor, Lars," said I. "My pal is not here yet. Mind the store for a few minutes; I have to step out." Our eyes met. He showed a glance of anticipation. I tried to be casual. "Make sure nobody gets in here," I ordered, walked out and closed the door behind me.

When I returned, Lars reported, "Nobody came, the phone didn't ring either." The tone of his voice sounded relieved. I wondered whether he had had a peek in the desk drawer.

A couple of days later we were told a visitor from the German high command would hold an inspection on Friday at 1500 hours in the front yard of the headquarters building. Everybody had to attend, except the sergeant-at-arms who would hold down the fort.

Was this another attempt to further reduce the occupying forces in Norway, I speculated. In March of that year, we had been decimated from almost five hundred thousand personnel to slightly over three hundred thousand.

My concern was not justified. The visitor gave us a summarized version of our military efforts at both major fronts. He could have been in public relations. The few desperate counterattacks we had managed to launch in the West were successful frontal offensives. In cases where we had to retreat in haste, he used the phrase "regroup to restrengthen." He used quite clever language, almost reversing our actual desperate military situation in the minds of those who still believed in final victory.

Toward the end of his address he praised the loyalty with which our allies were fighting side by side with our troops. By "allies" he referred to troops from countries such as

Yugoslavia, Romania, Czechoslovakia and particularly Hungary, who were valiantly fighting with us. With that, his pep talk ended.

The following Monday, 13 November, we received a special report admitting that several thousand Hungarian troop formations, after having murdered their officers, deserted to the Soviet side. This was only one of a number of reports which directly contradicted the official portrayal of our war propaganda and came as no surprise to me, the skeptic. We were briefed and reminded one day later, to be on the lookout. Any Norwegian should be considered a potential enemy.

For several days in the middle of November, I had a foreboding that something unprecedented or even bizarre would happen soon. I could not explain my feeling, and after a week or so it vanished. "False alarm," I thought, whatever it was. I was only partially correct, though. My great anxiety during that time had had a base, as time would tell.

What I did not know then was that the Western Allies had gotten wind of the purpose and objective of the inspection tour along the Norwegian coast last August. The possibility of seriously considering Norway's use as Hitler's last fortress had to be discussed.

In September and October, a series of situation meetings were held in London. Options open to the Allies for taking positive steps were deliberated. By the beginning of November, a tentative target date for an Allied invasion of Norway was set for Sunday, 19 November.

Two days prior to that date at the eleventh hour, so to say, Mr. Lange, Norway's foreign minister in exile, talked the Allies out of an invasion, backed by a substantial group of like-minded politicians and military experts.

Lange was convinced that Hitler would not flee to Norway but would remain in Berlin. He emphasized with conviction and logic that an unnecessary invasion would likely cost ten thousands of lives: those of the invaders, the defenders and the Norwegian population.

The pending invasion never took place.

Lord How How

A flyer went around early in December announcing that William Joyce, better know as Lord How How, would hold an address at the theater off Kirkegata on the fourteenth. I had often heard him making inflammatory statements against Britain at the Bremen broadcasting station. Now I could see him in person. Even though the man was a charlatan in my book, I was curious enough to buy a couple of tickets for Victor and myself from Commander Brinkman, who would also attend the lecture.

Victor and I went quite early; one hour early, in fact. As soon as we had entered Kirkegata we encountered a swarm of Gestapo agents and SS men. Against the moonlit sky, several dark shadows could be seen crouching on rooftops all around, machine guns poised. I knew the reason for this extra-tight security: We had received a tip from one of our snitches that an attempt on the life of Joyce would be made. His coming to Stavanger had been made public by placing advertisements on pillars all over town.

We had to produce our IDs six times until we eventually arrived at the half-moon shaped plaza in front of the theater. We joined the milling crowd which was mostly military but also contained a considerable number of civilians, more than I had anticipated. The speech was scheduled for 2000 hours. The voice over the public address system informed us that no one was allowed to enter the theater before the guest speaker arrived.

At 1940 hours, a chain of cars came through the small lane leading to the plaza. They were all black limousines, the first two carrying the standard flag of the SS. I counted seven vehicles. Six SS men peeled themselves out of the first car. They were joined by five civilians with the typical black leather coats, apparently Gestapo agents, who had vacated the first car of the convoy. They all entered the theater building. I assumed they would comb through the building with a fine-tooth comb. Five minutes went by. Then four SS men reappeared, posting themselves left and right of the entrance.

After having glanced at the buildings nearby, one of them gave sort of a signal. The passengers of the second, third, fifth and sixth car emerged. They quickly formed two half-circles around the fourth car, whose doors opened. Five civilians came into sight. Four of them kept the fifth person in their midst, a rather slim man with dark features. It was the guest speaker.

He was hurriedly ushered into the building. Following another five minutes of waiting, we were admitted, but again screened at the door; military personnel by the SS, civilians by the Gestapo.

Victor and I had a couple of seats close to the center of the third row from the front. It was an opportunity to see William Joyce's gestures, together with hearing his voice which had become relatively familiar to me over the years.

Having taken my seat barely ten minutes, I looked over my shoulder and noticed the theater filled to capacity. It had about two thousand seats at the time and equally served for theater performances and the showing of feature films.

Nowadays, besides owning several movie houses, Stavangerians enjoy theater productions and stage shows in its *teatert* on Teaterveien downtown. Concerts of various nature are held at the Stavanger Konserthus, located in Bjergsted Park close to the old Stavanger town.

At three minutes past the hour the curtain went up. Although Joyce had been formally invited by the local office of Goebbels' propaganda ministry, the city commandant acted as host. Since Joyce could not converse in German, only those understanding English had been admitted as members of the audience.

The commandant stepped forward to the speaker's desk which had been set up in the center-front part of the stage. He provided a brief background of Joyce, explaining the man had become disillusioned with the British government, and had joined the ranks of German national socialists. During the next hour or so, the audience would find interest in what Joyce would have to say. The announcer did not mention anything about a question and answer period.

Joyce came on stage receiving polite applause from the spectators. The two men shook hands. Joyce took his stand behind the lectern and the city commander withdrew. After some initial hesitation, Joyce launched into a prolonged tirade and mix of bitter and blunt denunciation of the Allies. He had nothing but praise for the "determined Germany" for counteracting the ruse and schemes of international Jewry and other diverse elements shunning the light.

It could well have been one of Hitler's or Goebbels' denunciations except for the fact that the English language was used. He did not use any notes, and it occurred to me that he well may have followed the same pattern of speech many times before.

His propaganda included "evidence" that Germany was not about to give up her fight. He repeated his adopted master's claim of miraculous weapons that would yet turn war events into our favor and assure final victory. I had the distinct impression that he actually believed what he wanted us to believe.

The whole lecture more or less turned out to be a pep talk with upbeat exaggerations designed to revive a dying body. He closed his presentation with a couple of statements, unbelievably simplistic and even silly:

"In conclusion, then, ladies and gentlemen, members of the German armed forces, accept my absolute assurance and conviction," he said, "very soon I will have the satisfaction of returning to England (he did not say Great Britain), heading large party contingents of national socialists, freeing my country from the yoke of suppression. We shall be victorious. Heil Hitler!"

Clearly he had the majority of the audience in a spell and they jumped to their feet and applauded vigorously. Lord How How took a few bows, then left the stage.

I had kind of hoped a question period would follow. Maybe I could corner him behind the stage and raise a few questions, was my wishful thinking. Asking Victor to wait for me, I rushed forward, passing the few rows that lay ahead and mounted several steps to the side of the stage, only to almost stumble into the arms of an SS man.

"What do you want here?" he demanded belligerently, while his hand moved to his holster.

When I told him what I had in mind, he looked at me as if I had arrived from Mars. "You must be a bit cracked up. Mr. Joyce does not grant interviews. Scram, but fast!"

Well, at least I had seen the man once in person. Since Victor and I were convinced the war would soon be over, I knew I had seen Joyce for the first and last time. On Thursday, 3 January 1946, William Joyce, better known as Lord How How, was executed for treason in London.

WITHDRAWAL TO BJERGSTED PARK

The Beginning Of The End

Since the factory was blown up, security was tightened. Even at naval headquarters, which was located in a so-far peaceful area, additional night guards were introduced. Any elements that could be hostile to us had to be kept at arm's length. Again, we were reminded that Norwegians were natural enemies of our occupying troops. Those on watch were instructed to shoot without hesitation if foul play were suspected. Easier said than done. That order proved to be disastrous.

Identifying code words were changed daily, rather than twice weekly as before. Nothing wrong with that in itself. Naval personnel on guard after 1800 hours would request the current identifying code word from anybody, who approached the main entrance way to the headquarters building.

One day shortly before Christmas a guard saw a shadow of a figure coming in his direction. It was about fifteen minutes to midnight. "Code word!" the guard demanded, poising his rifle in the path of the stranger. The oncomer responded with a code word that had been obsolete for two days. It had been changed twice.

Later on, the guard testified he gave a warning shot over the head of the approaching silhouette. He also claimed to have picked out a foreign accent in the voice of the stranger. In any case, the intended warning shot drilled itself into the victim's skull, causing instant death.

The deceased was a petty officer from a submarine. The man had the mandate to contact naval headquarters on behalf of his commander in a matter of some urgency. However, the poor man had been given an outdated code word by the harbor police, resulting in an unfortunate accident.

On Friday, 28 December, Commodore Mayer-Pantin announced that he and his aide, Lieutenant Commander Wunderlich, had received their transfer papers to Germany. A new commandant would take over the regional command at the beginning of the New Year. It hit us like a shock wave. We knew the war was really winding down and we had hoped that our team would be kept intact to the end.

The new man arrived with his aide on Wednesday, 3 January. He was the antithesis of Mayer-Pantin, declaring himself to be a loyal follower of Hitler's ideology. To prove a point, he had brought with him, as his aide-de-camp, a national socialistic leading officer. From now on, the wind would be blowing from another direction.

When discussing this change with Victor in the evening, after we knew what the new score would be, he said, "Don't worry, Sigy. Look at it from the positive side. It's a darn good thing this pair was not sent to us earlier. At this stage of the game, they cannot do anymore harm. If they are not absolutely stupid, they will step rather quietly. The war is going to end in two to three months anyway."

My colleague from the top secret department and I were given the priority task of singling out and presenting all reports which had anything to do with activities of the Norwegian Underground. By Friday noon, 5 January, the task was completed. The commandant's desk was covered with piles of files.

I must say, it did not take him long to make a decision. He had painfully studied all reports over the weekend at his residence. Early Monday morning, he called a special meeting of all officers reporting to headquarters. The situation room, where the meeting was about to be held, allowed standing room only for the forty-six officers. My pal and I were called in as resource persons, since we were most familiar with the subject at hand. We had acquired a deep knowledge of each report's content and would be called upon to answer some questions from the floor.

The main purpose of the meeting was to acquaint everybody with the comparative sensitivity of different post locations and decide which of these should either be relocated or additionally fortified against any possible attacks.

Twenty-four hours after the situation briefing a decision was made. Artillery installations along the coast between Haugesund and Flekkefjord would remain untouched, with exception of a few outpost bases. The Stabs and Wachkompanie would have more guards and sentries. The company also would be equipped with high-voltage electric fences to keep out unwanted visitors.

Within Stavanger, there would be two major changes. Naval headquarters would be relocated to the northern end of town in Bjergsted Park, a somewhat elevated terrain and easier to protect than the downtown building we occupied now. The naval officers mess on Ny Olavskleiv was to be closed as soon as the alternative mess was operational in Bjergsted Park. That is where I would come in. I thought, "Yet another assignment. Now I have to start a new operation practically from scratch."

It sounds easy to move from point A to point B, but it seldom is. To dismantle, disconnect, rebuild and reconnect all the equipment belonging to centralized communications was a monumental task in itself. But since we had practically unlimited manpower available from the Kompanie, it worked quite well. Nevertheless, it did take two full days to complete the move.

Having a look at the house in Bjergsted Park designated to become the new officers casino, I was certain that a maximum of only about twenty officers could be accommodated for meal service. That was not the sole problem. Meals had to be prepared off the premises, but I had sufficient people to assist me with solving some of the problems. It took only a few days to work out the logistics. Put a few good brains together and almost anything can be overcome.

By the eighteenth, everything ran like a clock, although I had picked the shorter end of the stick. Sure, I had been replaced at the top secret department to put my full attention to the casino, but for a while I got stuck with terrible hours of duty.

I had to rise at 0615 hours to prepare for breakfast service. Luncheon was served between 1200 and 1330 hours; dinner from 1800-1930 hours. In between service, I assisted in keeping the premises in shape. And that went on seven days a week.

By the end of the month I felt as if my eyes were popping out of their sockets from lack of sleep. I took all the courage I had, and that was not much in the first place, and presented my problem to the Nazi adjutant. To my astonishment, he responded well. "You should have come to us earlier with your request for relief. We have to change this." He did. The one hundred plus hours per week would be divided by two.

There was yet another annoying problem for everybody. Nearby at Sandviga, located at the northwestern part off Strandkeien, almost adjacent to the Stavanger *dampkipselskap* was a fish-processing plant. The overpowering twenty-four-hour stench of fish smell penetrated everything.

On the second day after having taken residence at the park, we decided to seal off all windows. But not even this eased the foul smell. If anything, it made matters worse, because we now came close to choking on the combined fish and human body stink. Before the end of one week, some chaps nearly blacked out from a lack of oxygen. The sealing strips were removed, and after a while it became somewhat better, or at least it seemed that way. I guess the human nose can endure just as well as the body as a whole.

When these numerous reorganizations took place, the B Band had to be dissolved. There was no chance for us to get together and keep the troops entertained. The main reason for giving up on that effort was the fact that Kvitsøy, our main listening post off Stavanger, had suffered a considerable manpower loss due to the beefing up of surrounding bases. It felt kind of like having lost my family but I was compensated a bit by occasionally calling Werner Boes and the boys from our new communication center at the park.

Our administrative functions continued as before, but a lot of comrades were just going through the motions knowing that the beginning of the end had arrived. As far as security was concerned, it was decided not to overreact by building a wall around the base. Along the northwestern and southwestern edge of the park there was already a wall, dividing the park from Rosenberggata and Tastgata. We drew a six-foot fence at the southern perimeter along Byberggata, and a second one, not more than a chicken fence, at the eastern border, alongside Bjergstedveien. The base entrance at Byberggata had a sentry house outside and a traffic control hut immediately inside.

Nothing much happened during the next several weeks. The Norwegian Resistance refrained from any unfriendly acts and a suspicious quiet had set in. Some voiced concern that this would only be the quiet before the storm. I did not believe in this theory, but rather guessed (correctly, as I later found out) that the leaders of the Resistance had given instructions to their members to simply wait us out.

Events in and around Germany chased each other. While British and American forces advanced from the west, their Russian Allies moved in from the east. Hitler's narrow escape on the twentieth of July convinced him more than ever before that God had chosen him to lead the German people. He retreated to Berlin assuring himself that as long as he was present there the nation would not fall.

Since the assassination attempt, Hitler suffered from what his quack doctor called paralysis agitatis, a progressively worsening nervous disease. By April 1945, he had received an enormous amount of injections of sedatives, hormones, vitamins and stimulants, which threw the man into mounting fits and depressive stages. While his generals stood by helplessly, not daring to report anything unfavorable to their supreme commander, he ordered armies that did not exist to attack and dispatched twelve-year-old youth to defeat the encircling enemy, the Red Army.

For twelve years he had kept from the German people his relationship with Eva Braun, his mistress. But, on 15 April, coming nearer to the end, he permitted her to be with him. On the twentieth, he celebrated his fifty-sixth and last birthday. In the early hours of the twenty-ninth the two were married.

In the afternoon on the same day, he sat down and drew up his last will and testament. In it, he blamed the war on "the poisoner of all people, international Jewry." At the end of his will, he once more expressed confidence in the German navy by appointing Gross Admiral Karl Doenitz as Supreme Commander of all German forces.

On the next day, he poisoned his wife and took his own life. Upon his prior instructions, his body was dumped into a trough, doused with gasoline, and set afire. He had taken potassium cyanide. To insure his death, his valet gave him a *coup de grâce*.

Doenitz had maintained his headquarters in Flensburg for some time. He knew the actual military situation much better than his former boss. On 3 May, Doenitz drafted the first peace overture of the Third Reich, and sent it to Field Marshal Montgomery. The offer was of very limited character which was a good reason for Montgomery to refuse acceptance of it as a basis for discussions.

Doenitz immediately went back to the drawing board, and sent his special emissary, Admiral Hans G. Friedenburg, the next day again to Montgomery's headquarters. He was given authority to surrender all German forces in northern Germany, Holland, Denmark, and Schleswig-Holstein.

On the fifth of May, Montgomery formally accepted the offer for his front and ordered his troops to cease fire. On the same day, the Germans surrendered to the British Army in Copenhagen.

Two days later, on 7 May, the official document was signed at supreme headquarters in Reins. At the same time, upon the insistence of the Russians, a second ceremony of the formal surrender of Germany was signed in Berlin. The war had ended in Europe.

Most personnel belonging to our headquarters had their living quarters within the base, but not all. The members of convoy guidance and a number of guards protecting harbor installations had their quarters at a sturdy barrack building located only about a five minute walk south of headquarters, on Christen Tranes Gate.

By the first of May, several departments suddenly developed a feverish activity which nobody could explain. A further degeneration of matters was caused by a shortage of experienced key personnel, those who had specific expertise. I was told to temporarily leave my domain at the casino, where I had a small room as living quarters opposite the end of the rectangular dining room. "We have to reassign you for a while to convoy guidance until things quiet down," the lieutenant commander told me, "which means you will have room and board down the road, and essentially cover the night shift at the guidance office." I did not really care too much one way or another at this stage, now that I knew I would survive the war.

From the third through the sixth of May, I observed an unusually high number of submarines harboring in Norwegian ports. What I did not know was that Doenitz had sent out orders to all submarine commanders in any waters to converge their boats in Norwegian coastal areas.

Some had promptly followed these instructions, while others took a wait and see attitude by lingering in international waters. Others still had high-ranking Nazi officials and officers aboard and were sailing to South America, never to be seen again. That was part of a plan which had been worked out only weeks after the Western Allies started their invasion of the European continent.

I had listened to *Soldatensender* West (Soldiers' Broadcast West), an Allied transmission program, which started providing news in German as soon as they had occupied Paris, France. Among others, the broadcaster announced the names and ranks of German officials, mainly highest-ranking party members and SS members, who had been supplied with false identity papers in preparation for leaving Germany. How the Allies were able to get hold of most confidential information shortly after the processing of such documents remains a mystery to me. The plan would make it possible for political fanatics to travel to Italy and board with their papers any ship that would leave for South America. As history has shown, most of them were successful. The old story prevails that the big fish get away, while the small ones get caught.

On Tuesday, 8 May, I came off duty at 0800 hours, had a light breakfast, and immediately went to sleep. At 1430 hours I woke up from a deafening noise which came from outside the front windows. Looking out I saw several teenage boys carrying a wooden upside down cupboard between them. Others marched beside with big sticks, using the back of the cupboard as a drum. While marching up and down along our quarters, they peeked triumphantly through our windows, smiling broadly. I knew then that the war was over. It could not be anything else.

The Surrender

Not long after that, headquarters called ordering us to leave the premises and report to the base. Guards who were protecting harbor installations and other strategic points were told to stay put until further notice.

When we arrived at headquarters, the commandant called a general information meeting which everybody had to attend. He unfolded a lengthy cablegram, advising that General Jodl had formally declared the surrender of all German troops stationed in Norway. This news had been channeled to us through the regional coastal commanding officer, Admiral Von Schrader in Bergen. "Stand by for further instructions," was the last sentence of the cable.

An interesting point should be made here: The fact that we had surrendered after Germany's formal capitulation had positive results for us. Since we did not surrender while hostilities were still going on, our status automatically became quite different from that of POWs. As a matter of course we were declared to be interned soldiers and even had the right to protect ourselves and our bases from external threat. I simply mention this here for the record, because few Europeans and hardly any Canadians and Americans are aware of that status.

On direct orders from Admiral Von Schrader, all commanding officers were urged to submit the names of those familiar with the English language so they could function as interpreters when the Allies landed in Norway.

At headquarters, we had only two people familiar with English, Lieutenant Doehle and myself. Because of his background, Werner Boes was called in from our listening post on the island of Kvitsøy to serve as our chief translator. Formally, because of rank, Lieutenant Doehle would be leading the team.

As a long-standing order and directive from the OKW (*Oberkommando der Wehrmacht*, or high command of the armed forces), in case of a pending surrender, two orders had priority: one, the shredding and burning of top secret documents, and two, the destruction of military installations and weapons.

Since we were facing a totally different situation from the ones during wartime, Doehle, Werner and I saw it as our first major task to discuss any options available to us. I had one particularly major concern which I brought forward during our first informal meeting late that evening. Our commandant had already decided that any documents we could get our hands on would have to be destroyed. That, in my opinion, was outright dangerous. At this stage of the game, there was no purpose in destroying classified material; besides, there was no "German High Command" anymore.

"Let's face it," I declared to Doehle and Werner, "we have to clean up our own mess. Since we have lost the war, the Allies will not, for example, sweep the mines for us which we have laid during the war along the Norwegian coast. If we destroy our mine location documents, our own boys who will have to sweep the mines might be blown up."

That argument hit fruitful grounds. We agreed to pull a fast one without the commandant's knowledge. All Gekados documents were instantly confiscated for review from the department and then stored at Doehle's residence. The mine situation papers were separated from the others, and hid in yet another safe place.

Then we focused our attention on another matter that was important to everybody. A lot of food provisions had to be secured. Special requisitions had to be made out to obtain additional food supplies from the rations warehouses. They were usually filled up to their ceilings and it would have been a shame not to claim a decent portion of these for ourselves. But somebody of higher authority had to be in on this stunt. Doehle contacted the adjutant by telephone. By now it was almost midnight. He had just retired but joined us after five minutes went by. Yes, he equally saw the need for obtaining additional food supplies. We had better rely on our own organizational talents than that of the Allies. Besides, who knew when they would appear on the scene.

The aide used his pass keys to get into the administration office building to secure a few pieces of letterhead. Then we sat down and drafted requisition lists on behalf of headquarters and signed by the scrawl of the commandant, which appeared between impressive-looking stamps and a seal. The Germans just love and actually only recognize documents as legitimate when they carry stamps. The scrawl was that of the adjutant, and Doehle could not resist kidding him about his talents as a forger. Nobody, however, would pay too much attention to the signature anyway.

The next day, Wednesday, 9 May, produced several unexpected developments. Doehle contacted the naval truck division and requisitioned a pickup truck with driver to report around 0830 hours at the main food provision warehouse on Skansegata. Then he opened our weapon arsenal and selected some firepower for the three of us. One never knew who we would run into.

Werner got a brand-new 0815, while Doehle chose to pick up several clips for his sidearm and handed me a Mauser, which I slung over my shoulder. My own Walthers was nicely hidden under my coat, just in case.

The commandant's driver took out the Adler BMW limousine. We wanted our own transportation, and this fairly long car had plenty of space to stow some stuff away on which we were especially sold, such as good brandy, liqueurs and cigarettes.

We arrived at the warehouse before the truck did and were met by four guards who had been posted there by Inspector Pohlmann. They were supposed to prevent any illegitimate looting of the military magazine. Doehle produced our authorized requisition papers and we passed but not without the guards taking a puzzled look at my armory, his Mauser.

The warehouse was a good place to spend a couple of hours. It was literally bursting with foodstuffs and sin goods. The building had three floors with layers in between stacked with crates and cartons. I had not seen that much food in years. Even Doehle, who received different portions and foodstuffs than the ordinary soldier, shook his head at one point in time and said, "By golly, a lot of this I haven't seen during the entire war. All the best stuff had been kept hidden from us. Our time has finally come when we can get into the act and enjoy some of these things before the Tommies cash in on them."

He did not get any arguments from Werner and me. The ration master, a sergeant I knew from my service at the officers casino, allowed us to even extend our requisition with items we did not even know existed. "Soon we will be swamped by every unit in the vicinity, I am sure," he added. "Take whatever you can manage. Who knows what meager rations the Tommies will allow us."

By 1100 hours the truck was fully loaded with the assistance of warehouse personnel. We packed some special items in the Adler BMW limousine. Doehle told the sergeant we would return soon to pick up a bunch of items that did not fit into the two vehicles the first time. We had stacked them along one wall of the anteroom. Doehle had painted and attached a placard with the word *Seekommandant* underlined, and pinned it conspicuously in front of a pile of crates.

Back at the base, space was a problem. We knew this and selected to have all crates and sturdy cartons placed on wooden slats behind the officers casino. Tobacco bales, cigarette cartons and containers with big chocolate bars and liquor-filled fancy chocolates were distributed in the lounge room for the time being.

We were just about finished placing the first load when the commandant and his aide came and had a look. "Born," I was told, "with this change of events you had better take over here at the casino. Our ship's reporting service is put on ice for the moment. You will be responsible for the security of all extra provisions."

Did I have a choice? Of course not. However, I requested that some of my comrades be detailed to stand guard at and around the casino, and this request was granted.

Right after lunch time, we made a second trip to the warehouse. Our goods were still there, although we first had to worm ourselves through a lineup of trucks from other units. By the looks they cast at us, some guys did not like the idea of us driving to the front. But when they recognized the commandant's limousine with its standard flag at its front fender, they did not dare to cause an uproar. An additional discouraging factor, of course, was the way we were armed.

We loaded up again, beginning with the truck, then the limousine. We thanked the warehouse sergeant for his courtesy and help, and took off. The truck had already left.

As we set ourselves in motion, Doehle suggested, "You know, fellows, we have so much stuff now. Maybe we can part from some and carry out a public relations move." We did not know what he was driving at and said so. "Wait and see," was his reply.

When we arrived at the open square at the tip of the harbor inlet, which is now called *Torget* (marketplace), Doehle instructed the driver to stop. It was a nice day; we had rolled back the cover of the cabriolet to enjoy the fresh air. Doehle told me to stay put and got out of the car with Werner and the driver. I heard them rummaging around in the back; then they reappeared with two small crates and several cartons, some with cigarettes, others with chocolates.

As this went on, some curious Norwegians looked on, wondering what we were up to. Doehle, who was fairly fluent in the language (he spoke five altogether) waved with both arms, inviting the civilians to come closer. I laid the machine pistol at my feet.

Werner and the driver opened one crate, which was loaded with canned pork meat and several cartons with cigarettes and chocolates. In the meantime, Doehle played good Samaritan, passing the goods around. A swelling sound of surprise could be heard. The crowd was friendly. I heard one man say with sincere astonishment in his voice, while his eyebrows went upward, "Good Germans."

Suddenly, I recognized a familiar face in the crowd, Lars Hansen. He had not reported for work this morning nor yesterday morning. He navigated through the throng of spectators in my direction. I had left the car and met him halfway. "Sigy," he exclaimed jubilantly, "we can all be friends now. The war is over!" We hugged like brothers and slapped each other's back.

Then he turned around and addressed the gathering people a couple of minutes in his native tongue, which I could not follow. One man beside Lars commented, "Yes, we believe you, good Germans." It seemed Lars had done some positive advertising for us.

"We've missed you at headquarters," I said to Lars. Then I asked, "Where were you?"

He answered in a low voice, looking at the lieutenant, "I cannot explain now, Sigy. I was kind of busy with other things. By the way, some of my friends and I are going to celebrate the end of the war tonight. We would like you to join us. Can you get away?"

I turned around to question Doehle, who had just given away the last piece of goodies we had. "No sweat," he replied. "You will receive a special pass and have to wear an armband inscribed with 'Interpreter,' '*Dolmetscher*' and '*Tolk*.' That should do it."

"Great," said Lars, who understood German quite well. "We'll pick you up at the front gate around 1900 hours."

We got back into the car and drove off while the crowd still chanted "many thanks, many thanks" until their voices faded away.

I had hardly entered my quarters at the casino when the telephone rang. I picked up the receiver and heard Doehle's distinctive voice, "Sigy, don't mention anything to anybody. Get out to the front gate and meet me at the traffic control hut." He hung up, not waiting for my reply.

When I arrived at the hut, Doehle and Werner were waiting for me. "We have a problem," Doehle said unceremoniously. "Three guys are waiting outside, asking for refuge here. I don't think they are legitimate. Something is wrong with their IDs. Let's have a look at them."

We went outside the gate. The sentry was still viewing their papers. He called Doehle for help. All three of them saluted us with outstretched hands. Doehle, Werner and I had agreed to switch back to the traditional international soldier's salute the previous day, without formally asking anybody for permission. "Not anymore," I jumped the gun, not waiting for Doehle to comment. "The Nazi salute is out the window as far as we are concerned."

They wore different uniforms. One was an air force sergeant and the second an able seaman like myself. The third wore the uniform of an army corporal. I had recognized two of them but waited for Doehle to scrutinize their papers which matched the uniforms they were wearing. Doehle asked each man a number of questions, receiving rapid replies. They must have practiced their stories well.

Before Doehle could return the identity papers, I took him far enough aside so that the three could not hear our conversation. "Herr Oberleutnant," I said, "they are not what they pretend to be. One of them is a Gestapo agent, whose face I remember well in spite of his army corporal uniform. When the Terboven reception was held in November 1943, he lingered around the lobby examining any civilian entering the building.

"The air force sergeant is equally a phony. He was the SS officer who screened me in the lobby on that same day at the desk before I was allowed to go upstairs for the dinner service.

"The third man I don't know. But I'll bet you anything he is also a Nazi in disguise. It is your decision, of course; but if these three birds are permitted to find refuge with us, we will sooner or later be held responsible for our action by the Brits."

Doehle put his hand on my shoulder. "I appreciate your letting me in on this, and I agree. How do you think we should best handle this? You know that our commandant very likely would let them hide."

"Since you ask me, Herr Oberleutnant, I would not mention this to him at all. I would tell these three that their cover has been exposed and that the best we can do for them is to let them fend for themselves. They don't deserve our assistance. These kingpins have haunted and persecuted people for years. It might do them some good for a change to swallow some of their own medicine." He agreed and sent them on their way.

As we retreated through the gate, a navy truck pulled up. The driver stayed inside, but two MPs got out with a prisoner in shackles, an able seaman like myself. The man would have to be court-martialed since he had shot and fatally wounded his superior officer the day before.

He was brought to a confinement room at the end of a barrack, but other arrangements would be made immediately. By order of the commandant, a couple of men familiar with carpentry work were assigned to build a special cell for the prisoner. When we found out what that special cell was going to be, a great debate ensued among the men, most of whom got up in arms about the event. One could not even call this a cell. The lame explanation that the man did not deserve better did not satisfy the personnel, regardless of the prisoner's crime. It was called a stand-up cell, having just sufficient room for the prisoner to get in, but he could not sit or lie down!

Discussing this situation with Doehle, he said, "We can solve that soon, when the first British land. Like everything else of importance, they will have to be informed of this. In the meantime, I will urge the adjutant, who is a more reasonable man that I expected, to join me and ask our men to play it cool."

Around 1600 hours, the daytime base messenger came to the casino with my special pass for the evening. My colleague would not have any problem covering the dinner service on his own. The pass indicated unlimited shore leave. I took a nap before Lars picked me up.

The telephone rang at 1850 hours. "I have a few strange-looking Norwegians here at the gate who are asking for you," he said.

There were four of them, including Lars, who was wearing a windbreaker and multicolored pants I had not seen on him before. The others wore combat fatigues. That I did find strange, but I refrained from asking any questions.

Lars introduced his friends by first names, Erik, Jens, and Harald. Their handshakes were firm, with scrutinizing eye contact which proved to me I was dealing with people of action, who know their goals.

Lars and his friends led me around the corner into Tastgata, where a jeep-type vehicle was waiting. I detected that the license plate was quite different from other Norwegian vehicles, with several letters and numbers. It looked as if it had been recently attached to the automobile.

The trip took barely twenty minutes southward from Tastgata, then continued the same direction all the way down Lokkeveien, passing our former naval truck service division. We made a half-turn at the end of the street, that brought us to Madlaveien. I used to call it my favorite avenue. During summer, I had pedaled down that avenue many times on a bicycle until I would reach Mosvatnet, a lake where I would lie in the sun and dip in the water to cool off.

The Underground

Close to the west end of the lake, we turned left onto a small gravel road, winding about four minutes through bush land. A land house that looked like a large summer cottage came into view. It was situated close to the lake, yet hidden from direct view. A circled driveway in front of the building was accentuated by a central fountain depicting four imaginary figures from the *Peer Gynt Suite*. The four men were standing close to the rim of the fountain, each one facing inward. They bowed to the center of the fountain with outstretched arms, paying homage to a taller statue in the center, which portrayed the great Norwegian composer Edward Grieg. The four admirers had their hats in hand, out of which water bubbled, keeping the fountain filled.

Having stepped out of the car, I stopped for a moment to look at the peaceful exhibit. Lars talked at my side. "Sigy," he introduced, "meet the composer you like so much. His features have been made larger than life. He was a rather small person, as you know. But his looks are amazingly real." I had to agree.

I had seen two identical oil paintings of the man, one in an Oslo art gallery, the other in Trondheim, when returning from the north. It was all there, his hairstyle, his nose with the somewhat widening end of the side of the nose, the intensive stare of his eyes, and the drooping mustache. Even his arms were folded as if sitting in a chair.

We went inside the house. The vestibule gave away a whiff of fresh paint, suggesting it had been recently painted. Lars opened the second door to the left and we entered.

I was not prepared for this at all. A couple of dozen people, including two women, rose from their chairs and saluted smartly. With exception of one man who wore a British army uniform bearing the rank of a colonel, they were all similarly dressed in battle fatigues like Lars' companions. My brain clicked into third gear. What was going on? I automatically had returned their salute, of course, but as if in a trance. Lars broke the spell.

"Sigy," he explained, "since the hatchet is buried now, let me acquaint you with my group." He emphasized "my." "These people are all key members of what used to be the Rogaland Division of Resistance Fighters."

The man in British uniform had come forward. "This here," Lars continued, "is Colonel Kristen Hyllesand, who just arrived from England. He coordinated our efforts to give you people a hard time. His new mandate is to assist us here in maintaining order in this county. That includes a cease and desist order from any further acts of sabotage."

"Glad to hear that, Colonel," I commented. "We have no intention, nor the means, for that matter, to give you anymore problems either. I am personally saddened to have been a member of the occupying forces. I would have rather preferred to get to know your country under friendlier circumstances. But the past cannot be changed. In spite of the fact that I was a member of unwelcome intruders, I have learned to respect your people, Colonel Hyllesand."

"We know that from Lars, Sigy," he confirmed. "And call me Kristen. Ranks do not matter anymore. Besides, we owe you."

I had no idea what he was driving at. The explanation came later.

The members of the group had formed a half-circle around the huge oak table that dominated the room. Lars went with me from person to person, like during a reception. I exchanged a few words with each one. Since they seemed to know that my knowledge of their language was more than limited, they conversed with me in German or English. I know it is rather difficult to explain, but I did not feel like an outsider among these people.

As we approached the end of the line, I suddenly stopped. I had concluded chatting with one of the two female participants and turned my attention to the third last member in the line. His presence hit me like a cleaver in the neck! "Impossible," went through my mind. "It must be a great likeness." But it was not.

The face I was looking at was that of Petty Officer Erich Wallach who, in November 1943, had been transferred from Germany to Stavanger, taking over the *Marinepeilstelle* (naval directional radio service) at Stavanger Harbor. The first three days of his new assignment he had spent on Kvitsøy Island, at our principal naval listening station, to study the type of listening devices we used, and the overall operation in general. The first time I met the man was on that weekend when I had joined the boys on Kvitsøy to rehearse with the B Band.

The second time I met him was when Lieutenant Commander Schubert took me on a round trip through the harbor. It had included a division that reported to Schubert as Harbor Master, the *Marinepeilstelle*.

All this rushed through my mind, plus something else. Since the end of 1943 it had become more and more difficult for our convoys to leave Stavanger in any direction without the British almost instantly being aware of it. There were dozens of cases that indicated an immediate feeding of naval moves to the other side. I probably would not be too far off in connecting this man with these events.

Lars Hansen had intensively watched my face during the time I stared at Erich Wallach. Wallach was, of course, not wearing his German uniform, but wore similar combat garments like the others. There was one exception. His left arm sleeve displayed the British Crown, underlined with a black inscription on yellowish background, MI-Six.

With a slightly theatrical gesture, Lars announced, "And this gentleman, who you know as Petty Officer Wallach, is Lieutenant Alexander Spencer from MI-Six." Even though I had easily identified Spencer's insignia on his sleeve, hearing Lars' revelation almost knocked my socks off. I had to find out more about this "traitor."

It was about 2000 hours when we withdrew to another room across the corridor to sit down for what my host called a celebration dinner. "Why not be part of it?" I thought. While these people celebrated their newfound freedom, I had something to celebrate also: the end of the bloody war!

Lars knew how curious I was about Spencer. So he arranged for me to be flanked by Spencer and himself. During dinner I had to chuckle a few times. Here I was, having dinner with members of the former Underground, Lars to my left, the jack-of-all-trades at naval headquarters, and in reality the second in command of the regional movement, and the naval petty officer, a British spy in disguise!

Before the service of the dessert course, Hyllesand clinked his wine glass with the dessert spoon and rose from his seat. "Permit me, ladies and gentlemen," he announced, "to address a few words to our guest on behalf of all of us." He looked straight at me and began, "We are eternally grateful, my friend, for the concern and courage you demonstrated last year when you received that list of suspected members of our movement. You don't even have to admit that you made it available for Lars when you briefly left your office at the time. There wasn't sufficient time to make a copy of the document, but you left long enough for Lars to take a couple of pictures with his microfilm camera he always carried with him. Your action enabled us to bring our comrades to safety before your field operators could arrest them.

"Only a fool could believe that the decision you made was an easy one. You must have wrestled with your conscience, being drawn back and forth between duty and human considerations." He described my feelings extremely well! "Anyway, you came through on the side of humanity, knowing full well that the suspects on the list would be arrested and exposed to torture, or even death. That's what I meant before when I said we owe you. By your action you have become one of us."

He looked around the table and added, "And so we all salute you. Please accept our gratitude and friendship. With this, I raise my glass." Everyone had risen from his or her seat. Then I heard the chorus I was about to hear many more times on other occasions.

"Hip, hip hurrah; hip, hip hurrah," followed by, "for he is a jolly good fellow." I felt overwhelmed by emotion, coming close to tears. At the same time, embarrassment got hold of me caused by the outpour of friendliness. Everyone had sat down again and looked at me expectantly. A reply was in order.

I made it brief, downplaying the importance of my role in the affair in question. Yes, I admitted, I had had mixed thoughts but I was convinced my final decision did not differ from anyone's in the room who would have faced the same situation. I thanked Hyllesand for his kind words and the honor bestowed upon me. I expressed deep appreciation for their feelings and accepted those outstretched hands in reciprocation.

As soon as I had resumed my seat, Hyllesand rose, looked at me once more, and said, "We have no reason to withhold anything from you, Sigy. Four members of our group whose names appeared on the list are with us tonight. The four would like to formally thank you for your deed."

Four men got up and joined Hyllesand at the lectern. One of them carried a dark box embroidered with emeralds around the rim, which he sat down in front of Hyllesand. The size of the receptacle was not much larger than that of a snuffbox, which I had seen my grandfather carrying around when I was a small boy. The front of the box displayed an emblem, depicting two Vikings in the foreground shaking hands. The background showed a Northern Light with a raising sun in the East, identifying Scandinavia.

When I reached the five men, Hyllesand reintroduced each of the four by name. We exchanged firm handshakes while sternly looking into each other's faces, like brothers or good friends who had been apart for a long time. Each man said clearly, *"Jeg er Dem stor takk skyldig,"* the Norwegian equivalent of "I am much obliged to you," a phrase with which I was fairly familiar. It touched me so deeply that I was unable to reply.

The names of the first two men rang a bell with me, but I was not sure where to place them. One added in English, "My dad was the one who cut your hair, the barber on Erlands Gate."

"I," declared the second man, "am the son of the dentist on Ny Olavskleiv." I had not been mistaken when I had read the blacklist the second time.

While I shook hands with the third and fourth man, Hyllesand opened the small container and removed from it a gold-coated coin, about three and a half centimeters in diameter, attached to a neck chain.

Hyllesand lifted the coin with the chain and placed it around my neck, saying, "Please accept this friendship badge from us as a sign of appreciation and thankfulness."

After dinner we proceeded to a room adjoining the dining room. It had the atmosphere of a private club, very British. There was a fireplace quite similar to the one we had had at the officers casino on Ny Olavskleiv. It also contained deep lounge chairs which, when one sat too long in them, would tempt one to fall asleep.

The Traitor

I sat again beside Wallach, alias Spencer, an opportune time to hear the rest of his story, part of which I had dragged out of him during dinner.

As a young man, he had attended Cambridge University. His tutors discovered his reception for foreign languages, four of which he mastered with speed and accuracy within four years. The ground work was laid for service in the foreign office, a goal his father had motivated him to follow. When World War II broke out, Alex was twenty-eight.

He mustered as a future member of the widespread army communication service, but because of his language skills and a couple of favorable circumstances, he had caught the attention of MI-Six.

A high-ranking official of that intelligence service paid Alex a visit before his introduction to the armed forces and asked if he would he be interested in special training, involving intelligence work. It would be dangerous but also rewarding.

"Why not?" Alex said. Adventure was what he was looking for. He knew, though, this was invariably associated with danger.

His training began soon after. He was familiarized with all tricks of the trade, the knowledge of which is a must for survival when operating behind enemy lines.

In May 1942, he was considered fit to travel. His bogus identity papers were second to none. His name and the rank of able seaman (corporal) were that of a member of the German navy, who had actually died of natural causes in 1938 and who was buried in a small community called Haffkrug near the Baltic Sea. Members of MI-Five and Six, who floated around Germany before the outbreak of the war, had provided lists of names with personal data that could be used comparatively easily and with minute chance of discovery for almost any purpose, on the military as well as the industrial level.

Alex was flown to Germany and parachuted near Wilhelmshaven by the North Sea during the early morning hours. He was to report to the Wilhelmshaven signal corps as a wizardly communication expert, as his sealed personal file indicated.

After about one year of service with the unit, headquarters in Kiel called him in to serve as technical advisor for improving the range of sending messages and also to sophisticate the coding and decoding system. By September 1943, he had carried out several improvements, including the ability to almost double the WATTS range of sending messages by using a device which was built by the naval technical application branch, based on his design.

The following two months he spent training other peers in the use of the upgraded equipment. Then, immediately after his promotion to petty officer (sergeant), he was sent to Stavanger to introduce the same technique, based upon a request by Dr. Carlos Mayer-Pantin, our commandant.

That was the moment for which the British Admiralty and the MI-Six had been waiting. Alex had unlimited access to the radio, Morse and other wireless equipment to make these technical improvements. But he did more than his German superiors were asking. He integrated a switch-system only known to him that enabled the sender to communicate directly with relay stations operated by the British. The ruse was laid! Now I knew why the British seemed to be so much more alert than before the end of 1943.

Even though it was past history, I could not help telling Alex my misadventure as a courier in September 1944. He knew the whole story, of course. The report of the incident had been distributed to all naval units, leaving out the name of the courier. That I was the one in question, Alex knew from Werner Boes.

During the dinner table conversation we had switched back and forth between German and English, depending on the subject at hand. It seems to be natural for people who are equally comfortable in both languages, though Alex's command of German was much better than mine of English.

For a moment I was tempted to hold him, if only half-jokingly, responsible for the ordeal I had gone through. But I changed my mind for two reasons: He did not know me that well, and after all, he was British, working against us, while I had shielded, as a German, potential enemies of Germany from arrest. In comparison, he likely would have come out on top. (However, I never harbored any regrets about my activities, not then, and not now!)

It was around midnight when I decided I had already overstayed my welcome, and it was time to retreat. Lars offered to drive me back to the base. I gladly accepted, since the distance would have taken me longer than one hour to walk, at best. Before vacating the group, I accepted another rain check from Alex, who was eager to show and demonstrate to me the communication installations at the harbor, after the arrival of the British.

When we crossed the entrance hall, Lars walked over to a coat rack near the exit door, took a gray British Macintosh off the hook, and handed it to me with the statement, "Wear this any time you wish. That way, all you have to do is take off your navy cap, and you will look like any other civilian." He added, "And this here is a special ID which should enable you to walk around freely without difficulties."

I looked at the laminated card, which bore my name with the statement that I should be given any assistance I needed. On the left-hand bottom of the card appeared the effective date with the emblem of the organization. The signature to the right was that of Colonel Kristen Hyllesand. It looked as if I had it made!

Returning to the base, I found half the gang still wide awake. Girls had shown up at the front gate in the late afternoon and evening, asking us for protection. There were a dozen of them, all wearing scarves over their heads, which had been clean-shaven by members of the former Resistance. The girls were known to have collaborated with us, the term used for being friendly with the enemy. Some had gone steady with Germans and in some isolated cases, had even borne them babies.

I could not possibly agree with the conduct of the persecutors, though I understood their frustrations and the anger they must have felt in all those years of our domination. Unfortunately, too often the less guilty or the innocent suffer most. One good thing, though, was that none of the girls had been harmed physically.

Formally, we could not offer any protection to them. Our jurisdiction over the population had ceased once and for all. Likewise, we could not allow them to stay at the base. It simply would not be proper nor condoned by our leaders.

Doehle, having been given the mandate to use his discretion in matters concerning us, the Norwegian population, and our future communication with the Allies, worked out a compromise. The girls would have to leave the base by 0100 hours, but could return during the day. The fence along Bjergsted Veien was manipulated so that it could easily be opened from the outside and closed from the inside without causing any attention. That way, the girls did not have to submit to further harassment by entering through the entrance of the base, but could enter and leave undetected.

Meet The Enemy

The following morning, Thursday, 10 May, the telephone rang during breakfast service at the casino. "Sigy," the front gate guard said, somewhat out of breath, "you are the only one I can fetch. I did not want to disturb Oberleutnant Doehle, and Werner is not in his quarters. There are a lot of leaflets floating from the sky. As you know, I cannot leave my post . . ."

I cut him off. "O.K., I'll be out in a minute."

Crossing the yard, I picked up two leaflets which rested side by side on a lower branch in one of the birch trees I had to pass on the way to the entrance. They both were the same, printed in English and Norwegian. From their content, it was apparent they were directed to the civilian population as a whole but they also addressed the former Resistance.

The message appealed to the population to stay calm and await the arrival of the Allies. The Resistance was urged to immediately cease and desist from acts of sabotage against the Germans. All military installations and strategic bases would now be under the control and ownership of the Allied Forces. The flyer also pointed out that the Germans were simultaneously instructed to abide by the Geneva Agreement, and terminate any unfriendly acts. It was signed by a general on behalf of the Allied headquarters in Great Britain.

I assumed correctly that this was not the only leaflet that had been dropped, since it had mentioned us as well. When passing through the gate, the sentry pointed to a few dozen leaflets which were strewn about, some of them still fluttering in the light breeze. Several youngsters were playing in front of the gate where Tasta Gata and Christen Tranes Gate merge.

Some of the kids had leaflets in their hands, and the elder ones read the contents aloud. I crisscrossed the opening and collected altogether six of the leaflets. Two were the same as the ones I had picked up from inside the base. The other four were printed in German and English, evidently meant for us.

They bore the same identification and signature. I remember the text quite well. It said, "Attention! Attention! All German soldiers in Norway, the war is over! Soon, members of the Allied Forces will land and discuss with your commanders future action that must be taken in order to carry out the peaceful transfer of all war-type installations. Remain calm, and continue to follow the orders of your superiors. The Norwegian population is to be left alone. The former Norwegian Resistance has been instructed to cease any hostile acts against you. You are expected to collect all handguns and firearms, which should be kept secure and under the supervision of your base commanders, until our troops arrive. The first contingent of Allied Forces will land within twenty-four hours and advise you of permissible food provisions."

When I returned, Doehle was at the casino. I retained one copy of each message, and yielded the remaining ones to him. The reference regarding food provisions at the end of the message loomed in my mind.

Doehle went to see the commandant, and it did not take long for two things to happen. At 1100 hours, a general assembly was ordered to take place in the courtyard. The commandant had directives for us, based on the content of the leaflets. Secondly, I was summoned to his quarters.

"Able Seaman Born," he began, in a friendlier tone of voice than customary, "since you are in charge and responsible for extra food supplies, I want to hear your suggestions. How can we hide them from the English, who will undoubtedly put us on a diet about which we might not be keen?"

He caught me by surprise by the question itself and also by his unconventional way of expressing himself. Maybe he was not so sure about himself anymore, because of the substantial change of events.

"May I have a couple of hours to discuss this topic with some of my comrades, Herr Kapitaen?" I requested. He agreed.

Doehle, Werner Boes, and I held a blitz meeting with the base chef and the second steward discussing the possible options. We arrived at a comparatively simple solution to the problem. First we would stock up to the hilt present inventories in holding storerooms. Next, we would line up all perishable foods for immediate consumption. Thirdly, we would unpack canned foods from crates, wrap them in tent squares, and bury the load in different locations around the base. I would get in touch with gardener Berg, who was located on Ovre Stokkavei West and ask him to camouflage the top of the buried treasures with *gres matte*, a Scandinavian forerunner to what we call a grass mat now. Swedish scientists had come up with something close to it in 1944. I was positive that Berg would gladly help us out. In all these years I had bought flower bouquets and centerpieces for different occasions from him. Besides, both his teenage sons belonged to the youth wing of the former Resistance, of which I now had become the only honorable German member. That should count in Berg's book.

The officers casino building had a huge loft on the second floor, right above the ground floor facilities. When I moved into the building in December, I had detected a trapdoor in the ceiling right beside the entrance door to my quarters. Curiosity led me to investigate what was up there, which turned out to be nothing but loads of open space, that could now be utilized for storing entire crates.

It was 1330 hours when Doehle called the commandant, who received us without delay. I had asked Doehle to accompany me for three reasons. As the formal senior interpreter he had to be in on practically everything that was going on within the confinements of the base-turned-internment camp.

I knew Doehle's ability to influence the commandant, in spite of the fact that their political views differed. In case something went wrong with this business of hiding these extra supplies from the British, I needed a reliable witness who could testify to the approval of this act.

The commandant did not have a problem with points one and two but didn't like three and four. We assured him the appearance would be such that nobody would ever suspect anything buried in these target spots.

As far as point four was concerned, I had to admit there was some danger involved, the outcome of which I could not predict or guarantee. I intended to explain to the British inspectors that if we landed upon the loft in the first place, all crates stored up there were empty.

The plan was to pile up different rows of empty crates in front and in the more accessible storage lanes, and hide the contraband behind. Nobody could predict in advance whether this deception would work. I personally had strong doubts, but did not mention anything, not even to Doehle or Werner. After all, the ability to beef up our nutrition for weeks to come was too important for everybody on the base. But I had no illusions I would have to do the dirty work on my own and put my head in the noose. Oh, hell, no wager, no win.

After some hesitation, the commandant gave the green light.

At 1500 hours we lined up and surrendered our carbines and sidearms, which we had received at the beginning of our basic training. Those who possessed personal handguns, like myself, had to relinquish these also. One room at the center-staged barrack on the base had been cleared of junk, and all arms were placed in there. The room was fitted with a new lock, just in case. There were two keys: the commandant had one; Doehle the other.

The girls returned in the afternoon and most of my pals decided to use this as an excuse for celebrating. I guess we had various reasons for feeling elated. The greatest bulk of the unpacked illegal whiskey ended up in my quarters, but not because I consumed more than anybody else. On the contrary, the stuff was safe with me. One could see bottles all over the place, in cupboards, along wall shelves, in the hand-wash sink, and even under my bed.

When I had finished with dinner service, I cut loose a few bottles and walked with them, well-camouflaged, to a semi-secret meeting place.

"Here comes a generous guy," an already inebriated pal shouted, when seeing me with the "fire-water."

"Don't be fooled," replied another chap. "He's got more of the stuff than any one of us. Let's kill it!" The girls joined in the echo.

Early the next morning, eight work crews were digging graves all over the place. By noon, all treasures were buried safely. Covering them with grass mats was done within twenty minutes under the supervision of Gardener Berg, whom I had called in the morning.

All storage rooms were close to overflowing with perishables and goods of limited lifetime. When everything was calculated, we concluded having at least four additional weeks of food supplies available for consumption. That did not include our secret supply up in the loft.

The carpenters had the noble task of erecting a wooden wall in the loft after the crates were carefully stacked as planned. The decision to have a lockable door added close to the center of the wall turned out to be a blunder, as I was about to experience.

On Doehle's advice, I reported to the commandant that all foodstuff had been secured. To my astonishment, he asked me to take him on a tour "to visit the graves."

When we returned, he was visibly pleased and seemed to be more at ease. Why not? If something bad happened I would have to face the music and get clobbered. He declined, though, upon my invitation to also inspect the hidden crates in the loft. Before leaving, I provided him with a detailed list of the entire inventory, including our estimate of how long it would last. He actually praised our organizational work, which I did not expect. The man had noticeably mellowed since our surrender.

I was about to take an afternoon nap when the phone rang. Habitually, I glanced at my watch. It was 1348 hours. Picking up the receiver, I heard two excited voices talking at the same time, the sentry outside the gate, and the guard in the guardhouse. "Come quick, Sigy. Three Englishmen are here who probably want something."

"Keep cool," I replied and hung up. Then I rang Werner and Doehle, who wanted us to pass by his quarters first.

"Let's impress these fellows in an unexpected way," Doehle suggested. "You take the lead, Werner, as the most fluent of us, with your American drawl. Sigy and I will throw in an occasional appropriate remark, playing it by ear." That suited me fine.

We checked our uniforms to look our best, and marched, keeping step with each other, until we reached our first visitors from the other side of the fence. They had not demanded entry to the base from the sentry and seemed to wait patiently for us. Two of them smoked cigarettes. The sweet smell of an English brand hit my nostrils before we came to a stop. We saluted the British way, keeping our hands close to our headgear. Werner had his welcome speech ready. With his sonorous voice, he said, "Gentlemen, as representatives of the German Navy, we greet and welcome you to the shores of Norway. We shall fully cooperate with you and follow your instructions."

The three in British uniform, a second lieutenant, a warrant officer and a corporal, had returned our salute politely. When Werner had ended his salutation, the three looked at each other, thoroughly perplexed, then cracked broad smiles and began laughing heartily.

Getting ahead of Doehle, I threw in the question, "What is so funny? Why are you laughing?" as if our conduct and handling of the situation were perfectly normal.

"By Jove," exclaimed the lieutenant, "the first Germans we meet on Norway's soil talk like Americans! What kind of birds are you?"

The ice was broken. If anything, it was the beginning of an unusually cordial relationship between conqueror and defeated. We chatted a few minutes. They had just been disembarked as members of the initial British contingent sent to set our demobilization process in motion, but were momentarily on a cruise to inspect the general scene without entering any bases at the time. In parting, Doehle extended an open invitation to the trio, encouraging them to visit the base any time. What we did not know then was that the lieutenant would be commissioned later by the British city commandant to lead the first formal inspection tour of our base, a coincident that assisted in creating an unruffled relationship between the two parties.

Passing the inner guardhouse, the guard had a message for me. "A guy with the name of Wallach called a couple of minutes ago, saying he would pick you up at 1600 hours to inspect the *Marinepeilstelle* at the harbor. He did not tell me his rank."

"He lost it recently," I said loudly, more or less joking to myself, realizing the guard would not know what I was talking about. I thanked him without clarifying my remark. It would not serve any purpose to explain that situation, thereby making things seem more complicated than they were. Besides, sooner or later the real identity of Wallach would come to light anyway.

On the way back to the officers casino, I had to pass headquarters' major communication center barrack. Something was up. Different messengers entered and left the building in droves, an unusual activity. I would soon find out why.

Even though there was only an hour and a quarter left until Wallach, alias Spencer, would appear, I decided to have a quick snooze. The phone rang again.

"Listen," Doehle said, not wasting any time. "Have the dining room available immediately for a special meeting of the officer corps. You and Werner are to attend as observers. We received a cablegram this very instant advising of the death of Admiral Von Schrader. Our present and future structure of command and administrative obligations for winding down activities will be revised."

My colleague and I had just stripped the tables that had been set up for dinner already, when the officers filed in. The meeting was short and snappy. Our territorial responsibilities would automatically be enlarged to include the city of Bergen and vicinity. "How bad that is," the commandant remarked, "is not clear at this time. We should know more tomorrow when the first British military representatives are expected to pay us a visit. They will have to inform us what is expected, but I doubt we will be permitted to have more manpower."

He added that Doehle, Werner, and I should hold ourselves available to interpret. Three or four Brits would join the German officer corps for luncheon the next day.

Wallach picked me up at the appointed time. He was alone. We spent two hours at the harbor communication centers, and the time flew by fast. Though I knew literally nothing about electronics, the demonstrations Wallach made were fascinating. He had added an apparatus to the core of the equipment in December 1943 and unnoticed by anybody else, it was doing a fantastic job. Coded Morse messages were sent and received without interference, with and without relay stations. It included a built-in radio facility with an improved direction finder, a sophisticated (now obsolete) wire recorder, a type of magnetic recorder using steel wire, and Ham operator-type equipment, boosted to a capacity of sending messages using two thousand kilowatts of power.

All this was pretty much Greek to me, but seeing the actual performance and results was stunning. He had installed all this additional equipment without anybody's detection. In answer to my question of how he had accomplished this feat, he replied quite casually, "Easy. Since I took charge, I had access any time. I did the installations over the weekend, 11 and 12 December 1943. I usually sent covert messages during the day from my own office via satellite transmitter, which fed into the main transmission apparatus. Less urgent messages I sent in the late evening through the regular scrambler." It sounded simple enough.

In the same evening during dinner service, I spotted three officers bearing their handguns again while everyone else had surrendered their weapons the previous afternoon. I did not like these exemptions and told Doehle so, while Werner and I deliberated a number of other strategy matters with him. He did not respond to my complaint. "Fine," I thought, "I'll find a way to get mine back."

Doehle held another meeting with us around 2100 hours. In anticipation of meeting the British soon, we had to concoct a plan of action which would involve a unified reply to certain questions that might be asked.

We divided up the territory, determining who would guide the Tommies around where within the base. My role was to accommodate the inspector(s) by explaining the functions of the officers casino, the food preparation facilities, in the presence of the base chef, and the communication center.

It was agreed that the first two points of discussion with the Allies should be the incarcerated man in the stand-up cell, and the content of top secret intelligence material, especially the positioning of German mines along the Norwegian coast. We let it rest there, for the time being.

Werner and I had almost reached the door, when Doehle said like an afterthought, "You may want to have a look at the collected weapons, making sure everything is in order." Then he handed me his key with the remark, "I don't think I am going to miss it before tomorrow morning," and smiled knowingly.

That was good timing. I wanted to get my Walthers 7.65 caliber pistol back before the British arrived. It was getting dark, but not dark enough to go on an expedition trip. Besides, too many men were crawling all over. I spent the next two hours at Werner's quarters, taking advantage of the time by learning from him a few more American phrases.

Shortly after midnight, we shadowed around three barracks and landed opposite the conspicuously center-staged building in which the arms were held. When the coast seemed to be clear, we swished across the foreground and quickly entered.

I was glad about Doehle's decision to lend us the key. An original key was much superior to getting hold of a locksmith-comrade to assist in entering. That would have been a witness to a crime.

Once inside, we did not have to be overcautious, since nobody was living in that building. Since we did not dare to switch on the electricity for fear of being noticed from the outside, Werner had taken a flashlight with him. He had applied his ingenuity by having ripped strips of electricians tape and maneuvered it around the front head of the flashlight. This way, light would limit itself to a small ring, similar to a burglar's spotlight.

"Hang it!" I said under my breath, seeing a mountain of arms. "I'll never find that darn gun here."

"Don't worry, Sigy," Werner retorted, "I'll help you with the search while I steal one for myself. I don't want a fancy gun like yours, but I intend to look for that heavy 0815, which can kill the strongest horse in one shot." He used a German phrase referring to horses but he talked about a handgun which even then could have been compared to a Magnum. It left holes big enough for the sun to shine through.

It was easier than I had thought. Barely five minutes after we had entered the room, I found what I was looking for. It rested right in front of me on a center shelf, in its holster, the handle reflecting the moonlight that shone on it. It still contained the loaded clip as surrendered.

Not far away from there sat two more loaded clips of the same caliber. I made up my mind to search for one or two boxes of the 7.65 millimeters. I promptly discovered them in the farthest corner of the room. The date on the boxes indicated the ammunition was manufactured one year ago. Not that I was going on a shooting spree, but it had become a habit with me to check on quality when buying something.

In the meantime, Werner had found a fairly new-looking 0815, and pocketed the big ugly thing in his belt under his jacket. He also swiped a couple of boxes of shells, wrapping them in canvas that had partially surrounded an automatic weapon. We left, locked the door, and sneaked out of the barrack reversing our tracks.

Early the next morning I discussed with Doehle and the base chef the luncheon menu. My first thought had been to prepare a four-course gourmet meal in honor of our expected guests, but discarded the idea for fear they might think we were living high on the hog. The succeeding inspection team would probably be instructed to go over the whole base with a fine-tooth comb.

The visitors arrived at 1120 hours and were greeted by our commandant, his aide, and Doehle at the gate. There were three of them, all from the British Army: a brigadier who had been commissioned as the new city commander of Stavanger; his aide, a major; and a captain, who was introduced as a logistics expert.

They withdrew to our commandant's quarters, where an initial briefing took place. The brigadier explained under which conditions he intended to communicate with us. His basic thought, according to Doehle, was to deal with us in mutual trust and respect. Naval matters, he emphasized, would be settled in conjunction with the Royal Navy, who would lay out our future role in winding up specific operations. Some matters related to naval action would be assigned to us in due time.

By 1150 hours, all base officers had assembled in the casino lounge in anticipation of meeting the first former enemies. Werner Boes and I had posted ourselves at the entrance door. The sextet arrived at noon sharp. The air was balmy, so we had left the door open. My co-steward had stationed himself in the dining room.

Werner and I put on our best faces and saluted smartly. Doehle introduced us as his interpreter colleagues. He added that I was wearing a second hat, that of a steward.

I had heard many times how reserved the British are. Unexpectedly, though, the brigadier and his two companions shook hands firmly with us. At that moment, Werner remarked with his distinctive drawl, "Brigadier, sir, it will be our honor and pleasure to assist you with all we can."

A flash of sincere astonishment flew over the brigadier's face. "Aha," he uttered with a tone of discovery in his voice, "you must be the ones my first excursion team told me about yesterday. They reported having met a few Germans who speak English like Americans. I want to meet with you and Lieutenant Doehle after luncheon."

We served oxtail soup, a combination cold cuts dish, decorated with vegetables and fish delicacies. As we set in the *Kommisbrot*, a canned U-boat bread, made from light rye, our commandant remarked we thought our guests would like to taste something different from their traditional soft white bread. They sure did.

Bringing our visitors "back home," we served plum pudding for dessert, topped with Turkish coffee. This luncheon was tasty but, of course, not nearly as sumptuous as what we had originally in mind.

Everybody left the dining room at 1325 hours. Doehle had explained to our commandant that the brigadier and his men would meet with us to get an idea of our present structure of operation. So the six of us withdrew and proceeded to the lounge.

Doehle and Werner did most of the talking. We began by reporting that we had a prisoner in a stand-up cell. The brigadier's aide started making notes. The captain interjected, stating that this matter was of considerable urgency and would have to be corrected immediately. The prisoner would be taken into custody by the Allies and hearings would take place soon to get all the facts. That would include the interrogation of those who had been present when the act occurred. The captain gave us a brief rundown of the British legal system, emphasizing the importance of providing due process of law for the accused. I had done some studies on the subject when typing out translations and realized that the idea of presuming a suspect innocent until proven guilty was indeed quite different, if not opposite, from our present German legal interpretation.

As a next step, Doehle opened his briefcase and withdrew copies of a number of documents, including the position maps of mines we had anchored and those that floated along the Norwegian coastline.

The brigadier knew, naturally, that according to Hitler's directives these maps should have been destroyed. I opened my mouth for the first time, commenting that we were not foolish enough to believe when having lost the war the Allies would sweep our mines for us. The brigadier did not hold back in praising us for using common sense. "The British Royal Naval mine sweeping commander will be grateful for this and will give you high marks for your action, gentlemen. That makes his task much easier, and many of your comrades' lives can now be saved." He was echoing what we had told ourselves when we were faced with this crucial decision.

He shuffled through some papers in front of him while we answered his queries. His tone of voice, which had not sounded distant before, now became almost friendly. Apparently we had made a positive impression on him. It occurred to me that the entire atmosphere of this meeting was not at all as one between foes. There was practically no tension, as one would expect. It was my first experience of what group and teamwork is all about, a behavior totally foreign to the government system under which we Germans had grown up.

As the gathering came to a close, the brigadier placed a copy of the British Common Law on the table. "From now on," he stated, looking at Doehle, "this will be your guide or Bible, if you wish, for general conduct of communication and also for determining legal situations. The most important chapters had been marked for translation. Have this done on a priority basis, as all German internment camps in the region have to have copies as soon as possible. Thank you."

We rose and led our visitors through the main communication center facilities, which the brigadier wanted to view.

On the way to the exit, Doehle asked when the first official base inspection team could be expected. "Probably tomorrow," replied the brigadier, "but you will be contacted ahead of time." He added as an afterthought, "By the by, make sure you are all disarmed. Weapons and ammunition must be securely stored."

At 1930 hours the sentry called Werner out. Two members of the Royal Navy requested entry to the base. One was a commanding officer who introduced himself as Engineer May; the other man had the rank of a midshipman with the name of Fairfield. He was being groomed to become a commissioned officer. They had no specific assignment, but were just on shore leave and wanted to get acquainted with some German navy men.

That was our first contact with the Royal Navy, but not the last. During the ensuing weeks we developed a sort of friendship which led to other contacts with the British. They were all indications that we had a great start with the former enemy.

The Inspection

In anticipation of a base inspection, I had worked with the chef on a food inventory list that corresponded with the open supply. Naturally, it did not include any hoarded items, those buried and those stacked up in the loft. Providing a list proved to be good foresight. I had learned it is always better to attack first, taking the initiative oneself rather than wondering what the other party will come up with. I kept the documented inventory list in my quarters, handy to be presented when needed.

The following day was a Sunday. Doehle, Werner, and I met immediately after breakfast to discuss strategy. It was a good move. At 1000 hours we were advised that the first inspection would take place early in the afternoon. Obviously, the British disregarded the Lord's Day Act, not that we cared.

At 1100 hours, the entire military staff was informed. The commandant launched an appeal to show the British that we are disciplined and orderly people, having everything in tiptop shape, spit and polished, as usual.

Since this was another balmy day, Doehle, Werner, and I chose to loiter around in front of the base after luncheon. Doehle had drafted a list, which I had typed out and made copies, showing who would accompany which inspection team, and was to be made public to all. As planned before, I was to cover the food preparation facilities, the casino, and the communication complex.

The inspection teams arrived at 1340 hours. The first man climbing out of the jeep was the army lieutenant, whom we had met with his two comrades at the gate two days earlier. "Great," Werner remarked, before we greeted the visitors. "We don't have much to worry about." But Doehle threw in a word of caution not to be overoptimistic.

There were six men altogether. The leader of the group was an army captain who, with a sergeant at his side, would be accompanied by Doehle. Werner led a warrant officer and a corporal on his inspection territory. I ended up with another sergeant and a private.

Wasting no time, I went straight with them to the communication center, where our petty officer in charge was waiting to answer any questions.

My maiden assignment as an interpreter went rather smoothly, only having problems with a couple of technical expressions, that had to be explained by demonstration. We spent about twenty minutes there, then proceeded to the cooking facilities, which consisted of a main preparation kitchen, a bake shop, a small pastry room, and several storage facilities.

The English private started asking some simple questions in German, like "What is this here?" apparently wanting to practice some of his German. The chef, pleasantly surprised, responded fluently, but by the private's face I noticed he probably understood only part of the chef's answers. So I filled in the loopholes.

When we arrived at the officers casino, I took the two into my humble quarters. I was aware that once the inspection took place, we were not allowed to have any alcoholic beverages. Most of what was in my quarters had been consumed by my comrades. However, I had kept three bottles prominently displayed on a wall shelf, one bottle of German brandy, one plum liqueur, and one Aalborg Akvavit.

Before I could hear a lecture, I quickly volunteered, "I know we are not supposed to have any Schnapps, but I must give you chaps a chance to compare this booze with yours."

Without waiting for a reply, I offered them seats, took three shot glasses from a shelf underneath my small writing desk, and poured us some Akvavit.

"Cheers to you," I lifted my glass, "and bottoms up."

"Darn good stuff," commented the sergeant when setting down the jigger. "It almost tastes like gin, but with an additional taste. What is it?"

"Very close, sir, isn't it?" I retorted. "Only this liquor is flavored with caraway seeds. I have kept this bottle for special occasions since 1943, when I last visited the Aalborg Akvavit Distillery."

We drank another round with some more "cheers" and talked a few minutes about the war being over. They were just as happy as I was that there would be no more slaughter.

I showed them the dining room facilities and the lounge, which was all there was to see. "Easy going," I exulted in my mind. While we made the short round I had purposely avoided to looking up, fearing they would notice the trapdoor in the ceiling of the small hallway.

"That's about all here, gentlemen," I commented, turning to the exit door, when the sergeant turned around once more and pointed to the ceiling.

"What's up there?" he asked.

"Just an ordinary loft," I retorted, trying to sound unconcerned. But I was not going to get them out the door yet.

Turning to the private, the sergeant ordered, "You stay down here. Is there a ladder somewhere so we can go up and have a look?"

No sense in trying to bide time. The situation would not alter. "Of course," I replied cheerily, as if there was absolutely nothing to hide. I returned to my chambers and retrieved an adjustable ladder which I had carefully hidden underneath my bed. I stretched it out so it would reach the trapdoor and began climbing the eight steps leading to the ceiling of the hall, while pushing the trapdoor open and upward.

When we had reached the upper floor landing, the sergeant looked around. "What is so valuable behind that wall and the locked door?" he inquired, cocking his head a bit to the side.

"Nothing but empty crates, sir," I replied, but not feeling so confident anymore. Withdrawing the key from my pocket, I had trouble even with both hands guiding it into the lock. My body shook like a leaf in the wind. Soon the ax would come down on me. I knew it! That blasted wooden wall and especially the locked door were stupid mistakes, for which I could get burned.

Once inside, I started kicking the empty crates about, frantic to demonstrate the legitimacy of my claims. When we had passed two rows, the sergeant suddenly put one hand on my shoulder and asked, "Are they really empty?" He looked me straight in the eye, but I noticed a roguish grin on his face.

"Yes," I lied, putting everything on one card, but my voice lacked that convincing sound. My armpits started to sweat, which happened every time I skated on thin ice. "Except some that contain leftover packing material," I added unnecessarily, though it was a half-truth.

"I believe you this time," he remarked, adding good-humoredly, "provided you pour us another glass of booze before we leave."

Not for the first time, and probably not for the last, I felt that heavy "one-stone weight" sliding off my shoulders and thudding to the floor. It seemed my execution had been postponed.

We chatted for another fifteen minutes or so while enjoying a plum liqueur this time. Then I handed over a copy of our up-to-date official inventory list, and we left the building.

Coincidentally, the other two inspection teams had also concluded their tasks. Werner had been instructed to have a complete inventory list of all confiscated weapons ready. Our makeshift armory would be emptied the next day by a special contingent, including demolition and bomb-defusing experts. All collected weapons would be carted off.

When the Allies had left the base, Doehle, Werner, and I had to report the outcome of the inspection to the commandant. When my turn came, I dramatically withdrew my handkerchief from my pocket and wiped my face while describing our visit to the loft. The best news of all, however, was that not one grave had been discovered! We could live like kings for another five or six weeks.

The Skull

Tuesday after the inspection, on 15 May, Lars called me with a personal request from Colonel Hyllesand. He asked if I would be interested in assisting the British in adjusting to driving on the right side of the road? Since they had landed in Norway they underwent a number of accidents, some of them serious, because of their left-hand-side driving habits.

"Delighted to be of help," I replied, "if I get permission to leave the base, assuming this will involve several days. But I cannot drive a car myself, Lars."

"Not necessary," he replied. "All you have to do is sit beside the driver. You are right, though. Hyllesand has a plan to reduce accidents over and above instructing the drivers. He will fill you in on details. A written request will be forwarded to your base commander by courier before the day is over."

He left his number where he could be reached. I informed Doehle of the request, and only then did I give him a sketchy outline of my previous encounter with the colonel. He was all ears and then commented, "I was wondering where you spent all evening on the ninth. The sentry had told me that four strange-looking individuals had picked you up. It sounded as if you had been kidnapped or something."

The courier arrived at 1700 hours with Hyllesand's request for my release for a few days. He brought four copies: one for our commandant to sign; the second one was for him to retain; the third went to Doehle; and one was for me in case somebody asked me any questions before I reported to Hyllesand.

I called Lars after dinner and established a pick-up time for me to report to their headquarters. I was told 0700 hours would be O.K. for them, but not for me. It was a bit early for my taste, but what the heck.

Erik picked me up with the same vehicle the four had used a week before. The streets were deserted, and Erik did not waste any time. Houses seemed to swish by rather fast. No wonder; when glancing at the speedometer it showed sixty miles per hour, twice the allowable speed. "It's a good thing you are used to left-hand driving," I commented to Erik. "Otherwise I would need an ejection seat and a parachute." He only grinned and laughed.

Colonel Hyllesand's plan was like this: Four different jeep convoys would comb through routes that were traveled most often. He presented a Rogaland map to me on which the four routes had been traced in red ink, reminding me of human arteries. He allowed me to pick the one I preferred. I decided on the twin-route via Sandness, Byrne, and then along the coast to Egersund. The return trip would be made further inland. It practically retraced the excursion route I had made with Heinz Marzi during our bartering trip in May 1942.

Our team commanded two ordinary-sized jeeps with three men in each. The back seat of each jeep was piled high with all kinds of transparencies and warning signs, which we would install in appropriate and particularly dangerous spots in order to be plainly seen by drivers of approaching vehicles.

By the time we arrived in Egersund, we had used twenty-seven of them. Some were quite funny–Keep right, dummy!; Stay right and stay alive!; This is not Great Britain, remember?; The bright keep right!; Got brains? Remain with an arrow pointing to the right.

At Egersund British base, a message awaited us. We were ordered to advance further eastward to the town of Moi, at the northern tip of Lundevatnet (Lunde Lake). The first documentary film about German concentration camps had arrived in a camp nearby Moi. Viewing was arranged for all Germans and British troops over the next ten days.

We overnighted in a British Army compound in Egersund and continued our journey the next morning. The distance to Moi is only forty kilometers, but we carried a sufficient number of signs with us to make several stops on the way. We arrived in Moi shortly before noon.

Transport trucks were arriving in droves, bringing German internees together from all surrounding areas. My English companions and I had luncheon together in one of the two base mess halls. This kept me busy, even during the meal, translating back and forth for some of my comrades who had not yet rubbed elbows with the former enemy.

Naturally, the conversation zeroed in on concentration camps. I could see by their faces that my English companions did not believe that we simply did not know what actually went on in these camps. We knew about them, but that was all.

It is inconceivable for people who grow up in a democratic and open society that any government would be able to keep crimes like these from the people, but let me remind you how long it took the Soviets to find out how many millions Stalin had slaughtered during his reign of total terror! Six million Ukrainians alone were systematically starved to death in the early thirties in the breadbasket of the Soviet socialist republics!

The film presentation lasted about eighteen minutes. I sat there, mesmerized, crying like a baby! Only then did I fully realize how rotten our system of governing (for which I never had any use in the first place) really was! The greatest irony of these acts was that these despicable crimes were committed in the name of the German people. What a blessing it is to live in a free society!

I took the opportunity to chat a while with a couple of chaps who had left Stavanger bases to accept special assignments in Moi. One of them was Inspector Pohlmann, who had presented felt-covered boots to me when I had to leave for the Arctic. Now he had the task of providing food and supplies to the British for distribution to several base camps right down to Farsund. He was as jovial as ever. He gave me a box of fine cigars and some Weinbrant (Brandy) for myself and my English friends. "Tell them," he said, "that the Scots are not the only ones who can make good booze." He also gave me his home address, and suggested to "look me up one of these days." Unfortunately, I lost it in the bustle of demobilization in Mandal later on.

Returning to Stavanger was a cinch, except for the second part of the ninety-five-kilometer stretch, where we had to pass through mountainous regions. Accidents were more likely to happen there than anywhere else.

We had saved some of the more dramatic reminders, of which we made liberal use. At two particularly hair-raising spots where there were high-rising mountains to one side and precipitous declivity on the other side with winding roads, we spanned huge transparencies right across the roads before and after a sharp curve. The more than candid inscription on the banner started with a realistic-looking skull shouting at the approaching driver, "Why hurry? The closest hospital is right around the next corner!" Some grim humor all right!

We checked in with Hyllesand in early afternoon for a debriefing. He did not want to hear a word from me about quickly returning to my base but kept me there at headquarters for a roast beef dinner. I met a number of group members for the second time, and some others I had not yet met. Short of being able to reciprocate, I passed my box of cigars around after dinner, which was quite appreciated. Most were cigar smokers, but not by accident. For reasons unknown to me, members of underground organizations and revolutionaries, even when coming to power, seem to be more hooked on cigars than on cigarettes. Fidel Castro is not alone!

FACING DEMOBILIZATION

Move With Bag And Baggage

By 24 May, our new role was clearly defined. We were about to become responsible for the supervision and administration of assembled German convoys, which included all German U-boats which entered Stavanger Harbor since our surrender. We also were expected to supply sufficient minesweepers and naval personnel to clear all German mines from Flekkefjord, south of Stavanger, to Bergen in the north. It sounded like a piece of cake, but the trouble was we had to move from Bjergsted Park with all our equipment and furniture to Buøy, the southern part of a twin island. The northern part is named Hundvag and is the largest island within a clustered group located east-northeast of Stavanger. With its Strait of Pynte and the two islands of Engoy and Solist nearby, the surrounding waterways were ideally suited to serve as a haven for all types of vessels.

Formal permission was granted by the Allies to prepare for the move. There were no conditions set. We could take everything with us we found necessary to resume operations at our new post.

We began assembling material, equipment and furniture during the night from Thursday to Friday, since we had to be in operating position by Sunday, 27 May.

All those accumulated empty crates in the casino loft came in handy now. It appeared as if we were in for a rather rainy weekend, so it was only prudent to protect all items as assiduously as possible. Besides, there was an added reason for being cautious: The southern part of the strait of Byfjorden had to be crossed where it ended in the bay of Vagen. And we knew from the failed attempt of the British to sink the *Tirpitz* what sea water can do to equipment.

At about 0100 hours in the morning of the twenty-fifth, when we crated a few of Doehle's items and set up a chesterfield outside his quarters, two bright lights shone into our eyes. A voice demanded, "Stop! What are you doing here?"

We shielded our eyes with our hands, while Doehle replied in English, "What does it look like? We are packing to relocate. And take your damn lights out of our faces."

That helped. The lights went out. In the moonlight we made out two huge, tall figures staring at us. Both were Canadians in British uniforms. "Keep your hands in sight," said the man who had spoken before. "Do you have any weapons?"

Werner got fed up. "First of all," he retorted, "how did you get in here without an invitation? Second, our weapons were carted off by your pals two weeks ago. You are out of touch and out of order. Third, we are moving to an island close by in a couple of days by order of your city commandant and your naval commanding officer. Any other questions? If not, leave us alone. We have better things to do than to answer silly questions."

During his tirade, I had elbowed Werner in his ribs, but he did not take notice. In any case, his boldness had worked. The two towering men changed their tune. No, they were not on official inspection. They had passed by the base and, seeing all the movements, suspected that something fishy was going on. The reason for not having been announced by our sentry was they had sneaked into the base by the side fence which had not been correctly secured.

A couple of small boats were lined up to transport our stuff to the island. About 1400 hours, we started loading the first one. We were barely halfway through, when suddenly, as if out of nowhere, more than a dozen Norwegians, dressed in semi-battle fatigues, swarmed upon us and demanded to inspect our goods. Not one of them looked familiar to me, which I found strange.

I was responsible at the time for the loading procedures at the harbor. Werner and Doehle were up at the base. Several comrades were about to move some furniture in crates onto the boat, when one of the visitors came with a cleaver and a big knife. He started chopping at one of the crates.

"We are searching for weapons and other things you are not supposed to have," one of the men declared.

That made me angry, but not angry enough to assault the man with the knife and the cleaver. I wasn't that stupid. Too bad I did not have the friendship coin with me which could have ended the debate in no time.

I rushed up the hill to the base and tried to get in touch with Lars. Nobody answered the phone. Werner, in the meantime, had contacted the city commandant's office and complained about the harassment by Norwegians who, after all, had not defeated us and had no business flexing their muscles now.

Returning to the quay, I saw another man starting to work on a chesterfield, cutting the upholstery apart. Again, I decided to be chicken, rather than turning up dead. Five minutes later, a jeep screeched to a halt about twenty steps away from where we stood. Six British MPs jumped off the vehicle, four of them wearing submachine guns. They quickly surrounded the Norwegians and led them halfway to the jeep.

The leader of the MP team, a lieutenant, came over to me. I gave him a quick account of the event and produced the loading permit from the commandant. He amazed me by asking whether we wanted to press charges. I declined, for Lars' sake. Minutes later, a pickup truck arrived on the scene and drove the intruders away.

Later in the evening, Doehle called the city commandant and thanked him for the assistance. The latter apologized for the inconvenience and assured us this would not repeat itself. It was after 2000 hours when I finally got hold of Lars. He had already heard about the incident. "It didn't take you long to solve that problem," he commented lightly. "We found out that splinter group used to belong to the Hardanger territory. The area commander expelled them for previous infractions, but now has no control over them. Detailed information is now in the hands of the British, who will take it from there."

I told Lars we were moving to Buøy and gave him an open invitation to visit there as soon as we were settled in. Doehle did not set any restrictions on me for inviting people. He kind of admired and very much approved of me having become a connecting link to the former Resistance.

The next morning I was sent over to the island with the second boat. My mandate was to survey the terrain and select a suitable building for utilization as an officers casino. What else? I had to start yet another operation from scratch. Five men were assigned to me to get things moving fast. By the same evening, 26 May, the mess was operational. "If this continues," I told myself, "I will soon be able to do this in my sleep."

Brush With Death

The following day was bright and sunny. Since I had not taken a dip in the ocean for almost a year, I decided to skip luncheon, and went to the more western part of the island. I had neglected swimming in the fjords, which I loved very much.

A fifteen-minute walk brought me to an area where rocks rimmed the island. Slight slopes ended up on sandy beaches. I sat for a while on my beach towel, sunglasses on, enjoying nature. Occasionally, a PT boat would pass by in the distance. Otherwise, it was as quiet as during church service.

I soaked up sun for about forty minutes, then went down the slopes in preparation for a swim, my favorite pastime. I had become a good swimmer after my dad removed my fear of deep water. The temperature was cold, maybe about nineteen degrees Celsius, but I was used to that. Applying wide breast strokes, occasionally turning around to float on my back, I cruised away from land.

Suddenly I noticed a small boat approaching from the northeast and steering in the opposite direction. The sound of German voices told me that some of my comrades were on a pleasure cruise. I thought it might not be a bad idea to join them. Keeping on course, and judging from their course and speed, I would be able to be near them at a triangle, the logical meeting point.

After a few minutes, though, I became nonplused. I did not appear to be making any headway. Was I that slow? Then it dawned on me; they had changed course and were now moving away from the island, rather than sailing horizontally with it. I turned around. I was too far away from the island now to make it back! For a moment, I panicked but told myself that would bring certain death.

I began shouting to the men in the boat and gesticulating with my arms, only to see them waving back. There was no other alternative but to turn around. Luckily I never suffered from spasms in my legs when swimming. But to be on the safe side, I turned around on my back, gently paddling with my legs and hands to save energy, as my father had taught me so well.

Ten minutes went by. When I looked toward the island, I knew I could not conquer that distance. "What a lousy way to die," flashed through my mind for the third time in my life. The first time I was sitting like a duck in the basement while bombs fell all around. Next was trying to stay afloat in the minesweeper while the Tommies attacked front, back and sideways. And now this! Too bad I was not a cat with nine lives.

I was still approximately four kilometers away from shore. My strokes became weaker and weaker. Once I had already swallowed sea water from an uncontrolled dip. How long could I last?

Lifting my head, I saw a couple of men coming over the rocks from the same spot from where I had descended. Hallelujah! Rescue was on the way. I started shouting, "Help! Help!" as loudly as I could and moved my arms alternately up and down. They were too far away to hear what I was shouting and just waved back.

Panic grasped me again. So close to the rescue, and yet no help? I involuntarily dipped again and, coming up, began coughing water from my lungs. The two men fixed a startled stare at me, then looked at each other and jumped into the fjord waters. I had submerged renewed and felt close to the end. "Hold on a bit longer," a voice told me. It seemed, though, as if I was going to blackout at any moment. My lungs and heart hurt like they had needles sticking in them. The pain had a paralyzing effect on me. I sank once more and lost consciousness. Everything went black.

I did not know it then, but I regained consciousness after a few seconds, feeling clamps around my arms and upper body. The two comrades had me in tow, dragging me to the beach. I find it hard to describe how I felt when I realized I had been saved after all. The two placed me face-down and pumped some water out of my lungs. I sat up, dazed and coughing, but otherwise still alive, although I felt like I was broken in several places.

I had been more than lucky–again!

The two were looking for a good spot to lie in the sun and swim like I had done and, coincidentally, had selected the same spot. Their ship had thrown anchor the previous night at Engoy Vagnet south of Buøy. In search of a good beach, they had swam across the Strait of Pynte to Buøy.

Nowadays, the islands of Buøy, Engoy, Solyst and Grasholmen are connected with each other by bridges and a highway that ends on the mainland, Stavanger East, at an open-air swimming pool.

It took me a few days to get over the shock. Four days after the near-drowning, a couple of comrades invited me to swim across Pynte Sundet to Engoy Sorvagen, the southern bay of Engoy, where a friend of theirs served on an oil tanker. The friend had announced his arrival in port by wireless.

When we approached the strait, its water did not look too clean to me, but I did not pay any great attention to it. A good shower after the swim would fix that. At least that is what I thought.

Crossing the strait was quite easy. The only thing that bothered me a bit was an intensive oil smell. Otherwise, the water carried my body extremely well.

After twelve minutes we waded ashore on the north center of Engoy. We put on our board shoes, which we had carried over our shoulders in airtight bags during the swim. We had to cross the island now in a southeasterly course in order to reach Sorvagen Bay. The more we walked, the more uncomfortable my skin felt. It was as if everything was tightening up. But I did not say a peep for fear of appearing too sensitive.

Having received permission to come aboard, our host greeted us on deck with raised eyebrows. "What is this?" he inquired, ogling at our swimming trunks. "Did you not come by boat?" Without waiting for an answer, he criticized, "You have to be nuts to swim across the strait. Didn't you see the oil slicks?"

"We didn't pay any attention to it," one of my companions replied. "But now that you mention it, my skin feels as if it continues to shrink." Aha, I thought; I am not alone.

We remained aboard for an hour, hardly daring to sit down anywhere. Ordinarily, wet swimming trunks cling to the body. This was different. They were gliding and sliding. I had already turned the waistline around a couple of times, but that did not help much either. There was the danger they would suddenly slip down and not get caught anywhere.

The ship's captain arranged for us to be taken back to Buøy with a lifeboat, but the damage was done. The three of us got special permission to rub our bodies with turpentine, followed by soapy showers. That gradually replaced the oil smell, but then we smelled like walking paint thinner. After a while, I had to laugh. I could not help thinking about a funny German feature film I had seen some years hence. Its title was *Die Drei von der Tankstelle (Three Guys from the Petrol Station).* If we had not assumed their roles, we certainly smelled like them!

Hospitalized

The next day we received a special message from the Allied high command in Oslo. It was addressed to all German base units, indicating that several thousands of German naval personnel and officers would be needed to conclude the dismantling of all fortifications, the sweeping of mines, and other related operations. Volunteers were sought to carry out these projects and to stay in Norway for an additional eighteen months.

My first reaction was to go for it. The war was over. What could be more pleasant than spending some extra time in a country I had learned to love?

We had the weekend to mull over this offer. By Monday, I had decided against the idea for two main reasons; I was anxious and curious to find out whether my parents had survived the war, and it had to be assumed, as a logical conclusion, because of extensive bombings in Germany, there would not be enough jobs to go around for everybody. Delaying my demobilization could mean that a lot of other comrades would snatch up the jobs available. By the time I showed up, I would get the shorter end of the stick, or no stick at all.

During that week my hay fever started like clockwork. Since there was no antihistamine medication available on the island, it got progressively worse. On the weekend of 15-16 June, I could not open my eyelids any longer. The base physician determined that I had a case of acute conjunctivitis. He made arrangements for me to be transported to the area major army-air force-navy hospital, which was located at the time near Aalgard, south of Stavanger and the town of Sandness.

My co-steward and another chap packed a few things for me in the evening, including the raincoat from Lars Hansen. The following afternoon, a medical orderly accompanied me, my head all bandaged up, to the quay where a small motorboat was waiting.

We cast off immediately, crossed the Strait of Byfjorden, and docked at Strandkaien, the western part of Vagen inlet. A navy transport truck awaited us and several other patients who could not be treated at the regular naval hospital. All suffered acute illnesses of some kind or another.

As soon as I had climbed into the truck and sat on a bench, we were set in motion, in the real sense of the word. The springs of the truck must have been shot to pieces, and shock absorbers appeared nonexistent.

Being thrown from side to side, back and forth, was bad enough, while we traveled on a paved main road. But the real fun began when we reached the outskirts of Stavanger and hit a gravel road. "If this takes long," I thought, "I will have a second illness by the time we arrive at our destination: hemorrhoids." No matter how careful the driver tried to be, and he really tried, we were shaken up like potatoes on a train.

When the arrival was announced, one could hear a sigh of relief. The less than forty-kilometer trip had lasted two hours.

Having been assigned to a bed, I thanked the orderly for taking good care of me and almost immediately fell asleep.

I woke up when someone shook my arm. It was dinner time. From the sounds around me I figured I had been placed in a ward, together with another dozen or so soldiers. This was nothing unusual for a military hospital. Semiprivate accommodations are only available for the brass.

The next several days were an ordeal. Every morning, after breakfast, two orderlies would pick me up and guide me to one of the base hospital's treatment rooms. On the first morning after he had removed the bandage, I heard the chief of staff explaining to several other doctors who gathered around me, "Here, gentlemen, you can see a typical case of acute conjunctivitis."

I was sitting on an adjustable stool with a small lumbar backrest. The medic forced one eyelid open at a time, carefully lifted one eyeball out of the socket, and treated the socket with a cauterizing liquid, using what looked like a fine bakers brush. Then he repeated the same procedure with the other eye.

I was given a medium-sized bowl, which I used to collect tears that flowed from my eyes caused by the tincture and pain, which is hard to describe. Of course, the details of this procedure I could only see on the fourth day of this treatment, when some improvements in my condition had taken place.

Four times a day I had to take antihistamine tablets, which did their part to ease the itching somewhat.

On Sunday, 24 June, the chief indicated that I could leave in a couple of days. That was O.K. with me. I was an ambulatory patient now, free to move around without any assistance. And there was a shortage of beds on the base anyway.

Monday evening, when I just had sat down for dinner, I was called to the telephone. My base commandant's adjutant was on the line. "When are you going to return?" he asked.

"Maybe tomorrow," I replied.

"The reason I ask," he explained, "is our base will be dissolved tomorrow. You'd better make it tomorrow. Talk to your doctor. Otherwise, we may not be here anymore and you will be in limbo. Your papers are already made out. As a next step, we will be transferred further south to a reception camp before ending up in Mandal for debriefing and demobilization." He hung up, not awaiting my response.

I went to the dispensary and asked for the physician on call. Luck was with me. One of the young internists who had witnessed my first treatment came within five minutes. He supplied me with medication for about four weeks. It would last long enough for the remainder of the hay fever season. Then he checked with his superior, asking for permission to make out my discharge papers. "You are in luck," he said. "Three other soldiers will leave tomorrow also, all of them for Stavanger. A bus has been ordered. Be ready by 1000 hours."

Prince Olav

The next morning after breakfast, I said good-bye to the gang with whom I had shared accommodations for over a week. The bus pulled up as scheduled, and away we went.

Halfway between Sandness and Stavanger the vehicle broke down. Now what? I got nervous. What if I did not make it to the base in time before everybody flew the coop? We were about eight kilometers short of Stavanger.

My three companions decided to start walking. I joined them for a while, but got fed up. With that gravel road I was going to ruin the only halfway decent pair of oxfords I had left. I picked a milestone beside the road and leaned against it, waiting for something to happen.

After waiting twenty minutes, an ox cart came into view, moving in my direction. The open cart was full of milk cans. The farmer on the riding box sucked at his Briar pipe. He seemed to be engrossed in nature around him. When he was close enough, I asked whether he could give me a ride. That would be fine with him if I had plenty of time. He had to make close to twenty stops before reaching Stavanger and the oxen could not be pushed. They had only one speed, slow. Besides, he had to use some side roads.

I did some quick arithmetic. It was 1050 hours and I had about seven kilometers to go. I could walk these in about one and a quarter hours. Add an extra hour and a half and it would be about 1330 hours by the time we entered the harbor area. Why not enjoy the fresh air and save my precious shoes?

I boarded the riding board beside him. Every time a milk can had to be unloaded I jumped off and placed it beside the receiver's mail box at the road entrance to a farm. His German was limited, but not as much as my Norwegian. We got along fine. I enjoyed his company. The man radiated a complacency that became infectious. I was quite content with the way things were going. Nothing beats the power of positive thinking.

It was 1320 hours when he let me off at the harbor. To be less conspicuous, I removed my navy cap and put on Lars Hansen's raincoat. Now I looked like a civilian with my oxfords. There were no other German uniforms around. Since the surrender, all German military had been confined to their bases. Interpreters were the exception, because sometimes their assignments made it necessary to go ashore, as we say in the navy.

I walked the few steps to the building on Skagen, where the harbor control complex used to be located, which I assumed would now be operated by the British. My assumption was correct.

Entering the main entrance, I walked through the familiar corridor until I reached the door of the receptionist, who used to announce visitors and invitees to Captain Schubert. Before I knocked, I craned my neck a bit to see the inscription on the next door. Captain Schubert's nameplate had been covered with a white paper reading, "Commander MacIntosh." The German word *Hafenkapitaen* for Harbor Captain had not been changed. Either MacIntosh was not a particular man or he wanted his men to use their own imagination a bit.

The door in front of me bore a new sign, "Reception–Harbor Administration." A piece of paper was pinned underneath, "Knock and walk in." There was no one in the hallway, nor had I seen one British uniform anywhere outside the building.

I walked in. A petty officer first class sat behind a desk, his feet resting on the edge. He put down the newspaper he had been reading on the desk and slowly disengaged himself from a comfortable swivel chair. To my friendly "Good afternoon," he replied with "Good day," adding, "what can I do for you?" He looked a bit lost. Apparently, he could not place me.

Not to let him dangle in the air, I identified myself and asked if I could use his telephone to contact my unit on Buøy Island. I wanted to let them know that I had returned and was prepared to be picked up by boat.

"Of course," the sergeant replied accommodatingly, and moved the counter telephone toward me. I picked up the receiver, dialed, and received a busy signal. After two minutes I made another attempt and got through.

The chap at the communication center instantly recognized my voice and said, "Hold a few seconds." Then the commandant's aide came on the line.

"There is a problem with picking you up," he stated. "We have been instructed to put all naval movements on hold until about 1730 hours. Nobody is allowed to come close to the harbor. We have no idea why not, but as soon as the restriction is lifted we shall send a boat to Skagenkaien. Stick around."

Before he could hang up, I threw in for good measure, trying to be funny, "Do I have a choice?"

I told the sergeant about the restriction and asked for the reason. "I cannot comment on that except to say that a general naval inspection of two destroyers, which are tied up outside right now, will take place. But I guess it's all right if you watch, since you don't stick out like a sore thumb among other civilians, who probably will watch the parade as well."

I thanked him for letting me use the phone, and turned to the door. Prior to my touching the door handle (they don't use knobs in European countries) he asked, as if on second thought, "By the bye, where did you learn English?" I told him about the Berlitz School and mentioned Werner Boes, which seemed to satisfy his curiosity.

Coming outside, I stepped into bright sunlight. The two destroyers looked threatening, tied up side by side at the quay. A bunch of sailors disembarked from both vessels, all dressed spic and span for the upcoming occasion. The men took different positions. Two groups of about forty men each stood in four rows in front of their vessels.

A couple of minutes went by. Two acting sublieutenants came down the ship's planks, baton in hand. "Great," I thought. "They are going to give an open-air concert." While this went on, I noticed a step-by-step gathering of about two hundred or so Norwegian civilians taking place on the quay. Both quays at Stavanger inlet, Strandkaien and Skagenkaien, are wide and spacious allowing a considerable number of ships to be loaded and/or unloaded simultaneously without encumbrance. I looked at my watch; it was 1425 hours.

I found it strange that if there was a parade or an inspection to take place, nobody seemed to bother with cordoning off the area for security reasons.

One of the two conductors had raised his baton. The choir bellowed out what for years I had considered to be a German song whose title and first line of lyrics was "*Wochenend und Sonnenschein" (*"Weekend and Sunshine*")*. Only the lyrics were different: "Happy Days are Here Again." I could not believe what my ears were hearing.

I had another surprise coming. When the first choir had ended its song, the second one started with "Roll out the barrel, we'll have a barrel of fun," the German title of which is *Rosamunde.* Both songs struck a familiar chord in me. Until that day, I thought the only song with cosmopolitan flavor was the one Lale Anderson had made so popular, the song about Lily Marlene. How much I had to learn! The crowd applauded jubilantly.

The two choirs continued to sing alternately for about twenty minutes. Then a company of Norwegian soldiers in British uniforms came marching from the courtyard of our former headquarters. They carried the Norwegian national flag on one side, and a British standard with an army emblem with which I was not familiar on the other side. These were all men who had left Norway when her legitimate government went into exile, and had served as members of a battalion within the British Army. A small half-moon shaped label on the upper arm sleeve with the word *Norsk* was their identification mark.

They marched right by where we stood and lined up further down Skagenkaien, close to one of the four huge loading cranes.

Several Norwegian policemen appeared on the scene, asking us politely to leave about ten paces space between us and the navy men, whom we were facing. More naval personnel had shown up to join their comrades on the quay, who had stopped singing. No doubt there was an inspection in the wind.

Ten minutes went by. Then we could see a motorcade of three vehicles approaching from around the harbor inlet and entering Skagenkaien. Four motorcyclists in Norwegian King's Guard uniform, two on each side, led the small convoy.

They advanced slowly, probably not faster than ten kilometers per hour, and came to a full stop approximately thirty meters to the left of where we stood. The crowd had swelled to several hundred people. I had wormed myself to the front row of spectators for a vantage point, expecting something special to happen.

The four cyclists dismounted and were joined by generals who had been passengers of the second and third car. At that moment I noticed that the first passenger car was flying two different flags, one each mounted on the left and right front fender. One fender carried the Union Jack and on the other front fender fluttered the Norwegian Royal Standard, clearly distinguishable by the stand-up lion in the center of the flag, wearing the royal crown on his head, and holding a tomahawk-like hatchet up in his front paws.

Four figures emerged from the car as soon as two of the King's Guardsmen had opened the car doors to one side. The first figure stepping out of the vehicle was an imposing and ascetic-looking man, over six feet tall. He wore a British Army uniform with the Basque-like cap made popular by Field Marshal Montgomery, the identification mark of the green berets.

But that did not fool me. I had seen his picture and that of his dad many times in homes of Norwegian friends. The man who had vacated the automobile was Norwegian Prince Olav, the man who today reigns as King of Norway!

Following on his heels, an admiral of the Royal Navy peeled himself out of the car; then an army general with the *Norsk* arm label, and finally a brigadier with the typical huge armlets, indicating the function of an aide-de-camp.

The Prince and his entourage advanced slowly. He returned the salute of the naval honor guard to his left, alternately greeting the civilian assembly to his right with a friendly wave of his hand. When he came to where I stood, I instinctively raised my right hand to salute, but, remembering that I was supposed to be a civilian, caught myself in midair and waved with my palm outward. He looked directly at me with a natural smile and hesitated for a moment as if he was about to stop in order to ask me a question. I had seen him doing this further up the line on a few occasions, but he continued his walk. For a few seconds, only two steps had divided us. Exhilarated by the experience, I had something to tell my children and grandchildren, having been that close to the Prince who was destined to become the King of Norway, Haakon VII!

My boat arrived at 1745 hours. We reached Buøy fifteen minutes later. The whole base appeared like a swarm of bees. I was instantly engaged to translate German travel documents with Lieutenant Doehle. While I was hospitalized, Werner Boes had left the base for Mandal, the actual demobilization camp where all German soldiers had to pass before being released to Germany. At 0100 hours everything was in order. We were ready to be shipped out that same day.

Welcome To Feda

We had our last breakfast on Buøy and boarded two small boats. When entering Stavanger Vagens inlet, it was clear we were not the only ones being sent off. Skansekaien, Skagenkaien and Strandkaien were swarming with German uniforms: army, air force and navy. It almost looked as if we just had successfully landed an invasion force. I had never seen that many members of Armed Forces congregating in Stavanger. There were over two thousand men.

Apparently a number of area bases had been dissolved. A rather large convoy was in the making. What amazed me most, certainly not for the last time, was that one could see barely a dozen British uniforms. I was about to discover that the British knew so well their instructions would be followed to the letter. They refused to worry about our conduct. Drilled-in German obedience did not allow for any variations. It was in sharp contrast to our own experience with other nationals, who could not be trusted to obey our orders unless we constantly were breathing down their necks!

Our destiny was an internment camp situated near the community of Feda, between Flekkefjord and Lyngdal, a distance of about ninety kilometers southeast of Stavanger. It was the major holding camp of soldiers who were expecting demobilization at the camp in Mandal, the most southern point of Norway, before being shipped to Germany. The Feda Camp would supply Mandal with German soldiers based on the speed with which Mandal could manage demobilizing German troops. The ones released would be substituted by others arriving from northerly territories.

Feda Camp was like a small town. At any given time, in excess of seven thousand men lived there. Some of us were received with a big hello, as comrades who had not seen each other for some time became unexpectedly reunited.

Accommodations were surprisingly well-kept and clean. Of course, we had to look after the upkeep ourselves. Chambermaids or housekeepers were not available.

After a couple of days, I became acquainted with a jovial Scottish sergeant from the camp administration. He was kind enough to chat with me and supply me with English newspapers, providing me with something to do in my leisure time, which was most of the time. Sure, the occasional work commandos were put together, assisting with repairs on barracks and roads. But overall it was evident the camp administration had difficulties keeping us busy.

I was there about a week when I took an extended stroll with some other comrades through the whole camp. We were curious whether there was any way by which we could make our stay more interesting, besides meeting girls who did not exist in this environment. Sure enough, we found what we were looking for.

Two buildings close to the center point of the camp advertised in big bold letters "Troop Entertainment." We went into the first one and investigated what entertainment was being offered. In answer to our queries the officer in charge explained that several stage shows, some theatrical, others light sketches, were offered on a weekly rotating basis. On Wednesdays the huge hall was used for skat game tournaments and chess competitions.

The second building we entered was only about to open up at the end of the current week for the first time. Stage directors, cameramen, decorators, those in charge of lighting, and program directors were in the process of setting up a cabaret show. It just so happened they were still looking for some additional talents, including members of the pit orchestra. But I would have to see the producer if I was interested. I was.

His office was located at the end of the long-stretched building. The nameplate on the door indicated that Hans-Dieter Kleinbartz was the *Produzent*, or producer.

We entered and saluted an air force squadron leader with a chest full of decorations. He sported a semi-handlebar mustache. His shirt collar was wide open and revealed rust-brown chest hair sticking out. His smile, overall appearance, and relaxed informality with which he offered us seats signaled to me an unconventional character. He was my kind of person.

I told him my intention to join the pit orchestra, adding I could read. He knew what I meant, even though I had purposely left out the word notes. He smiled broadly.

"Good," he replied, sounding interested. "We have another mandolin and one mandola player. You could help beef up the third mandolin section which is rather weak. Starting tomorrow we will hold daily rehearsals until opening day. So far we have rounded up forty-two musicians: strings, brass, woodwinds, reeds, cello, two string bassists, a great pianist and, not to forget, a terrific percussionist." He handed a small parcel to me. "Here," he added, "is a set of third mandolin charts with all show tunes for you to practice. Report to the program director at 0900 hours sharp tomorrow."

The premier performance of our cabaret show was scheduled for Saturday, 14 July. Every morning I would march with my instrument to rehearsal, which would often last four hours. Producers and directors had not spared the horses to come up with a performance that would have been acceptable in a big city theater. Besides the sizable pit orchestra, whose terrific percussionist turned out to be our Teddy Paris from Stavanger, the talent finders had managed to get hold of a juggler, two acrobats, a high-wire act trio, comics, a dandy MC, who would crack jokes between acts, and a full-fledged chorus line, consisting of twenty-seven men acting as chorus girls with dance costumes, professional makeup, the necessary "roundings," and nicely-shaved legs. Nothing was missing. This promised to be fun!

Every late afternoon I hid in the basement of the barrack and practice the charts, driving everybody nuts with endless scales.

Two performances were scheduled each day until we could measure the response of the audience. It was simply overwhelming! A third performance had to be scheduled. After the third day, tickets were sold out for three weeks in advance. That could turn out to be a headache for the organizers, as some of us undoubtedly would have been moved to Mandal by then. But the show had to go on, as they say in Hollywood.

The camp was jointly administered by British and German officers. They decided we deserved extra food rations for our extra efforts. We did not object. What was of real importance to us was that we had found a way to break monotony and take our minds off troublesome thoughts.

When word came through on 7 August, that the first atom bomb had been dropped on Hiroshima, a sobering chill went through the camp. Nobody had expected that much horrifying and devastating force to be unleashed upon mankind. Maybe it should have been clear that viciousness had no limit in war! Everything is relative to something else, of course. If President Truman did not decide upon this drastic action, ten thousand or more American lives might have been lost during an invasion of Japan. Who is to say?

In the meantime, the men with whom I had arrived at the camp at the end of June had been moved to the top of the list of those due for transfer to Mandal, the official demobilization camp.

Our turn to be moved to Mandal came on Sunday, 12 August.

Mandal

After March 1944 when one hundred thirty thousand troops had been withdrawn from Norway to replace front-line casualties, about three hundred and fifty thousand servicemen remained. Regardless of where they had been stationed at the end of the war, or to which part of the armed forces they belonged, all had to pass through Mandal Camp.

The main purpose was to provide for an orderly demobilization of each soldier, which included a debriefing. Mandal's southern location and its proximity to the European mainland were not the only reasons for its function as the only demobilization camp. Because of the centralization of this activity, an intensified and uniform screening of individuals was made possible. For good measure, some ideological questions were asked during the screening process in the hope that disguised members of the SS, the SD, or the Gestapo would get confused and spill the beans.

Upon arrival, it became evident that this time somebody had miscalculated the number of empty berths in the camp. About two hundred of us had to sleep in ordinary tents. The fact that 185 men would arrive with their Norwegian brides, whom they had married close to and after the end of the war, had been overlooked.

The British camp personnel confined themselves pretty well to the screening and administration building. One could hardly see any British uniforms anywhere else. German camp police wearing white armbands with the appropriate inscriptions had been assigned by the Allies to maintain order and discipline. This time it did not surprise me. I now knew the philosophy of the Allies, which was so much opposite of ours in the past.

The next morning we lined up for inspection by the German officer who was detailed to look after our group. Naval personnel were informed that some additional mine sweeping personnel was needed to speed up the removal of mines along the coast. Two small British vessels had been slightly damaged by floating mines north of Aalesund and west of Bomlø, an island off the west coast north of Haugesund. The task of mine sweeping, however, was preferably assigned to those who volunteered for it. About three hundred men were needed as crew members.

I suppose it was a sign of adventurous spirit among naval personnel that more volunteered within a few minutes than were required. Three cheers for the navy! The officer was visibly impressed. "This is quite a group," he commented. "We have one more special assignment for which we need about a dozen men. I cannot disclose what it is about, except to say it includes daily routine."

Throwing my previous principle never to volunteer for anything overboard, I lifted my arm and was chosen with another thirteen men. Some useful work was necessary to keep one going in a big camp like this. It was unlikely that it would turn out to be dangerous work at this stage of the game. I had had my share of that!

While we stepped aside, the rest of the gang had been given various job assignments. Then we were told what our task would be: cleaning the administrative offices and the camp commandant's quarters every morning before the daily activities began.

The officer went with us to the building. There were eleven offices to look after. Two tools and cleaning supply rooms were centrally located. The previous cleaning crew had been demobilized. Keys for the supply rooms and a semi-master key for the offices were handed to a master able seaman, who also happened to be the eldest of the group. We were ready to go.

The good thing with this assignment was that it took us only two to two and a half hours to complete the job. We assembled at 0600 hours, went to the building, and usually were out again by 0830 hours, when the administrative personnel arrived. The rest of the day we were off.

On the fourth day we had two accidents. It had worked well that two in each team would cover different areas. That Friday, one team spilled a pail of dirty water over a carpeted floor while another man tripped over a container of wax on the landing of a set of stairs that led to the main office area. It caused quite a mess!

Even though we all took off our boots in the process of removing the wax, we were sliding all over the place. This was an easy way to break one's neck. The situation had to be adjusted before the British administrative personnel arrived or they would be prone to serious injury. We certainly did not want to arouse the anger of our former adversaries.

We were still trying to clean up the mess when a staff sergeant arrived with two other men on the scene. One man on our team had stationed himself at the bottom of the staircase, expecting their arrival. As the three passed me by, the sergeant said to his companions "These Krauts must have had a problem this morning," looking at his watch.

I could not let this go by without giving a "Darn right, Sergeant, sir, we did have two problems this morning. This could be Friday the thirteenth, which it isn't, but we had to clean up this muddle, rather than risking that you Tommies would break your necks."

For a moment I thought his eyes were popping out of his head. He had not expected us to understand his "Kraut" reference and did not count on such a reply. His laugh was a mixture of embarrassment and surprise. "I guess I had that tit for tat coming," he commented. "Why are you not with the screening teams with your knowledge of English, rather than cleaning offices?"

"Simple," I replied. "Nobody asked me."

"We could use your help with the debriefing of your comrades," he suggested. "Would you be interested?"

"Sounds like a good promotion," I agreed willingly. "All right with me, unless I cannot be replaced here. Do I get a formal invitation, and how would that change my own situation?"

"You would be screened immediately, rather than several weeks from now," he explained, "and join our team of interpreters until such time as you want to be formally demobbed yourself."

"Fine. Let's do it," I consented graciously, as if I was the one making the final decision on it.

He had prepared a cup of coffee–real coffee–before he began chatting with me. Other members of his administrative team appeared now, looking kind of puzzled to see their boss sitting with the Kraut, having an amiable conversation.

"Wait a minute," he ordered, picking up the telephone on the nearest desk to his. I heard him mention my name and rank. When he hung up he told me that Knudson, a Norwegian cadet, had instructions to have me put through the mill at 1400 hours today. I thanked him for his consideration and turned to leave. "See you later," he shouted after me when I had reached the door.

Returning to my group, I advised the officer in charge of the turn of events. "Lucky you," he commented. When the rest of the gang heard about it during lunch time, some accused me of pulling strings, but good-naturedly. I abstained from a reply but grinned from ear to ear.

The cadet had expected me when I walked into the screening compound. He knew the Germans were hardly ever late. Before I could identify myself, he addressed me in German, "You must be Sigy. Our staff sergeant was talking about you this morning. Our commandant is aware of your appearance and wants to interview you personally."

My wheels began to turn. Why did this cadet talk in German to me? Maybe he intended to give me an indirect message, indicating he would be able to know if I interpreted incorrectly for whatever reason. Who cares? I had absolutely nothing to hide and could easily prove my attitude by producing the special ID from Hyllesand. But no, let them find out about me firsthand.

"Follow me," the cadet ordered, and steered in the direction of a door off the main hall, which looked almost spacious enough to house a couple of light airplanes. The doorplate told me that this was the office of the commanding officer in charge of debriefing and demobilization. There was no name. Knudson knocked briefly and went in, shoving me in front.

Captain Cornish

A tall gentleman with rather marked features, standing in front of a huge desk with a folder in his hand, looked up expectantly. "Captain, sir," Knudson reported, "this is the German the chief mentioned this morning as a good candidate for aiding with our tasks."

I dug up my smartest salute, which the captain acknowledged suavely. "Thank you, Knudson. Check with me in another fifteen minutes or so," the captain instructed. Turning to me he offered his hand and said. "I am Captain Cornish, MI-Six."

He seemed to watch my face for a reaction, but I purposely did not drop an eyelid, as if his introduction was either Greek to me or the order of the day. He offered me a chair and sat close by, halfway facing me. Then, to my astonishment, he switched to German. "Able Seaman Born, where were you born?"

"In Wuppertal, Herr Kapitaen," I replied.

"Hm, Wuppertal," he reiterated. "Elberfeld or Barmen?"

It took me a few seconds to get over that shock. How the devil did this man know that Wuppertal consisted of several communities, interlocked with each other?

Loudly I said, "Elberfeld."

His next question stunned me even more. "What was your last employment?"

I told him. He nodded his head up and down. "A fine hotel," he approved. I just did not believe what I heard, and could not help myself asking, "You know Wuppertal, Captain, sir?"

"Quite well indeed," he replied, diverting to English, in all likelihood to test my fluency in his mother tongue. He asked me a few more questions about my parents and where I had learned English. He finally challenged me to give him a couple of examples that would differentiate between a dictatorship and a democratic government. I highlighted the restrictions set by the first versus the individual freedom of choice offered by the latter.

I could not resist offering a specific illustration, proving that not everything that goes on is acceptable in a democratic society. Quoting my former American teacher, I said, "I understand, sir, that my freedom to use my elbows stops where somebody else's nose begins."

He kind of liked that, chuckled, and replied, "That statement describes it well. Here is something I want you to be aware of," he emphasized. "As an interpreter you will have full access to all files regardless of the origin or type of information. You are not to discuss their content with anybody outside this building. And one more thing, we have a dual mandate here, the major one being the debriefing and demobilization of hundreds of thousands of your comrades. Proportionally lower, but certainly not of lesser importance, is our mandate to catch war criminals who may try to sneak through here in disguise. If the latter activity should make you feel uncomfortable for whatever reason, you don't have to accept our offer to assist us."

He had cocked his head slightly to one side as if waiting for a reply, which I gave without hesitation.

"Captain, sir," I assured, "I am just as interested as you are to see these people punished for their crimes. Catching some of them would not disturb my conscience at all. As far as keeping secrets under a lid, I have some experience in these matters due to my stint as administrative assistant with Naval Intelligence at former German naval headquarters in Stavanger."

We had a deal. He chatted with me a few more minutes, after which Knudson reappeared to lead me out of the complex.

On the same evening I moved into one of the barracks with my seven things. Enough Germans had been demobilized by now to eliminate the squatting in tents. It was purely coincidental, having nothing to do with my promotion.

On Saturdays the screening was reduced to half a day. The Norwegian cadet had asked me to report a half-hour earlier so he could introduce me to all members of the interrogation teams. The largest proportion of the hangar complex was used for the actual debriefing of soldiers. One corner of the hall was completely separated from the rest, since it served as a "delousing station." This was just a matter of health precaution. Shower and bath facilities were very limited on camp, allowing each person only one bath or shower a week. All newcomers went through this process first, as most of them had been hanging around for some time in other camps where personal hygiene was equally difficult to maintain.

There were fourteen interviewing stations, each manned by two teams of members of the British forces and two interpreters. Each station was separated from the next by partitions, providing a certain flexibility.

A number of resource persons floated around. They were brought into action in cases where it appeared that somebody had something to hide. Others served as fact finders. Their function was to provide confidential reports and other material for the interviewers. Most of this information originated from files of MI-Five, MI-Six, and the OSS. After a few days of working in this environment, I was amazed and impressed with the quality and quantity of information which enabled us to sort out fiction from facts.

When we had finished our round, passing all interview stations, Knudson said, "Now I want you to meet our resource people. They are known to the interviewers, of course, but it doesn't do you any harm to also know who they are."

He crossed the hall to the north side of the hangar, where several doors along the wall revealed offices. Assorted conspicuous signs bore the inscription "Authorized Personnel Only."

A stand-up sign was posted in front of the center door, with an arrow pointing to it and the words "Enter Here." Knudson opened it without first knocking. We had entered what was obviously a shared office area. Over twenty desks were sprinkled all over the area, each one divided from the next by about ten feet.

"Wait here," he ordered, "I'll round them up to meet you." He went from table to table and quietly talked to each person at the desks, who followed him to where I was standing. As they came closer, I counted twenty-one men and one woman, an impressive number of resource people. Looking closer at their faces, I incredulously recognized some of them.

They lined up in reception-line fashion. Knudson went with me to the front of the line and began introducing me to each member. The first two I did not know. The third was Eklund, the general manager of Holmenkollen in Oslo, whom I had initially met at the end of November 1942. He could not be here by accident, I was sure. His role as a loyal Quisling follower had been a phony one.

The conversation we had had on that certain Sunday in November crossed my mind. I had offered him to converse in English and had remarked, "Who is to know, if you do not have any listening devices planted in your hotel?" He had not given himself away then, but that was exactly what he had done all these years. Whenever the Germans held a high-level meeting in his hotel, he had taped the conversations and passed on the information through the Resistance to the Allies.

There was more to come. Further down the line, Messrs. Berger and Sandborg were standing side by side smiling at me. Herbert Kaufmann and I had dated their daughters, Astrid and Victoria. The two had been our hosts in 1941. I remembered Berger being a coordinating diplomat between the Quisling government and ours at the time, while Sandborg controlled security at the heavy water plant.

In reality, both had worked on behalf of the self-exiled Norwegian government. I met with them on my Sunday off and finally received an answer to a question I had raised in my mind in 1941, why they bothered with little fish like Herbert and me. The answer was simple. They did not want to arouse suspicion of having ulterior motives by dealing with German brass only. Astrid and Victoria knew their fathers' roles and assisted in playing the game of being sympathetic to the Germans.

When I had packed my things on the island of Buøy, I had put in a call to Lars Hansen, announcing my sudden departure from Stavanger for good. Asking for Erich Wallach, alias Alexander Spencer, Lars told me he had been sent southbound on special assignment.

Seeing him in the line-up told me what this was about. Alex became my main contact man for the group with whom I worked. He had a close to photographic memory and could find files with specific information for us in a jiffy.

The only female member in the line was a woman in her forties. She had been a special agent of MI-Five special branch and was thoroughly familiar with most intelligence matters referring to the European theater and North Africa.

Coming to the end of the line, Knudson emphasized, "And this, Sigy, is Konrad, our man from Berlin. He is here to assist with assessing and reevaluating British and American intelligence information, regarding war criminals." We shook hands. Later I discovered his real background. Konrad (not his real name) had been a widely-traveled German foreign correspondent fluent in five different languages. He had been recommended to Hitler by Dr. Joseph Goebbels and Admiral Canaris who, later in the war became chief of military counterintelligence. Konrad became Hitler's special stenographer. He had A-I top security clearance and could move about freely at Hitler's headquarters. Being above suspicion, it was not difficult for him to leak information to any source he chose.

He attended all situation meetings/discussions, took notes, and formulated many of Hitler's directives and proclamations. Because of his brilliant articulation, Goebbels, his former boss, frequently called upon him to assist with drafting propaganda material. All the time, though, Konrad hated the Nazi system and functioned as an Allied "sleeper" in Berlin.

Before Berlin became completely sealed off during the last three weeks of the European war, Konrad set himself in westward motion and made it without major difficulties to Denmark. There he offered his services to the Allies, which was easy since he could be quickly identified. He brought with him additional files of interest to the West.

Konrad, Alex, and I held numerous interesting powwows exchanging notes until my own formal demobilization was due.

I started my new assignment on Monday, 20 August. By the end of that day, we had screened seventy men. All teams combined had handled over eight hundred cases. A couple of teams were held up because they had several cases where additional information was needed for processing by reviewing files. However, nothing unusual was reported by any team.

During the first week, three men came to my quarters asking for my assistance. They represented a group of married couples, some of whom had small children. The British had arranged to provide these families with extra milk, cereal and chocolate rations. A week ago those in charge of distribution had told them these rations had been discontinued. Something was fishy.

I made a few notes regarding previous delivery dates, how much was involved, and what exactly they had been told. Armed with this information, I reported the complaint to the administrative staff sergeant, the man who had called us Krauts and whom everybody called the chief.

"One thing is for sure," he commented. "we have not changed these rations. Leave it with me. Our capo supervision will investigate. Don't mention anything to anybody."

That same night a raid took place across the camp. We all had to leave our quarters while the raiders, British MPs, combed through the barracks.

Most of the missing food was promptly found before it could reach the black market. Two major distributors and a number of capos had worked hand in glove. They were arrested, interrogated, and incarcerated for fourteen days. But that was not all. The British had an effective way of dealing with such elements as these chiselers. First it surfaced as a rumor but later it was established as fact that those who had shown lack of ethics, and there were quite a few, were sent to Bremerhaven, Germany. There they were received by Moroccan troops and sent immediately to France to work at reconstruction projects. Crookedness did not pay off for them.

It was about a week after this event that I met Adolf, my former drill sergeant from Haon. The story he had to tell was hair-raising! Having spent over a year inside the Arctic Circle, he was one of a few who survived the terrible German retreat after the Soviets marched in. Practically the entire theater which the Norwegians call Finnmark had been destroyed by following Hitler's insane policy of *verbrannte Erde* (burnt earth, meaning destroy and retreat). Military and strategic installations were defended from the advancing Soviet troops until the last minute, then blown up, often together with part of civilian communities. This was just one of many prime examples of what political and religious fanaticism can do around this world.

Finnmark is the northern-most county in Norway, with an acreage of approximately forty-eight thousand kilometers and a population of about seventy-seven thousand, or two percent of Norway's population, Laplanders (or Lapps) not included. It shares a common border with the Soviets of 196 kilometers, and another Finnish border 616 kilometers long.

Although totally destroyed in the fall of 1944, the reconstruction process has been finished a long time. Nowadays, the county is part of the modern Norway.

As could be foreseen during the process of retreat, the Germans temporarily secured the *Tirpitz* by moving the crippled vessel further south to Tromsö. She was finally sunk right at the pier by the RAF. Three blockbuster hits by Lancaster heavy bombers caused her to turn bottoms up with hundreds of her crew members trapped inside. The event was later dramatized in a pretty accurate feature film.

Some time during Friday, 31 August, the debriefing commando expected to process the two hundred thousandth soldier. This called for a celebration, to which we interpreters were also invited. It was then that I found out from Captain Cornish's orderly what the Captain's background was.

He had entered Germany undercover in the mid thirties and actually remained there right through until the end of World War II, a feat unequaled. Cornish became an outstanding intelligence provider for the British Empire, right, left, and center. Surviving in a climate of totalitarianism, such as we had in Germany at the time, deserves, to say the least, special recognition. I am one of those who give great credit to the men and women who for democracy and freedom have put their heads on the block. Quite often, the results achieved by these comparatively few people outweigh the effectiveness of entire armies.

Sunday, 2 September, was a fine sunny day. I was strolling along the camp with several other comrades speculating about the future when I saw coming in our direction a figure that struck me as familiar. The man was one-legged and used crutches. Coming closer, I recognized that he was a school buddy with whom I had shared a school bench for four years, Herbert Bardolatzki.

From him I heard another tragic story that shook me with emotion. He had volunteered and joined the navy when he was barely eighteen years old. His first attachment was with the battleship *Bluecher*, which the British promptly sank in the Skagerrak after our invasion of Scandinavia on Wednesday, 22 May 1940. Herbert survived without a scratch.

"It seemed," Herbert described, "as if any vessel to which I was assigned was destined to be sank. I served on two destroyers which faced the same fate as the *Bismarck*. Only the last ship, a torpedo boat, made it to the end of the war. I really rejoiced when the war came to an end. But it wasn't over for me yet, Sigy, as you can see. I was with the first six crews going out to sweep our mines, when one bastard blew up while we were in the process of deactivating it. That's when I lost this limb. But everything considered, I am still grateful to be alive!"

To be sorry when something like this happens is totally insufficient, as we all know. There was not anything one could say. I met Herbert once more on one of my European holidays in the sixties. He was doing all right, happily married, and had a good job. Still my heart is filled with sadness when I think about how ironic life can be at times. It is a good thing that we do not know when our bell tolls.

The fourteen screening teams worked closely together. As a matter of fact, I was amazed and at the same time delighted to see such a closeness develop between former enemies. It shows what happens when people really get to know each other. At times we discussed what would have happened if we met during the war, eye-to-eye, and we all came to the same conclusion. How insane it is of people to kill each other when they do not even carry a personal grudge.

During the following weeks we caught the occasional person who had committed war crimes. There was a U-boat commander, for instance, whose record was on file. Documented with clarity and substantiated by several of his former crew members, he had torpedoed a vessel off the coast of North Africa and ordered his crew to shoot the swimming survivors! His excuse? You guessed it. "I was just following orders." However, he was one who did not get away with it. He had unmistakably overstepped his orders and acted in disregard of international war ethics.

The Last Leg

It was Monday, 29 October, when my own demobilization papers were prepared. I was now itching to find out whether my parents were still alive. The commendation I received for my services was a verbal one but nevertheless appreciated. Somehow I felt good in the knowledge that I had made a worthwhile contribution to the process that could be considered the first step of normalization for a lot of my comrades.

The next day eleven hundred of us boarded a boat with a normal capacity of four hundred passengers. That in itself would not have been too bad. The distance between Mandal Harbor and Bremerhaven, our destiny, was about three hundred statute miles, or two hundred-sixty nautical miles. With an average speed of about eighteen knots, we could arrive within fifteen hours of sailing time. This was nothing to complain about when comparing it to the inconveniences of the war years.

But there was a hitch. The ship's cooking crew had prepared yellow pea soup which had not cooked long enough. The peas were still hard, but we ate anyway. Right after lunch time, the trouble started. Almost everybody complained with stomach cramps. Soon passengers and crew members sprinted in all directions to vomit all over the vessel. In many cases, including my own, one had to expose oneself for a bowel movement and vomit at the same time. It was positively the messiest thing I had ever seen, short of the scenes I witnessed during the convoy attack. The board planks and gullies had to be flushed for hours, and there were no germicides aboard. Luckily, not one case of actual cholera came to light. This was simply a case of undercooked food without adding the presence of Vibrio comma, the bacterium which causes cholera.

Our ship threw anchor at 1500 hours at Bremerhaven the next day. A British escort ship took us into harbor. Several trucks were waiting for those of us who would be sent off to Neumuenster, one of the major demobilization camps in Germany at the time. The Brits scrutinized our papers from Mandal, and we were told that we could be on our own now and go home if we wanted to. Any train would take us to our destination without charge upon producing our documents. That is exactly what I should have done!

Those who would prefer to be taken closer to their homes could remain and make use of different transport convoys. I opted for that alternative. Regrets come always after the fact.

I left two days later with a large contingent, all of whom had relatives living in the center of the western part of Germany, primarily in Westphalia and the Rhineland. But we were dumped in another holding camp close by Hannover. We were told plans had changed for the time being. Why the heck did I not scram for Neumuenster?

Days went by and no logical explanation was offered for this holdup. On the twelfth, a large convoy of POWs from Russia arrived. If we thought we were bad off, we had news coming! The POWs were kept in a camp area divided by barbed wire. These poor chaps were clothed in rags. Most of them did not have footwear but had substituted with rags wrapped around their feet. They were a pitiful sight! Many of them looked like walking skeletons. Men taller than I, six feet or more, would weigh barely one hundred pounds.

We went to meet these comrades of ours and to chat with them through the wire. Whatever we could spare, including cigarettes, we shared with these poor souls. A few British soldiers were moving about them. Close to where I stood, a couple of them shook their heads from side to side. They stood close enough for me to overhear one of them commenting, "They look like concentration camp survivors, just terrible!"

"Darn right!" I could not help barging in. "As you can see for yourself, this whole war was not a matter of strictly black and white. These people have suffered immeasurably and have come close to starvation, thanks to your Allies!"

On the twenty-second we were newly enumerated for the purpose of establishing who would be transported to his final destination when, depending on the administrative district to which we wanted to go. This process was expected to last four days.

I did some thinking. Believing that we would be moved in alphabetical order, district by district, I opted for the district of Arnsberg (Westphalia), rather than Rhineland. Too bad if they started at the end of the alphabet!

The next day proved me right. I was listed with the third truck transport group leaving in the afternoon. "Nothing else could happen," I thought. Wrong again! Rather than being put on a train rolling homebound, we ended up in yet another holding camp, this time in Muenster. We were herded to a vacated school complex, the same one where at the beginning of the war several members of Jehovah's Witnesses who refused to serve in the armed forces had been shot.

We received a meager food portion, barely enough to fill one cavity, and were told to find a place to lie down anywhere within those buildings. Easier said than done. All we could do was to spread out our blankets on the floor, including in hallways.

At 0600 hours we were ordered to line up for inspection by the regional coordinator. What nerve; it was raining cats and dogs! My watch showed 0715 hours when the inspection finally took place. At first, a German Army sergeant still in full uniform bellowed out some threats. With typical megalomania and delusions of grandeur, he shouted, "If you think the dance is over, you are wrong!"

A few minutes later a British sergeant joined him. I had counted twenty-three rows of men, leaving sufficient space between them for a person to walk through. The two marched through the thoroughfares, one by one. Occasionally they would stop and tell a soldier to step aside. When they passed me by from behind, I had the feeling my back hair was standing up, fearing that I would be told to step aside. But nothing happened.

When they had finished their rounds, we were informed that a final entry would have to be made in our papers on Monday for administrative purposes. Red tape never seems to end. That entry would include the city of our destiny and a notation regarding the day, the time, and the train to board.

I got more edgy by the minute. Should I just fly the coop and manage on my own? Why take another risk that close to home? Maybe that last entry was important, so I stayed put.

My turn came on Monday afternoon. I was accorded a release code number with a stamp reading Schwelm as the goal town. The time of departure by train early Tuesday morning was quoted at 0530 hours.

The last night in the camp I hardly slept in anticipation of my reunion with my parents. Besides, my bones ached from sleeping on the hard marble floor for days. Breathing was not quite easy either. It was more of an ordeal. Over one thousand bodies who had not seen a bath for weeks poisoned the air.

We rose at 0430 hours, received a cup of coffee with a hard bun, probably old enough to start molding soon. But at this stage who cared about anything but getting moving?

They brought us in time to a secondary railway station. The train departed as planned. It would end up in Cologne, but would stop at many little towns on the way. I was reminded of my first railway journey when I was drafted in 1941. That train stopped at what we felt like was every mailbox collecting draftees, but this time it was in reverse. Come to think of it, I had waited for this day for four years, one month, and twenty-seven days!

The train rumbled into the familiar railway station of Schwelm at 0715 hours. I said good-bye to my comrades for the last time, took my leftover things, and vacated the station. None of the civilians around seemed to take any notice of me. Seeing guys like me reappearing after the war was the order of the day and not worth noticing. After all, everybody had his own mounting personal problems of getting by day-by-day.

Taking my time, I strolled up Bahnhofstrasse and took the left fork to Schulstrasse, where my parents, as I found out later, had been assigned a modest apartment by the railway late in 1944. I rang the outer doorbell and pushed against the door as soon as I heard the door release hum. The first door to the left on the ground floor was slightly ajar. The nameplate read Heinrich Born. Before I could push the door further open, it moved to the inside and my mother stood in the door frame.

"My boy, my boy," she cried and we fell into each other's arms with shouts of joy. My father, in full railway uniform apparently ready to go to work, sprinted out of a side door, and the three of us embraced. What a wonderful homecoming! And the timing could be called immaculate: it was Mother's fifty-fifth birthday.

EPILOGUE

The country lay in ruins. The Nazi machine had been crushed. We were in for some belt-tightening but we also learned for the first time in German history, disregarding the ill-conceived reign of the Weimar Republic between 1919 and 1933, the difference between a totalitarian and a democratic government.

It was time to hitch up our socks, spit on our hands, roll up our sleeves, and build a new Germany on the ashes of the old.

The tremendous monetary infusion of the Marshall Plan availed the rebuilding of Europe. Ideological differences did not prevent the Germans from utilizing the resources of the Marshall Plan wisely and effectively. Within one decade, the world would call Germany's economic recovery a miracle, or *Wirtschaftswunder* in German. Decisive for the upswing was the overall willingness to work hard coupled with the application of ingenuity.

Not only have German postwar generations benefited from the fruits of democratization, but they also with very few exceptions appreciate their newfound freedoms: individual freedom, economic freedom, and political freedom.

As ideological differences between East and West seem to become less rigid, it is my greatest wish to see Germany reunited, and function as a full partner within a peaceful and united Europe!

Summer of 1989.

S.B.

MILITARY PLAYERS

Anton - Our guide in Oslo.

Anton - Groom at the fourth battery.

Apfel, Erich - Cellar master at naval officers casino.

Assmann - Second in command of the *Tirpitz*.

Baer, Hans Fregattenkapitaen - Captain, second in command at Stavanger naval headquarters.

Ballzuweit, Fritz - Private. Company armorer; former trainer of Herbert Runge, only Wuppertal heavyweight gold medal winner, Berlin Olympics 1936.

Boes, Werner - Jazz musician extraordinaire and chief interpreter after World War II.

Born - Vice Admiral, naval headquarters, Oslo; instrumental in my transfer from the Arctic to Stavanger. (No relation)

Boschetto, Victor - Austrian comrade who hated the Nazis.

Brinkman, Korvettenkapiteen - Commander, technical advisor, liaison between naval headquarters and Abwehr.

Cameron - British Commander of X-Six craft, the mini-sub which attacked the *Tirpitz*.

Cornish - Captain, spent several years in Germany before and during World War II as MI-Six operative. In charge of demobilization process in Mandal, Norway 1945.

Doehle - Lieutenant. Official chief interpreter in Stavanger after surrender of German troops in Norway.

Eckler, Dr. - Chief naval staff physician in Stavanger.

Eye, Erich - Chef at naval officers casino in Stavanger; former high-ranking executive with HAPAG Line (Hamburg-America Line).

Friedberg, Harald - Commanding officer of speedboat *Stavanger II*.

Kaufmann, Herbert - Petty officer second class; in charge of food and beverage supplies, preparation and service on island of Haon.

Von der Knesebrecht, Oberleutnant - Specialist in naval protection, defense and camouflage.

Knudson - Norwegian cadet working as coordinator and administrative assistant to Captain Cornish, MI-Six.

Kretchmar, Kapitaenleutnant - successful German U-boat commandant.

Mankievicz, Lieutenant - Hands-on expert for convoy guidance.

Marquart, Dietrich Oberleutnant - Navy artillery commander; military upgrader.

Marzi, Heinz Hauptgefreiter - Master Private, chief steward, Stavanger naval officers casino; former world adventurer.

Mayer-Pantin, Dr. Carlos - Seekommandant NACO.

Meyer - Commander of the *Tirpitz*.

Pohlmann, Fritz - Chief inspector, commanding officer for all food and beverage supplies and provisions.

Schmidt, Kapitaenleutnant - Staff and guard company base commander.

Schmucker, Dr. - Medical doctor and surgeon aboard minesweeper number 456.

Von Schrader - Rear Admiral. Chief of naval deployment Norwegian west coast.

Schubert - Korvettenkapitaen, Stavanger Harbor master.

Skorzeny, Otto - Adventurer and daredevil. Freed Mussolini in September of 1943 from Mount Grosso, where Il Duce was held captive under guard.

Tossati, Ernesto - Comrade and Jesuit friend at the fourth battery.

Tuleweit, Lieutenant - Commander of minesweeper number 456.

Waldgruber - Petty officer; main slave driver on Haon boot hill.

Wallach, Erich - Petty officer at naval directional station in Stavanger Harbor. Real name: Alexander Spencer, our "mold."

Walters, Engineer - Planner of strategic defense installations.

Witzfeld, Lieutenant Commander - Commandant of basic training base on Haon.

Wunderlich, Eberhard - Kapitaenleutnant; adjutant and aide-de-camp to Mayer-Pantin.

OTHER PLAYERS - Nonmilitary

Berger - Emissary of Quisling government; liaison between Norway and Germany; diplomat.

Bjornson, Jorg - Norwegian Antarctic explorer.

Bohr, Niels - Danish nuclear physicist.

Borgerlige Partisaner - Danish Resistance organization.

Campani, Joe - Business wizard of the Dutch Shultz Gang.

Dempster, Cramp - Top aide of Dutch Shultz.

Eklund - General manager of Holmenkollen Ski Resort, Oslo.

Garcia - Mexican Captain; also called Capitano Sangre, or Captain Blood. One-eyed smuggler and Heinz Marzi's mentor.

Hansen, Lars - Factotum at naval headquarters in Stavanger.

Hyllesand, Kristen - Norwegian member of British MI-Five; coordinator of Norwegian Resistance.

Joyce, William - Better known as Lord How How. British Nazi propagandist living in Germany.

Kardialgi - Top aide to Vidkum Quisling, Norwegian Nazi leader. Kardialgi's name means "heartburn" in Norwegian.

Konrad - The man from Berlin.

Lange - Norwegian foreign minister in exile; talked Allies out of invading Norway in mid November 1944.

Loehndorff, Ernst - German adventurer and trailblazer for Ross Sitwell's international capers.

Lyngby Group - Danish Resistance organization.

Marlene - Friend at the "house of pleasure"

O'Brian, Chuck - Irish-American navigator.

Olav, Prince - The present King of Norway (1989).

Olson, Hans - Swedish geologist.

Rethmeier, Fritz - School friend. Served with Rommel's Panzer Corps in Africa.

Sandborg - Norwegian nuclear physicist responsible for security at heavy water plant in northern Norway.

Shalburg Corps - Traitors in the eyes of Danes. Pro-Nazi Danish volunteers, mostly criminals, serving with Germans at the Eastern Front.

Sitwell, Ross - British engineer and exhibition leader.

Toriani, Arturo - Called "Angel." Procurer of whiskey smugglers; foreign agent of Dutch Shultz Group.

Van Buren, Jan - Dutch anthropologist.

GLOSSARY

I A - Second in command.

Abwehr - German Military Counterintelligence.

Ad Akta - Inactive files, saved for future reference.

Aft - To the end of a boat or vessel.

Akvavit - Distinctively clear and zesty gin distilled at Aalborg Akvavit Distillery.

Amidship - In or toward the middle part of a vessel.

Astern - Toward the stern or end of a vessel.

Backbord - German for port side (the left) of a ship.

Bergen - "Europe's rainiest city." Headquarters of Admiral Von Schrader.

Bjergsted Park - Located near "Old Stavanger." Used as Naval Headquarters after December 1944. Now accommodates the Stavanger Concert Hall.

Bow - Forward part of a boat or vessel.

Bukt - Norwegian for bay or inlet.

Bulkhead - Wall-like construction inside a ship for forming watertight compartments.

Bulkroom head - The top of a "hold" where the cargo is stored.

Buøy - Largest island located east-northeast of Stavanger.

Convoy - A group of vessels, including small armed ships, forming a convoy. Also used for a consecutive number of automobiles, such as in a parade.

Deck - Any platform suggesting a deck of a ship.

Fallreep - Adopted by the Germans from Old English meaning a rope ladder, gangway, or jack.

Finnmark - The northernmost county in Norway.

Flak - German abbreviation for "*Fliegerabwehrkanonen*" or antiaircraft guns.

Fourth Battery - Antiaircraft artillery base defending the *Tirpitz*, stationed on a plateau nearby, overlooking Kafjord inlet.

Galley - A kitchen aboard a vessel; also used as a pantry.

Gata or Gate - Norwegian for street.

Geheimregistratur - German for Confidential/Secret Department.

Gekados - German abbreviation for "*Geheime Kommandosache*" or Top Secret.

Gestapo - German abbreviation for "*Geheime Staatspolizei*" or Secret State Police.

Godvilje Band - Goodwill band. Jazz combo at "Det Jazzhus" on Karl Johans Gate in Oslo.

Hold - The space below the deck of a vessel where cargo is stored.

Holmen - Norwegian for inlet.

Holmenkollen - Famous Norwegian ski resort at the outskirts of Oslo.

H.Q. - Abbreviation for headquarters.

Ja - Norwegian for yes, well, indeed.

Ja takk - Norwegian for yes, please!

Kafjord - Norwegian fjord within the Arctic Circle. The fjord sheltered the *Tirpitz* in 1943/44.

Kaien - Norwegian for quay or wharf.

Karl Johans Gate - Oslo's main street and promenade.

Klamotten - German slang for oldies, old things, or rags.

Knot - Speed of one nautical mile, equivalent to 1.1516 statute mile per hour.

Kripo - German abbreviation for "*Kriminalpolizei.*"

Kvitsøy - Island northwest of Stavanger. Was used as the German Navy's main listening post in the area.

Lapp or Laplander - Nomadic people living in North Scandinavia and the Kola Peninsula of the Soviet Union.

Leitstand - German antiaircraft guidance system, estimating height, distance and speed of approaching enemy aircraft.

Luftschutzbunker - German for air raid shelter.

Marineheim - Mess and entertainment center for Navy men, operated away from regular bases.

Mauser - Automatic German pistol.

Midship - Pertaining to, or situation in the middle of a ship.

N.S.D.A.P. - National Sozialistische deutsche Arbeiterpartei, or National Socialist German Workers Party. The Nazi Party.

OKW - Oberkommado der Wehrmacht or High Command of the Armed Forces.

Operation Greif - Operation "Grab," special German commando under Otto Skorzeny causing confusion behind Western Allies invasion lines in France and Belgium.

0815 - Clumsy looking but powerful German handgun.

Oslo - Capital of and largest city in Norway.

Pelerine - Water-repellent, raincoat-type cape. A sleeveless garment hanging loosely over the shoulders. Mostly used by fishermen.

Rogaland - County in which Stavanger is located.

S.A. - Political uniformed paramilitary organization. Also called "Braunhemden" or Brownshirts.

S.D. - Sicherheitsdienst or Security Service. A civilian police force.

S.S. - Originally meaning "Saalschutz" or Hall Protection. Developed into a uniformed political terror organization. Members were drawn from the German elite.

Sieben Sachen - German for "seven things" meaning a few things, usually worthless.

Stavanger 2 - Diesel-engined speedboat, capable of making forty-two knots plus per hour.

Stern - The aft or end of a ship or boat.

Steuerbord - German for starboard (right side) of a vessel.

Storting - Norwegian Parliament.

Sundet - Norwegian for strait or sound.

Takk - Norwegian for thanks or thank you.

Tirpitz - Germany's biggest and last battleship left in 1944. Tonnage: 42,000. Crew: 2,500.

Torget - Norwegian for marketplace.

Trondheim - Trondjhem in Norwegian. City dividing South Norway from North Norway.

Vatnet - Norwegian for pond or small lake.

Veien - Norwegian for road.

Walthers - A 7.65mm (.32-caliber) semiautomatic pistol; often called a Luger.

Weihnachtsbaeume - German for Christmas trees. So named for light flares used by RAF, parachuted and hanging from balloons; they lighted up target areas to be bombed.

Zwischendeck - German for "between decks."